LAKE MICHIGAN

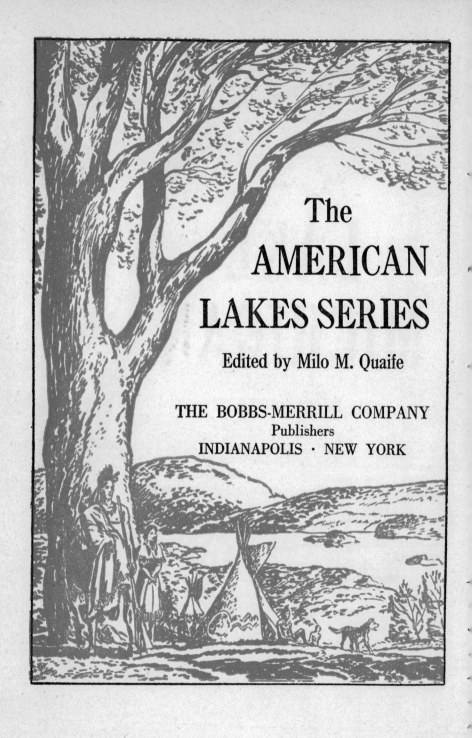

The AMERICAN LAKES SERIES

Edited by Milo M. Quaife

THE BOBBS-MERRILL COMPANY
Publishers
INDIANAPOLIS · NEW YORK

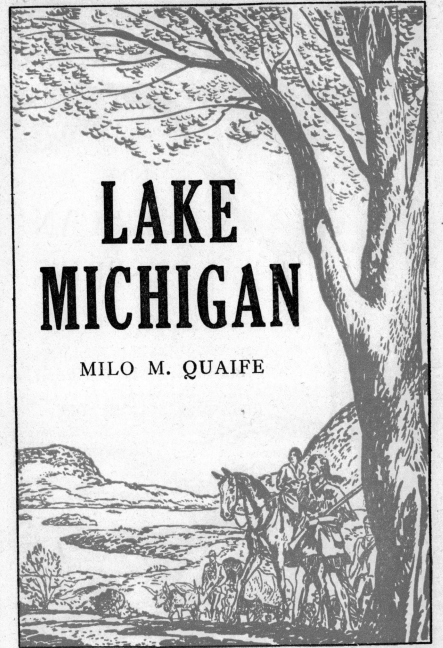

LAKE
MICHIGAN

MILO M. QUAIFE

To Letitia

PILOT OF MY MATRIMONIAL BARK

I remember the black wharves and the slips,
  And the sea-tides tossing free;

. . . .

And the beauty and mystery of the ships
  And the magic of the sea.

—LONGFELLOW, "My Lost Youth"

PRELUDE

In the Book of Genesis we are told that the Lord created the earth in six days. Modern science, however, teaches that uncounted millions of years were required to accomplish the task. Almost at the end of this long period the Glacial Epoch dawned, during which much of North America was buried under one vast sheet of ice. Repeated periods of milder temperatures intervened to destroy the ice altogether or to reduce materially its volume. As the ice receded it left lakes of water in the lower depressions, which at one time drained southward through the Chicago-Illinois River Valley to the Mississippi, and at another eastward through the Mohawk-Hudson Valley. Eventually the glaciers retired for the last time, leaving in the preglacial river valleys the five Great Lakes of the present day.

Geologic time is long and human life is short. The white man came to the Great Lakes less than 400 years ago, and his entire sojourn here comprises but a fraction of a second of geologic time. Meanwhile the forces of erosion and of successive elevation and depression continue to operate. West of Lake Michigan the Continental Divide is so low that at Portage great levees have been built to keep the Wisconsin River from deserting its own bed to flow eastward down the Fox into Green Bay, while at Chicago men have long since reversed the flow of the Chicago, which now finds its way to the Mexican Gulf instead of to the Gulf of St. Lawrence. A relatively minor change of elevation, it is obvious, would once more send the waters of the Great Lakes down their ancient Chicago-Illinois outlet, shrinking Canada's mighty river to an insignificant fraction of its present magnitude; a return of the Glacial Age would destroy all existing life and turn the Great Lakes Basin once more into an icy waste as dreary as the interior of Greenland.

The Lake Michigan drainage basin is but twice as large as the lake itself, and its rivers are of necessity comparatively small. In its primitive state the lake possessed few harbors, and none at all in its southerly 200 miles of extent. Regularity of shore line and absence of islands account in large part for this native paucity of harbors. One commonly looks for a harbor at the mouth of a river, but on Lake Michigan these were clogged with sand through the action of the lake current which flows southward along the western coast and northward along the eastern. The harbors which today serve such busy cities as Racine, Kenosha, Chicago, Gary and Muskegon are all artificial, made either by building breakwaters in the open lake or by cutting stabilized channels from it into the rivers, whose banks answer the purposes of a harbor.

There are seasonal and long-time variations in the surface levels of the Great Lakes, so that both their area and their elevation above sea level can be stated only approximately. Records kept since 1860 for Lake Michigan disclose an extreme surface variation of about 5 feet (from 578.3 to 583.4 feet above sea level), with a mean elevation of about 581 feet. Lake Huron, connected with Michigan by a broad open strait, has practically the same elevation. Superior is about 21 feet higher, while Lake Erie is about 8 feet, and Ontario 335 feet, lower.[1]

The bottom of Lake Michigan presents much the same gently rolling series of hills and depressions as the adjacent mainland. Between Chicago and Grand Haven the depth of the lake is about 200 feet; between Racine and Holland it is 500 feet, and northward from the Milwaukee-Muskegon line it attains a maximum depth of 870 feet. Most of the lake bottom is thus above sea level, while its extreme depression is less than 300 feet below.

Although Lake Michigan is materially smaller than Lake Superior, and slightly smaller than Lake Huron, its 300-mile extent from north to south has given it a greater influence upon the economic and political development of America than is exercised by any of the other lakes. St. Ignace, at the north, is closer to the Pole than Montreal or than much of New Brunswick, while Michigan City, at the south, occupies the latitude of New Bedford and the southern coast of Cape Cod. If we exclude from consideration the westerly reach of Long Island Sound, Lake Michigan extends through more degrees of latitude than the entire New England coast, and the climatic range between its northern and southern ends is correspondingly great. Even more significant in the development of our country has been its influence in forcing the lines of travel and transportation between East and West to diverge southward in order to by-pass the obstacle which the lake presents.

The story of Lake Michigan has many ramifications, involving not only the life which goes on upon and beneath its surface but the influence it exerts upon the adjacent land area and the people who inhabit it. The habits of the latter, in turn, determine the shipping and other activities of the lake itself. So our present volume endeavors to supply a picture of the lake in its historical and human setting. The complete picture would be too vast, of course, for any one volume to limn. In the present one an earnest effort has been made to condense something of the grandeur that is Lake Michigan; with what degree of success the reader alone must determine.

M. M. QUAIFE,
Detroit Public Library

---

[1] Observations recorded by the U. S. Coast Survey disclose that in the summer of 1943 the lake levels were close to their maximum for the eighty-three-year period. Michigan was at its highest since 1887, and Huron since 1927. Ontario's elevation had been equaled once since 1860; Superior's had been equaled but twice.

TABLE OF CONTENTS

Part I

FROM BARK CANOE TO STEEL LEVIATHAN

Part II

TALK OF MANY THINGS

TABLE OF CONTENTS—*Continued*

Part III

ALL AROUND THE COAST

LIST OF ILLUSTRATIONS

Part I

FROM BARK CANOE TO STEEL LEVIATHAN

Chapter 1

China in Wisconsin

No scenario out of Hollywood was ever stranger than the true story of the discovery of Lake Michigan. It really begins with Genghis Khan, the twelfth-century forerunner of Adolf Hitler, who dreamed of conquering the world and actually ravaged and overran a large part of the Orient. The conquest of China, which he began, was completed by his grandson Kublai Khan, in the years from 1260 to 1279. A few years before this, two Venetian merchants, Maffeo and Nicolo Polo, had wandered into the then mysterious Orient and found their way to Peking, the capital city of Kublai. Before long they won the Emperor's confidence, and when he became ready to provide his new empire with a ready-made religion they sold him on the superior merits of Christianity. So in 1269 he sent them back to Venice, charged with the curious mission of bringing him 100 priests whom he proposed to utilize in establishing Christianity in China. They found all Italy in a state of turmoil, however, and so great was the confusion of public affairs that they were quite unable to fulfill their errand; they returned to China without even a single priest, and Kublai turned to Buddhism, whose salesmen proved ready to deliver.

But the Polo brothers made their mark upon the future in another and wholly unintended way by taking back to China Maffeo's son, Marco, then a youth of fifteen. He, too, won the favor of the Khan, rose to important station and after a quarter of a century returned once more to his native Venice. The people of Italy were just emerging from the Dark Ages which for centuries had spread their mantle over western Europe. Like the mountaineers of eastern Kentucky today, they had become isolated from the center of culture and civilization, and their standards of living had become almost incredibly coarse and mean. From the mysterious East over long and hazardous trade routes came the silks and spices and other objects of use or luxury which they eagerly coveted but were unable themselves to

15

produce. The home-coming adventurer had the greatest story in all the world to tell, and never did a storyteller find more eager listeners. Glib of tongue and loaded with information, he talked, and the tales he related were so marvelous that he was soon dubbed "Marco of the Millions," or "Marco the Blowhard." Even in prison he continued to talk, for in 1298, as the result of a disastrous naval battle, Marco, along with thousands of other Venetians, became a prisoner of war in Genoa. There, either to gain relief from his talking or because they were impressed by it, his jailers produced a scribe to write it all down.

So *The Book of Marco Polo* was produced, about the year 1300. It was soon translated into other languages and for centuries it comprised practically all that the people of western Europe knew about the Far East. It is one of the most remarkable travel books ever written, and after 650 years it is still being republished and widely read.

One eager reader of the fifteenth century was a Genoese navigator named Christopher Columbus. He adopted the theory that the East could be reached by sailing westward across the Sea of Darkness which washed the western coast of Europe, and when in October 1492 he landed on the island of San Salvador, he mistakenly believed that he had arrived off the coast of eastern Asia and that the fabulous Indies lay just beyond. So the red men were dubbed Indians, and the search for the realm of Marco's patron, Kublai Khan, was begun.

Never was there a ruder geographical awakening. As the result of successive expeditions, it finally dawned upon the explorers that instead of eastern Asia Columbus had found a New World; but their chief concern was how to find a way around or through it, to continue the voyage to the Indies. This search went on for centuries and it supplied the motive for most of the exploration of interior America. Our immediate interest, however, is in the efforts of the French, who early effected a lodgment at the Gulf of St. Lawrence. Jacques Cartier in 1535 discovered the Great River of Canada, and ascended it as far as Montreal. Here, atop the mountain which overhangs the great city of today, he gazed westward upon the broad waters of the upper St. Lawrence and the Ottawa, and listened eagerly to the red men's stories of the sea to which these rivers led. The Old World offers no parallel to our own Great Lakes, and Cartier could not know that the seas the savages told about were in fact fresh-water lakes.

In 1608 Champlain founded the city of Quebec, as an advance station on the route to the Indies, and until his death in 1635 he omitted no opportunity to prosecute the search for an open water-way which would lead him to the western ocean. In the summer of 1615 he visited the Huron Indians at the head of Georgian Bay, and here listened to tales of a land, forty days' journey to the westward, where the buffalo roamed, some of whose skins were displayed to him by his hosts. He planned to visit it in the coming spring, and had he done so he would probably have become the white discoverer of Lake Michigan. But an inopportune brawl between the Huron and their Algonquin neighbors demanded his services as peacemaker until the season for the departure of the expedition was past. Deeply disappointed, he returned to Quebec and never again found the freedom to resume his personal explorations. "If ever anyone was greatly disheartened," he wrote, "it was myself, since I had been waiting to see this year what I had been seeking during many preceding ones with great toil and effort and through many fatigues and risks of my life."

But the western forests were to know him no more, for until his death in 1635 his time was divided between the administration of affairs at Quebec and in France. About this time, however, he hit upon the plan of sending young men of promise into the wilderness to live among the natives, to win their friendship and to master their language and way of life. At the same time these men could incidentally accumulate for their chief a fund of valuable geographical information.

One of the youths thus selected, "forasmuch as his nature and excellent memory inspired good hopes of him," was Jean Nicolet, who in 1618, at the age of twenty, came out from Old to New France. Champlain at once sent him up the Ottawa River, where he remained two years among the savages, sharing their hunts and war raids and "undergoing such fatigues as none but eye witnesses can conceive; he often passed seven or eight days without food, and once full seven weeks with only bark from the trees for nourishment." So records his personal friend and chronicler, Father Vimont.[1]

The two-year apprenticeship in the arts of savagery was interrupted when Nicolet accompanied his hosts upon a foray against the Iroquois, with the happy consequence that he was instrumental in restoring peace between the two warring nations. After this he retired still farther into the western wilderness, going this time to the Nipissings, who lived north of the great lake which still bears their name. Here he passed the next eight or nine years, "taking part in the very frequent councils of these tribes, having his own separate cabin and household, and fishing and trading for himself." But he did not forget meanwhile the object of his mission, for he kept a memoir (now unfortunately lost) of the habits and customs of the Nipissings.

After such a wilderness schooling he was recalled to Quebec and given the office of interpreter. Meanwhile reports grapevined down to Quebec of a people who dwelt beside the Stinking Water, far to the westward of the Huron, by whom they were called "People of the Sea." About the year 1633 the Huron fell out with their western neighbors, and Nicolet was the man best fitted to restore peace between the warring tribes. To Champlain "Stinking Water" and "People of the Sea" obviously meant the western ocean and the residents of Marco Polo's Tartary, or China. Under this belief, Nicolet, before leaving Quebec, was provided with a gorgeous robe of China damask "all strewn with flowers and birds of many colors" to don when he should approach the oriental monarch, and early in 1634 he set out from Quebec for Georgian Bay and the city of Peking.

As far as Huronia the route was already a familiar one; beyond, it was as mysterious and unknown as the Sea of Darkness had been to Columbus in 1492. But Columbus had three sturdy ships and their crews; Nicolet had a single canoe, paper-thin and paddled by half a dozen Huron savages, which must hug the coast line lest it be overwhelmed by a sudden storm before its occupants could flee ashore. Past the Manitoulin chain of islands, which separates the North Channel from Lake Huron, the voyagers pushed, landing at nightfall to consume their meal of sagamite or Indian corn hastily crushed and boiled, and to seek repose under the open sky or, in stormy weather, beneath their upturned canoe.

In due course they skirted Point Detour, threaded beautiful Les Cheneaux Islands, and caught their first glimpse of the green-clad heights of Mackinac. We have no journal of the voyage,[2] but it is easy to imagine that Nicolet thrilled to the vision of the "Fairy Island," looming up in the distance; even more did he thrill, no doubt, when the savages informed him that just beyond lay the broad Strait of Mackinac, the entrance to still another vast sweet-water sea on whose farther shore dwelt the People of the Stinking Water.

Father Vimont writes:

"He embarked in the Huron country with seven savages, and they passed by many small nations, both going and coming. When they reached their destination they fastened two sticks in the earth and hung gifts on them, so as to prevent those tribes from mistaking them for enemies to be massacred. When he was two days' journey from that nation, he sent one of those savages to bear tidings of the peace, which word was especially well received when they heard that it was a white man who carried the message."

The natives sent forward a delegation of their young men to greet Nicolet.

"They meet him; they escort him, and carry all his baggage. He wore a grand robe of China damask, all strewn with flowers and birds of many colors. No sooner did they perceive him than the women and children fled, at the sight of a man who carried thunder in both hands, for this they called the two pistols that he held."

The natives received him hospitably, gathering in large numbers and providing many feasts of beaver meat and other forest delicacies. But instead of the squint-eyed dwellers of Cathay, Nicolet had found only the skin-clad savages of Wisconsin, and their hospitality did not atone for the revelation he must carry back to his master at Quebec that America was a vaster continent than the people of Europe had imagined, and that the fabled Indies lay hidden somewhere far beyond the Wisconsin coast of Lake Michigan.

So the great lake was discovered in 1634 as the incidental by-product of a search for something else, at a time when the English were still confined to the vicinity of Boston harbor and New York was an infant settlement of wooden-shod Dutchmen. Jean Nicolet, the discoverer, went back to Three Rivers to resume his duties as interpreter. In 1637 he married a young girl who was the godchild of Champlain and whose descendants were destined to become notable in Canada and the Northwest.

In 1642 Nicolet's career was terminated with an act as noble as his life had been adventurous. Some Algonquin Indians had come to Three Rivers with a prisoner whom they proposed to torture. Word of the affair was sent to Nicolet, temporarily absent at Quebec, and he promptly returned to rescue the doomed wretch. Near Sillery the boat in which he had embarked was swamped by a sudden tempest, leaving Nicolet and his companion struggling in the wind-swept St. Lawrence. "Save yourself," he cried, "you can swim but I cannot. Take care of my wife and daughter. I must go to meet my maker." Nor was this the only time, records Father Vimont, that Nicolet had risked his life for the welfare of the savages; "he did so very often."

---

[1] R. G. Thwaites (ed.), *The Jesuit Relations and Allied Documents* (Cleveland, 1896-1901), XXIII, 272-281.

[2] Because of this, we can only tentatively reconstruct the route taken by Nicolet. Mr. Louis Burbey of Detroit, a keen student of the subject and period, thinks that on his outward journey Nicolet went westward from the Sault along the south coast of Lake Superior, crossing the Michigan Upper Peninsula by one of the river highways of that area. Such a route, however, does not affect the question of his priority in the discovery of Lake Michigan.

Chapter 2

Black Robe and Red Skin

Aᴌᴛʜᴏᴜɢʜ Lake Michigan had been discovered in 1634, for a generation nothing was done to explore it. Then in a few years' time a group of intrepid Frenchmen extended the rule of France over all the Great Lakes and the Mississippi Valley, from the dim-lighted forests of Minnesota to the sun-bathed shore of the Gulf of Mexico. As an incident in this great advance Lake Michigan was explored and its shores were occupied. Why this was so long delayed and then so speedily accomplished are matters which must now receive attention.

Before the founding of Quebec the Huron, who had formerly lived on the lower St. Lawrence, had removed hundreds of miles inland to the southern end of Georgian Bay, around which they had established many fortified villages. Here they had become a sedentary tribe, devoted chiefly to agriculture. Although they were an Iroquoian people they had long since quarreled with their kinsmen who lived south of Lake Ontario. Upon the founding of Quebec they promptly established an alliance with Champlain, who in consequence became embroiled with the Iroquois. Thus the future expansion of New France southward toward New York was effectively blocked, while its westward extension up the Ottawa was promoted. In the summer of 1615 Champlain himself visited Huronia and from there accompanied the warriors upon an expedition eastward against the Iroquois in central New York. Since the time of Jacques Cartier, seventy years earlier, the French had known of the Great Lakes by Indian report, but there is no record that until now any Frenchman had actually visited them. So the way to Huronia was opened in 1615, and Lakes Huron and Ontario were discovered.[1]

In 1615 three Récollet priests came out to Quebec to begin the tremendous task of Christianizing the red men. Father Le Caron, one of the number, accompanied an advanced detachment of Cham-

21

plain's expedition to Huronia, where he was welcomed by the natives and provided with a cabin. Here on August 12, 1615, the first Mass in what is now the great province of Ontario was celebrated.

Thus the Huron Mission was established, and for a decade the Récollets labored to develop it. Finding the field too vast for successful cultivation, they invited the more powerful Jesuits to share it with them, and in 1625 the first of the Black Robes arrived. The English conquest of 1629 caused the withdrawal of all the priests from Canada, but in 1633 Champlain returned to Quebec; with him came four Jesuit fathers, three of whom were assigned to Huronia. For a decade and a half they labored to convert and civilize their charges, their numbers being increased by the arrival from time to time of additional priests and lay brothers. In 1640 the Jesuit superior decided to establish fortified headquarters to serve as the mother station and as a safe retreat for the missionaries and their converts. It was built on the little river Wye, near present-day Midland, and was named Ste. Marie in honor of the mother of Christ. Here today its ruins may be seen, and close at hand a great Catholic church and religious shrine is maintained, to which thousands of devotees resort annually.[2]

For about a decade Ste. Marie was a flourishing cultural and religious center, where blacksmiths, farmers, and other artisans labored, and from which the fathers conducted missions to neighboring nations. In 1641 two of them journeyed to the Sault, where they preached to 2,000 assembled savages, the first introduction of Christianity to Michigan; and in honor of Saint Mary they gave to the river and its rapids the names they still retain.[3]

At the Sault the fathers obtained some information from the natives concerning Lake Superior, which was "larger than our fresh water sea [Lake Huron], into which it discharges by a very large and very rapid river." Half a dozen years later they provided a more comprehensive report on the Upper Lakes, in which the name "Superior" is employed for the first time.[4]

"This superior lake extends toward the northwest. . . . A Peninsula, or a rather narrow strip of Land [the Upper Michigan Peninsula] separates this superior Lake from a third [Lake Michigan] which we call the Lake of the Puants, which also flows into our fresh water sea by a mouth [Strait of Mackinac] on the other side of the Peninsula about ten leagues farther west than the Sault. This third lake extends between the West and Southwest ... and is almost equal in size to our freshwater sea. On its shores dwell other nations whose language is unknown. . . . These People are called Puants [Stinkers] not because of any bad odor that is peculiar to them, but because they say they come from the shores of a far-distant sea toward the North, the water of which is salt, they are called 'the people of the Stinking Water.' "

So Lake Michigan was first named "Lake of the Stinking Water," and as early as 1648 the fathers had gained some conception of its approximate size. But over Huronia a dreadful fate impended and the day of doom was now at hand. As long as all the tribes were equipped only with their Stone Age weapons the Huron had been able to maintain the struggle with the Iroquois. But the Dutch were now at New York and Albany, and from them the Iroquois obtained guns and axes, traps and other implements whose possession enabled them to pass at one bound from the Stone to the Iron Age. Thus equipped, they began a series of murderous forays upon their Stone Age neighbors, which went on for several decades. The turn of the Huron came in 1648 and in two short seasons the destruction of Huronia was accomplished. It was the Golgotha of a nation. In 1650 the fathers abandoned the mission and accompanied by a few hundred converts sadly retraced the long route to Quebec. For the rest, such of the Huron as were not slaughtered or carried into captivity scattered to the islands of Lake Huron or disappeared in the wilderness of the adjacent mainland. One considerable group fled along the southern shore of Lake Superior to its western end, where for twenty years they found asylum in the wilds of northern Wisconsin.

Huronia was the stepping-stone from Quebec to our own North-west, the Jesuits' wilderness university. Here they learned the language and condition of life of the savages, and this experience was indispensable to their further advance over the Great Lakes and the Mississippi Valley. The mission perished, drowned in a sea of blood, but the hard-won knowledge gained in it survived. A decade later (1660) Father René Ménard was sent out from Quebec in search of the lost remnant of the Huron, which had found refuge in northern Wisconsin. He perished en route, and five more years passed before a successor, in the person of Father Claude Allouez, was sent out. At Chequamegon Bay, near present-day Ashland, Wisconsin, were two villages of Ottawa and Huron, numbering several hundred souls. In addition, the place was a crossroads of travel, to which savages from far and wide resorted. It was an excellent site for a mission, therefore, and here Allouez remained for several years, although laboring with but indifferent success. In 1668 Father Jacques Marquette was sent to relieve him, and Father Allouez transferred his activities to the tribes clustered around Green Bay and along Fox River. While laboring at Chequamegon, Allouez had eagerly collected Indian reports of the Great River of the West, which he conjectured emptied into the ocean "somewhere near Virginia." At the Fox River towns he was told that it was called the "Messi-Sipi," and that one could reach it by a six-day journey. This information, subsequently enlarged by later reports, Allouez carried straightway to Quebec, where his eager hearers puzzled over the problem whether the Great River found outlet in the "Gulf of Florida" or in that of California.

Meanwhile Father Marquette at Chequamegon had developed an ambition to go in search of the Great River, and Louis XIV at Paris had taken New France under his personal protection and had instituted a far-reaching reform of its administration. Among other things, the Iroquois were thoroughly humbled by the splendid Carignan Regiment, dispatched to Canada for this purpose, and in 1667 a peace was concluded which endured for a decade and a half. A great executive, Intendant Jean Talon, was sent to Canada and a brilliant period of reorganization and expansion dawned upon New France. On June 14, 1671, on the pine-girt hill overlooking the waters of Sault Ste. Marie, a cross was erected bearing the arms of

France; and with imposing ceremonial, formal possession was taken of all the Upper Country, together with the vast region stretching to the Arctic Ocean on one side and to the Pacific on the other.

About this time the Huron and Ottawa charges of Father Marquette at Chequamegon became involved in a war with their Sioux neighbors and to escape imminent destruction fled eastward toward the Sault. The missionary had no choice but to accompany them, and after a short stay on Mackinac Island he established on the northern mainland the mission of St. Ignace, on the site of the modern city of this name. Since the time of his arrival at Chequamegon he had not ceased to invoke the Blessed Virgin for permission to visit the natives of the Mississippi. The eastward flight of his charges in 1671 seemed to banish forever any prospect of such an enterprise, but in December 1672 a canoe drew ashore at St. Ignace bearing Louis Jolliet with the welcome news that he had been commissioned to go in search of the Mississippi, and that he brought the permission of Marquette's superior for the father to accompany him on the journey.

The departure could not be made until spring, and the intervening months at the isolated mission were devoted to final preparations. The material equipment for the voyage was small, but the leadership was well-nigh perfect. Jolliet was already an explorer of proved capacity and experience while Father Marquette had eagerly mastered all that could be learned concerning the language and the country of the Illinois. So the two men set forth in May 1673 in two bark canoes with five French voyageurs and a little smoked meat and Indian corn on a voyage "whose duration they could not forsee."

The story of the great exploration has been many times retold[5] and here need only be summarized. Crossing Wisconsin by the Fox-Wisconsin waterway, the explorers came on June 17 to the Great River, a mile wide and flowing between walls of towering cliffs. Down it they paddled for days without sight of human beings until at length a path was found on the western bank and followed to an Illinois village. "How beautiful is the sun, oh Frenchmen," exclaimed the chief of the village, "when thou comest to visit us." The feast which followed, the first in the state of Iowa ever recorded, began with a platter of corn-meal mush!

Days of paddling followed, until the steady southward trend of the river convinced them that its course was to the Gulf of Mexico and not to the Sea of California. So, near the mouth of the Arkansas, fearing to fall into the hands of the Spaniards if they continued, the explorers turned back. At the mouth of the Illinois they turned aside up that stream and, crossing the Chicago Portage, arrived at Lake Michigan and coasted its western shore until they came once more to the Mission House at De Pere on the lower Fox, a few miles above the city of Green Bay. In four months' time they had traversed 3,000 miles of wilderness in two bark canoes without accident or loss and had brought the greatest river and the richest wilderness in the world within the ken of civilized man.

Father Marquette remained at the mission, worn down by illness, while Jolliet busied himself with further explorations of Lake Michigan.[6] The following spring he returned to Canada to carry to the Governor the news of his great discovery, but his canoe was overturned in the rapids above Montreal and all of his records were lost. From memory he drew a map of the continent, on which Lake Michigan in its entirety was drawn for the first time.[7] Marquette meanwhile remained in the West, to perish beside the Stinking Water Lake at the site of present-day Ludington in May 1675. Six years later Melchisidek Thevenot published at Paris his map of the voyage, on which only the western shore line of Lake Michigan appears[8]. On both maps the name Stinking Water is limited to Green Bay (Baye des Puans), while Lake Michigan itself is labeled "Michigan or Illinois."[9] On both, also, the general north and south trend of the lake and the distinction between it and Green Bay are shown for the first time.

So through the explorations of Jolliet and Marquette in 1673-1675 the Lake of the Stinking Water received the name of Michigan or Illinois, while its extent and general contour were for the first time established. For Father Marquette, the exploration constitutes his chief claim to fame; for Jolliet it marks the untimely close of a brilliant career. The man who before the age of thirty had added to the map the Detroit, Wisconsin, Illinois and Mississippi rivers, together with the sites of future St. Louis, Milwaukee, Chicago and Detroit and the entire shore line of Lake Michigan, was never again permitted to visit the West. The further development of the country to which he led the way fell to the lot of others.

---

1 It is probable that Etienne Brulé, like Nicolet a protégé of Champlain, had already visited both Lake Huron and Lake Superior. However, he left no records, and we lack definite knowledge of his discoveries.

2 For the fuller story of the Mission, here briefly summarized, see Fred Landon, *Lake Huron* (Indianapolis, 1944).

3 The fathers, of course, spoke French. With characteristic disregard of logic, American usage has retained the French form of Sault Ste. Marie, while transforming the name of the river to Saint Marys.

4 *Relation* of 1647-1648, printed in *Jesuit Relations,* XXXIII, 149-151.

5 For Marquette's own journal of the expedition, together with additional contemporary documents, see *Jesuit Relations,* LVIII and LIX.

6 This statement is an inference based upon the data contained in the maps which he subsequently drew.

7 It remained unpublished for two hundred years, but the data it contained were known to the Governor and other officials and leaders of New France. For it see *Jesuit Relations,* LIX, 85-86.

8 Although Thevenot ascribed this map to Marquette, it seems probable that some of the data on it came from Jolliet.

9 Spelled "Michigami" by Marquette and "Misschiganin" by Jolliet.

Chapter 3

Dreamer of Empire

Hardly had the bones of Father Marquette been deposited in their final resting place at St. Ignace[1] when a man of radically different temperament and character assumed the leading role in the unfolding drama of Lake Michigan. He was a dreamer no less than Marquette, but unlike the latter, his visions dealt wholly with the affairs of this world. Although he perished in the wilderness, shot down by assassins over a quarter of a millennium ago, within the last half-dozen years half a dozen books have been written about him. The entire period of his activity in this region covered but half a decade, yet his influence over it still abides.

Robert Cavelier, Sieur de la Salle, was a native of Rouen, who in early manhood followed an elder brother to Canada and Montreal. Here he obtained a tract of land beside the rushing Lachine Rapids and began the task of developing it as a feudal seigniory. But the great river which swept past his door beckoned him irresistibly to the interior, and before long he sold his seigniory to embark upon the career of western exploration which was to bring him undying fame.

For La Salle, the return of Jolliet to Canada from the western exploration of 1673-1674 marked the opening of the door of opportunity upon his new career. He had already undergone his preliminary wilderness schooling and was ready for a rendezvous with Destiny. Despite the brilliance of Jolliet's achievements, Governor Frontenac had no further use for the explorer. The Governor had come out to Canada two years before, intent upon recouping his ruined fortune, and this could be accomplished only through his manipulation of the Indian trade. New France was rent by feuds and one of the bitterest was the quarrel between the Jesuits and the State. The Jesuits had already gained firm control over Lake Huron and Lake Superior and were eager to extend their influence southward over the new-found Mississippi country. This prize, however,

Count Frontenac intended to monopolize and he required an agent wholly unassociated with the order. So Jolliet was brushed aside and the opportunity of exploiting the country to the west and south of Lake Michigan was awarded to La Salle.

The new favorite was no humdrum toiler, satisfied to lead a life of contented obscurity. Instead his restless mind entertained visions of breath-taking projects, the scope of which is conveniently suggested by the name Lachine, or China, which still remains attached to the site of his first Canadian enterprise. The newcomer was intent on solving the age-old puzzle of a water route to China; and whether he himself named his estate or the name originated as a derisive jibe of his enemies, its significance remains the same.

For a few years La Salle and his patron were busy developing Fort Frontenac on Lake Ontario, on the site of future Kingston, to serve as an advance base for his real western push. The summer of 1679 found this task completed, and with a grant of authority from the King and with two small sailing vessels on Lake Ontario (the first ever built on the Great Lakes) to convey supplies and furs between Fort Frontenac and Niagara, La Salle was ready to undertake the winning of the valley of the Mississippi for France and civilization. Long since, the Spaniards had gained a secure foothold south of the United States with claims extending indefinitely northward from Florida and the Gulf of Mexico, while the English had founded a row of colonies along the Atlantic Coast, with claims to dominion inland from sea to sea. The significance of La Salle's design lay in the fact that the richest valley in the world was still unoccupied and the question remained whether it should become the seat of a Spanish, French or English civilization.

It was La Salle's plan to establish a colony in the Illinois country to serve as the base for prosecuting his commercial and imperial designs, and to find for it an outlet to the sea and to Europe by way of the still unexplored lower Mississippi. Thus New France would extend from the St. Lawrence to the Mexican Gulf, the English colonies would be surrounded and those of Spain in North America would be neatly cut in twain.

In the autumn of 1678 an advance party of fifteen men was sent out to Lake Michigan to accumulate a cargo of furs from the Indians. The following January La Salle himself dispatched a force of workmen who established a shipyard above the Falls of Niagara, and with materials forwarded from Fort Frontenac built a ship of forty-five tons for use on the Upper Lakes.[2] With the ships La Salle already had on Lake Ontario, he was thus provided with transportation, unbroken save at Niagara, from Fort Frontenac to the southern end of Lake Michigan. This was vital to the prosecution of his design, since until he should find an outlet by way of the Gulf of Mexico, supplies for his colony and the furs with which he expected to finance it must be carried by water between Illinois and Lower Canada.

In August 1679 the vessel was ready, and with her sails spread to the breeze and aided at times by men tugging on a rope ashore, she breasted the rapid current of the river and entered Lake Erie. Three days and nights of sailing brought the ship to the mouth of the Detroit at what is now Amherstburg, where La Salle found the river current as strong as the tide at his native Rouen. The ascent of the strait to Port Huron was made without particular difficulty, however, save for the search for a navigable channel at the St. Clair Flats. At the exit into Lake Huron the current is normally rapid, and a strong north wind blowing for some time had piled up the water to make it "violent as the bar at Caudebec." Although a good wind now blew from the south, La Salle had again to send a tow rope ashore, manned by twelve sailors, to enable the ship to breast the current and enter the lake. Today a steady procession of great ships, carrying the ore which maintains the freedom of the world, passes beneath the Blue Water Bridge into and out of Lake Huron, where once taut sails and straining sailors labored together to transport La Salle's tiny vessel.

Somewhere off Thunder Bay a violent storm was encountered and Father Hennepin records (although La Salle does not) that all on board took to their knees in prayer, save for the pilot, a veteran salt-water tar, who instead "did nothing all that while but curse and swear against M. La Salle, who as he said had brought him thither to make him perish in a nasty lake, and lose the glory he had acquired by his long and happy navigations on the ocean." But the pilot's

Courtesy of the U.S. Coast Guard

AN ICEBREAKER IN ACTION

The ice crusher in the foreground is opening a pathway for the *Thomas W. Lamont* and an unidentified freighter in background. Picture taken at the Straits of Mackinac in April 1943

Courtesy of the U.S. Coast Guard

GUARDING THE WAY OF THE SAILOR

Lighted buoy No. 24 in foreground and Hills Point Lighthouse in background. For lack of such safeguards scores of Great Lakes ships went to destruction less than a century ago.

hour had not yet struck; whether because of the prayers or the curses the ship rode out the tempest and on August 27, twenty days out from Niagara, cast anchor before the Jesuit mission at St. Ignace.

Here was an Indian village, and here, to his surprise, La Salle found several of the men he had sent on the preceding autumn to trade with the Illinois for furs. Six of the men had deserted, having wasted or embezzled the supplies La Salle had entrusted to them, while the others had become discouraged by adverse rumors and false reports. Henry de Tonty, his faithful lieutenant, was sent with a party of six men to the Sault, where he seized two of the deserters and recovered the goods still in their possession. Moved by the lateness of the season and the fear of winter storms on the lake, La Salle pushed on to the Green Bay Peninsula, without awaiting their return. At a Potawatomi village on Washington Island he found some more of his men with a considerable quantity of furs, and he dispatched the vessel loaded with the furs to Niagara. On arriving there and discharging the cargo the ship was to return with all speed to the mouth of the St. Joseph, to which place, meanwhile, La Salle was to proceed by canoe around the western and southern shore of the lake, while Tonty's party would descend the eastern shore from St. Ignace to the appointed rendezvous.

The *Griffin* set sail from Washington Island September 18, 1679, "with a light and very favorable wind from the west." Having seen it off, La Salle, with fourteen men and four canoes, laden with a forge and carpenters' and sawyers' tools, struck southward across the Death Door entrance to Green Bay for the Door County mainland. When halfway across, immediately after a complete calm, he encountered a sudden tempest which raged for four days "furiously as the greatest storms at sea." Although La Salle and his company made the land in safety the men on the *Griffin* did not, for after the ship's departure from Washington Island no white man ever saw her again. The natives afterward related that she had anchored somewhere along the north shore of the lake, and despite their warnings of an impending storm her pilot had set sail to vanish from their sight amid the storm-tossed seas. Thus Lake Michigan gained her first maritime mystery. To this day the unhappy fate of the

Griffin fascinates the minds of men, and from time to time hopeful enthusiasts still announce their supposed discovery and identification of her rotting remains.

The journey of La Salle and his men down the western shore of Lake Michigan proved difficult enough. Not until September 25 did the lake subside enough to permit them to leave the spot where they were marooned on the nineteenth. After paddling all day and into the night of the twenty-fifth, they escaped a fresh tempest by landing on a "bare rock" where they remained two days, exposed to the rain and snow and warmed only by a little fire of driftwood. Another spurt from noon until late into the night of September 28 was terminated by another storm. For two days they were stranded on a rocky point, where the last of the corn and pumpkins they had obtained from the Potawatomi were consumed. Next day they paddled ten leagues on empty stomachs and finally came to another village. Here the bank was high and a strong wind was driving heavy seas on shore. La Salle and his three companions in the leading canoe leaped into the water and bore the boat ashore despite the waves which at times completely covered them. Then they plunged back into the lake to assist in rescuing the remaining canoes.

So the journey continued, past present-day Milwaukee, Kenosha, Chicago and Michigan City with alternate alarms from tempests a-sea and savages ashore, and with food so scarce that aged Father Gabriel, who accompanied the expedition, several times fainted away, until on November 1 they came to the appointed rendezvous at the mouth of the St. Joseph. Neither the *Griffin* nor Tonty's party were there, and La Salle improved the period of waiting by erecting on the bluff beside the river mouth a stockaded fort, the first such structure west of Kingston. Since the St. Joseph was then called the Miami, this name was given the fort. The site today adjoins the business center of St. Joseph, while in front, beneath the face of the bluff where the vessel was to have found anchorage, stretches sandy Silver Beach, popular playground for resorters from Chicago and other midland cities.

Throughout November the men toiled steadily, save on Sundays and Feast days, when the two fathers took turns at preaching to the entire company. On the twentieth Tonty arrived with his party of twenty men from Mackinac. The joy which greeted his coming was tempered by the report that the *Griffin* had not returned to Mackinac from Niagara, and that all his inquiries of the Indians concerning her had proved fruitless. Despite this heavy blow to his enterprise La Salle determined to persevere in his plan of proceeding to the Illinois by way of the St. Joseph and the Kankakee, and on December 3, with thirty men and eight canoes, the journey was begun. At South Bend, within easy sight today of the golden dome of Notre Dame University, the portage to the Kankakee was begun. Although the country normally abounded in buffaloes, deer and smaller game, the natives had fired the grass which covered the Kankakee marshes and the wild animals had fled before the flames, compelling the explorers to journey with tightened belts and empty stomachs through this veritable wilderness Eden.

On January 1, 1680, they came to the great village near Starved Rock, where five years earlier Father Marquette had opened the Illinois Mission. Finding the villagers all absent on their winter hunt, and pressed by his urgent necessity for food, La Salle helped himself to thirty bushels of corn from their underground store, planning to explain his action and pay for the food at the first opportunity. Four days later, on January 5, they entered Lake Peoria and rounding a projecting point came suddenly upon another village. Women, children and old men fled in terror to the woods, while the warriors rushed to arms. In the midst of this confusion the white men swept to the landing and leaped ashore, in readiness for instant battle. Instead, a parley ensued, at which La Salle explained his peaceful intentions and his desire to build a "great wooden canoe" in their midst which would go down to the sea and return laden with the white man's goods they so eagerly desired.

A night or two later all of the sawyers whom La Salle had brought along to build the ship deserted to the wilderness. Despite this setback, he began the erection of Fort Crevecoeur on a hill overlooking the foot of the lake, and by the first of the month had all the lumber in readiness for putting a forty-two-foot vessel on the stocks. The site of the fort, the first fixed establishment built by white men in the entire Mississippi Valley, is today marked by a historical monument. Below, as of old, the placid river slips past; but the wilderness to which the affrighted squaws and children fled for refuge in 1680 is now replaced by the factories and homes of busy Peoria.

Although the fort was completed and the lumber for the ship was in readiness, there was still no news of the *Griffin,* which was to have brought to St. Joseph the materials for ironwork, sails and rigging. Since vain waiting was useless, La Salle now reached the desperate resolve to return on foot through the snows and floods of springtime to Fort Frontenac to make new arrangements for the supplies he needed. During March and April the terrible journey was performed, and in August 1680, having ordered his affairs in Canada, he set out once more for the West, traveling by way of Mackinac and the east coast of Lake Michigan to Fort Miami and thence, as before, by way of the St. Joseph and the Kankakee to the Illinois.

Meanwhile Tonty had gone from Lake Peoria to fortify Starved Rock, and the men he left behind at Fort Crevecoeur took advantage of his absence to scuttle the fort and desert to the wilderness. Of more far-reaching consequence than this desertion, the Iroquois Indians, at peace with the French since 1667, seeing in the enterprise of La Salle and Count Frontenac a threat to their own prosperity, had raided the Illinois country, several hundred strong, and destroyed or driven in flight across the Mississippi the villagers at Starved Rock and Lake Peoria.

In Huronia in earlier decades the French had done nothing to protect their native allies, who had fallen easy victims to the Iroquois. Now, however, La Salle proposed to organize the western tribes into a confederation, which with French supplies and guidance should repel the murderous raiders; in return for the furs which his western allies would supply, he would provide the goods they needed and pay the cost of supporting his colony.

Another year was spent in gathering his scattered resources and in making further journeys to and fro around Lake Michigan. Late in 1681 he was again at Fort Miami in readiness for the grand push down the Mississippi. This time his party made its way in canoes around the end of the lake to Chicago. Here, the river being frozen, the canoes were placed on sleds and hauled across the portage and down the Des Plaines and the Illinois as far as Lake Peoria, where open water was encountered. The Mississippi was entered on February 6, 1682, and two months later the explorers gazed upon the waters of the Gulf of Mexico. Near Memphis, La Salle had paused to erect a small fort; farther down river he had planted a cross and formally claimed the country for his king; and now, beside the gulf, the ceremonial enacted eleven years earlier by St. Lusson at Sault Ste. Marie was repeated. A cross bearing the arms of France was planted, the *Vexilla regis* and the *Te Deum* were chanted and a volley of musketry was fired; in the presence of a handful of Frenchmen and a few savages all of the country drained by the Mississippi and its many tributaries was claimed for the King of France. Thus, on April 9, 1682, the imperial province of Louisiana was born.

On the return journey to Illinois, La Salle fell ill and lay for several weeks at the fort near Memphis, while Tonty with five companions pressed on to Mackinac to forward to Governor Frontenac a report of the successful outcome of the expedition. Here La Salle joined him in September, intending to go on to France, but the Iroquois were again invading the country and he was forced to postpone the journey until the Illinois country could be made secure against the invaders. During the ensuing winter Fort St. Louis was constructed on Starved Rock and soon the lodges of several thousand natives, gathered from half a dozen tribes, were clustered around it.

Already, however, a new and crushing disaster to La Salle's enterprise impended. Count Frontenac, his stanch supporter, was recalled to France and La Barre, the new Governor, pursued a policy of determined hostility toward him. His supplies and ammunition were detained, lying reports about him were sent to the home government and an agent was sent to supersede him in the command of Fort St. Louis.

La Salle's only remedy against such an enemy was to appeal in person to the King of France. He left the Illinois country for the last time in 1683, and two letters written at Chicago on June 4 and September 2 of this year indicate either that he tarried there a considerable period, or that he twice paused there on his journeys to and fro. In France, he was completely successful. His command and honors in New France were restored by the king and he was lionized by the Court. His requests for colonists and supplies needed to establish his Mississippi colony were granted and in July 1684 he sailed with a fleet of vessels for the Gulf of Mexico.

Unable to locate the mouth of the Mississippi, however, his colonists were landed far to the westward on the coast of Texas. We need not enter into the tragic story of the leader's vain efforts to find again the Mississippi and re-establish connection with his Illinois colony. On March 19, 1687, somewhere on the Brazos River, he was murdered and his body was left to the vultures and wild beasts. Although the dreamer perished, his vision endured, and before many years the colony of Louisiana became a reality. Largely through his efforts the work which Jolliet and Marquette had begun of bringing Lake Michigan within the ken of civilization was completed. Its general contour and its geographical relation to the chain of Great Lakes and the upper Mississippi were clarified; its shore line now embraced in the states of Wisconsin, Illinois, Indiana and Michigan, was repeatedly traversed. Missions at Chicago and St. Joseph were presently added to those at St. Ignace and De Pere. All of these places became centers of trade and settlement, being numbered among the earliest centers of white civilization in the interior of the United States. At Starved Rock, which continued to be occupied for many years after La Salle's departure, the earliest land grants in the State of Illinois—quite possibly the earliest west of Niagara—were made. Finally, the travel narrative of the mendacious Father Hennepin, an associate of La Salle, which was first published at Paris in 1683 and reprinted in many editions and languages, advertised the western country throughout the length and breadth of Europe.

---

[1] Marquette died and was buried by his voyageur companions on the lake shore at Ludington in the spring of 1675. Two years later some savages visited the spot and having exhumed the body and cleaned the bones in accordance with ancient tribal custom, they carried them to St. Ignace where they were reinterred under the Mission House. Two hundred years later, the supposed site of this burial was located, and a monument to Marquette now marks the spot. Some tiny bits of bones taken from it are preserved at Marquette University in Milwaukee.

[2] According to Father Hennepin, who accompanied the expedition, La Salle named the ship the *Griffin* in compliment to Count Frontenac, whose coat of arms bore two griffins as supporters. La Salle himself nowhere names the vessel and Jean Delanglez surmises that the name is one of the many inventions of Hennepin when his narrative was being prepared in Paris several years later. See his "Hennepin's Description of Louisiana," *Mid-America*, XII, 120.

Chapter 4

Itching Foot and Iron Hand

Among the followers of La Salle, two achieved lasting fame, imprinting their memory forever upon the Great Lakes and the Mississippi Valley. One was a soldier, the other a priest. Henry de Tonty, the soldier, was loyal and honest, self-reliant and brave. Father Louis Hennepin, the priest, was a vain and boastful vagabond, treacherous, vengeful and dishonest. Both sleep in unknown graves, which the snows of almost 250 winters have covered, yet the character and personality of each remains as sharp and clear today as it was to their contemporary associates.

Father Hennepin was a native of Ath in Belgium, where to this day a street bears his name. At its head is a public watering place, erected long since as a memorial to him, and inscribed with the preposterous statement that he "discovered the Mississippi River in 1680."[1] Throughout his life the father was driven by a demon of restlessness and an itch for travel and adventure which he was powerless to control. He has himself related that a sister whom he dearly loved labored to discourage his wandering propensities, but all her solicitations were in vain, for he would not and probably could not endure a life of humdrum routine.

For such a man to enter the priesthood was a tragic mistake. At one time he was stationed at the ancient seaport town of Calais. He relates:

"Being there, I was passionately in love with hearing the Relations that Masters of Ships gave of their Voyages. Afterwards I returned to our Convent at Biez, by way of Dunkirk; But I used ofttimes to sculk behind the Doors of Victualling-Houses to hear the Seamen give an account of their Adventures. The Smoak of Tobacco was offensive to me, and created Pain in my Stomach, while I was thus intent upon giving ear to their Relations: But for all [that] I was very attentive to the accounts they gave of their Encounters by Sea, the Perils they had gone through, and all the accidents which befell them in their long Voyages. This Occupation was so agreeable and engaging that I have spent whole Days and Nights at it without eating; for hereby I always came to understand some new thing concerning the Customs and Ways of Living in remote Places; and concerning the Pleasantness, Fertility, and Riches of the Countries where these Men had been."

The war between France and Holland was now raging and Hennepin was drawn into it as a chaplain. At Maestricht in 1673 he "administered the Sacraments to above 3000 wounded Men." He modestly continues:

"The singular zeal I had for promoting the Good of Souls engaged me the year following to be present at the Battle of Seneffe, where I was busied in administering comfort to the poor wounded Men: Till at length, after having endured all manner of Fatigue and Toil, and having run the risk of extreme Dangers at Sieges of Towns in the Trenches, and in Fields of Battel (where I never ceased to expose myself for the good of Men's Souls) while those bloody Men were breathing nothing but Slaughter and Blood, I happily found myself in a condition to satisfie my first Inclination."

In 1675, at the request of Governor Frontenac, several Récollet priests were sent out to Canada, and to the great joy of Hennepin he was included among the number. A fellow passenger on the ship that bore the friars to Quebec was La Salle, returning to Canada with his newly won patent of nobility and his plans for the development of Fort Frontenac. On such a voyage he could scarcely escape becoming acquainted with Hennepin, of whom he seems to have formed a good opinion. At any rate, in 1678 when he again returned from France to Canada in readiness to launch his westward push for Lake Michigan and the Illinois country, he brought an order for Hennepin to accompany him; and when a few months later at Lake Peoria La Salle decided to send a party of three men to explore the upper Mississippi, the father was one of the number. Eventually he made his way back to Canada and to France, where with commendable enterprise he made haste to bring out, in 1683, his book called *Description de la Louisiane*.

La Salle was at this time very much alive, although still in the Illinois wilderness. In 1697, when the explorer had been dead for a decade, Father Hennepin reissued his *Louisiane,* under the title *A New Discovery of A Vast Country in America.* In addition to the new title, the book now contained an addendum in which, with amazing audacity, Hennepin related that he had himself descended the Mississippi to its mouth in 1680, thereby robbing La Salle of the credit for his greatest achievement, the tracing of the Mississippi to the gulf in the spring of 1682.

It would be idle to relate in detail the father's diverting narrative of the perils he endured and the travels and discoveries he made. Although he was never the leader, even on the three-man expedition to the upper Mississippi, he calmly ascribes this role to himself throughout his narrative. He served as chaplain to the men engaged in building the *Griffin* at Niagara, and when this ship was in readiness to sail for the Upper Lakes in the summer of 1679 Hennepin was a member of her company. He accompanied La Salle on his canoe voyage down the western shore of Lake Michigan and on the descent of the Kankakee and the Illinois to Fort Crevecoeur. From here, at the end of February 1680, he set out in the company of two men, Michael Accau and Antoine Augel, for the upper Mississippi.

Although Accau was the leader of the party, Hennepin, who was the only educated member of it, enjoyed an opportunity for which any modern reporter would almost give his soul. Marquette, on his descent of the Mississippi in 1673, had described it only briefly; to Hennepin was reserved the opportunity of giving to the world its first detailed picture of the great river from the Illinois northward to far above St. Paul.

The result of his effort was a confused, although lively relation of experiences, commonly impossible to identify with the known geography of the region. Somewhere upriver a Sioux war party made prisoners of the white men, whom they carried back to their own Minnesota homeland. Although the friar makes much of the dangers and hardships they underwent, their captors seem to have treated them kindly on the whole. At Lake Pepin they wept over them so profusely that Hennepin called this the Lake of Tears.[2]

Eventually Hennepin and Augel separated from Accau and began the descent of the Mississippi, passing the falls which Hennepin named in honor of his patron saint, Saint Anthony of Padua. Frequently they were so desperate for food that they eagerly watched the eagles flying overhead to salvage the fish which occasionally slipped from their beaks. The river swarmed with fish and they had a supply of hooks, yet they were seldom able to catch any. Once, after fishing two days without success, they prayed fervently to Saint Anthony to come to their aid. Before the prayer was ended a commotion arose, and while the father continued to pray his companion ran to the hooks where he found two catfish so large that he could not pull them from the water until the friar concluded his prayer and came to his aid.

At length a man of sterner stuff than the father appeared on the scene in the person of the woodranger, Daniel Greysolon Duluth. Somewhere in the vicinity of Lake Superior he had heard of the three Frenchmen on the Mississippi and with only four companions had set out in search of them. Sternly rebuking the Sioux for their ill-treatment of his countrymen, he took charge of the Frenchmen, and proceeding down river as far as the Wisconsin, crossed by that waterway to Green Bay. In due time Father Hennepin made his way back to Quebec, where his colleagues, supposing him long since dead, received him with amazement.

Returning to France, Hennepin prepared his book by the simple process of plagiarizing wholesale from the Memoir of La Salle, eking it out, of course, with variations and contributions of his own. Niagara Falls, for example, which the father had really visited, was "above" 600 feet in height. His fictional description of the mouth of the Mississippi provoked the comment of a French scholar in 1699, following Iberville's Mississippi voyage: "If Father Hennepin had not hidden himself already, he would have to do so on the appearance of this authentic description of the mouth of the Mississippi, so totally different from what he says he saw."[3] Yet it remained for a diligent Catholic scholar of our own day to expose the full measure of the friar's mendacity, and to strip from him the last shred of any claim to common honesty.[4]

Despite his defects of character, however, Hennepin's place in the history of the Northwest is secure. The spirit of adventure which led him into strange and unknown places enabled him to provide a public avid for information about America with one of our earliest and liveliest descriptions of the new land and its strange and savage inhabitants. The simple truth about his travels and observations was enough to confer both fame and prosperity upon him. Because he departed from it, his period of success was brief; his braggart and dishonest character was exposed, and he died in obscurity and want.

Henry de Tonty was an Italian who was taken in infancy to France. At the age of eighteen he entered the army, where he remained for a decade, serving much of the time on naval expeditions. On one of these, while attempting to board a hostile ship, his right hand was mangled by a grenade. He finished the job of cutting it off without awaiting the aid of a surgeon, and presently replaced the missing member with one made of iron. Like Captain Hook of Barrie's fairy tale, he occasionally mowed down an obstreperous opponent with it, and after coming to America the Indians far and wide knew him as The Man with the Iron Hand. In 1678, when the war in Europe was over for a time and Tonty was in want of employment, he was introduced to La Salle, in whose service he immediately enlisted. Never was there a happier meeting, for until La Salle's death almost a decade later Tonty served him with singular fidelity and skill.

Returning from France to America in the summer of 1678, La Salle, accompanied by Tonty, pushed on to Fort Frontenac, where he pressed the preparations for launching his western enterprise the following year. The first important task was the building of the ship to be used in navigating the Upper Lakes. This consumed the winter and spring of 1678-1679, and Tonty superintended the construction of the vessel in the shipyard at Niagara. When it was completed he tried to navigate it up the river into Lake Erie, but contrary winds and current and the smallness of his crew defeated his effort. La Salle now came on with more men and an extra anchor, and with their aid the ship, which is commonly called the *Griffin*, was worked up the rapids.

La Salle had sent a band of hunters on ahead the previous autumn to procure a store of furs for a return cargo for his ship, and he now dispatched Tonty and five men in an open boat to locate them and await the arrival of the *Griffin* at the mouth of the Detroit. Tonty was a veteran soldier in Europe but he was still a tenderfoot in the American wilderness, and it took him nearly three weeks to traverse Lake Erie. During all this time practically the only food his little party had consisted of a few edible herbs they found in the woods along the lake shore.

Early in August they reached the Detroit and went into camp on a low point just below modern Amherstburg, where lake and river meet. During the night they were forced from their beds by the waves of the lake which an onshore gale was driving over their camping ground. The rude awakening proved fortunate, however, for at dawn they saw the *Griffin* in the distance, and by building a signal fire they brought her to anchor and were taken on board.

At St. Ignace, La Salle learned that some of his hunters had absconded and sought asylum with the savages at Sault Ste. Marie. Tonty was dispatched in pursuit of them, while La Salle himself continued his journey to Green Bay and thence around the lake to the St. Joseph. With characteristic efficiency and brevity of speech, Tonty "captured the said deserters" and returned with them to St. Ignace. While he tarried here (probably awaiting the return of the *Griffin* from Green Bay) one of his men was wounded by an Indian. Although he had but seventeen Frenchmen in his party he calmly demanded satisfaction of the savages and when it was not forthcoming prepared to storm their fortified town. The warriors poured out to meet the attackers and a bloody conflict was only averted at the last moment by the Jesuit missionary, who persuaded the chiefs to ask for pardon and to "cover" the Frenchman's wound with the present of a few furs.

With peace restored but with the *Griffin* still missing, Tonty set out southward along the shore of western Michigan to the appointed rendezvous with his chief at St. Joseph. Winter was now at hand and provisions were again lacking. Some of the men were left behind to hunt for food while Tonty himself pushed on to St. Joseph. There La Salle, impatient to be off for the Illinois, sent him back to find the missing hunters. A storm on the lake drove him to seek shelter in the river mouth at South Haven, but before it could be reached the canoe capsized in the pounding billows. The occupants made the shore drenched to the skin and half frozen, and for several days their only food was the acorns they found beneath the snow.

La Salle's return to Lower Canada in the spring of 1680 and the scuttling of Fort Crevecoeur and the vessel during the absence of Tonty at Starved Rock have already been described. Tonty returned to Peoria to be met by this scene of destruction. Save for himself and the two priests, only five men had remained loyal to La Salle. He dispatched two of them to carry to La Salle the news of the fresh disaster, while he, with the others, remained at Crevecoeur awaiting the return of their leader. So the summer weeks passed by slowly, with the imperial interests of the King of France upheld in the Mississippi Valley by one Italian, two priests and three other Frenchmen. One of these three was a mere youth and one of the priests was old and feeble, worn out by the wilderness hardships he had for years undergone.

Autumn came on lovely as a poet's dream in the heart of one of the world's richest valleys, but with it came 600 Iroquois warriors, ravenous as tiger sharks. They had been at peace with the government of New France since 1667, but they were determined to prevent La Salle from establishing a direct trade with the Illinois and the one way to accomplish this was to "shoot them up." Although the invaders came armed with guns, while the Illinois had only such Stone Age weapons as bows and arrows and war clubs, about 400 warriors rallied in defense of their homeland.

With the two armies face to face and with some irregular fighting already beginning, Tonty pushed forward, accompanied by a single Illinois spokesman, on the desperate errand of averting the combat. Despite the wampum strings which the two ambassadors displayed to signify their peaceful purpose, they were greeted by a volley from the Iroquois guns as soon as they came within range. At this, Tonty told his companion to return, and he himself walked steadily on toward the foe. In the hostile camp mixed counsels prevailed, and while one of the chiefs embraced him a warrior drove a dagger at his heart. A protecting rib turned the knife point aside but streams of blood poured from his side and his mouth. Another warrior snatched his hat and held it aloft on the muzzle of his gun, while the Illinois and their trio of French allies, supposing him to have been slain, pressed the attack with fresh vigor. But now the Iroquois chiefs closed in a circle around him and demanded to know the object of his errand. "Never was I in such perplexity before," he wrote at a later time; for while the chiefs were telling him he had no reason for fear, a warrior standing behind him fingered his knife with one hand and ran the other through Tonty's hair, momentarily lifting it in readiness to remove the scalp.

Although the Frenchman was wondering whether he would meet with instant slaughter or be reserved for the more dreadful end of death by torture, his self-possession won his escape from both of these fates. The chiefs demanded to know the numbers of their opponents, and Tonty's answer trebled the Illinois warriors and multiplied the Frenchmen by ten. This deceit planted a doubt in the minds of his captors over the outcome of the battle and induced them to send Tonty back to the Illinois with a request for a further parley. Fainting from shock and loss of blood, he staggered back across the open space to meet the two fathers, coming to administer to him the rite for the dying.

The Iroquois peace proffer was about as sincere as a Hitlerite solemn oath, yet two or three days passed in mutual palavering. Tonty, meanwhile, steadily warned the Illinois that they were marked for destruction and that only instant departure from the vicinity would save them. The presence of such a counselor was inconvenient to the invaders, who sought by "covering" his wound with a gift of beaver skins to induce him to set out at once for Canada. He insisted, however, on first knowing when they themselves proposed to leave Illinois, upon which angry murmurs arose and some of the warriors shouted that before they left they meant to drink Illinois blood. At this Tonty, in the midst of 600 snarling warriors, kicked the proffered beaver skins violently aside and informed the chiefs that he would have none of their presents while they were planning to kill the allies of his King.

This act was a deadly insult to the Iroquois and except for its sheer audacity he would probably have been instantly slain. As it was, the enraged chiefs drove him from the council, and the six Frenchmen passed the night in their cabin in momentary expectation of being put to death. In the morning they were harshly ordered to be gone, and since further resistance seemed futile they made haste to place their scanty supplies along with aged Father Gabriel in a canoe which two of the men poled upriver, while Tonty and the remaining two walked along the shore.

Measured by any sensible standard the six men were already as good as dead. Around them swarmed hundreds of Iroquois, to say nothing of Potawatomi, Miami and other skulking local bands of savages. With winter close at hand, with a single paper-thin canoe, burdened by a feeble old man and singularly unburdened with food and other necessities of life, they must make their way through half a thousand miles of wilderness before reaching the nearest white refuge at Green Bay, Wisconsin, or its neighbor, somewhat farther removed, at St. Ignace. Even today, with all the resources of modern engineering skill expended upon ships hundreds of feet in length and driven by engines as powerful as any in the world, men do not lightly brave the stormy waters of Lake Michigan in midwinter. The only possible hope for the survival of Tonty's little party rested in the wholly intangible iron will of the leader.

Within a few hours after the start, tragedy, not unmixed with mercy, visited the little band of fugitives. A pause was made to repair a leak in the canoe, and Father Gabriel improved the time, despite Tonty's earnest warning, to withdraw into the prairie for secret prayer. He did not return, night came on, guns were fired and a signal fire blazed to guide the lost man back to camp. But all was in vain. In the morning Tonty followed his footsteps in the prairie grass until they became mingled with the tracks of many savages. Sadly the searchers gave their companion up for dead, and months later this conclusion was verified when his bones were found in a sinkhole, the skull broken by blows of a savage war club. However grievous his fate seemed at the moment, before many weeks the five survivors were viewing it as a providential escape from the more prolonged miseries they were undergoing.

There were now five Frenchmen left to continue the flight, including one priest and one youth. At the forks of the Illinois they kept to the left up the Des Plaines, and crossing the portage descended the

Chicago to the shore of Lake Michigan. Here, where the towers of Michigan Boulevard today look down upon Grant Park, they again repaired their canoe and launched forth upon the Inland Sea, sorely beset by hunger and exposed to the strong gales of late autumn. With frequent landings to hunt for food, they struggled northward until on November 1 their boat was driven shoreward and utterly wrecked somewhere north of Milwaukee.

Father Membré and the boy had been with La Salle on his descent of the Wisconsin shore line the year before, and they recalled that somewhere farther north was a Potawatomi village. This now became their goal, and for days the fugitives, now reduced to four since Boisrondet, the strongest man in the party, had become separated from the others, pushed desperately ahead, frequently becoming lost and finding themselves at the end of a day of toil back at their place of departure in the morning. At length on November 11, faint from hunger and with feet and legs cut and bleeding from repeatedly breaking through the ice which covered the marshes, they came upon a path which led in the direction of the Indian town. With hope renewed they stumbled onward, only to find on emerging from the forest upon the lake shore the cold and empty huts of a silent and deserted village whose inmates had all departed upon their annual winter hunt.

They were saved for the time being, notwithstanding, for the lodges afforded shelter from the cold and the refuse dumps and cornfields gave a scanty supply of food. On the shore, too, was a canoe, and Tonty now proposed that they remain in the village until they could find enough food to enable them to make the voyage to St. Ignace. Although an entire day of searching turned up "hardly two handfuls of Indian corn," they fell to work with a will and day by day noted the slow increase of their precious hoard.

But now a fresh disaster occurred to dash their plans. The missing Boisrondet staggered into the village while all were absent hunting for food, and supposing the provisions had been left behind for him, recruited his famished body upon them, and by the time the others returned from a three-day absence in the fields the precious store they had accumulated was sadly diminished.

The project of continuing the voyage in the canoe to St. Ignace was now abandoned and in its stead the effort was made to follow the natives to their winter hunting camp. Their trail led toward Sturgeon Bay, and carrying the canoe for possible future use, the fugitives went doggedly onward. On reaching the bay they again embarked but soon were forced ashore where they were wind-bound for many days. With their provisions now entirely gone and in despair of overtaking the savages, they decided to return to the last village they had passed, where there was a supply of wood and where they might at least die warm. The wind went down and with this resolve they again embarked. Before long they came upon the embers of a campfire which some savage had only recently abandoned. Here was the prospect of help, but their strength and their resolution were both at an end. "None of us could stand from weakness, all of us were like skeletons," wrote Father Membré. Even now Tonty sought to inspire them to make one more effort, but in vain. Resigned to death, they were only awaiting its arrival when two Ottawa hunters stumbled upon the spot and conducted them to the camp of the Potawatomi, which was not far away.

The chief, who had established friendly relations with La Salle the year before, extended all the resources of savage hospitality to the fugitives. Safe at last, they slowly recruited their strength while their cut and frozen limbs were healing. Within a few days Father Membré was able to go on to the Jesuit Mission at Green Bay. Tonty, still ill, remained with the Indians until summer, when he was at length reunited with La Salle at St. Ignace.

For more than twenty years longer he remained in Illinois, where from his fortified station atop Starved Rock he conducted a trade in furs, pausing from time to time to make a journey to the Gulf of Mexico or to lead his western warriors eastward to wage war against the Iroquois. During all these years he enjoyed throughout the vast valley a reputation for tenacity and bravery which endures to the present day. A random illustration of it is afforded by the testimony of Father St. Cosme who in 1698 journeyed from Mackinac to the lower Mississippi in Tonty's company. Not only was he "universally beloved by all the voyageurs," wrote the father to his superior, but he was highly esteemed by all the savages. "He had only to be in one's company," he added, "to prevent any insult being offered." When some disaffected savages were muttering dark threats of violence, he reminded them that they had seen him among the Iroquois and "knew how many men he could kill," calmly adding that "he feared not men."

So, in a land of abject savagery, he maintained for almost two decades a center of civilization, fairly earning for himself, meanwhile, the title of First Settler of Illinois. At length in 1700 he left to join the new colony which Iberville in pursuance of La Salle's dream had founded on the gulf, east of the mouth of the Mississippi. He died there, probably from yellow fever, four years later. No man ever looked upon death with more contempt or faced the duties of life more steadfastly than Henry de Tonty.

---

[1] Edward C. Gale, "On the Hennepin Trail," *Minnesota History*, XI, 3-4.

[2] The Sioux of 1680, like a Hollywood actress today, could weep copiously whenever the occasion demanded. Such demonstrations were frequent, and to the object of their attentions were more or less devastating. The outpour at Lake Pepin was apparently unusually torrential.

[3] See Grace L. Nute, "Father Hennepin's Later Years," *Minnesota History*, XIX, 397.

[4] Jean Delanglez, "Hennepin's Description of Louisiana," *Mid-America*, XII, 3-44, 99-137.

Chapter 5

Cities in Embryo

IN THE footsteps of the explorer came the trader and the priest, and both followed the highways of travel which led to the Indian towns. Trader and missionary alike must find customers for their wares, and like any modern merchant they sought the centers of savage life and activity.

The earliest missions on Lake Michigan were those of St. Ignace at Mackinac and St. Francis Xavier on Green Bay, both begun in the winter of 1669-1670. Some twenty years later the Mission of St. Joseph was founded at present-day Niles, and in 1696 the Mission of the Guardian Angel at the northern edge of Chicago's throbbing Loop. *Coureurs de bois* or outlaw traders had preceded the missionaries at these sites, and all were strategic centers of trade and travel where government forts were presently established.

The closing decades of the seventeenth century thus witnessed Lake Michigan bracketed at either end by incipient metropolises, the earliest centers of civilization in all the tributary region. The Mission of St. Ignace was begun by Father Dablon on Mackinac Island in the winter of 1669-1670. A year later when the Huron and Ottawa bands fled eastward from Chequamegon to escape destruction at the hands of the Sioux they established two fortified towns on the curving bay shore which indents the Northern Peninsula, and Father Marquette, who came with them, located the mission close by. The traders who were attracted to the place built their houses on the other side of the mission and St. Ignace thus became the site of three distinct towns. To these and the mission in 1690 was added a garrisoned fort, which immediately became the most important French post in the Upper Country.

In 1689 the first in the long series of wars between France and England in North America began, and finding New France on the verge of ruin, Louis XIV sent Louis de Buade, Count de Frontenac out as governor, charged with the mission of conquering the Colony's

49

enemies. These were chiefly the English and the Iroquois, but under the misrule of Frontenac's incompetent predecessors, the tribes of the Upper Lakes, traditional allies of France and foes of the Iroquois, were on the point of going over to the enemy. To prevent this disaster Count Frontenac's first act was to dispatch a strong force to Mackinac; the disaffected warriors were overawed and Fort De Buade, named for the governor himself, was established. In 1694 Lamothe Cadillac, one of the most brilliant Frenchmen of his day, was placed in command of Fort De Buade. During his three-year stay at St. Ignace he found time not only to dispatch repeated parties of warriors eastward to fight against the Iroquois but also to pen an exhaustive geographical and sociological *Memoir* upon the Upper Country which is one of the most revealing records of its time.[1]

It describes the Huron and Ottawa towns, surrounded by triple stockades of logs. Within these enclosures were rows of two-storied cabins 100 feet or more long and 24 feet wide, the interiors divided into small family compartments antedating by 200 years the twentieth-century city dweller's flat. In the French town the houses were built of logs laid "one upon another" and roofed with cedar bark, while the Jesuit Mission, also built of logs, had a roof made of planks. From another authority we learn that there were 60 houses in the French town, suggesting a probable population of several hundred; the Huron and Ottawa villages contained 7,000 inhabitants, and in addition numerous Indians from distant points habitually camped at St. Ignace during the summer months.

Thus in the final decade of the seventeenth century St. Ignace was an important and thriving governmental and civil center. But unknown to officials and townsmen the seeds of its early decline were already sown. Not only had Cadillac quarreled bitterly with the Jesuits, but with statesmanlike vision he had fixed upon the waterway by which Lake Huron empties into Lake Erie as the strategic center for the control of all the Upper Country. When the King, yielding to the Jesuit influence, issued the decree commanding the evacuation of the forts and the return of the garrisons and traders to Lower Canada, Cadillac hastened to France, where he pleaded for permission to begin the reversal of the decree by establishing a fort and a colony at Detroit.

This was accomplished in 1701 and the natives far and wide were urged to remove to the new center of French influence. The founding of Detroit marked the doom of St. Ignace, and in 1706 the fathers themselves sadly burned the mission and set out for another field of labor. The garrison had departed in 1698, in obedience to the Evacuation Decree, and with the migration of the Indians there was scant inducement for the traders to remain. So the forest resumed its sway over the abandoned site, and although the French reoccupied the strait a decade later, instead of returning to St. Ignace they built a new establishment on its southern shore, at what is now Mackinaw City. With the inrush of Yankee settlement to Michigan in the nineteenth century the present city developed on the long abandoned site of St. Ignace.

On a summer day of 1877 a pious Catholic resident rushed excitedly to his priest with the report that in clearing a plot of land at the easterly edge of the town he had uncovered ashes and charred remains indicating the ruins of a building. Further digging disclosed some bits of human bones, which were hopefully identified as the remains of Father Marquette, who had been buried beneath the church 200 years before. Today St. Ignace is a pleasant resort center through which all of the traffic between Michigan's Upper and Lower Peninsulas flows. Close beside the main highway leading northward toward the Sault is the town's principal historical treasure, a modest monument marking the supposed site of the ancient mission and the grave of Father Marquette.

The first mission west of Lake Huron was founded by Father Allouez at La Pointe on Chequamegon Bay near modern Ashland, Wisconsin, in 1665. But the early-day Ashlanders proved to be tough customers, and after laboring among them for three years with slight visible signs of success the father indignantly shook the dust of the place from his shoes in true Biblical fashion and departed in search of greener pastures. During his years at La Pointe he had established friendly relations with some natives from Green Bay. Hither, late in 1669, he directed his course, and on December 3 somewhere in the vicinity of Oconto he celebrated Mass for eight French traders whom he found there and named his new mission in honor of St.

Francis Xavier. A year later he located it permanently at the rapids of the lower Fox, six miles upriver from Green Bay. They have ever since been known as the De Pere Rapids—Rapids of the Fathers—and the city which today occupies the site is called De Pere.

Past the newly established mission ran the principal highway connecting Lake Michigan with the Mississippi; close by was Green Bay, while within easy traveling distance dwelt thousands of savages representing half a score of tribes. These considerations had induced Allouez to locate his mission here, and for like reasons the traders were attracted. The settlement grew more slowly than the one at St. Ignace but it proved more permanent. The Fox Wars of the early eighteenth century caused the mission to be abandoned for a time, but they also induced the French Government to establish Fort La Baye in the heart of modern Green Bay City in 1717. Thus Green Bay became a military center as well as a resort for traders and missionaries. In 1728 an army was sent from Canada against the Foxes at the Bay but the invasion ended disastrously with the burning of the fort and the withdrawal of the garrison. In 1730 a new fort was established and was maintained until the conquest of New France and the arrival of British redcoats in 1761.

The newcomers departed in 1763 at the opening of the Pontiac War, never to return. But the French settlers and traders remained, continuing to dominate the community until they were gradually overmatched by the incoming Yankees barely one hundred years ago. Their culture and influence still abide in the community, which proudly cherishes the associations and memories of its historic past.

Although St. Joseph was the chief center of civilization at the south end of Lake Michigan for practically a century, the real history of the place is still unwritten.[2] Jolliet learned of the St. Joseph River on his return from his Mississippi voyage of 1673 and featured it prominently on the map he drew for Count Frontenac upon his return to Quebec.[3] During the next few years the location and importance of the St. Joseph as affording, with the Kankakee, a highway from Lake Michigan to the Mississippi must have become widely known in Canada, for La Salle upon his first journey to the western country appointed a rendezvous with Tonty at its mouth and while awaiting his arrival built Fort Miami on the bluff overlooking the lake, to serve as his base of operations at the lower end of Lake Michigan. His fort was soon destroyed by his disloyal followers, but before many years a new center of French-Indian influence and activity was established some twenty leagues up the winding river, at the southern outskirts of the Niles of today. Near here the important Indian trails leading from Fort Wayne and Detroit to the southern end of Lake Michigan came together, and a fort and trading center at this point controlled not only the traffic over these interior trails but all travel between Canada and the Mississippi by way of the St. Joseph-Kankakee highway as well.

St. Joseph was the patron saint of Canada, and although La Salle had called his fort and the river on which he built it "Miami," the name which the Jesuits gave their mission soon became permanently attached to the river. The St. Joseph drains a rich and charming countryside, which as long ago as 1718 a French scout described to the officials at Quebec as "the best adapted of any to be seen for purposes of living and as regards the soil. There are pheasants like those in France," he continued; "quail and perroquets; the finest vines in the world, which produce a vast quantity of very excellent grapes, both white and black. . . . It is the richest district in all that country."[4] Today the region which aroused the enthusiasm of the traveler of 1718 is the heart of the lower Michigan fruit belt, and Berrien County is one of the richest horticultural areas in all North America.

"Somewhere in this earthly paradise," writes Father Paré, "the missionaries selected a spot for their house and chapel." Oddly enough we do not know the name of the founder, nor have we any certain record of the original site, although the presumption is strong that it was the same place where the fort was presently located, just outside of Niles. The date, too, remains unknown, although it was not later than 1690, and an ancient although undocumented tradition points to a somewhat earlier year. The first American settlers in the region found a large wooden cross standing on a bluff near the river, and the Indians told them that it marked the grave of a missionary and had been replaced by them from time to time. The only missionary to whom this could apply was Father Allouez, who is known to have died in the western country in the summer of 1689. The

American Indian has a tenacious memory, and if the tradition concerning the cross was correct, it points both to the burial place of the famous missionary, and to the founding of the St. Joseph Mission not later than 1689.[5]

In 1691 Count Frontenac sent the Sieur de Courtemanche to establish a fort among the Miami at St. Joseph, and he remained as commandant for several years.[6] The location near the southern end of Lake Michigan was in the direct pathway of the westward-raiding Iroquois, and Cadillac characterized it as "the key of all the tribes bordering the north of Lake Michigan," adding that fear of the Iroquois prevented them from occupying the country at its southern end.[7] Courtemanche was a gallant soldier whose time of testing came in the spring of 1694 when a band of Iroquois, several hundred in number, suddenly swooped down upon St. Joseph.[8] They surprised and cut off several of the savages who were at work in their cornfields. They then rushed to the fort and were already thrusting their guns between the palisades when a volley fired by the defenders drove them into a disorderly retreat, leaving their dead behind. From their camp near by they now sent an invitation to Courtemanche to pay them a visit, on the pretext of wishing to surrender the unfortunate captives they had taken. Not believing in Iroquois good faith, the commandant countered with an invitation to them to conduct the exchange at the fort and a promise that they would not be harmed. This offer was answered only with insults after which the invaders withdrew. By his spirited defense of St. Joseph, Courtemanche had discouraged them from pushing their invasion farther westward.

Although Count Frontenac in 1695 was planning to strengthen St. Joseph to serve as a surer defense of the southern country against the Iroquois, the King's Evacuation Decree of May 1696 compelled instead its abandonment. Sadly, we may be sure, both missionaries and the friendly Miami bade their protectors farewell as Courtemanche and his men embarked in their canoes to begin the long journey across the lakes and down the tumultuous Ottawa to far-off Quebec. Left behind were the outlaw traders and the missionaries and it is to the latter that we now return.

In 1690, although possibly some years earlier, Father Claude Aveneau was sent to the St. Joseph Mission, where he labored alone until in 1699 he was given an assistant in the person of Father Jean Mermet. Mermet remained until 1702 when he went to a new post on the Ohio near present-day Cairo. Somewhere about this time a band of Potawatomi established a town across the river from the Miami village at St. Joseph, and in 1705 Father Jean-Baptiste Chardon became their missionary, remaining until the outbreak of the Fox War compelled his withdrawal in 1712.

From 1705 onward, therefore, Father Aveneau and Father Chardon were laboring together at St. Joseph, one among the Miami, the other among the Potawatomi. In 1708, however, Cadillac at Detroit summarily dismissed Father Aveneau, to the great anger of the Jesuits.[9] In 1711 Father Gabriel Marest, missionary at Kaskaskia, undertook a journey to Mackinac to visit his brother Joseph, whom he had not seen for fifteen years. While he was about it, he concluded that he might as well take in St. Joseph en route and pay a visit to Father Chardon. A nine-day journey brought him to the place, at which point we will let the father continue the story:[10]

"As I approached the Pouteautamis village, the Lord deigned to recompense me for all my pains by one of those unexpected happenings which he sometimes reserves for the consolation of His servants. Some Indians who were seeding their land, having seen me from afar, went to advise Father Chardon of my approach. The Father came straightway to meet me, accompanied by another Jesuit. What a joyful surprise it was to see my brother, who fell on my neck to embrace me. For fifteen years we had been separated without any hope of ever seeing each other. It is true I was on my way to meet him; but our reunion was to be at Michilimackinac and not a hundred leagues below. We both thanked the divine Mercy which brought us together from such widely separated places to give us a consolation which is better felt than expressed."

After an eight-day sojourn at the mission the brothers went on to Mackinac, and on his return journey Father Gabriel again remained with Father Chardon for a fortnight. "He is a missionary full of zeal," his friend records. "He knows nearly every Indian tongue spoken on the Lakes; he has even learned enough Illinois to make himself understood, although he sees these Illinois only occasionally when they come to visit his village." So sorrows and disappointments, joys and friendly intercourse combined to spin the thread of life beside the winding St. Joseph two centuries and more ago. Although Father Chardon left the mission in 1712, he long continued his labors among the red men. In 1735 he was back at Quebec "infirm and old," and there he died in 1743 at the age of ninety-two.[11]

Prior to 1720 (the precise year unknown) Fort St. Joseph was reoccupied, to be continuously garrisoned until the defenders were blotted out in the Pontiac War of 1763. About the same time, apparently, the missionaries returned to St. Joseph; the records in the baptismal register which is still preserved, save for some opening missing leaves, begin with 1720. Father Charlevoix, who had been sent to Canada on a mission of inspection by the French Government, visited St. Joseph in 1721 and his published journal sheds much interesting light upon the life which went on there.[12] He came down the lake shore from Mackinac, and while ascending the St. Joseph became the near victim of a curious accident. Having camped for the night, which was very hot, unknown to his companions he went for a walk along the river bank, attended only by his dog. The faithful animal plunged into the river after a stick which the father chanced to throw into the water and the noise that was made caught the ear of two of the men in camp, one of whom was an irresponsible nitwit. Thinking the noise they heard had been made by a deer swimming the river, both started out to waylay it, but fortunately for the father's welfare the simpleton was ordered to remain behind. The other man in the darkness with three balls in his gun was stealthily creeping upon Charlevoix, when the father sensed his approach and called out to know if he was mistaking him for a bear. Receiving no answer, he advanced to the hunter, to find him stricken speechless with horror at the thought of the tragedy he had been about to perpetrate.

In 1724 Lieutenant Nicolas Coulon de Villiers came to Fort St. Joseph as commandant, to remain for the next six years. His wife was Angélique Verchères, sister of the heroine whose story is still familiar to every Canadian schoolboy, and they were the parents of a numerous brood. Several of the children were boys, the oldest seventeen in 1724, and when their years of play on the banks of the St. Joseph were ended, they found careers as had their father in the army. One of the boys, as well as the husband of one of the girls, was slain at Green Bay, along with the father, in 1733.

But our present interest is in Louis and Joseph de Villiers, the latter surnamed Jumonville, whose destiny was curiously linked with that of a young Virginian named George Washington. Years passed, and our two St. Joseph boys had long since become veteran officers, when the Seven Years' War began on the upper Ohio. As its opening act young Washington was dispatched with a small army across the mountains to occupy the site of Pittsburgh and uphold the cause of England on the Ohio. In the opposite camp at Fort Duquesne were Louis de Villiers and his brother, and Jumonville was dispatched with a small escort to carry a message of warning and protest to Washington. The latter, meanwhile, had arrived at a place called the Great Meadows, where, on learning that the French were advancing, he halted and threw up a rude stockade which he ominously named Fort Necessity. An Indian scout now arrived bringing the news of Jumonville's party to Washington, who believed, apparently mistakenly, that it was in reality engaged on a spying mission. With youthful ardor he set out at the head of fifty men in search of the party, and coming upon it at dawn, opened fire. The Frenchmen, taken by surprise, were quickly killed or captured; as at ancient Thermopylae, only one escaped to carry the story of their fate to Fort Duquesne. In this first battle of his career, Washington's success was overwhelming, and his exultation over the victory unbounded. "I heard the bullets whistle," he wrote to his brother, "and, believe me, they made a pleasant sound."[13]

But Washington's triumph was short-lived. Among the slain was Jumonville, and when Louis de Villiers at Fort Duquesne learned of his brother's massacre he led an army of several hundred men to avenge it. On the evening of July 3, Washington surrendered pitiful Fort Necessity to him, signing articles of capitulation which recited that he was unlawfully invading the realm of France in a time of peace, and that he had "assassinated" the dead Frenchmen in violation of the recognized laws of war. A year or two later the French Government pilloried him before the world in a series of atrocity accusations. In defense, Washington asserted that Jumonville had forfeited the protection which all nations accord a flag of truce, and that his own interpreter had not correctly expressed to him the meaning of the unfortunate admissions in the articles of surrender. Perhaps the best defense his admirers can make of his action is to admit that he was an ardent greenhorn who had been given a position of responsibility which his youthful inexperience was incapable of discharging. To the present day, however, Frenchmen continue to regard him as the assassin of Jumonville, in plain disregard of the rules of honorable warfare.[14]

Although the garrison at St. Joseph was never large, it contributed an interesting element to the population of the post. The soldiers were permitted to have their wives, who might be brought from Canada or obtained from the Indian population, since the French readily cohabited with women of the native race. The earliest entry in the existing parish register records the baptism on August 15, 1720, of Magdelene Collet, "born this same day," whose parents were Claude Collet, "soldier in the troops of the parish of Albin Diocese of Chalon sur Marne," and Marguerite Faucher of the parish of Lachine. On May 2, 1723, Marie Joseph, "daughter of Sieur Estienne de Villedonne captain of a company of the marine detachment and at present commanding for the king," and of Dame Frances Roussel, native of "Kebec," was baptized. Although the godfather was Pierre de Villedonne, apparently a son of the commandant, he could not sign his name to the register. In May 1727, "because of evil reports spread by people coming from the illinois country that Marie Catherine Sagatchioua who is married here to jean baptiste baron is not baptized," the priest rebaptized her conditionally, thereby setting at rest, at least momentarily, the tongue of scandal in the little community.

These are typical examples of entries in the parish register. On October 1, 1721, the parents of little Magdelene Collet presented her with a brother, to whom the name Charles-Ange was given. In due time the boy was sent to Montreal to school and subsequently to Quebec, where he was ordained as a priest in September 1744. The first native of Michigan to enter the priesthood, he rose to prominence, became a member of the staff of Quebec Seminary and was one of three canons who witnessed the interment of Montcalm following the untimely death of that hero in 1759.[15]

Thus, although St. Joseph was but a small outpost of France buried in the western wilderness, the flower of French culture was not permitted to wither. The missionaries and army officers represented the best society of New France and they as well as the traders were in the habit of traveling far and wide. They were in constant touch with the activities of all New France, and their influence pervaded the life of the community. One of the commandants, the Sieur de Muy, was a man of studious tastes who on returning to France in 1736 carried with him a collection of flora of the St. Joseph valley, which he had made while stationed there. He subsequently commanded at Detroit, where he died in May 1758 "at the end of a life that was always most useful," as his friend the parish priest gratefully recorded.

Although precise statistics are lacking it seems probable that from 1740 to 1750 fifty or more families were living at St. Joseph. Wars and turmoil lasting for two generations now succeeded, and although the settlement never perished, it underwent a marked decline. Massacres, surrenders and plundering raids all took their heavy toll, inducing many of the settlers who survived to abandon the place. The baptismal register ends significantly in 1773 and the years of revolution which followed found St. Joseph occupying the border line between the British and rebel armies in the Northwest. A census made June 25, 1780, lists eight families, numbering forty-one persons, besides eight individuals living "each one in his own house"—a total of forty-nine in sixteen houses. Five of the number were Indian slaves. The nadir of St. Joseph's fortunes was reached after the two plundering raids of December-February 1780-1781.

Following the Revolution several new traders settled at St. Joseph, the most celebrated among them being John Kinzie, erstwhile of Detroit and the Maumee, who after a sojourn of several years removed in 1804 to Chicago, there to win the proud title of "father" of that city. But others remained at St. Joseph, which continued to be a center of Indian trade as long as the red men remained in this region.

Late in 1822 the Reverend Isaac McCoy, who conducted an Indian school at Fort Wayne, removed it to St. Joseph, where he obtained a grant of land from the Potawatomi a short distance west of the present business section of Niles. A gristmill was erected, fields were cleared, and for almost a decade a flourishing agricultural establishment was maintained, serving as a center of attraction for the settlers who in the early 1820's began moving into the rich St. Joseph River Valley. So ancient French-Indian St. Joseph became metamorphosed into nineteenth-century Yankee-settled Niles, which has long been one of the flourishing cities of southwestern Michigan.

---

[1] Printed in Pierre Margry, *Découvertes et établissements des Français* . . . (Paris, 1876-1886), Vol. V. An English translation of the *Memoir* is in the Detroit Public Library.

[2] Two recent contributions of importance are the St. Joseph Baptismal Register, edited by Rev. George Paré and the present writer and printed in *Mississippi Valley Historical Review*, XIII, 201-239 (Sept. 1926) ; and "The St. Joseph Mission" by George Paré, *Ibid.*, XVII, 24-54 (June 1930).

[3] Reproduced in *Jesuit Relations*, LIX, 86.

[4] *Mississippi Valley Historical Review*, XVII, 26.

[5] *Mississippi Valley Historical Review*, XVII, 30-32. In 1918 an imposing cross of granite was erected beside the highway leading southward from Niles, suitably inscribed to the memory of Father Allouez, to replace the last wooden cross.

[6] Letter of Count Frontenac, Oct. 20, 1691, printed in Margry, *Découvertes*, V, 54.

[7] Margry, *Découvertes*, V, 124.

[8] For this affair see Margry, *Découvertes*, V, 62 ; also, E. B. O'Callaghan (ed.), *Documents Relating to the Colonial History of New York*, IX, 603-604.

[9] For the removal order and the resulting complaints see *Michigan Pioneer Collections*, XXXIII, 369, 382-383, 409-410.

[10] Quoted in *Mississippi Valley Historical Review*, XVII, 35.

[11] *Mississippi Valley Historical Review*, XIII, 212.

[12] See Louise P. Kellogg (ed.), *Journal of a Voyage to North America* (Chicago, 1923), Vol. II.

[13] When this was reported to King George II, that crusty veteran of the wars in Europe remarked: "He would not say so, if he had been used to hear many." See Rupert Hughes, *George Washington* (New York, 1926), I, 120.

[14] For the best discussion of the incident by an American writer, see Rupert Hughes, *George Washington*, Vol. I. For a recent study by a French spokesman see Abbé George Robitaille, *Washington et Jumonville. Etude Critique* (Montreal, 1933).

[15] Another priest, Father Luke Collet, devoted his life to the western missions, and in 1760 signed his name as "Chaplain of the Ohio river country." He may have been an older brother of Rev. Charles-Ange Collet, and also born at St. Joseph. If so, to him belongs the distinction of being Michigan's first native-born priest. See "The St. Joseph Mission," *Mississippi Valley Historical Review*, XVII, 37-38.

Chapter 6

Garlic River Beginnings

"THE post at Chicagou comes next," wrote Cadillac in his *Memoir* upon the Upper Country at the close of the seventeenth century. "The word means 'Garlic River' because a very large quantity of garlic grows wild there, without any attention." A decade earlier, in the autumn of 1687, the survivors of La Salle's disastrous Texan expedition reached Chicago, "which, according to what we were told, has been so named on account of the quantity of garlic which grows there in the woods." So wrote Joutel, the journalist of the expedition.[1] Although Cadillac and Joutel were contemporary observers, we do not think their explanation entirely adequate.[2] But more important is the fact that it has persisted to the present day, and the further fact that for almost 300 years most travelers in the interior of the continent have sooner or later found their way to the post on Garlic River.

Before the first white man came to the place the sluggish river entered the lake through an outlet choked by the drifting sands of the lake shore.[3] Periodically the growing sand bar would completely dam the current, but for this situation nature had provided her own remedy. Half a dozen miles inland the South Branch oozed out of a swamp which the early American settlers dignified by the name of Mud Lake, and a mile from the lake shore united with the North Branch to form the main Chicago River.

In midsummer Mud Lake was often completely dry, but a heavy rainstorm or the melting snows of spring transformed it into a shallow lake which drained eastward into the South Branch and westward across the imperceptible Continental Divide into the Des Plaines. At such times the entire countryside was flooded and the waters flowing to the St. Lawrence mingled indistinguishably with those flowing to the Gulf of Mexico. Occasionally, too, the Des Plaines would desert its usual channel and rush in a wild flood through Mud Lake and down the South Branch to Lake Michigan, sweeping sand bars and all else before it; a new channel into the lake would be opened, and the Chicago would again resume its placid flow until the drifting sands once more choked its channel and another flood rushed down from the Des Plaines to sweep it clean.

In this situation lies the explanation of the existence of America's second city. For at the divide which separated Mud Lake from the Des Plaines began the famed Chicago Portage, by which the transit from the Mississippi to the Great Lakes-St. Lawrence system might be made with relative ease, although the length of the portage might vary with the seasons from nothing at all to a distance of 100 miles.

This is nowhere better illustrated than in the experience of Joutel, whose party in the autumn of 1687 had to carry their goods from Fort St. Louis to Chicago, and, repeating the journey in March of 1688, were compelled to wade in the water much of the way, in order to force their boats upward against the heavy current.

To this same early visitor we are indebted for a clear description of the Chicago portage.

"There is a small river [at Chicago] formed by the drainage from a great plain or prairie, which flows straight into the lake called ... the Lake of the Illinois or Michigan. At about three or four leagues' distance, on the other side of the great plain, the waters run into the River of the Illinois which is formed by them; and the higher the waters the less is the distance things have to be carried."

Chicago's recorded history begins with the passage of Jolliet and Marquette in 1673 northward from the lower Mississippi toward St. Ignace and Canada. They found no Indians here, and if the place had a name they did not learn it, for Marquette on his second visit in December 1674 merely identified it as the "River of the portage." But Jolliet did not fail to take note of the strategic importance of the site, and in his report to Count Frontenac he dwelt upon the ease with which ships could sail from Niagara to the Gulf of Mexico if only a canal of half a league were cut across the prairie at Chicago. In this he was much too optimistic, as La Salle subsequently took pains rather sharply to point out, at the same time providing the best brief description of the portage route ever penned.[4] The discussion thus opened by the earliest white visitors has continued to our own

MAJOR ROBERT ROGERS, THE RANGER

OLD FORT DEARBORN

This replica of old Fort Dearborn formed a part of the Century of Progress.

PAINTING SHOWING MILWAUKEE IN 1852

day, and the improvement of the Chicago-Illinois water highway between Lake Michigan and the Mississippi still remains a vital national problem.

Father Marquette fell ill at Chicago on the occasion of his second visit and was compelled to pass the winter of 1674-1675 in a cabin built by his two lay companions several miles up the South Branch. A dozen or more leagues to the southward two bootleg traders were also passing the winter. One of them was a doctor, and when he learned of the priest's condition he came with food and medicine for the sick man. He remained to worship, and thus outlawry and charity, sanctity and trade, were strangely united for the moment in the rude hut beside the South Branch. Here the medical annals of Chicago begin, with a patient who was a charity case and an outlaw physician whose name the sick man carefully refrained from recording.

Toward the end of March 1675 the ice began to move in the river, a gorge formed, and Marquette's cabin was suddenly flooded. The inmates had barely time to hang their belongings on the limbs of trees and then flee to a near-by hillock where they spent the night, with the water steadily rising until, as the priest noted, it was twelve feet higher than in 1673. Next day, however, the gorge broke and Marquette prepared to resume his journey to the Illinois. A few weeks later, returning to St. Ignace, he again passed through Chicago where he had cached some of his goods on the outward journey. This time he passed down the eastern shore of Lake Michigan, dying en route at the site of modern Ludington.

Marquette's successor in the Illinois Mission was Father Allouez, who came up the lake shore from Green Bay to Chicago in the autumn of 1676. Apart from his missionary labors he supplied the future city with its first examples of two widely divergent practices, iceboating and oratory. For when winter overtook him and the water in the lake turned to ice he placed his canoe upon it and with the aid of a sail and a favoring wind "made it go as on the water"; at the mouth of the Chicago he was met by a party of eighty Indians whose chief compelled him to submit to an address of welcome.

The advent of La Salle in Illinois emphasized anew the strategic importance of Chicago. Beginning in the autumn of 1679 he frequently visited the place; almost immediately he pointed out the need of a post for protection of the traffic which must here change from land to water carriage; before leaving Illinois for the last time in 1683, he twice wrote letters here, and one of them, a fragile bit of paper marked with ink, is still preserved in the city where it was written over 250 years ago. Although La Salle's own visits ceased in 1683, his followers remained and until the end of the century were active in the Illinois country.

It was one such group, fugitives from the wreck of the Texan enterprise, which came with Joutel to Chicago in 1687, homeward bound to Canada and France. Although they found an abandoned canoe on the lake shore, contrary winds and stormy seas held them in camp for more than a week. Meanwhile winter was approaching and their supply of food was rapidly dwindling. Their state of mind is naïvely shown by the report of one of the number who burst his gun while shooting at a turkey and was so affected by the accident that it made him ill. At length the party embarked, with the town of the Wisconsin Potawatomi where Tonty and his companions had sought refuge half a dozen years earlier their immediate goal. After advancing a few leagues, however, the specter of starvation induced them to give up the enterprise and return to Fort St. Louis for the winter.

Placing their canoe on a scaffold at Chicago, and concealing their goods in a cache in the ground, they retreated to the fort, and Joutel's journal preserves a lively description of the life that went on here during the ensuing winter; in particular, a diverting picture of the bathing habits of the natives is presented. Every morning throughout the winter they bathed in the river, and the mothers even inflicted these icy baths upon their little children. "I saw them some times; they bawled like ogres and were as red as lobsters," the narrator tersely observes.

On March 29, 1688, they were again at Chicago, and hastening to their cache were dismayed to find the wolves had got at it and destroyed some of the contents. Joutel, whose bundle had been placed on top, was the principal sufferer, losing in addition to a number of skins several cravats and a shirt, "of which one sleeve was carried off whole." Recovering the remainder of their goods, the party once more embarked and this time successfully completed the journey to Canada.

About the year 1690 a band of Miami settled at Chicago, locating their village on the main river between the forks and the lake, and soon afterward a second Miami village was established a league away on the South Branch. In their wake came traders, missionaries and soldiers, and for a few years there was much activity on the banks of the placid Garlic. Before long Count Frontenac established a garrison of soldiery here, under the command of the Sieur de Mantet; and in 1696 Father Pinet established his Mission of the Guardian Angel, also on the main river, close to the fort and the Indian town.[4]

Indians and soldiers, traders and priests, together made the town at the mouth of the Garlic a characteristic center of French-Indian life and activity, of which the paucity of the still existing records affords but occasional tantalizing glimpses. One Chicagoan of several years' residence in this early period was the Sieur Deliette, nephew of Henry de Tonty, who came out to Illinois as a mere youth in 1687 and remained in the country for more than a dozen years, spending most of his time among the Illinois at Starved Rock and Lake Peoria. The period of his stay at Chicago seems to have been from 1698 to 1702. His *Memoir* presents the best picture of the Illinois Indians ever written, and although he says little directly concerning the Miami he expressly states that he found "no difference" between their manners and language and those of the Illinois. His description of the latter, therefore, applies also to the Miami who dwelt at Chicago.[5] At Lake Peoria the Illinois had a village of 260 cabins, with from one to four "fires" or families in each. Estimating two as the average number, Deliette calculated a population of 800 warriors between the ages of twenty and forty years. This would indicate a total population of 3,000 or more. Father St. Cosme, who visited Chicago in 1698, reports that there were over 150 cabins in the village on the main river and almost as many in the one on the South Branch. According to Deliette's calculation there were about 300 families in each village, with a total population in both of perhaps 3,000 to 4,000 souls.

In the midst of this turbulent population, exposed at all times to the hazards of Iroquois raids, lived missionary, soldier and trader. For the Jesuit father there was still another hazard, the enmity of Count Frontenac, inspired, as the Jesuits claimed, by the fact that the priest's opposition to the sale of firewater to the natives interfered with the profits of the Indian trade.

François Pinet, the founder of the mission and Chicago's first resident clergyman, was a native of Limoges, a city of importance in France since the days of Julius Caesar. He came to Canada in 1694 and for two years was stationed at St. Ignace, during the period of Cadillac's administration as commandant. In 1696 he was sent to Chicago, where he located his mission at the northern border of today's noisy Loop. Although his work opened "auspiciously," a year later he was ordered by Count Frontenac to leave the place. But the quarrel ended in the triumph of the church. An appeal to Bishop Laval at Quebec brought a cessation of Frontenac's opposition and in 1698 Pinet returned to his mission.

This same year a delegation of seminary priests passed through Chicago, en route to the lower Mississippi, and the lengthy letters written by them to the Bishop of Quebec supply considerable information about the mission and other conditions at Garlic River.[6] They found the missionaries "overburdened with work," and Father Binneteau of Peoria, who was visiting Chicago at the time, "quite exhausted" from illness. Each winter the Miami, whom Deliette praises as good hunters, left Chicago to take up their annual hunt, and Father Pinet, bereft for the time being of his charges, would spend the winter with his colleagues at Lake Peoria, returning to Chicago for the ensuing summer season. Thus he seems to deserve the title of Chicago's first commuter. As for the red men he served, they were admittedly "hardened in profligacy" and deaf to the appeals of the missionary; but the visitor emphasized his success in baptizing the children and expressed the optimistic hope that when the elders should die off "they will be a new and entirely Christian people."

Five years later Father Pinet again abandoned his mission, this time voluntarily, going to live among the Illinois near St. Louis, where he died in 1702. The Guardian Angel Mission at Chicago was continued for a short time by Father Jean Mermet, but he, too, left in 1701 or 1702 and for the space of 130 years Chicago remained without a resident clergyman.

With the seminary priests was a boy of twelve or fourteen years of age who had been given to them by the Sieur de Muy and who probably was a slave. While they were crossing the portage the lad, "having started on alone although he had been told to wait," became lost. For two days Father St. Cosme and five others searched for him, hallooing and firing guns, but in vain. The next day was the Feast of All Souls, for which they returned to the mission, but after the devotions were performed the day was again devoted to the search. The prairie was covered with a rank growth of tall dry grass in which a child might readily be concealed, but they dared not fire it for fear of burning him. The season was already late and the priests now felt compelled to continue their journey after giving orders to Brother Alexander, who was to remain at Chicago in charge of their goods, to continue the search and to enlist the help of "some Frenchmen who were at Chicago."

Although the hunters did not find him, the boy stumbled into the mission after an absence of thirteen days, utterly exhausted and "out of his head." His sad experience as Chicago's first runaway should serve as a warning to all future disobedient children! Apart from this, the story serves to shed a further ray of light upon seventeenth-century Chicago. The Frenchmen whose aid was enlisted were probably illicit traders residing at Chicago. Whichever be the case, and whatever their occupations, their presence points to the existence of a considerable white settlement, besides the two Indian towns on the banks of the Garlic.

Like St. Ignace, with the opening of the eighteenth century the promising settlement whose origin we have been tracing underwent an abrupt decline, and French-Indian Chicago became a memory. Father Garraghan writes:

"Over this narrow ribbon of land passed most of the freight and passenger traffic between Canada and the Mississippi Valley in the last quarter of the seventeenth century. Furs for Paris, despatches for Quebec or Versailles, supplies for the French forts in the Illinois country, traders and trappers, military officers and troops, Indian warriors, missionaries coming down from or returning to the St. Lawrence—these were factors in the picturesque tide of travel and traffic that flowed for a spell across the Chicago Portage. As long as the portage route, the key to Canada, was kept open by military protection or other means, Chicago was a place of note in the contemporary scene; when the portage route fell into the hands of the Indians, as it did at the turn of the seventeenth century, Chicago again became virtually a blank in history and remained so until a century later. . . ."[7]

Although red dwellers and white had departed, the sluggish Garlic and the Chicago Portage remained, to offer to traders and warriors of a future century a convenient highway from Lake Michigan to the Mississippi and to guarantee the development of another and greater city on the site.

---

[1] Joutel's narrative is printed in Margry, *Découvertes,* Vol. III. The portion dealing with Chicago has been printed in English translation by the present writer in *The Development of Chicago* (Chicago, 1916), 21-36.

[2] For a more adequate discussion of the meaning of the word "Chicago," see M. M. Quaife, *Checagou. From Indian Wigwam to Modern City* (Chicago, 1933), 17-19. Jonas Shawanessee, an Ottawa of Harbor Springs, states that the Ottawa name for Chicago, as handed down from his ancestors, was "Jigagong," meaning a place of shelter or of refuge from storms. This might be either a harbor or a protecting point of land. He firmly repudiates, insofar as the Ottawa are concerned, the wild onion and skunk interpretations of the name. Interview of January 14, 1944.

[3] When the company of American soldiers arrived at Chicago in the summer of 1803 to begin the construction of Fort Dearborn, the troops walked across the river to the north side "dry shod" on the sand bar at the mouth, within which they found the water "dead" and unfit for use. See M. M. Quaife, *Chicago and the Old Northwest* (Chicago, 1913), 133, 376.

[4] See M. M. Quaife, *Chicago and the Old Northwest,* 5-7.

[5] Our knowledge of both fort and mission at Chicago is relatively limited. For a fuller discussion of the French fort see Gilbert J. Garraghan, *Chapters in Frontier History* (Milwaukee, 1934), 41-47; M. M. Quaife, *Chicago and the Old Northwest,* 42-50. Notwithstanding the conclusion which I expressed in the foregoing reference thirty years ago, I am now of the opinion that the French had a commandant stationed among the Miami at Chicago during portions of the decade 1690-1700; what manner of fortification, if any, was maintained remains still uncertain.

[5] Deliette's *Memorial* is printed in *Illinois Historical Collections,* XXIII, 302-395. For the comparison of the Miami and the Illinois see pp. 392-393.

[6] For them see John G. Shea, *Early Voyages Up and Down the Mississippi* (Albany, 1861), especially the letter of Father St. Cosme. A more accurate translation of this letter is supplied in M. M. Quaife, *Development of Chicago,* 37-46.

[7] Garraghan, *Chapters in Frontier History,* 28-29.

Chapter 7

Wilderness Ishmaelites

THE decline of eighteenth-century Chicago was but one result of the long warfare waged between the French and the Foxes which for a generation deluged the Lake Michigan wilderness with marching armies, sudden massacres and gory slaughter. The earliest Jesuit missionaries in the Upper Country found the Foxes living in Lower Michigan, neighbors of the Sauk, whose name still remains attached to Saginaw Bay and River. Driven westward by the conquering Iroquois, the Foxes found an asylum on the upper Wolf River in northern Wisconsin, where the trader Perrot found them in 1666, living in a great village of 600 cabins. As yet they had had no direct contact with white traders and they were just beginning to emerge from their rude Stone Age culture. Father Allouez labored among them during much of the following decade, but they were little impressed by his teachings. Evidently they were a strong-willed, self-reliant people who clung to their ancient beliefs and habits.

The coming of La Salle to Illinois resulted in the migration of many tribes to new locations, and as a part of this general shifting the Foxes moved down from the upper Wolf to the Fox River valley, where they planted themselves astride the strategic Fox-Wisconsin water route to the Mississippi. About the same time the French were opening a trade with the Sioux on the upper Mississippi, with whom the Foxes had been at war for some years. Two influences, the desire to monopolize the traffic over the waterway and the disinclination to permit the French to supply the Sioux with guns and other Iron Age implements, set them in fundamental opposition to the policies of France in the Upper Country. Before the close of the century the Fox-Wisconsin highway was effectively closed to the French, and although overt hostilities were long postponed, the seeds had been sown which in due season were to produce an ample crop of blood and horror.

The withdrawal of the French from the Upper Country in pursuance of the Evacuation Decree of 1696 played into the hands of the Foxes, who now carried on their war with the Sioux unhindered. To repress such disorders and bring the western tribes again under French control the founding of the colony at Detroit was determined upon.

Cadillac, the founder of the colony, had seen long years of service in New France, including several as commandant of the important post of Michilimackinac. To a thorough familiarity with the western country he added a statesmanlike grasp of the situation and a breadth of vision which was shared by few, if any, of his contemporaries. His project for the establishment of Detroit contemplated a veritable revolution in the western country. He proposed to make of it a self-sustaining agricultural colony around which the tribes of the Upper Country should be invited to settle in friendly alliance. By so doing they would be enabled to procure the white man's goods on which they had come to depend, and through contact and observation would imbibe his religion and civilized way of life.

The Foxes of Wisconsin ignored for several years the proposals of Cadillac that they remove to Detroit and place themselves under his protection. At length in 1710 a large portion of the tribe, over 1,000 in number, turned their backs on the Fox River valley where they had dwelt for a generation and began the long overland migration southward around Lake Michigan to Detroit. It proved to be a fatal move for all concerned. Cadillac had stirred up powerful enemies in Canada who had at length succeeded in effecting his downfall, and the Foxes arrived to find all his policies repudiated and the post of commandant filled by another, the Sieur Dubisson. Whether they had any adequate comprehension of the changed situation may well be doubted. In any event they had never been noted for docility, and they soon became embroiled with their neighbors.

In 1711 the Governor of Canada summoned several Fox chiefs, together with representatives of several other tribes, to Montreal. To the Foxes he expressed in vigorous language his dissatisfaction with their conduct:

"I learned last year, Outagamies, that you had come to take up your abode with my children at Detroit. I thought you would at the

EARLY CHICAGO

The Corner of Jackson and Michigan Boulevards in the '60's.

THE FRINK AND WALKER STAGE OFFICE

In the pre-railroad era the Frink and Walker Company operated an extensive system of stage lines.

THE NEWBERRY AND DOLE WAREHOUSE

The first cargo of grain exported from Chicago being loaded on the brig *Osceola*. Note the use of "Irish power" to convey the grain to the hold.

same time adopt their spirit and would obey the will of him I have set there to command and to rule all the tribes of those districts. I learned today from the mouth of all men that you think yourselves masters of that place, and far from having brought peace there you have brought nothing but disorder, and have shed the blood of my children there. I am very glad to tell you, Outagamies, that I wish the country of Detroit to be peaceful. . . . It will only depend on you whether there shall be rest and peace in those parts. . . . Pay attention to what I have just said to you; do not draw down upon you all the tribes in the land. My opinion is that you would do better to go back to your old village, where the bones of your fathers are . . . rather than try to settle in a strange land where you may be insulted by all the tribes. Reflect once more, Outagamies, on what I have just said to you, for it is for your preservation."

They did not return, however, and the French soon began to entertain a lively fear that they were being won over to the English cause. In the winter of 1711-1712, therefore, a plot was hatched for their destruction. The Foxes had no historian, and for what followed we must depend upon the French accounts, which for obvious reasons put the best possible face on their own course of action. To sift the exact truth from them at this late date is perhaps impossible, but even the French reports show clearly that the Foxes were not the aggressors. Dubisson represents that the Huron and other tribes were determined to destroy the Foxes, and that he sought to induce them to be satisfied with merely driving them away; but the documents leave no room for doubt that he himself incited his savage allies to the plot in whose execution they acted merely as his agents.

From such a tangled web of greed, politics and cross-purposes came in 1712 the tragic Fox "siege" of Detroit. The Foxes were encamped on the hill which now is covered by the city's greatest offices and banks, less than a stone's throw from the City Hall and the palatial Federal Building. In front, the ground sloped gently down to the Savoyard River, today transformed into a great underground sewer, on whose opposite rise stood the stockaded town and fort. About the middle of May the "army of the nations of the south"— Illinois, Missouri, Osage, Potawatomi and other tribes—issued from

the forest which surrounded Detroit. The Huron and other war
bands were already on the ground, and with the arrival of the new
army everything was in readiness for the attack. The French black-
smith had prepared a supply of iron slugs for Dubisson's two cannon, while the priest held himself in readiness to give a general
absolution in case of need. The French allies poured into the fort,
where speeches were exchanged, ammunition distributed and the
attack opened. According to Dubisson, "the very earth trembled"
under the tumult and the bullets flew like hail.

The Foxes were clearly amazed at the turn events had taken.
"What does this mean, my Father?" demanded one of their chiefs
as the discharge of musketry from the fort began.

"Thou didst invite us to come to dwell near thee; thy word is even
now fresh in our pouches. And yet thou declarest war against us.
What cause have we given for it? My Father, thou seemest no longer
to remember that there are no nations among those thou callest thy
children who have not wet their hands with the blood of Frenchmen.
I am the only one thou canst not reproach, and yet thou art joining
our enemies to eat us. But know that the Foxes are immortal, and
that if in defending myself I shed the blood of Frenchmen my Father
cannot reproach me."[1]

Much else did the chieftain utter which the chronicler neglected
to record. If we may judge by the fragment of the address which has
been preserved the omission was a sad loss to world literature. In
fewer words than Lincoln employed at Gettysburg, the untutored
Wisconsin savage provided a defense of his people which his civilized
opponent in a score of labored pages signally fails to overthrow; the
proud boast, "Know that the Foxes are immortal," uttered in the
face of certain destruction, quickens the pulse of the reader like a
trumpet blast from the Homeric age.

For many days the messengers of death flew back and forth across
the sluggish Savoyard. The Fox warriors, taken by surprise, outnumbered four to one and handicapped by the presence of several
hundred women and children, were soon in sore straits, but their
reputation for bravery was not belied. Starvation, thirst and disease
decimated their number, while the slugs from Dubisson's cannon

played havoc in their ranks. The French erected towers from which to fire down upon them, driving them to seek shelter in holes in the ground. At one time, desperate from lack of water, they resorted to a maneuver in keeping with their tribal name. Covering their ramparts with scarlet blankets and erecting twelve red standards to attract attention, they addressed their foes with taunting insults. The great war chief of the Potawatomi mounted one of the towers and began a boastful reply, in which the character of the English, who were thought to be sponsors of the Foxes, was severely handled. Meanwhile, under cover of this oratorical deluge the Foxes crept down to the river to procure a supply of water. Seeing this, Dubisson cut short his spokesman's oratory with an order to recommence firing and the chieftain's further opinion of the English was forever lost to the world.

In the end, the Foxes were compelled to surrender. No quarter was granted the vanquished warriors; all but a hundred were killed and these were tied and reserved for future torture. All of them made their escape, but the victors for days "amused" themselves with the torture of the captive women and children. "In this manner," concludes Dubisson's report, "came to an end, Sir, these two wicked nations; our Reverend Father chanted a grand mass to render thanks to God for having preserved us from the enemy."

But this pious thanksgiving proved premature. The Foxes had suffered a terrible defeat but only a portion of the tribe was involved. The survivors waged relentless war upon the French and their red allies, and the proud defiance uttered by the Fox chief was much closer to the truth than Dubisson's foolish boast.

The warfare thus begun at Detroit was waged intermittently for a generation. The rulers of New France determined upon the extermination of the obnoxious nation. Repeatedly they dispatched French-Indian armies from Montreal to invade the homeland of the Foxes in distant Wisconsin, meanwhile urging all the neighboring tribes to join in the work of destruction. Of these, only the Sauk, ancient neighbors of the Foxes on Saginaw Bay, declined the French alliance, and made common cause with the persecuted tribe.[2]

At length in 1730 the Foxes determined to abandon their homeland and cast their lot with the Iroquois, their ancient enemy. To accomplish this they must move southward around Lake Michigan and then east across the states of Indiana and Ohio to New York. Such a migration of over a thousand men, women and children could not long be concealed from their enemies. While the French and their allies converged upon them from all the adjacent posts—Cahokia, St. Joseph, Fort Wayne and Ouiatanon—the Foxes fortified themselves as best they could a few miles south of Starved Rock. A three-week siege ensued, ending in a disaster to the Foxes second only to their earlier defeat at Detroit.[3]

The day and night of September 8, 1730, were marked by a violent autumnal storm, and under its cover the Foxes undertook to escape. They were closely pursued by their enemies but in the darkness friend could not be distinguished from foe. At dawn the French Indians began an indiscriminate slaughter, but the Fox warriors maintained their indomitable spirit to the end. The women and children and the old men walked in front and the warriors remained in the rear to protect them from the enemy. But their line was soon broken and the great majority of the doomed company were slain or captured to be reserved for torture or reduced to slavery. So important did the triumph seem to De Villiers, the leader of the St. Joseph contingent in the siege, that he sent his own son, the future conqueror of George Washington, to carry the news to Canada, and in due time he was rewarded for his part in the victory by promotion to the rank of captain and the command of the fort at Green Bay.

Other disasters followed, and the Foxes, reduced to despair, begged the victors for mercy. In their extremity a hero whose memory should not be allowed to perish emerged from the Wisconsin forests. The war chief Kiala, who had been an implacable enemy of the French, voluntarily came in to Green Bay to offer himself as a scapegoat for his people. De Villiers carried him to Montreal, where the Governor consigned him to tropical Martinique. Here, chained in a slave gang, his proud heart soon burst. His people were illiterate and only from the lips of his enemies has his story come down to us. Although they described him as the instigator of all the misdeeds of the Foxes, they could not withhold the tribute, "He was an intrepid man."

But De Villiers did not long outlive his captive. He returned to Green Bay with orders either to bring all the Foxes down to Montreal or to destroy them. If they persisted in resisting his ultimatum, he was "to kill them without thinking of making a single prisoner, so as not to leave one of the race alive in the Upper Country." Those who might surrender were destined to share the fate of Kiala. But the Sauk, who also had a fortified town at Green Bay, were unwilling to see the Foxes destroyed, and in a rash attempt upon the Sauk camp De Villiers was shot down and a son and a son-in-law along with half a score of his escort perished with him.

This tragic affair occurred in the heart of Green Bay City on September 16, 1733. The French, however, soon rallied their forces, the Sauk retreated and in an inconclusive battle a few days later many were killed and wounded on both sides. For some obscure reason this fight made a deep impression upon the local memory, and in succeeding decades the busy tongue of tradition magnified it out of all semblance to the actual affair. The place where it occurred still bears the mournful name of Butte des Morts—Hill of the Dead.

In the end, the French design to destroy the Foxes terminated, after a generation of effort, in utter failure. Although the Foxes and their Sauk allies were driven from their stronghold at Green Bay, the only practical effect of this removal was to establish them in a new homeland along the Mississippi, in southwestern Wisconsin and eastern Iowa. A world war, known to history as the Austrian Succession War, was precipitated by the ambitious greed of an upstart German dictator in 1740, and faced with this vastly greater struggle, the French abandoned their war upon the Foxes. Even without the coming of the war, the policy of exterminating the Foxes was doomed to early abandonment. The long struggle had strained the resources of New France to the utmost and French control over all the Upper Country was tottering.

"You may imagine," wrote the Governor of New France in answer to the King's indignant demand for an explanation of the failure, "that the savages have their policy, as we have ours, and that they are not greatly pleased at seeing a nation destroyed, for fear that their turn may follow. They manifest much ardor toward the French, and act quite differently."

Two decades later, in 1759, Montcalm and New France together received their death wound on the Plains of Abraham at Quebec. All Canada was surrendered to the conqueror the following year, and British redcoats occupied Mackinac and Green Bay and all the other posts of the Upper Country. The defiant boast of the chieftain at Detroit in 1712, "Know that the Foxes are immortal," seemed now to be fulfilled. Although New France had become one with history, the Sauk and Foxes remained.

In 1766, when Jonathan Carver descended the Wisconsin, at present-day Prairie du Sac he came upon a Sauk village which he describes as "the largest and best-built Indian town I ever saw. It contained ninety houses built of hewn plank, and each large enough for several families. Before the doors were comfortable sheds, in which the inhabitants sit, when the weather will permit, and smoke their pipes." The streets were regular and spacious, and on the fertile Sauk prairie adjoining the town great quantities of corn, beans, melons, etc., were raised, making it the best market for traders to procure provisions for 800 miles around.

Today the almost incredibly beautiful prairie has become a huge munitions base where vast quantities of explosives are stored in readiness for use in the struggle to subdue the mad dictators of Europe and Asia.

---

[1] Narrative of Chaussegros de Lery, chief engineer of Canada, printed in *Wisconsin Historical Collections*, XVI, 293-295.

[2] The Sauk-Fox alliance proved permanent. Even today a remnant of the two tribes resides on a reservation in central Iowa.

[3] For the site and the siege see Stanley Faye, "The Foxes Fort," in Illinois State Historical Society *Journal*, XXVIII, 123-163.

Chapter 8

Red Rebellion

Hardly had the red-clad soldiers of King George become settled in their lonely wilderness outposts when far and wide arose the mutterings of redskin revolt. The natives had never considered themselves the subjects of France and they recognized no authority in the French king to transfer their country to another. Although the English had come in the role of military conquerors, their actual display of martial might was slight, and the untutored savages had but the dimmest comprehension of the power of the Empire which lay behind it. At Green Bay a garrison of seventeen soldiers was expected to maintain order among numerous powerful and warlike tribes occupying a vast extent of country; at St. Joseph, Ouiatanon and Fort Miami the garrisons were even smaller. At Mackinac and Detroit considerably larger forces were maintained. They were ludicrously inadequate really to dominate the western country, however, while the French inhabitants, recently conquered and even now in process of being crowded out of the Indian trade, had many reasons for seeking to stir up trouble for their despoilers.

To these underlying factors of discord the English contributed their own generous share. They neither understood nor respected the natives, and the latter were not slow to resent the contempt in which they were held. Close upon the heels of the army came also a swarm of adventurers and fortune seekers eager to procure wealth by any means. Some of them were honorable men, judged by the standards of the time, but far too many were rascals of deepest dye who viewed the Indians as on a par with the quadrupeds of the forest and regarded no law of God or man in dealing with them.[1] Meanwhile the savages, no less haughty, resented the intrusion of the British officials and looked with alarm upon the tide of settlers pouring over the Alleghenies to occupy their lands.

So the two races, addicted to ways of life which were mutually antagonistic, came into collision, and since neither would tamely submit to the other, a war for survival was inevitable. Throughout a thousand-mile frontier the seeds of native revolt were sown to ripen in an early and devastating harvest.

Upon the stage thus set, suddenly appeared the man of the hour in the person of the Ottawa chief Pontiac. The story of his earlier career is shrouded in the mists of the savagery from which he sprang. Like a ship encountered in the night he loomed briefly upon the horizon, only to play out his brief role and sink again into obscurity and an unknown grave. Although much that took place in the war which bears his name was independent of his orders and even contrary to his will, from his central station at Detroit he dominated the local contemporary scene to a surprising degree, considering the nature of savage society.

His plan was simple and comprehensive and probably far from original. To expel the hated newcomers and restore the once happy state of the red man, all of the tribes were to be welded into one common confederacy which at the appointed time would raise the hatchet against all the English forts from Green Bay and St. Joseph to Niagara and Fort Pitt. The uprising was appointed for the month of May and Pontiac himself undertook the conquest of Detroit, the chief of all the western forts.

So, from Wisconsin to Pennsylvania the wilderness blazed up. Along the Pennsylvania-Virginia frontier some 2,000 settlers were slaughtered and of all the posts only Niagara, Fort Pitt and Detroit held fast. The three which immediately commanded Lake Michigan were Green Bay, Mackinac and St. Joseph, while somewhat farther removed were Ouiatanon (now Lafayette, Indiana), and Miami, at Fort Wayne; our immediate attention is confined to the course of events at these stations.

The fate of the three southern forts can be quickly told. Before St. Joseph, with its fifteen-man garrison, appeared, on the morning of May 25, 1763, a band of Potawatomi from Detroit. Mingling with their local fellow tribesmen, they soon manifested signs of hostility, and while Ensign Schlosser, the commandant, was rallying his garrison and the French inhabitants of the place for defense, the attack was begun. In barely two minutes' time, it was over; eleven of the soldiers lay dead, Schlosser and the three remaining survivors were captives and the fort was being expertly looted by the delirious victors. The four captives were carried back to Detroit, where on June 15 they were exchanged for some prisoners whom Major Gladwin had taken. Fort St. Joseph was never permanently reoccupied following its downfall of May 25, although the settlement became the scene of lively military operations and of temporary occupation during the stormy years of the American Revolution.

Forts Miami and Ouiatanon were both taken by stratagem, the first on May 27, the second on June 1. Ensign Holmes, who commanded Fort Miami, was forewarned of trouble and the garrison was on the alert. His vigilance was overcome by the appeal of an Indian girl, who lived with him as his mistress, to visit and minister to a sick squaw who lived in a cabin near the fort. While on this errand of mercy, he was shot down by two men who awaited in concealment behind the hut. The sergeant in the fort, hearing the guns discharged, went out to investigate the reason and was seized and bound by the Indians. Several Frenchmen now neared the fort and induced the tiny and leaderless garrison under threat of impending destruction to open the gate to the Indians. At least four of the soldiers eventually made their way to Detroit, where their testimony came close to encircling the necks of the French traitors with hempen halters.

The story of Ouiatanon's downfall is equally brief and considerably less gory. Here on June 1, Lieutenant Jenkins was invited to visit the hut of some friendly Indians where he was seized and bound and under threat of death was induced to order the surrender of the garrison. Apparently the Indians had planned to slaughter the soldiers, but for some reason they now refrained; the captives were quartered in the homes of the French settlers and treated "very well," their captors explaining that they were sorry for their misconduct, to which they had been driven by the other tribes.[2]

From Detroit in the autumn of 1761 a body of troops set out for Lake Michigan, intending to leave detachments at Mackinac, Green Bay and St. Joseph. The garrison of Green Bay—now renamed Fort Edward Augustus—consisted of Lieutenant James Gorrell, one sergeant and fifteen private soldiers. Although he was to uphold the authority of Great Britain in all the country west of Lake Michigan, Gorrell was given almost no supplies and even fewer instructions to govern his conduct. Throughout the winter the natives of the bay region were chiefly absent on their winter hunt and Gorrell improved the time to repair the fort which he had found in a ruinous condition. Meanwhile the French settlers plied him with awesome tales of the design of the natives, upon their return in the spring, to destroy the English. The Indians proved wholly friendly, however, and in a council held by Gorrell their spokesmen merely asked for rum and for a gunsmith to be stationed among them to repair their guns and other tools. In reply, Gorrell delivered one of the earliest temperance lectures west of Lake Michigan on record. "I told them," he writes, "that their Great Father, King George, knowing that they were poor, ... had ordered no rum be brought amongst them to sell, lest they should neglect their clothing, their wives and children, until such time as they might be clothed."[3]

To Green Bay came numerous delegations of savages to powwow with King George's representative and receive from him their scanty dole of presents. A party of Sioux from the Mississippi, who came in the spring of 1763, evidently had learned of Pontiac's design, for they told Gorrell "with warmth" that if ever the Chippewa or any other Indians should undertake to obstruct the passage of traders who wished to visit them, they "would come and cut them off from the face of the earth"—significant evidence of the clash of economic interests within the ranks of Pontiac's confederacy, which is the characteristic curse of all international alliances.

Suddenly the protestations of friendship of the bay Indians was put to the acid test. At Mackinac the morning of June 2 dawned hot and clear, and the local Chippewa planned a game of lacrosse outside the fort with a visiting party of Sauk. Such contests commonly stirred both players and observers to a state of frenzy. Although ample warnings of impending mischief had been borne to Captain Etherington, the commandant, he had stubbornly ignored them. While the Chippewa squaws were judiciously scattered throughout the fort with tomahawks and sawed-off guns concealed beneath their blankets, the players outside improved the uproar to drive the ball over the stockade. Rushing headlong through the gate of the fort as if in pursuit of it, they seized the weapons from the women and began a ruthless slaughter of the unsuspecting soldiers. The French residents meanwhile calmly viewed the scene of destruction as neutrals.

When the work of death was ended, Captain Etherington, Lieutenant Leslie and eleven private soldiers remained alive. The massacre was the work of the Chippewa alone, who for some reason had left the neighboring Ottawa of L'Arbre Croche in ignorance of their plans. The Ottawa, although fellow tribesmen of Pontiac, were angry over their exclusion, and this situation played into the hands of the English. By some means the Ottawa obtained possession of the captives and conveyed them to their village, where on June 11 Captain Etherington wrote a letter to Gorrell summoning him to come to their assistance from Green Bay, with his garrison and any English traders whom he could reach.

In the council which Gorrell at once convened the natives readily responded to his appeal for help and soon the garrison set out in boats across Lake Michigan, escorted by a hundred or more tawny warriors representing several tribes. Throughout the journey they zealously guarded the English, and on arrival at the Ottawa town they exerted themselves to procure the release of the captives and to reinstate Captain Etherington as commandant of the fort. Although the Ottawa declined to assent to this, they agreed to permit the prisoners to accompany the Green Bay garrison to Montreal. On July 18 the combined party set out for Canada while the Wisconsin Indians, their mission accomplished, returned to their homes. With them, at their request, went several English traders. By their conduct they had signally nullified the design of Pontiac both west and northward of Lake Michigan, and to some extent, no doubt, they had furthered his ultimate failure at Detroit.

One of the first English traders to make his way to Lake Michigan, following the conquest of New France, was Alexander Henry. He was a native of New Jersey who had gone to Canada in the wake of General Amherst's invading army in 1760. There he fell in with a Frenchman from Mackinac who told alluring tales of the profits to be won in the western fur trade, and he promptly prepared to engage in it.

He arrived at Mackinac in 1761 in advance of the British army, and nowhere do we get a clearer picture of the attitude of the Indians toward the newcomers than his narrative affords.[4] "Although you have conquered the French," the Chippewa in formal council informed him, "you have not yet conquered us! We are not your slaves. These lakes, these woods and mountains were left to us by our ancestors. They are our inheritance; and we will part with them to none." Some of this talk may have been designed to frighten the young trader into making them generous presents, for they offered no opposition to the troops who arrived a short time afterward, and outward peace was maintained until the massacre.

Two years later, when it began, Henry was seated in his room writing letters. At the sound of the war whoop he sprang to the window to learn the cause of it. He writes:

"I saw a crowd of Indians within the fort furiously cutting down and scalping every Englishman they found. In particular I witnessed the fate of Lieutenant Jemette.

"I had in the room in which I was a fowling piece, loaded with swan-shot. This I immediately seized and held it for a few minutes, waiting to hear the drum beat to arms. In this dreadful interval I saw several of my countrymen fall, and more than one struggling between the knees of an Indian, who, holding him in this manner, scalped him while yet living."

No resistance was organized, as we have already learned. A friendly Indian slave led Henry to her master's garret, and from this hiding place he could look down through an aperture upon the interior of the fort, where he beheld:

"... in shapes the foulest and most terrible, the ferocious triumphs of barbarian conquerors. The dead were scalped and mangled; the dying were writhing and shrieking under the unsatiated knife and tomahawk; and from the bodies of some, ripped open, their butchers were drinking the blood, scooped up in the hollow of joined hands and quaffed amid shouts of rage and victory. I was shaken not only with horror, but with fear. The sufferings which I witnessed I seemed on the point of experiencing. No long time elapsed before everyone being destroyed who could be found, there was a general cry of 'All is finished!' At the same instant I heard some of the Indians enter the house in which I was."

The floor of the garret was a single layer of boards, and through it Henry heard the Indians in the room below asking whether any Englishmen were in the house. The owner, not knowing that Henry was hiding there, replied that they might look for themselves and led them to the door of the garret. In one corner was a heap of birch-bark vessels used in making maple sugar, and while the Indians were ascending Henry crept into a small opening at one end of the heap. Four warriors, armed with tomahawks and with their bodies smeared with blood, now entered and searched the garret from end to end. In the darkness of the room, which had no windows, Henry escaped discovery and the warriors departed. Toward night, however, the mistress of the house discovered him in the attic, and the next day, fearful that her own family would be slain if the Indians should find him in the house, she insisted on reporting his presence.

Again the warriors climbed up the stairway to the attic where Henry made no further effort to hide himself. At their head was a six-footer named Wenniway, whom he knew. All were intoxicated and practically naked, and Wenniway had his entire face and body covered with charcoal and grease save for a white spot which encircled each eye. "This man," writes Henry, "walking up to me, seized me with one hand by the collar of the coat, while in the other he held a large carving knife, as if to plunge it into my breast; his eyes, meanwhile, were fixed steadfastly on mine." But the blow did not fall, and the victim was spared for the moment.

After a number of further hair-raising escapes, Henry was placed in a canoe along with three other Englishmen and seven Indians, bound for the Beaver Islands forty miles or more to the westward. A thick fog compelled the canoe to hug the shore line, however, and off Waugoshance Point they were waylaid by a hundred Ottawa from L'Arbre Croche.

"We now believed that our last sufferings were approaching; but no sooner were we fairly on shore and on our legs than the chiefs of the party advanced and gave each of us their hands, telling us that they were our friends, and Ottawa, whom the Chipewa had insulted by destroying the English without consulting with them on the affair. They added that what they had done was for the purpose of saving our lives, the Chipewa having been carrying us to the Isles du Castor[5] only to kill and devour us."

But the wheel of fortune still continued to spin giddily for the prisoners. The Chippewa complained bitterly of the conduct of the Ottawa, and next day the latter, although they had already declared that the Chippewa intended to kill the prisoners "and make broth of them," returned them to their former captors. They were now taken back to the Chippewa village at Mackinaw City, where, tied two and two, they were thrust into a cabin along with a number of other captives. Here a horrible night was passed, with Henry clad only in a shirt, shivering with the cold and famishing for lack of food.

A year or so before, an Indian named Wawatam had come to Henry and related that he had dreamed of adopting an Englishman as his son and brother and that on his first sight of Henry he had recognized him as the person the Great Spirit had pointed out. Henry had yielded to his whim and with an exchange of presents the rite of blood brotherhood was consummated. Now Wawatam suddenly reappeared in the cabin, where several war chiefs were assembling in preparation for a council.

When it opened, Wawatam and his wife entered laden with merchandise which they deposited in a heap before the chiefs. After a suitable interval of silence Wawatam began an address to which Henry listened with "extraordinary interest":

"Friends and relations, what is it that I shall say? You know what I feel. You all have friends and brothers and children, whom as yourselves you love; and you—what would you experience, did you, like me behold your dearest friend—your brother—in the condition of a slave; a slave, exposed every moment to insult, and to menaces of death? This case, as you all know, is mine. See there [pointing to Henry] my friend and brother among slaves—himself a slave! ...

"He is my brother; and because I am your relation he is therefore your relation, too:—and how, being your relation, can he be your slave?

"On the day on which the war began you were fearful lest on this very account I should reveal your secret. You requested, therefore, that I would leave the fort, and even cross the lake. I did so; but I did it with reluctance ... notwithstanding that you, Menehwehna, who had the command in this enterprise, gave me your promise that you would protect my friend, delivering him from all danger, and giving him safely to me.

"The performance of this promise I now claim. I come not with empty hands to ask it. You, Menehwehna, best know whether or not, as it respects yourself, you have kept your word, but I bring these goods to buy off every claim which any man among you all may have on my brother, as his prisoner."

The appeal was successful, and Wawatam led his "brother" from the council and home to his lodge, where he was fed and treated as one of the family. But his trials were not yet ended. In the night several of the captives in the cabin from which he had been rescued by Wawatam were slain; next day the body of one of them was cut up and boiled in kettles in preparation for a feast. Even Wawatam attended this cannibal orgy, returning home with a human hand and a large piece of flesh in his dish. To Henry he simply explained that it was an ancient custom of the Indians on returning from war to make a feast from among the slain. This was believed to inspire the warriors with courage for battle and with the will to meet death calmly.

Expecting the arrival of an English expedition to punish them, the Chippewa now decided to remove to Mackinac Island, which would be more defensible against such an attack. A few days later a fleet of traders' canoes from Montreal drew in sight, laden with liquor on which the Indians became uproariously drunk. Wawatam shared in the debauch, but before doing so he conducted Henry into the island a short distance to the entrance of a cavern, where for the sake of his personal safety he was urged to remain. When morning dawned he discovered to his horror that the floor of the cave, which had been his bed, was covered with skulls and other human bones.

Indians now began arriving from Detroit with reports of the progress of the siege there and of their own loss of friends and relatives in battle. They were filled with hatred of the English, and to save Henry from becoming the victim of their vengeance Chief Menehwehna advised him to assume the garb of an Indian; with the help of Wawatam's family this was accomplished that same day.

"My hair was cut off and my head shaved with the exception of a spot on the crown of about twice the diameter of a crown-piece. My face was painted with three or four different colors, some parts of it red, and others black. A shirt was provided for me, painted with vermilion mixed with grease. A large collar of wampum was put round my neck, and another suspended on my breast. Both my arms were decorated with large bands of silver above the elbows, besides several smaller ones on the wrists; and my legs were covered with *mitasses,* a kind of hose made, as is the favorite fashion, of scarlet cloth. Over all I was to wear a scarlet blanket or mantle, and on my head a large bunch of feathers."

Thus changed to all outward appearance into an Indian, Henry lived the life of a savage in the family of his benefactor for almost a year. Then a band of savages arrived from Detroit, and finding him at Mackinac proposed to kill him in order to feast their friends on a mess of English "broth." To escape supplying the food for this banquet, Henry crossed to St. Ignace and from there fled eastward seeking an asylum at the Sault. After spending many years in the Far Northwest, he eventually returned to Montreal and there resided, a respected merchant and citizen, until his death in 1824, more than sixty years after he was slated to be "put in the kettle" by his Chippewa captors on the Beaver Islands. His personal narrative of the years he passed in the Indian trade around Lake Michigan and in the farther Northwest is a fascinating tale of enterprise and adventure. The story of Wawatam has become a familiar one to the residents of northern Michigan, and today a great car ferry which conveys travelers and railroad cars across the Straits of Mackinac bears the name of *Chief Wawatam.*

[1] A lively contemporary picture of this attitude is presented by a well-informed observer in Robert Rogers' *Ponteach or the Savages of America,* edited by Allan Nevins (Chicago, 1914).

[2] Lieutenant Jenkins' account of the affair, written the same day, is printed in Parkman, *Conspiracy of Pontiac,* I, 276-277.

[3] Lieutenant Gorrell's journal is printed in *Wisconsin Historical Collections,* I, 25-48.

[4] Henry's *Travels and Adventures in Canada and the Indian Territories Between the Years 1760 and 1776,* published at New York in 1809 and reprinted under the editorship of the present writer in the *Lakeside Classics Series* (Chicago, 1921) supplies our most detailed picture of affairs at Mackinac in this period.

[5] The French word for beaver is "castor"; hence, Beaver Islands.

Photograph by Works Project Administration

A VIEW OF SAND DUNES AND LAKE SHORE

This photograph was taken near Goodhart, Emmet County, Michigan.

Photograph by Automobile Club of Michigan

THE CREST OF SLEEPING BEAR

Summer tourists who climb this dune get a vivid conception of the combined
influence of wind and sand upon forests.

ALONG THE EMMET COUNTY, MICHIGAN, SHORE

Typical eastern shore line with sand dunes. Along such a coast early explorers plied their bark canoes for hundreds of miles.

Chapter 9

Treason and Sin at Old Mackinac

To BUT few Americans has it been given to rise so high and subsequently sink so low in the esteem of their fellow country-men as Major Robert Rogers. The span of his life (1731-1793) coincided closely with that of George Washington. Both men were soldiers who fought in the Seven Years' War, and at its close the fame of Rogers far outshone that of Washington. But the succeeding years brought a striking reversal in their relative situations; while Washington moved upward to the pinnacle of human fame, Rogers descended to the depths of popular infamy, to die in exile from his native land and sleep in an unknown grave. An enterprising and valiant soldier, he achieved spectacular success in the field of arms, but he sadly lacked the qualities of character and judgment which are requisite for success in domestic and civil life.

Rogers grew to manhood on the rough New Hampshire frontier, where individual enterprise and boldness were qualities highly prized, and early in the war he became the leader of a corps of rangers whose memory is honored today in the name of the soldiers who are trained for scouting and outpost service on the battlefields of Europe. The British redcoats were the equals in courage and discipline of any soldiers in the world, but their training did not fit them for the kind of warfare which confronted them in the American wilderness, and it was the task of Rogers' Rangers to perform the scouting and outpost duties which were essential to the efficient functioning of the regular regiments. So well did they discharge it that the name of Rogers became a synonym of terror throughout Canada and one of no less renown in England and the Colonies.

In September 1760 the surrender of Montreal and all Canada to General Amherst ended the war on the northern border. To Rogers was assigned the arduous duty of taking possession of the French posts in the Upper Country, and within forty-eight hours he embarked upon his mission. With a force of 200 Rangers in fifteen whaleboats he ascended the St. Lawrence and coasted the Ontario shore line to Niagara. Crossing by the portage route to Lake Erie, he followed its southern and western shores to the Detroit, and on November 29 pitched camp on the river front half a mile west of the fort.

Although Bellestre, the last French commandant of Detroit, had talked bravely to the red men of what he would do to the English and had even prepared a flag on which was depicted a raven pecking out the eyes of a man, explaining to the Indians that thus would he destroy the intruders, he yielded abjectly to Rogers' demand for the surrender of Detroit, and to the vast amazement of the natives the banner of England soon floated over the town. The advent of winter, however, made it impossible for Rogers to complete his mission by occupying Michilimackinac and the other Lake Michigan posts. Their transfer to British control was delayed until the summer of 1761.

Two years later, when the Pontiac War was at its height, Rogers again visited Detroit as a member of the little army brought there by Captain Dalyell, which was soon led to disastrous defeat in the battle of Bloody Run. Although Rogers had but a handful of his rangers present, he fought with his accustomed fiery valor, defending the retreating force until his little band was cut off and surrounded by 200 triumphant savages. They were saved from their predicament by two armed boats on the river which opened fire on the Indians, driving them to seek shelter long enough to permit the rangers to escape.

The return of peace left Rogers without an occupation, and, freed from the restraints imposed by army discipline, he succumbed to dissipation, mistreating his wife and engaging in extravagant and ruinous speculations which only resulted in involving him deeply in debt. In this dilemma he sailed for England in the spring of 1765, intent upon seeking a government appointment as a reward for his military service.

In London he quickly became a social lion; he wrote and published in rapid succession three books exploiting the current interest in America provoked by the recent war; and he obtained the appointment to command the important post of Michilimackinac. Accompanied by his wife and a secretary named Potter, he arrived at his distant station in the month of August 1766. The fort, rebuilt since the massacre of 1763, was garrisoned by two companies of soldiers commanded, until Rogers' arrival, by Captain Spiessmacher. Detroit, distant a two weeks' journey in summer and wholly inaccessible in winter, was the nearest civilized center; to north, west and southwest for a thousand leagues or more stretched a wilderness inhabited by numerous savage tribes, to all of whom Rogers represented the majesty of the British Empire. As military commandant and Indian agent, he wielded supreme governmental authority over the vast region, limited only by the instructions issued by General Gage and Sir William Johnson, his military and Indian Office superiors.

Johnson's instructions he promptly proceeded to ignore, while he paid scant heed to those of General Gage. To develop the trade of the region tributary to Mackinac and to gain the favor of the natives were his two principal concerns during the winter. But in direct contrast to Johnson's instructions to confine the Indian trade to the immediate vicinity of the fort, he undertook to establish a dominant influence over all the tribes of the upper Mississippi area. Agents were sent to Wisconsin, to Lake Superior and to the Sioux of the Mississippi country, while Rogers himself held frequent councils with the bands that came to Mackinac. All this intercourse with the natives required the giving of numerous presents of blankets, tobacco, rum and other things, which he procured from the traders, paying them with warrants drawn on the Indian Department. Within six weeks of his arrival he had spent £300 and throughout the autumn and winter his expenditures mounted at an accelerated pace. By the spring of 1767 he was ready to launch the grand design he had conceived of procuring the establishment of a separate government at Mackinac which would free him from all dependence upon his "troublesome" eastern superiors. In effect, a duel was about to be staged with Sir William Johnson which had for its object the freeing of the Northwest from all seaboard control. Its outcome must be determined by the decision of the Board of Trade in London, on which both the American officials were dependent.

In May 1767 Rogers transmitted his project, in the form of a petition to the Board of Trade. He endeavored to convince it that by adhering to Sir William's policy of confining the trade to the immediate vicinity of Mackinac the interior tribes would be subjected to great distress while the British would sacrifice a large and valuable commerce which was theirs for the taking. Already French and Spanish traders from Spanish Louisiana were at work among the Sioux and at some of the posts on Lake Michigan and Lake Superior. If the British should refuse to enter the Indian country they would not only lose the trade of 30,000 natives but they would lose their friendship as well, and attachment to the French and Spanish would increase. The commercial situation of Mackinac, he urged, differed from that at all the other western posts, and called for a different governmental policy.

"This is the outside or Frontier British Post in America. It is, or ought to be, a Barier to all that may come Westerly, North westerly, or South westerly to the Pacific Ocean. It is, or ought to be, a Beacon, from which a most extensive and as yet unknown Territory is watched and observed. It is, or ought to be, a Store House fraught with all manner of necessaries for the Constant Supply of almost innumerable Bands, Tribes and nations of Savages—Savages removed from it five, six, and eight hundred and some a thousand leagues, who cannot annually or ever in their Lives visit it as a market."

From the extensive argument presented, Rogers proceeded to draw the conclusion that the interests of the Empire called for the erection of a civil government at Mackinac independent of any other post. It should comprise a Governor and a Legislative Council with power to enact laws, subject only to the royal approval. The Governor should be both military commander and Indian superintendent, and to enforce his will should have under his command a body of rangers, while an adequate annual appropriation for the expenses of government should be provided.

Johnson promptly damned the project in a letter to Lord Shelburne, declaring it "too absurd to deserve any comment." Yet he devoted much comment to it notwithstanding. His influence with the home authorities was decisive and Rogers' plan for the government of the Northwest never advanced beyond the stage of a paper

project. In many respects his views were far in advance of the time
in which he lived, and one can only regret that his inability to win
the confidence of his superiors doomed them in advance to the waste
basket.

While awaiting the answer to his petition, Rogers convoked an
intertribal congress to which came hundreds of warriors from a
thousand miles around. For days the tawny delegates straggled in
by canoe to Mackinac, and when all was in readiness the great council
was convened on the sandy shore overlooking the blue waters of
the strait. Many speeches were made and peace pipes smoked. The
red men, on their part, agreed henceforth to live "in Harmony, Con-
cord, and Good Agreement like Brethren and children of the same
Father"; while Rogers promised that traders should be sent to carry
to their "distant Villages" the goods they so urgently desired.

But the fatal flaw in this bright peace program was the fact that
Rogers had exceeded his authority, and had incurred heavy expenses
in flagrant disobedience of Sir William Johnson's injunctions. On
learning of the course Rogers was pursuing, Johnson had sent Lieutenant Roberts to Mackinac as his personal representative charged
with the duty of checkmating Rogers' designs. In such a situation
friction between the two officers was inevitable. It reached a climax
when Potter, Rogers' secretary, after a violent quarrel with his employer, disclosed to Roberts that it had been occasioned by his own
virtuous refusal to join in a treasonable enterprise which Rogers was
contriving. Soon after this Potter shook the dust of Mackinac from
his feet and returned to Montreal, where in a lengthy affidavit he repeated his accusations against Rogers. They created a sensation and
of course played directly into Johnson's hand.

General Gage dispatched an order to Captain Spiessmacher at
Mackinac to arrest and confine his commander until he could be
conveyed to Montreal for trial. The arrest was made on November
6, 1767, and since winter was now at hand the disgraced commandant
languished in irons at his own post until the spring of 1768 when he
was taken down to Montreal to be tried for his life on the charge that
he had conspired to betray Mackinac and all the adjoining country
to the Spaniards. The evidence proved so weak, however, that before
the trial opened the charge was reduced to one of mutiny and em-

bezzlement of funds, and when the issue was joined even this accusation broke down utterly.

Although Rogers was triumphantly acquitted, he was ruined nevertheless, and his great design for the development of peace and commerce in the western country was never realized. Although the treasonable project imputed to him never had any existence outside the vengeful minds of his accusers, the home authorities could not restore him to office without at the same time repudiating Gage and Johnson, the two highest officials in British North America. They were, of course, sustained and Rogers' appeal for the redress of his wrongs was ignored.

One of the most interesting sides of Rogers' remarkable personality was his interest in the promotion of geographical knowledge. On his first visit to England in 1765 he laid before the ministry a project for an expedition which, under his leadership, should cross the continent "from the Great Lakes toward the head of the Mississippi, and from thence to the River called by the Indians Ouragon." The proposal anticipated by forty years the Lewis and Clark Expedition of 1803-1806 conducted under the patronage of President Jefferson; and it gave to the world the sonorous name of "Oregon," although to this day no scholar has ever succeeded in discovering how Rogers came upon it.

To Michilimackinac toward the close of Major Rogers' regime as commandant came Dr. Daniel Morison to serve as post surgeon for the next four years. Because he was a badly abused man and because he kept a journal, a lurid picture of the curious society of Lake Michigan's metropolis a century and three-quarters ago has been preserved.[1] The reader will be aided in understanding it by recalling that the remoteness from civilization of such wilderness outposts as Mackinac deprived their inmates of most of the safeguards of law and justice which a thousand years of development of British liberty had created. The military commandant had the power to enforce obedience to his will, and when he was disposed to act tyrannically none might dispute his decrees with impunity.

At old Michilimackinac on November 6, 1769, a social event of some consequence was being prepared. Isaac Todd, a prominent trader and later the partner and intimate friend of James McGill, the founder of McGill University at Montreal, had joined with Dr. Morison and Commissary William Maxwell of the garrison in inviting a number of congenial guests to an evening party at the home of Sergeant Major McMurray. Supper was served and "Decency and innocent mirth" resounded until the arrival of two traders, Forrest Oakes and John Chinn. Chinn was already pretty thoroughly stewed and as the evening progressed he "unhinged" the flow of merriment by forcing his unwelcome attentions upon various guests, insisting that they drink to excess with him.

About eleven o'clock Ensign Robert Johnston and two cronies crashed the party uninvited, and their talent for troublemaking was united to that of Chinn and Oakes. A great bowl of punch and sangaree[2] had been prepared, which all of the guests were imbibing, and after two or three hours had passed Johnston asked them how they liked the punch. After they had answered "well enough," he told them he had emptied four ounces of jalap[3] into the water that had been used to dilute it. More hours passed, the doctor went home and was sleeping soundly in his bed when about dawn Johnston and Oakes, followed by some more tipsy revelers, made a violent attack upon his house. They broke down the door, wrecked the interior of the room first entered and then assaulted the surgeon in his bed; while still entangled in the bedclothes "like a fish in the net," he was given a terrific beating, which his assailants stopped only when his servant and two soldiers arrived and drove them from the room.

At this juncture Chinn arrived on the scene, brandishing a hatchet and eager to join in the riot. Since it was already ended, however, he contented himself with demanding that the surgeon, who was yet wallowing in his own blood and gore, provide him a bowl of toddy. Some weeks later, while the victim of the murderous assault was still confined to his room by the wounds he had suffered, his assailants spread the report that he was keeping in seclusion merely to carry on a solitary drunken debauch.

Ensign Johnston is the major villain of our story, and Sergeant Thomas Carlile was one of his numerous victims. On Sunday forenoon, December 9, 1770, the garrison was attending divine service and Carlile was doing guard duty. Feeling thirsty, he stepped into his own house for a drink of spruce beer and in doing so interrupted Ensign Johnston engaged in dalliance with his wife. Far from feeling abashed over his exposure, the enraged officer fell upon the husband, beating him in the face and head and kicking him in the groin so cruelly that his swollen body turned "black as a hat." Although the ensign himself passed the time of church service in such fashion, he virtuously consigned to the black hole several private soldiers who remained away from the service.

Ensign Johnston also found time to indulge in attempts upon the virtue of women of higher social standing. One of them was the wife of Major Rogers. Another was Mrs. George McBeath, wife of a trader long prominent at Mackinac and Montreal. Johnston attempted by various stratagems to seduce the latter lady and "destroy her peace with her husband," offering among other things a bribe of £100 if she would submit to his desires; but the spirited woman indignantly repelled his advances and forbade him to enter her house again.

Eventually Sergeant Carlile's foolish wife yielded completely to her seducer, accompanying him to his quarters and there remaining for several weeks. The injured husband appealed to Captain Turnbull, the commandant, for protection, but the latter declined to interfere, although he was daily dining with Johnston and his mistress at the officers' mess. Goaded beyond self-control by the spectacle of his own humiliation, Carlile committed an offense which cannot be better retold than in the formal record of his trial by the military court.

"Proceedings of a Regimental Court Martial, 2nd Battn, 60th Regt. by order of Captain Turnbull, Commandant.
President, Lieut. Christie
Ensign Johnston, member.
Prisoner, Sergt. Carlile, confined by order of Ensign Strickland for being insolent and behaving with disrespect to him.
"Ensign Strickland informs the Court that he went a Carroling with a Woman under his Protection (namely Sergt. Carlile's wife and Ensign Johnston's mistress), that the prisoner came up and wished that the Carriole, horse and all might break in and go under

the ice, with other insolent language. The Prisoner being put to defence denys the crime and says he will not be tryed by a Regimental Court-martial, and desires a general one, and objects to Ensign Johnston for reasons he will not mention. The Court is of opinion that the prisoner is guilty of the crime laid to his Charge, therefore do sentence him to be reduced and serve as a private in the ranks.

"(Signed) Lieut. Christie, president.
"Approved George Turnbull,
"Commandant."

Within a few weeks the Ensign tired of his toy, and with the connivance of the commandant set about the task of forcing the husband to receive her again as his wife. Carlile was now restored to his rank of sergeant and the record of his court-martial was removed from the regimental orderly book and destroyed, after which the now broken man was required to sign this letter, dictated by Ensign Johnston and addressed to Captain Turnbull:

"Michilimackinac, 22d Feby, 1771.
"Sir:

"I hope you will pardon my taking this liberty to trouble you, but to ease my own mind I cannot avoid it. By the instigation of my own notions, I was so imprudent as to object to Ensign Johnston's being a member of my Court Martial, altho I am now well convinced that his own Honour would not allow him to do anything prejudicial to Justice. The only excuse I can make to him and to Ensign Strickland is that a woman I have the greatest regard for distracted me by imprudent behaviour; this, Sir, I hope in some part will Extenuate my crimes, and I shall only further beg leave to observe that Ensign Johnston has behaved to me as a good officer, and I have no ground of Complaint against him, and I am extremely sorry for and beg his forgiveness and Ensign Strickland's for my past behaveour, which I will never be guilty of again.

"I have the Honour to be Sir,
"Your most Dutiful and humble servant.
"Signed Thomas Carlile late Sergt.

"To Capt. Turnbull.
Commanding at Michilimackinac.

"The above is a copy of a letter dictated to Capt. Turnbull by order of Ensign Johnston.

"A true copy (signed) Thos. McMurray
"Acting Sergt Major."

Between beating up soldiers and voyageurs and seducing their wives and daughters,[4] the crew of merry villains found time to indulge in financial peculations. In April 1771 "a kind of a horse race" was held outside the fort and the entire garrison turned out to enjoy the show. Ensign Strickland rode his mare in a race with another man's horse, and Ensign Johnston was appointed one of the judges of the contest. But with the racers on the ground and with everyone impatient for the contest to begin, the judge did not appear. Several messengers were sent for him, but although they found his mare, their search for him was in vain; "and no wonder," relates Dr. Morison, "for he was then in Captain Collans marking barrels of Liquors to be rolled over to the Sutter's house." He finally appeared at the racing ground after the race had started. "The horse won and the mare lost the race, which is a surprizing circumstance according to the constitution of this fort," the journalist dryly concludes.

That the commandant was himself a party to the financial peculations of his subordinates is more than once clearly charged. For example, in June 1771 Johnston sold to "Jew Solomon"[5] ninety gallons of rum and the year before this fifty bundles of dried venison, "for the benefit of Captain Turnbull," the commandant.

About a month after the horse race James Coleman, a private soldier, was tried for desertion and sentenced to receive 1,000 lashes.[6] After about 500 had been inflicted the surgeon intervened to stop the torture, saying the culprit was unable to stand any more. That same evening, without consulting Dr. Morison, the commandant ordered Coleman to be brought to the "flogging post" to receive the remainder of his sentence and the entire garrison was called out to witness it. The soldier fell on his knees and pleaded with Captain Turnbull that his further whipping be postponed until he should be in condition to endure it, and the commandant now asked Dr. Morison for his opinion. He answered that the prisoner was in no condition to receive further punishment and two soldiers carried him back to the guardhouse. The next day, however, the surgeon was publicly humiliated for his humanity by an order issued by the commandant requiring the Officer of the Day to keep watch upon his care of prisoners and the sick and to report any neglect of duty by him.

Every bully meets his match sooner or later, and it is a pleasure to relate the retribution which overtook Ensign Johnston of His Majesty's Royal Americans in the summer of 1771. At Milford, Connecticut, lived Peter Pond, an enterprising Yankee who was one of the earliest British traders to come out to Detroit.[7] His son, also named Peter, followed his father's calling, having his headquarters for several years at Detroit and in 1770 removing to Mackinac. Peter Pond II became a notable figure in the fur trade, a founder of the great North West Company and a founder and charter member of Montreal's famous Beaver Club; the quaint journal he kept supplies vivid pictures of Mackinac and its commerce in the years we are discussing.[8] He was a stormy and ruthless character who at least twice killed rival traders in personal affrays. Of the first of these encounters he simply relates that his opponent abused him shamefully, "Knowing that if I Resented [it] he Could Shake me in Peaces, at the same time supposing I Dare not Sea [him] at the Pints [of a pistol] or at Leas I would not. But the Abuse was too Grate. We met the next morning Eariley and Discharged Pistels in which the Pore fellowe was unfortenat."

Peter Pond had a brother named Phineas, who also engaged in trade, and Dr. Morison's journal discloses that he was just the man to call the turn on Ensign Johnston. The story can best be told in the doctor's own quaint way:

"The 10th of June, 1771, Ensign Johnston quarreled with Phinehas Pond, a trader from New England, the dispute became very warm with high and insulting Expressions, at length in the height of their dispute Ensign Johnston took down a brace of pistols off the chimney brace, presented them to Pond at the Table challenging him to take up one of them, which Phinehas Pond did directly. Ensign Johnston in wrath desired Mr. Pond to give his Pistol to Mr. Howard, trader, to charge, he replyed he would not give his Pistol to any man to charge; upon which Pond began to charge his Pistol as fast as he could work. Ensign Johnston (observing that Mr. Pond was about charging so brisk) took hold of his own pistol by the barrell and pushed the butt of it forward violently and struck him with great fury in the Pit of the Stomach which staggered him surprisingly; this unexpected proceeding prevented Pond from loading his Pistol, which he was obliged to drop and make use of his hands in his own defense, which he played about so manfully that Ensign Johnston fell flat directly upon the floor. Phineas Pond gave him such terrible bruising, black eyes etc. that Ensign Johnston was obliged to keep his Room for several days and tho' this day is the 6th since his disaster, he is not yet recovered but walking about slowly with a pair of black Eyes; what the consequences of this uggly affair will turn out to be, I cannot determine."

The journal ends abruptly on July 2, 1772. The writer's persecution at the hands of his commanding officer continued to the end, the final entry recording that although he had been four years at Fort Michilimackinac he had received neither wood nor chairs and other furniture from the barrack master; nor had he at any time been granted lodgings in the King's barracks, which his office entitled him to receive. Instead, he had been forced "to lodge in old french Houses, not habitable, at a Vast expense out of my Pay, by Plastering, thatching, etc. to preserve myself from the Inclemency of the winter season, which is generally very intense here." Of his further fate we know nothing. His nephew, Charles Morison, who figures somewhat luridly in the journal as the victim of an outrageous assault which we have not taken time to describe, was for many years a trader at Mackinac; many of his letters, written in a beautiful hand, are preserved in the Detroit Public Library. He died and was buried at Niagara, where his tombstone may still be seen. Its inscription recites that he was "a native of Scotland, who resided many years at Michilimackinac as a merchant and magistrate, and since the cession of that post to the United States became a British subject by election—for loyalty to his Sovereign and integrity in his dealings he was ever remarkable."

---

1 A copy of Dr. Morison's "Narrative," apparently made a century or so ago, is preserved in the Burton Historical Collection, Detroit Public Library. The reader should note that there has been no opportunity to check his statements by the testimony of his opponents.

2 A mixture of wine and brandy, sweetened and spiced and diluted with water.

3 A purgative of which a few grains constitute a dose.

4 On one occasion Johnston attempted to rape a ten-year-old girl but was defeated in his enterprise when her outcries brought observers to the spot. Her mother, of whose seduction he publicly boasted, was the wife of a soldier who was employed by Johnston as a servant. Although the latter seems to have submitted to the seduction of his wife he remonstrated against the mistreatment of his stepdaughter; this merely provoked an assault upon him, causing him to "quit his service instantly."

5 Ezekiel Solomon was one of the earliest British traders in the Northwest, coming to Mackinac from Montreal in 1761. He was taken prisoner at the time of the massacre in 1763 but was subsequently ransomed and permitted to return to Montreal. He remained at Mackinac for at least a quarter of a century and probably removed to St. Joseph Island when the British garrison was established there in 1796. Solomon was a German Jew from Berlin. His descendants were long represented at St. Joseph and at Penetanguishine.

6 Whipping was a common mode of punishment in both the British and the American armies for decades after this time, but 1,000 lashes was a sentence of extraordinary severity. In Anthony Wayne's army 100 lashes were sometimes inflicted; at Fort Dearborn and other western posts in the early nineteenth century the number did not ordinarily exceed 25.

7 For the Pond family genealogy see the *Connecticut Magazine*, X (January-March, 1906), 161-176.

8 The still existing fragment of Pond's journal was rescued from impending destruction in a New England kitchen a generation ago, and printed because of its orthographical oddities in the *Connecticut Magazine*, Vol. X; reprinted in *Wisconsin Historical Collections*, Vol. XVIII.

Chapter 10

King George's Fresh-Water Navy

O NE of the enterprising traders who settled at Mackinac soon
after the British conquest of Canada was a young Scotch-
Irish soldier named John Askin. Askin had come to America as a member of a Highland regiment sent to serve in the Seven
Years' War, and on its termination he remained here to enter into a
trading partnership with Major Robert Rogers. The firm soon failed,
leaving a burden of debt which Askin struggled for ten years to discharge. Moving to Mackinac, he entered aggressively upon the Indian
trade and was soon one of the leading merchants of the Upper
Country, his operations extending from Montreal on the east to the
farthest reaches of Lake Superior, Lake Michigan and Lake Huron
on the west and south.

To facilitate the conduct of his widespread operations he either
built or otherwise acquired several small sailing ships, and he is the
first person of whom we have any knowledge who performed the
feat of passing such vessels from Lake Michigan into Lake Superior.
We do not know the precise year when he acquired his first ship,
but it seems probable it was in the early 1770's. In 1778 Captain
Samuel Robertson married Askin's daughter, and in a letter of the
time Askin speaks of his new son-in-law as having been the master of
his ship for several years. This same year, too, both Robertson and
one of Askin's ships were taken into the service of the Government,
while Askin dispatched the schooner *Archange,* another of his vessels,
to Green Bay and Milwaukee to buy as much corn as could be obtained there.[1]

The *Archange* thus became the first ship of which we have definite
record to enter Lake Michigan since La Salle's *Griffin* in 1679.
Yet there is excellent reason for believing that years before this
voyage of 1778, and probably before any voyages were made by
Askin's ships, the armed warships of King George's Royal Navy
had more than once cruised Lake Michigan. Barely had the con-

quest of Canada been completed in 1760 when the British realized the necessity of providing a naval establishment on the Upper Lakes to facilitate the maintenance of the scattered military posts and the transportation of troops, orders and supplies between them and the seat of government to the eastward. Accordingly a shipyard was established at Navy Island in the Niagara River in the summer of 1761 which remained for several years the eastern center of naval activities on the Upper Lakes. Ten years later a second shipyard was established at Detroit, where to the end of the British regime it was a prominent feature of the Detroit river front. Several ships were built at Navy Island prior to 1771 and several more at Detroit beginning with that date, and these comprised the navy which from 1761 onward dominated the lakes from Niagara westward to the head of Lake Michigan.[2]

The tiny navy, which in 1763 comprised but two ships, the *Huron* and the *Michigan,* was involved in the first overt act of the Pontiac War; in the spring of that year a small party under Lieutenant Robertson, engaged in conducting soundings of the channel in the St. Clair River, was overwhelmed and destroyed at present-day Port Huron. More ships were built before the war ended and they plied frequently between Detroit and Mackinac. However, since the two Lake Michigan garrisons of Green Bay and St. Joseph were not restored by the British after 1763, prior to the American Revolution the occasions for entering Lake Michigan were probably comparatively infrequent.

But with George Rogers Clark's conquest of the Illinois country and with the Spanish at St. Louis active enemies of Great Britain from 1778 onward, the entire region between these Spanish and American centers at the south and the line of British posts on the lakes became a no man's land across which the rival armies made repeated thrusts and counterthrusts against each other. Thus the Lake Michigan country became a battleground, and in the conduct of their extensive military operations the British derived signal advantage from their little navy based at Detroit, which on occasions of need could quickly strike at any point from Chicago to Niagara.

The commandants of the isolated posts were keenly aware of the aid which the navy could render them, and this is well illustrated by an appeal of Major De Peyster at Mackinac to his superior in 1779, urging that a vessel be kept in constant service between Detroit and that post.

"In the situation we are in, the Indians are in constant alarm, and are often [so] much persuaded that Detroit is taken that they are ready to leave their habitations. . . . The commanding officer at Detroit gives me all the intelligence he receives. But to hear often that all is well would be most essential service in the management of Indians."

During the summer of 1779 a report came to De Peyster from St. Joseph that the rebels were about to send 700 men against Detroit by way of the Wabash River, and that 400 cavalry were to come up the Illinois and thence by way of St. Joseph to co-operate with them. In an effort to check this invasion, De Peyster sent Lieutenant Bennett with twenty soldiers to go with sixty traders and canoemen and 200 Indians to intercept the Illinois contingent and "harass" them in every possible manner. Although the expedition encountered no enemy, Bennett threw up a fortification at St. Joseph and from there sent out detachments of warriors on scouting expeditions in several directions. Meanwhile the sloop *Welcome,* commanded by Lieutenant George Clowes, was sent to St. Joseph to the support of Bennett; Charles Langlade, the Mackinac half-breed leader, led a party of Winnebago and other warriors down the west shore of Lake Michigan under orders to unite with Bennett at Chicago, or, if the latter had gone on down the Illinois, to follow him as rapidly as possible.

The entire campaign miscarried. The desertion of Bennett's Indian allies forced him to retreat from St. Joseph; although Langlade arrived from Lake Michigan with sixty Chippewa warriors to join him, they proved even more "insolent" than Bennett's own Indians. After vainly trying to make contact with the *Welcome,* which had been sent to the mouth of the St. Joseph with provisions for his relief, he was compelled to beat a hasty overland retreat to Mackinac.

From this failure arose an operation which sheds much interesting light upon conditions around the Lake Michigan shore line in the autumn of 1779. When Lieutenant Bennett arrived at Mackinac with his report of Indian disaffection to the southward, Sinclair, who had succeeded to the command at Mackinac, dispatched His Majesty's sloop *Felicity* on a cruise around Lake Michigan to gather in all the corn and other provisions to keep them from falling into the hands of the rebels. The log kept by Samuel Robertson, commander of the *Felicity,* discloses that an exceedingly stormy cruise was experienced by the crew of the little vessel. Of more interest at the present day, it discloses the names of several traders plying their calling around the shore of Lake Michigan, of whom, but for this incidental record, we would have no knowledge. At the mouth of the Muskegon was established a group of Negro traders who thus early were engaged in this highly individual calling. They related that the traders on Grand River had a large quantity of corn in store, and the *Felicity* made for that place.

At Grand River, "we cam in the river about 2 cabbel lengths and moored her with the anchor on the shoar the Bank being steep too so that we stept from the vessels gunwale on the Shoar." A messenger was sent upriver to the first Indian town to see if canoes could be obtained to bring down the corn. But an epidemic had driven all of the surviving inhabitants into flight and the mission proved fruitless.

Sail was now set for the Kalamazoo, where it was expected a trader would be found. Robertson wrote that on coming abreast of the river

"... we hauld down the Main sail and Lay too with the jibb, and fired a swivell; in the span of half an hour we fired 3 swivels but saw no sign of any smoak or any person on the shoar. . . . I waited about an hour; Closs reefd the Main saile; as the wind kept hauling off the Lake and freshening up I thought it would be imprudent to make any delay as there was no certainty of finding any person contigious to the Lake at that place, besides it was impossible for us to send on shoar it Blowing a gale of wind."

Thus the quaint daily entries in the logbook continue. At the St. Joseph, with the wind "hauling to the west," the vessel could not lay to the windward of the river; so "we wore and stood closs upon a wind N. N. W. a verrey strong gale and hazey." At midnight the vessel wore again and at 7:00 A.M. "as the wind did not abate" the skipper abandoned hope of entering the river mouth at Michigan City, whence Baptiste Point Sable of early Chicago fame had recently been carried off a prisoner to Mackinac by Lieutenant Bennett; instead he "steared" west north west toward the Illinois shore. At sunset next day the *Felicity* was off "litel fort," or modern Waukegan; at midnight the crew "hauled the main sail and lay too" for fear of overrunning their destination; and at dawn "we sett the main sail and stood in shoar we just fetched into Mill wakey Bay" in "a verrey strong gale."

At Milwaukee as early as 1779 lived "a mixed Tribe of several nations," whose affections with respect to the war between the British and rebels were pretty thoroughly scrambled. There were also two French traders, Morong and St. Pierre, and at Two Rivers, eighteen leagues to the north, was another, Monsieur Fay. St. Pierre had been here as early as 1763 and insofar as available records disclose was the first resident trader of Milwaukee.

If the term "Fifth Column" had then been invented it would have found frequent place in the annals of Revolutionary Milwaukee. Presents of rum, tobacco and wampum were entrusted to St. Pierre to deliver to various groups of Indians who were supposed to be loyal to the British. One of them, a chief named Chambolee, was urged to bring his neighbor Siggenauk, who was tarred with rebel associations, to Mackinac by fair means or foul, for which service he would be "weall rewarded." St. Pierre related that Siggenauk "had received a Belt from the Rebels desiring him to doo his Endeavour to keep all the other indeans from going to ware upon either side, but Chambolee said that they had deceived him to often by telling him that their ancient father the french was going to send people to live and trade amongst them, but he would now no longer believe them, and that he would go this spring and fetch a prissonier or scaulp from [Peoria] and make peace with his father the English at Michlimakna."

Of the commerce of Milwaukee in this troubled period we obtain an interesting glimpse. The natives reported

". . . that they had but a very poor crop this year and that they understood that their father suffered no merchandise to come there this winter; they had hid away all their corn for this winter but would fetch it to Michilmakna and trade it in the spring without they had goods sent them; they also told us that they had sent for Monsieur Fay . . . he has 2 Canos of goods from the commetee but he said it was against his orders to go amongst them. . . . Before Monsieur St. Pierre said that he believed there might be between 200 and 300 bags of corn to trade there in the spring he said that he raised between 40 and 50 bags for his owen use which was all that him and his 2 men had to live upon this winter; he also said that the indeans owed him about 80 or 100 bags and that they waited untill such time as he had merchandize and then they would pay their old debts and take new."

The interview concluded with St. Pierre exchanging fifteen bags of corn for a "kegg" of rum, the Milwaukeeans went ashore and the *Felicity* "imeedatly weighed anchor and sett sail for Mitchilmakna, a fresh breeze from the S. S. W. and heazy." At noon next day the Manitou Islands appeared on the horizon and at sundown, records the pilot, "we cam too anchor under the lee of the Northmost these islands it looking verry blak to North I did not think it prudent to proceed farther, for there is severall shoalds off from Wabashans point which would be impossible to avoid in a dark night, at 12 this night the wind more moderate we weighed anchor and keept under Easey sail all this night."

At sunrise, Point Waugoshance came into view three leagues ahead, and the log of the stormy two-weeks' cruise around Lake Michigan came to its end when the vessel rounded the point on the morning of November 6.

The *Felicity* remained in service for many years. The British official records disclose that she was built in the King's Shipyard at Detroit in 1773 and was one of the small vessels of the naval establishment. A return of the establishment at Detroit in 1778 lists a crew of eight men and an armament of four swivels, while one made January 1, 1779, gives the ship six swivels and four four-pounders. This report seems to have been made up at Quebec and is probably inaccurate. Oliver Spencer, who spent some time as a boy captive at Detroit in 1793, in his old age remembered the *Felicity* as "a sloop of about 100 tons, armed only with 2 swivels." But old-age recollections are notoriously inaccurate, and an official return of 1783 shows her to have been a forty-five-ton vessel.

The vessels of the little fleet based at Detroit were likely to be ordered to any part of the Upper Lakes as the exigencies of the government service might require. An official return of 1778 indicates that the *Archangel,* another sloop, was assigned to service on Lake Michigan, which means that she was based for the time being at Mackinac. Following Clark's conquest of the Illinois towns, Lieutenant Governor Sinclair was in great fear lest a party of "rebels" should suddenly appear at Mackinac, in which event the garrison would quickly be starved into submission. To avert such a disaster he planned and eventually executed the abandonment of the existing fort at Mackinaw City, the scene of the massacre of 1763, and the transfer of the garrison and settlers to a new fort on Mackinac Island. This was an extensive and arduous enterprise, and for its execution the co-operation of the navy was essential. The extensive logbook of Captain Alexander Harrow, master successively of the *Welcome, Angelica, Dunmore* and *Gage,* is still preserved, and its pages constitute a moving picture of life on the Upper Lakes during this faraway and stormy period. For many months the *Angelica* and *Welcome* were engaged in transporting men and supplies for the building of the new fort. They even passed the winter of 1780-1781 at Mackinac. The *Angelica* had been sunk in the autumn, remaining in this condition throughout the winter.

On July 30, 1780, Harrow was placed under arrest by Lieutenant Governor Sinclair, who at one time or another quarreled with most of his contemporaries, and was not restored to his command until two months later. A year later, still at Mackinac in command of the *Welcome,* he was ordered to exchange ships with Captain Henry Ford, master of the *Angelica.* Years later he resigned the naval service in disgust over the petty bickering to which he was subjected and began the development of an extensive estate on the St. Clair River. Here he died in 1811 and here some of his descendants continued to reside until recent years.

Captain Samuel Robertson, skipper of the *Felicity* on its lonely cruise of 1779 around Lake Michigan, was a native of Scotland and an ocean sailor from his youth. In 1774 he was sent out to Detroit by the London firm of Phyn and Ellice to take command of a vessel in the interest of some merchants who were engaged in the Northwest fur trade. Then living at Mackinac with his Ottawa wife was John Askin, an early and prominent British trader in the Northwest. The young Scotch seaman fell in love with Catherine, the fifteen-year-old daughter of the Askins, who had recently returned from a sojourn of several years in a nunnery at Montreal. The jubilant father-in-law, reporting their marriage to a friend, described it as "a Match which pleases me well, as I never was acquainted with a more industrious, Sober, Honest man, a fine prospect, perhaps, to be a grandfather next year."[2] By way of honeymoon the young bride soon departed on a voyage to Detroit in her husband's tiny ship, while the fond father wrote a letter to Montreal to have a wedding gown "made for her the French fashion, of a light blue Sattin."

Despite Captain Robertson's sterling character he presently incurred the disfavor of Governor Sinclair, by whom he was arrested in the winter of 1779-1780 and sent to Montreal for trial. In 1782 he was at Quebec still awaiting trial, and he died not long afterward. The young widow, still in her teens, subsequently married Robert Hamilton, and the city of Hamilton, Ontario, is named in honor of one of their sons. The half-breed girl from L'Arbre Croche had developed into a splendid woman, and some of her descendants are still prominent in Toronto and elsewhere.

Spain's declaration of war against Great Britain in 1779 changed the authorities of Spanish Louisiana from an attitude of secret sympathy for the American colonists to one of open alliance. For the year 1780, therefore, the British planned a comprehensive campaign which would embrace such distant points as Mackinac and Green Bay in the north and New Orleans and Pensacola at the south and would complete the downfall of both Spanish and rebel power in the interior of the continent.

The chief feature of the northern portion of the campaign was the attack of May 26, 1780, upon St. Louis; memory of it still abides in that community. Sioux warriors from the upper Mississippi, Canadians from Mackinac, and Sauk and Winnebago from Wisconsin effected a junction at Prairie du Chien and over a thousand strong began the descent of the Mississippi; another contingent of Canadians and Indians assembled at Chicago to begin the descent of the Illinois;

and still another army from Detroit moved southward across Ohio to engage and hold Clark at Louisville.

Although Sinclair had hoped to surprise the Spaniards, news of the impending blow was carried to Governor De Leyba, who made such preparations as he could for defense; while from Cahokia, across the river, a messenger bore an appeal to Clark to come to the assistance of the villagers.

The outcome of the great effort was a humiliating failure. Governor De Leyba made a vigorous defense of his town, and the warriors soon abandoned their attack upon it to ravage the adjoining countryside, where the farmers at work in their fields were slain without mercy. With this work of destruction ended, the attackers retired in two divisions, one up the Mississippi, the other up the Illinois to Chicago. A combined Spanish-American force followed the latter as far as Peoria and then turned westward to strike the Sauk village at Rock Island. Meanwhile, the contingent which was descending the Illinois learned of these events and beat a hasty retreat to Chicago, where two ships which Sinclair had sent down Lake Michigan rescued it from threatened destruction.

At Prairie du Chien the British traders had a warehouse stored with hundreds of packs of furs. Fearful that the victorious Americans would soon arrive, about sixty Canadians and Indians set out from Mackinac in nine large canoes to convey the peltries back to that place. With the party went John Long, a trader who had spent many years in the desolate wilderness lying north of Lake Superior, and the abundance of deer, bear and other game encountered in Wisconsin provoked his wondering comment. At Prairie du Chien 200 Sauk and Fox warriors there assembled prepared a feast for the party, after which a powwow was held. On the bill of fare were Indian dogs, bear, beaver, deer, cats and raccoons boiled in bear's grease and mixed with huckleberries. The canoes were loaded with 300 packs of furs, while sixty remaining packs, which they could not carry, were burned to prevent their falling into the hands of the rebels.

"About noon Two Traders with a Party of Canadians who had repulsed and routed a Party of Rebells at St. Joseph arrived here bringing 3 Prisoniers." So wrote Captain Harrow in the log of His Majesty's sloop *Welcome* at Mackinac on January 27, 1781. Today a fine inn at Niles bears the name Four Flags Hotel. The two items are intimately related, for both are associated with the Spanish invasion of St. Joseph in the winter of 1780-1781. Since the departure of Lieutenant Bennett in 1778 the ancient French-Indian settlement had not been guarded, although the British traders kept a large stock of goods here and war parties of St. Joseph Potawatomi had conducted raids against the Americans. Evidently retaliation was in order, and in early December, while the savages were absent on their winter hunt, a small party of raiders from Cahokia overpowered the traders at St. Joseph, loaded their goods on pack horses and beat a retreat in the direction of Chicago. Opportunely for the traders, a British officer now appeared at St. Joseph and rallied enough Potawatomi to go in pursuit of the raiders. They were overtaken on December 5 somewhere between Michigan City and South Chicago and cut to pieces, and the three captives who appeared at Mackinac on January 27 were taken at this time.

Those who escaped from the battle of South Chicago made their way back to Cahokia, where the villagers promptly organized a second raid upon St. Joseph. This time they appealed to Governor Cruzat for assistance and he assigned thirty Spanish militia to join in the enterprise. Accompanied by the Cahokians and flying the Spanish flag, they set out upon the midwinter march of 300 miles across Illinois and Indiana. En route they were reinforced by a dozen Spanish soldiers stationed on the Illinois River and by 200 warriors, among whom were the Milwaukee Potawatomi led by Siggenauk and Nakewoin. Early on the morning of February 12, 1781, the little army crossed the St. Joseph River on the ice and occupied the town without resistance. The goods of the harried traders were again confiscated and distributed among the Indians of the place and the warriors of the invading army. For twenty-four hours the Spanish flag was kept flying, and formal possession of the country in the name of the King of Spain was taken; after this the party hastily retreated and arrived at St. Louis on March 2 without the loss of a single man.

Hardly had the fugitives from the St. Louis expedition of 1780 regained the shelter of Mackinac when Sinclair began laying plans for a new attack upon the Illinois settlements the following year. The aggressive policy of Governor Cruzat at St. Louis, of which the raid on St. Joseph supplies an illustration, combined with the threats of George Rogers Clark against Detroit to instill in the British officials a wholesome fear of their opponents. Cruzat maintained a garrison of forty men at the mouth of the Des Moines River and another force on Lake Peoria to afford timely warning against impending attack. The British, however, abandoned their plans and turned all their energies to the defensive. Clark continued to dream of attacking Detroit and for the year 1781 a force of 2,000 men had been promised him. But Washington was engrossed in his contest with Clinton and Cornwallis on the seaboard and the promised assistance never came.

Although in 1782 the British resumed the offensive, making it in local Kentucky memory a second "bloody year," the war ended in a practical stalemate. The British could conquer neither Kentucky nor Spanish Illinois, and the nearest the Americans ever came to the lakes was registered in the St. Joseph raids of the winter of 1780-1781. So the war ended with the British in complete control of all the country bordering the Upper Lakes. Their success in maintaining it was due in large measure to their fleet of little warships bearing such quaint names as *Felicity, Welcome, Angelica* and *Hope*.

---

[1] Diary and correspondence of Askin, printed in the *John Askin Papers,* Vol. I, edited by the present writer (Detroit, 1928).

[2] For the more comprehensive story of their activities see M. M. Quaife, "The Royal Navy of the Upper Lakes," *Burton Historical Collection Leaflet,* II, 49-64. The probability that the King's ships had visited Lake Michigan long in advance of the voyage of Askin's *Archange* in 1778 is obvious from the nature of the situation, and it was definitely suggested by Sir William Johnson in his report to the Board of Trade, Dec. 3, 1767 (printed in *N. Y. Col. Docs.,* VII, 795). Urging the re-establishment of a fort and garrison at Green Bay, he observes that it "can receive all its supplies in the King's ships which go to Michilimackinac without additional expense."

[3] Letter of April 27, 1778, printed in *John Askin Papers,* I, 68.

Chapter 11

Yankee Newcomers

THE treaty of peace made in 1783 fixed upon our present boundary between Canada and the United States and the British agreed to remove their garrisons and armies "with all convenient speed" from within the territory awarded to the new nation. Yet year succeeded year and redcoat garrisons continued to hold the chain of border posts extending from the Thousand Islands westward to Mackinac at the entrance to Lake Michigan. Finally, in the summer of 1796, in pursuance of a new treaty negotiated by John Jay, the posts were evacuated by the British, and American rule and American commerce for the first time gained entrance to the Great Lakes.

As usual, the army led the advance into the new frontier and the Americans, like the British before them, quickly discovered the necessity of a resort to water transportation. Since the government had no ships on the lakes it was compelled to procure the boats it needed from British private shipowners. In the Upper Lakes, the three posts taken over were Fort Miamis on the lower Maumee, Detroit and Michilimackinac. The treaty called for the transfer of the posts on June 1, 1796, but this date found the Americans unable to accept them, and the British remained in possession until they could do so.

Captain Schaumburgh, an American officer, had been sent on to Detroit to make advance arrangements for the transfer of this post, and he chartered two tiny vessels, the *Weazel* and the *Swan,* of about sixteen tons burden, each operated by three-men crews, for a voyage to the Maumee Rapids. There an advance detachment of sixty-five soldiers commanded by Captain Moses Porter was taken on board, and with artillery and ammunition for arming the fort, it was conveyed to Detroit where Captain Porter, we may feel sure, was the first man to step ashore on the King's Wharf. "He was a striking figure in his artillery officer's uniform," writes Professor F. C. Bald, a recent student of the period: "a cocked hat with red-tipped black plume; a blue coat with facings, collar, and cuffs of red; gold epaulets; and a sword with a gilded hilt. His waistcoat and his breeches were spotlessly white; and his black boots glistened in the sun."[1]

So the U. S. Army reached Detroit, the goal of George Rogers Clark's dreams, and there on July 11, 1796, at the foot of what is now Griswold Street the American flag was displayed for the first time in all the Great Lakes area.[2] Meanwhile Captain Schaumburgh had purchased the *Detroit,* a fifty-ton sloop, for the government,[3] and in it and eleven accompanying bateaux the main portion of Colonel Hamtramck's army of several hundred men was brought from the Maumee. A month later General Wayne reached Detroit and for some weeks the old French-British town was the headquarters of the entire U. S. Army. Familiar with shipping on the Delaware at Philadelphia, Wayne was astonished by the sight which the Detroit river front presented. "Here in the center of a wilderness," he wrote his son, "you see Ships or large Vessels of War and Merchantmen lying at the Wharf or sailing up and down a pleasant river of About One Mile wide as if passing and repassing from the ocean."

The scene thus described must have impressed the mind of the commander in chief, busy with his plans for the reorganization of the army, with the urgent need of supplementing its operations by developing a naval establishment on the Upper Lakes. A garrison must be sent to occupy Mackinac at once, and only by water could that distant fortress be reached, or maintained when once occupied. On August 19 Major Henry Burbeck sailed in the *Detroit* with a detachment of 110 soldiers for the northern outpost. A voyage of thirteen days brought him to Mackinac, which was transferred to the American army on the afternoon of September 1; the courtesy shown by the British at Detroit in lending the American army the supplies of food without which the expedition could not have sailed was repaid by an offer to convey the little British garrison back to Fort Malden on the *Detroit.*

The *Detroit* was too small, however, to answer the needs of the army in maintaining communications on the lakes. In 1797 the government established a shipyard on the River Rouge, where today the vast Ford automobile activities are centered, and here in 1799 the new brig *Adams* of 150 tons burden was built. We have no details of her construction, but a letter written in 1803 by John Askin, a competent judge, describes her as "a sound fine Vessel that cost from eight to ten thousand pounds." In some of the old manuscripts she is called a "snow," a name applied in the era of sailing ships to a brig having a certain arrangement of masts and sails. About the same time as the *Adams,* a second vessel, the sloop *Tracy,* was built at the Rouge shipyard, and named for Senator Uriah Tracy of Connecticut, who happened to be in Detroit at the time of her launching. The *Tracy* remained in government service for several years, and in 1803 conveyed Captain John Whistler to Chicago with his family and the artillery and other supplies used in founding Fort Dearborn. Eventually she passed into private ownership and in 1809 was wrecked on the reef at Fort Erie.

Until the summer of 1812 the *Adams* remained the mainstay of the "navy of the lakes," commanded all this time by Major Henry B. Brevoort. He was a New Yorker of Dutch descent, who entered the U. S. Army in early manhood and after a term of service on the lower Mississippi was assigned to the command of the *Adams* in 1802. At Detroit he married Catherine Navarre, descendant of one of the city's old French families, and the ancestral home of his wife became his permanent home. Here he died in 1858, and the estate, originally a feudal grant from the French Government to an earlier Navarre, is still known in Detroit as the Brevoort Farm.

When the War Department, early in 1803, decided upon the establishment of Fort Dearborn at Chicago, Captain John Whistler was dispatched from Detroit with an escort of six men to investigate the possibility of marching troops overland to the mouth of the St. Joseph and to find and mark the route. Upon the receipt of his report, a company of infantry with pack horses to carry the necessary baggage and provisions was sent to the mouth of the St. Joseph, where a temporary camp was to be maintained until preparations could be made for its reception at "Chickago."

Meanwhile, Captain Whistler himself embarked in the *Tracy* for the voyage around the lakes. With him were his eldest son, Lieutenant William Whistler, and the girl wife of the latter; with him, also, was George Washington Whistler, a child three years of age, who was destined to build the railroad from St. Petersburg to Moscow and to become the father of the noted artist, James A. McNeill Whistler.[4]

For some reason the plan to leave the troops in camp at the mouth of the St. Joseph was abandoned. At old Fort St. Joseph boats were procured from the traders in which a portion of the command and the baggage descended the river to its mouth, the remainder of the company marching by land. The river mouth was reached on July 28, and two weeks later the *Tracy* hove into view. Here Captain Whistler disembarked to accompany the soldiers around the end of the lake, while the *Tracy* resumed its voyage to Chicago. There, since there was no harbor to shelter the vessel from the autumnal gales, all haste was made to discharge her cargo and free her for the return journey to Detroit. Mrs. William Whistler in old age related that some 2,000 natives assembled to gaze upon "the big canoe with wings"; a secondary attraction, no doubt, was the prospect of begging or stealing some of the coveted food and other supplies the white strangers were sure to bring with them.

Chicago now became an important center of Indian trade as it had been in the days of New France more than a century earlier. An Indian agency and government factory were soon established, and private traders and government officials were alike dependent upon the lake ships for maintaining their contacts with the outside world. Throughout the season of navigation the *Adams* was engaged upon its far-flung journeys from Niagara to Chicago, and privately owned sailing vessels made such occasional voyages into Lake Michigan as the slight commerce of the time demanded. The principal ports of call on Lake Michigan were Green Bay, Milwaukee, Chicago and St. Joseph; between Detroit and Mackinac, the great interior fur-trade center, commerce was much heavier and vessel sailings correspondingly more frequent.

For the first three decades of the nineteenth century, however, the entire Lake Michigan area remained substantially a virgin wilderness, commercial needs of which were confined to the fur trade and the maintenance of the government posts. Even the sailing vessels of the period would be considered hardly more than toys today. The *Adams,* of 150 tons burden, was probably the largest ship. Vessels of 16, 20 and 30 tons were much commoner.

From some old customs manifests preserved in the Detroit Public Library we may obtain glimpses of the scanty commerce of Lake Michigan in the opening decades of the century. For example, on August 11, 1814, a bateau commanded by Joseph Rolette cleared the port of Mackinac for Prairie du Chien. Her cargo included such items as gunpowder, liquor, tobacco, coffee, butter, sugar, tea, vinegar, raisins, linseed oil, paint, glass, putty and guns. Obviously this shipment was intended chiefly for civilized customers. More characteristic was the "batoe" owned by George Schindler which cleared Mackinac for Grand River on August 16, 1800. On board were "8 balles [probably bales] of goods; also 1 barrel, 1 trunk, 6 kegs, 6 caarscks [casks], 1 basket, and 1 bale of tobacco." The "basket" meant a nest of copper kettles; the unitemized contents of the various kegs and other packages undoubtedly comprised the usual assortment of goods for Schindler's winter trade with the Indians of western Michigan. With the opening of navigation in the spring he would return to Mackinac with his season's accumulation of peltries and mococks of sugar for which he had exchanged his European wares.

Another manifest of the period, entered at Mackinac in June 1804 by Joseph Bailly, the Calumet River trader, incidentally reveals the type of men whose cheerful endurance of a life of extraordinary hardship made the conduct of the business possible. The crew of his boat, eight in number, bore these names: Pierre LeCompte, Noel Parrent, François Breau, Jacques LeMaine, Michel Bellaud, L^{is} Descary, François Branconnier, and L^{is} Morin—all hardy voyageurs of French-Canadian origin.

Illustrative of the small sailing vessels of the period is the schooner *Blacksnake* of Cuyahoga (now Cleveland), Captain Jacob Wilkinson, 21 tons burden, which cleared Detroit with a crew of two men on June 25, 1816, bound for Mackinac. Two days later the schooner *Diligence* with a burden of 32 tons and a crew of three men also cleared for Mackinac. Both ships carried the usual cargo of staples, the liquids listed including whisky, brandy, gin and "cherry bounce." Four months later, on October 30, 1816, the *Eagle,* of 20 39/95 tons burden, left Detroit for Mackinac; her late-season cargo numbered provisions of many sorts, besides eggs, onions, apples, chairs and chamber pots—in all, 183 articles of entry.

The sloop *General Hunter,* a "British bottom," navigated by four men, left Mackinac for "Chicawgo," May 8, 1805, carrying to Kinzie and Forsyth a barrel of gunpowder, 2 bars of iron, a box of tobacco, 19 bags of flour, and 1 trunk, 3 boxes and 8 kegs of undisclosed contents. On the return voyage, "inwards" bound from St. Joseph and "Chicawgo," the *Hunter* brought 321 packs of furs, of which 158 belonged to Kinzie and Forsyth and 68 to Forsyth alone. But this was far from constituting the total output of furs from Chicago this season. The sloop *Contractor* had left Mackinac for Chicago on June 6, with 65 barrels of pork, 120 of flour, 36 of whisky, 4 boxes of candles, and 4 "new saddles." She returned three weeks later with 474 packs of furs. About the same time (June 16) the *Adams* cleared Mackinac for Detroit and Fort Erie with a general cargo which included no less than 422 packs of furs.

An interesting glimpse of the upper Mississippi trade which crossed Lake Michigan on its way to and from Mackinac and the East is afforded by the manifests of the sloop *Saginah* of Sandwich the same season. She reached Mackinac on July 5, 1805, with a large shipment of goods, one of the largest consignees being Robert Dickson, who traded with the Sioux of the upper Mississippi. His consignment included 95 kegs of liquor alone. Eight days later the *Saginah* cleared for the return voyage to Sandwich with a cargo in which 9 packs of buffalo robes were included; although their ownership is not indicated, they evidently came from the upper Mississippi, and had been brought in open boats across Wisconsin and northern Lake Michigan to Mackinac.

On May 16, 1810, the *Adams* cleared Detroit with a cargo chiefly consigned to Mackinac, but with a portion destined for Chicago. Its contents embraced a wide variety of staple supplies which we need not trouble to enumerate. To Chicago went 4 barrels of whisky, 4 boxes of candles, 7 barrels of cider and 1 "plough complete." The whisky was the property of Dr. John Cooper, the Fort Dearborn surgeon, who had obtained permission to suttle at Fort Dearborn. In this rested the seeds of a quarrel which rocked infant Chicago to its foundations and scattered the official family of Fort Dearborn far and wide.

To "suttle" meant to supply the soldiers with articles not furnished them by the government. The privilege Dr. Cooper had obtained interfered with the profits of Matthew Irwin, the government contractor for furnishing supplies to the garrison, and also with the trade of John Kinzie, the "father" of Chicago. Irwin and Kinzie soon drew together in opposition to Captain Whistler, whom they regarded as the real power behind Cooper. For some reason Indian agent Charles Jouett and Lieutenant Thompson of the garrison joined the Kinzie-Irwin coalition, while Lieutenant Hamilton, the sole remaining commissioned officer at Fort Dearborn and a son-in-law of Captain Whistler, of course sided with the latter.

Here was a pretty kettle of fish, with all the men of importance in infant Chicago arrayed on one side or the other of a bitter factional feud. Whistler asserted that the "malignant wretches" opposed to him were guilty of defrauding the public; Lieutenant Thompson was a mere tool in the hands of his associates, who despised him even while they used him. Jouett had told of Thompson's running away to escape paying a debt to his landlord, and Whistler affirmed that he had acknowledged himself a "Liar" in the presence of all the gentlemen of the garrison. Dr. Cooper bore a challenge to a duel from Lieutenant Hamilton to Kinzie which the trader declined, contenting himself with roundly cursing both challenger and his second.

The coalition against Captain Whistler, determined to drive him from Chicago, preferred charges against him to Colonel Kingsbury, and demanded a court-martial. Among other misdeeds it was claimed that he had beaten a soldier for not trading with his son, and had defrauded the government by raising ten acres of corn with soldier labor. Although it is not now possible to determine the truth or falsity of the charges made, it is significant that Captain Whistler retained the confidence of his brother officers, who repeatedly testified their approval of his conduct.

Yet the feud eventuated in his downfall and the triumph of his enemies. Rather than undertake to bring Whistler and Lieutenant Thompson to trial on the charges preferred against them, the War Department decided upon a general scattering of the Fort Dearborn officers. Captain Whistler was sent to Detroit and Lieutenant Hamilton to Fort Wayne. Thompson and Cooper remained at Fort Dearborn but the latter's privilege to suttle was revoked by special order of the Secretary of War, and he soon resigned from the army in disgust over his treatment.

Captain Whistler was old and infirm and burdened with a large family of young children. Although the Chicago of 1803-1810 was no Riviera, he had become accustomed by seven years of residence to its drawbacks, and the cost of maintaining his family there was much less than at Detroit. But it is an ill wind that blows no good. By the removal he was spared undergoing with his family the horrors of the Chicago Massacre two years later.

We return to the story of the *Adams,* which for a decade constituted Chicago's chief official life line to the outside world. A commonplace illustration is supplied by the report of Captain Whistler to Colonel Kingsbury at Mackinac in July 1804 that his men were in urgent need of clothing and other supplies. Kingsbury responded by ordering them forwarded from Detroit on the *Adams.* The following spring he was assigned the task of establishing new Fort Bellefontaine opposite the mouth of the Illinois River above St. Louis, and the *Adams* on its first voyage of the season conveyed his company of soldiers from Mackinac to Chicago. Here he found two traders headed northward from the Illinois River to Mackinac in bateaux laden with their season's harvest of furs. A deal was made by which the traders and their furs were carried to Mackinac on the *Adams* by Major Brevoort, and Colonel Kingsbury acquired their bateaux in which to convey his troops down the Illinois River to his destination.

But the *Adams* was not always engaged upon purely military missions. In the autumn of 1808 Governor Hull of Michigan Territory went east to spend the winter, and the following spring he requested the War Department to direct the *Adams* to come to "Buffalo Creek" by May 10 in readiness to convey him back to Detroit.

Another type of service of the *Adams* during these years bears the odor of an ancient scandal. Not only did she convey government property and persons but she habitually carried goods for private citizens as well. In 1806 some censorious individual complained to the government that U. S. vessels on the lakes (this could only mean the *Adams*) frequently carried goods of a dutiable character for favored individuals. This provoked an order commanding Brevoort "without the smallest deviation" to enter and clear at Detroit and Mackinac all privately owned goods of a dutiable nature which the *Adams* in the future should transport. Presumably he did so, but he continued another practice which, however permissable then, has a curious aspect to modern eyes. On the voyage of May 1810 from Detroit to Mackinac, for example, the commander shipped on his own account 31½ bushels of corn, 13 barrels of cider, 18 barrels of flour, 10 barrels of pork and 1 box each of soap and of candles. In short, the commander of the "navy of the lakes" was entering into competition with private traders, and however honest he may have been, it seems obvious that his position as commander of the ship gave him an unfair advantage over them.

If any complaint was made, however, it is buried under the oblivion of a century and a half. Evidently the War Department approved of utilizing the *Adams* to convey private property and Major Brevoort's report of the ship's operations during the season of 1807 seems to supply the explanation. She had earned by carrying public property $1,481.67; by transporting private property, $421.93. Sundry items of expense incurred totaled $91.95, while some miscreant at Detroit had entered the unguarded "cabbin" and stolen $230. The net balance for the season's operations, therefore, was $1,581.65, while the pay roll of the crew for the year was $1,913.79, leaving a net deficit of $332.14, most of which was chargeable to the wretch who burglarized the "cabbin."

Such was the modest account of the navy of the lakes a century and a half ago. As these pages are written a $13,000,000,000 loan is being floated, and the daily expenditure of the government is said to amount to $250,000,000; in government spending as in many things else the years that have elapsed since 1807 have been marked by wondrous growth.

Over Lake Michigan the dread specter of bloody war was now impending, and Chicago and Mackinac became its focal points. On April 6, 1812, Jean Lalime, the government Indian interpreter at Fort Dearborn, was slain in a personal affray by trader Kinzie. Three months later, on July 5, Matthew Irwin, keeper of the government

factory, departed for Mackinac in search of a successor to the slain
interpreter, leaving the factory in the custody of surgeon Van Voorhis.
The *Erie* and the *Friend's Good Will,* two small ships from Black
Rock, shortly appeared at Chicago and Van Voorhis shipped on
board the latter ninety-nine packs of furs belonging to the factory.
At Mackinac both ships were seized by the British, who had captured the place in mid-July. Despite her Quakerish name, the
Friend's Good Will was renamed the *Little Belt,* armed with a cannon or two and added to the British fleet which Perry destroyed in
the Battle of Lake Erie.

Captain Nathan Heald, commandant of Fort Dearborn, and his
wife were both grievously wounded in the massacre of August 15.
Carried away as captives to St. Joseph, they eventually hired a friendly
Indian to convey them in an open canoe to Mackinac. Here Captain
Heald secured passage to Detroit on a small sailing vessel and on his
arrival there was permitted by Colonel Procter to continue on his
homeward way. Oddly enough, the ship on which the Healds found
passage to Buffalo was the *Adams,* which in happier days they had
eagerly welcomed at Chicago. When the war opened in 1812 the "old
Brigg" was undergoing extensive repairs at the Detroit shipyard.
Before she could be fitted for service Detroit fell, and the *Adams,*
now a British ship, was rechristened the *Detroit.* The captors completed her repairs and with six cannon and a crew of fifty-six men she
set out for Fort Erie on her maiden voyage with the Healds and a
considerable number of prisoners on board.

On October 8 she cast anchor alongside the *Caledonia* under the
protecting guns of British Fort Erie. At Black Rock, a few miles
away, Lieutenant Jesse D. Elliott was assembling the nucleus of the
fleet which a year later was to fight and win the Battle of Lake Erie.
Upon learning of the presence of the *Detroit* and the *Caledonia*
at Fort Erie, he conceived the bold design of boarding and captur-
ing them in a night assault. If he were successful, the two ships
added to the vessels he was already outfitting would, he hoped,
enable him to meet and conquer the remainder of the British force
on the Upper Lakes and thereby shorten the war in the West.

With fifty sailors and fifty soldiers in two open boats Elliott left
Buffalo Creek at one o'clock in the morning of October 9, and two

hours later was alongside the doomed vessels. Swarming aboard, his men made prisoners of the crews and within ten minutes' time had the topsails sheeted home and the vessels under way. But the wind was not strong enough to ascend against the heavy current into Lake Erie, and the *Caledonia* was beached on the American shore under the guns of a battery at Black Rock, to become one of the ships of Perry's fleet in the Battle of Lake Erie. The *Detroit,* meanwhile, drifted downstream until she went aground on Squaw Island. Here, exposed to the fire of the land batteries from both shores, she could be held by neither Americans nor British, and after an all-day bombardment, with "her sails in ribbons and her rigging all cut to pieces," the vessel was destroyed.

Thus gloriously perished the *Adams,* for almost a decade the sole representative of American naval power on the Upper Lakes. At the time of her capture, Lieutenant Elliott reported, she mounted six 6-pound long guns, and besides her crew of three officers and fifty-six men had thirty American prisoners on board. Had the wind been a little stronger that morning at the entrance to the Niagara, Elliott would have conveyed his prizes in triumph to Buffalo and been in position to undertake his further project of attacking the remaining British vessels on Lake Erie. In this event the world might never have heard of Oliver H. Perry, and William Henry Harrison might not have been President of the United States; and with supremacy on the lakes retained, the restoration of American rule at Detroit, Mackinac and Chicago as well as throughout all the Upper Lakes would have followed as a natural consequence.

---

1 Unpublished study by Professor F. Clever Bald which has kindly been placed at the present writer's disposal.

2 Fort Miamis, at the head of ship navigation on the Maumee a short distance above present-day Toledo was taken over the same day as Detroit.

3 The *Detroit* thus became the first ship of American ownership on the Great Lakes.

4 Whistler's desire to build the railroad of standard American gauge was overruled by the Czar's advisers with consequences that have remained momentous to the present day. Because of it, the German invaders of 1941 were unable to utilize the Russian railroads until they could relay the rails, while in like fashion Russian rolling stock is unusable outside its own country until after such a change has been made.

Chapter 12

American at Last

At Fort Dearborn in the autumn of 1811 youthful surgeon Van Voorhis sat down to commune, on paper, with a friend in the East. He wrote:

"I cannot but notice the villainy practiced in the Indian country by British agents and traders; you hear of it at a distance, but we near the scene of action are sensible of it. They labor by every unprincipaled means to instigate the savages against the Americans, to inculcate the idea that we intend to drive the Indians beyond the Mississippi, and that in every purchase of land the Government defrauds them. . . . Never till a prohibition to the entrance of all foreigners, and especially British subjects, into the Indian country takes place, will we enjoy lasting peace with the credulous, deluded cannibal savages."[1]

Here in a nutshell we have the contemporary indictment of British policy which roused western America to the pitch of warfare in 1812. For several years the frontiersmen had been frantic with anxiety over threatened Indian uprisings, and at the very moment Dr. Van Voorhis was writing his letter the army of Governor Harrison of Indiana Territory was marching northward toward Tippecanoe. The battle he fought on November 11 ended all hope of peace on the frontier and drove Tecumseh and his followers to seek open alliance with Great Britain.

Despite the eagerness of the West for war, its declaration in June 1812 found the nation woefully unprepared. In three years of campaigning the United States enlisted half a million soldiers and launched numerous futile invasions of Canada, conquest of which our orators had assured us would be an easy romp of only a few weeks' duration. At the end, Canada remained unconquered, powerful armies were invading the United States at Lake Champlain and the mouth of the Mississippi, and a relatively insignificant expedition had captured and ravaged our capital. By totally unexpected victories at Plattsburg and New Orleans the nation was saved, as if by a miracle, from dismemberment, and peace was made on the basis of a return to the status existing at the outbreak of hostilities.

The story of the war around Lake Michigan is one of monotonous American defeat and disaster. At the outset General Hull led an army composed chiefly of Ohio militia northward to Detroit, from which place the invasion of Canada was begun on July 11. It ended five weeks later with the surrender of the army and all Michigan Territory to British General Brock on August 16. Thus at the very outset of the war the British established control of the Upper Lakes, while the Americans were thrown back upon the line of the Maumee and the Wabash.

This initial disaster was intimately bound up with the fate of Mackinac and Fort Dearborn, the two forts on Lake Michigan. Many months before the actual declaration of war astute British General Brock had begun to prepare for it by laying plans for the capture of Mackinac as soon as war should be declared. During the winter of 1812 measures were concerted with Robert Dickson, an energetic British trader on the upper Mississippi, for the latter to raise a band of warriors in that area who were to co-operate in the projected enterprise.

In August 1811 Dickson had returned from Canada to the Mississippi with a large quantity of trade goods which he proceeded to distribute gratis to the natives with the object of strengthening their friendship for King George. In the spring of 1812 he again set out for Canada, going by way of Prairie du Chien and the Fox-Wisconsin highway to Lake Michigan and Mackinac. At the Wisconsin Portage he was met by two Indian runners bringing word from General Brock of the imminent prospect of war. They had come westward around Lake Michigan and at Chicago had been examined by Captain Heald, who suspected their true character. One of them managed to conceal Brock's letter in his moccasin, however, and so they had been turned loose to continue their journey. As a consequence, Dickson promptly set out with a party of 140 Wisconsin and Minnesota warriors for St. Joseph, where the British had maintained a garrison since their withdrawal from Mackinac in 1796.

Here Captain Charles Roberts, a veteran officer who commanded a small body of redcoats, had been promptly notified by General Brock of the declaration of war, and on July 15 had been informed that he might act at his discretion about attacking Mackinac. To a keen soldier such permission was as good as an order. Already Roberts had practically completed his preparations for the expedition, and early on July 16 it set out. Nucleus of the picturesque array was the contingent of redcoats, 46 in number. To them were added about 200 voyageurs, led by their *bourgeois* or employers, and perhaps 400 Indians. About one-third of these had been brought by Dickson from Wisconsin; the remainder were from the region adjacent to Mackinac and the Sault. The latter war bands, however, had been lukewarm in their attitude until they were infected by the zeal of Dickson's followers. The L'Arbre Croche Ottawa even held aloof from the British until after the fort had been taken and then tardily declared themselves for the victors.

The flotilla which bore the nondescript army over the forty miles of water which separated Fort St. Joseph from Mackinac comprised three types of vessels. The North West Company's trading schooner *Caledonia* served as flagship of the fleet. On it were the army officers and fur-trade leaders, two small brass cannon and a quantity of supplies. The regular soldiers, the voyageurs and such supplies as could not find room on the *Caledonia* were conveyed in the picturesque bateaux of the traders. Finally came the warriors, gay with feathers and paint, in their graceful bark canoes.

Meanwhile at Mackinac, Lieutenant Porter Hanks, ignorant as yet of the declaration of war but aware of the strained international situation, heard rumors of the impending attack brought to the island by an Indian. Michael Dousman, a leading American trader, was friendly with many of the British traders at St. Joseph and it was determined that he should visit there and bring back information concerning the state of affairs.

Summoning the crew of his personal canoe he departed upon his mission. The evening twilight changed to darkness and Dousman was lost in slumber while the voyageurs with steady stroke of their paddles urged the lone canoe onward through the night. Suddenly a babble of voices overspread the dark waters, the boat was surrounded by canoes filled with savages and Dousman awoke to find himself a prisoner. Carried aboard the *Caledonia* for questioning, he admitted the defenseless state of the American garrison and its ignorance of the impending attack. Moved by the desire to save the civilian population from pillage and massacre at the hands of his red allies, Captain Roberts obtained from Dousman a pledge not to inform the garrison and sent him back to warn the townsmen to withdraw secretly from their homes to another part of the island where they would be guarded from insult or harm by the Indians.

This program was faithfully carried out. While the garrison on the bluff slumbered peacefully the townsmen slipped away to the appointed rendezvous, an old distillery. Meanwhile the British flotilla, advancing steadily through the night, passed around the northern end of the island to debark in a sandy cove known ever since as "British Landing," almost directly across the island from the fort. From here in the early dawn voyageurs and soldiers drew the cannon to the top of a lofty height which looks down upon the fort from the rear. About this time the unwonted silence, together with the whoops of the exultant savages skulking in the woods, apprised Lieutenant Hanks of the situation. A flag of truce soon appeared with a demand for the surrender of the garrison, accompanied by the usual alternative that in case of noncompliance townsmen and garrison would be exposed to the horrors of Indian massacre. Honorable terms were offered which Lieutenant Hanks, convinced of the hopelessness of successful resistance, accepted. The soldiers were paroled and dispatched to Detroit. Not a gun had been fired nor had a civilian been harmed in either person or property. The efficient humanity of Captain Roberts in the taking of Mackinac stands in refreshing contrast to the subsequent callous indifference exhibited by General Procter at the River Raisin.

The fall of Mackinac unloosed upon the Americans in the Northwest a veritable Pandora's box of mischief. Fear of the "northern hordes" of savages, fresh from their triumph at that place, chilled the heart and palsied the will of General Hull at Detroit. His sorry surrender was induced in large part by his concern for the preservation of the townsmen from massacre; and news of the easy victory, spreading quickly across the western wilderness, convinced the natives that the British were about to win the war and filled them with a desire to share in the triumph and in the spoils of victory that would attend it.

Thus aroused, they trooped down upon Fort Madison, the advanced American outpost on the Mississippi, and subjected the place to a siege which impelled the defenders to fire the fort and make their escape by night. Even earlier than this, several hundred had swarmed into Chicago, where Captain Heald with half a hundred regular soldiers upheld the banner of civilization; when in obedience to an order received from General Hull he evacuated the fort and began a withdrawal to Fort Wayne, they were quick to strike.

The morning of August 15 dawned hot and cloudless. For several days such hasty preparations for the evacuation as were possible had been made, and at nine o'clock the south gate of the fort was thrown open and soldiers and settlers issued forth upon their hazardous journey. In the lead was Captain William Wells, famed scout for Mad Anthony Wayne, who had come from Fort Wayne with thirty friendly Miami to assist in the evacuation. In due array followed the garrison, the women, children old enough to walk and the "Chicago militia," twelve in number, made up of the men and older boys of the tiny settlement. Here also were two baggage wagons in one of which the younger children had been placed, attended, probably, by one or more of the women. The wives of Captain Heald and Lieutenant Helm were mounted and near or with their husbands, while in an open boat near the mouth of the river Mrs. Kinzie and her children waited in readiness to begin the voyage around the lake shore to St. Joseph.

> "I heard the muffled beat of drum,
>   The woman's wail of fife,
> The Dead March played for Dearborn's men
>   Just marching out of life."

So a local poet long afterward made verse of the strange story told by Mrs. Kinzie that the march began to the tune of the Dead March,

AN ARGOSY OF DOOM

The *Eastland,* which overturned at a Chicago dock in 1915, drowning 800. Today, remodeled and renamed the *Wilmette,* she serves as a training ship.

COAST GUARD PATROL BOAT

Few Americans know that the stripes on the Coast Guard flag are vertical instead of horizontal.

DISCHARGING A CARGO OF LIMESTONE AT GARY

The *B. H. Taylor* belongs to a fleet of "self-unloaders" which brings limestone from Calcite, Michigan, to the steel mills.

VIEW OF THE DOCKS AT GARY

The freighter *John G. Munson* is unloading limestone at the Gary Works Dock while the *Carrollton* loads steel for delivery to another lake port.

played by the soldier musicians. If this was intended as a prophecy it found quick fulfillment, for the warriors filing behind the sand ridges hastened ahead to a position suitable for ambush and there awaited the oncoming column.

When the attack began, the troops promptly charged into the dunes driving the warriors before them until they gained a spot on the prairie in their rear. Although half of the soldiers had fallen, the Indians showed no desire to come to close quarters in the open and refrained from following them. The day was already lost, notwithstanding, for in making the charge through the dunes the regulars had become separated from the baggage wagons in the rear where the women and children were gathered. Here, too, were the junior officers, Ronan and Van Voorhis, together with the Chicago militia. Outnumbered many times, the militia were cut down to a man in a furious hand-to-hand melee, and the two young officers shared the same fate. Even the soldiers' wives, armed with swords, hacked bravely away as long as they could.

While the conflict was raging a young warrior, eluding the defenders, sprang into the wagon containing the babies and young children and in the space of a few seconds slaughtered all but one. Among the infants slain was the child of Black Cicely, Mrs. Heald's Negro slave, and the mother also perished, being one of the two women who were killed. The other was Mrs. Fielding Corbin, wife of a private soldier. She had vowed never to be taken prisoner, dreading the indignities of Indian captivity worse than death itself, and although far advanced in pregnancy she fought until cut to pieces.

Although the regulars had fought off their attackers for the moment, the position of the survivors was hopeless and their only alternative to surrender was death. After a little delay the Indians sent a half-breed interpreter, who had gone over to their side at the moment of attack in the hope of saving his life, to propose a surrender. After some parleying this was agreed to on the promise that the lives of the prisoners would be spared. They were now conducted back to the beach and thence to the fort along the route over which they had marched so short a time before. On the way they passed the scene of slaughter at the baggage wagons and Lieutenant Helm records his horror at the sight of men, women and children "lying naked with principally all their heads off." Among the headless bodies he thought he perceived that of his wife and the sight almost overcame him. To his great joy, however, on reaching the fort he found her unharmed, sitting crying among some squaws.

The promise to spare the lives of the prisoners was promptly violated and several of the soldiers were put to death, some of them by the customary methods of Indian torture. Of the remaining capives, a few were quickly returned to civilization; many underwent a long and terrible captivity, from which some found release only in death; no record remains concerning the fate which befell many others. Some were taken in one direction and others in another by the various bands of natives into whose hands they had fallen. Lieutenant Helm, carried to an Illinois River village, was soon ransomed by Thomas Forsyth of Peoria by the payment of two mares and the additional promise of a keg of liquor "when practicable." The members of the Kinzie family, owing to the trader's influence with the Indians, were not regarded as prisoners; a few days after the massacre they journeyed by boat to St. Joseph, and after a stay of several weeks with friendly Potawatomi, they continued to Detroit, their former home.

Probably few voyages around Lake Michigan have ever been made in sorrier circumstances than those attending the flight from captivity of Captain and Mrs. Heald. During the battle both were repeatedly wounded and at its close they belonged to different bands of natives. The appeals of Mrs. Heald and the arguments of a friendly half-breed, reinforced by the latter's gift to her captors of "an old mule and a bottle of whiskey," effected her transfer to the company of her husband. Next day their captors set out by boat for St. Joseph. They had no food and the prisoners were suffering from many wounds. After paddling for hours around the end of the lake one of the Indians shot a deer on the shore. Encamping, they dressed the animal and using the hide as a kneading board Mrs. Heald stirred some flour which had been brought along into a thick paste which was wound around sticks and held over the fire to toast. This the captain later declared made the best bread he ever ate.

At St. Joseph they were allowed to stay in the house of the trader Burnett, where their wounds were treated by an Indian doctor.

Within a few days most of the Indians trooped off to participate in the attack on Fort Wayne, and Captain Heald improved the opportunity to persuade a friendly Indian, Alexander Robinson, to paddle them to Mackinac in his canoe. The distance was 300 miles and the journey consumed sixteen days. On their arrival the fugitives were accorded all possible consideration by Captain Roberts, the British commandant, to whom Heald appealed for protection from the Indians who, he feared, were pursuing him. He was given his parole and permitted to continue on to Detroit, traveling in a small sailboat. It is interesting to note that one of the witnesses to his parole was Robert Dickson, whose activities in rousing the Indians of the Northwest against the Americans we have already noted.

In the autumn following the massacre Dickson went to Montreal to advocate a program he had conceived for recruiting the western Indians to take part in the war. His plan was approved, and he returned to the West with the appointment of superintendent of the tribes west of Lake Michigan. Green Bay and Chicago were to be the centers for assembling the warriors and he estimated that he would be able to bring a thousand of them into the field. Early in June 1813 he led 600 warriors—Chippewa, Menominee, Winnebago, Sioux and others—to Mackinac, while 800 more were reported to be marching overland to Detroit from their rendezvous at Chicago.

The struggle for the recovery of Detroit by the Americans ended in complete victory with the naval triumph of Captain Perry on Lake Erie on September 10, 1813, followed by the destruction of the British-Indian army at the Battle of the Thames on October 5. These victories prepared the way for an attack upon Mackinac, made in August 1814, which met with disastrous defeat. Meanwhile from St. Louis the Americans struck at the center of British-Indian influence on the upper Mississippi by sending a force of 150 men to occupy Prairie du Chien at the mouth of the Wisconsin River in the early summer of 1814. There they erected a stockade fort which they named Fort Shelby in honor of the Governor of Kentucky. In it six cannon were mounted, while in the river near by lay the gunboat which had brought the expedition from St. Louis.

As soon as Colonel McDouall at Mackinac learned of this irruption of the Americans into Wisconsin he began organizing an expedition to dislodge them. Dickson had already come to Mackinac with 300 warriors from west of Lake Michigan, half of whom were retained to aid in the defense against the impending American attack. The remainder were assigned to the expedition against Prairie du Chien. To accompany them, two companies of volunteers were hastily organized from among the voyageurs at Mackinac and given the imposing designation of "Michigan Fencibles." The Indians especially urged that a "big gun" be supplied them, and McDouall assigned to the expedition a single regular artilleryman, Sergeant James Keating, with a three-pound gun. To command the whole he appointed Major William McKay, a brave and capable officer.

The little army, consisting of 95 Michigan Fencibles and 136 Indians, set out upon its 500-mile journey on June 28. Six days later it was at Green Bay where another company of voyageurs, known as the Mississippi Volunteers, was enrolled, bringing the white contingent to 120 men. At Green Bay and the portage additional bands of warriors joined the expedition, augmenting the redskin contingent to more than 500.

McKay reached Prairie du Chien on July 17 to find Fort Shelby, defended by six guns and 60 or 70 men, "perfectly safe against Indians," while the gunboat *General Clark* was "a floating block-house" whose defenders were securely protected from small-arms fire. Although he had already made the painful discovery that his red allies were "perfectly useless," McKay summoned the Americans to surrender or be ready to defend themselves "to the last man." Since they declined the former alternative the three-pound gun was dragged to a position where it commanded the gunboat and artilleryman Keating opened fire upon it. After three hours in the course of which eighty-six rounds had been fired, the *General Clark* cut her cable and sought shelter behind a near-by island. The cannon was now turned upon the fort, which was bombarded until the evening of July 19 at which time the garrison surrendered and Fort Shelby was occupied by the British.

Meanwhile early in July, in ignorance of the British invasion, a force of 120 men led by Lieutenant John Campbell left St. Louis to reinforce the garrison at Prairie du Chien. One of the boats became stranded at the mouth of Rock River, where on July 11 a vicious fire was opened upon it by Indians concealed on shore. The other two boats which had gone on ahead now came to its assistance, with the result that after some time one of them took fire and was abandoned, while the other fled down river leaving the occupants of the stranded boat to their fate. In this extremity the *General Clark,* descending from its inglorious battle at Prairie du Chien, opportunely appeared and taking off the beleaguered keelboaters continued its voyage to St. Louis. In this sharp battle the Americans had sustained a loss of sixteen killed and twenty-one wounded, practically one-third of the entire contingent.

When the survivors of Campbell's expedition returned to St. Louis with their story the American authorities began preparations to dispatch a more formidable force to chasten the hostile villagers at Rock Island. In August, therefore, Major Zachary Taylor set out for Rock Island with eight gunboats and 330 men. News of the coming attack had been carried to the Indians, however, and they had appealed to the British at Prairie du Chien for help, particularly requesting that some of the "big guns" of the white man be sent down. In response to this appeal a force of thirty men with three small guns was dispatched to Rock Island, to be presently followed by over 100 Sioux and Winnebago warriors from the upper Mississippi.

When Taylor's expedition arrived, in addition to the British detachment a force of savages variously estimated at 1,000 to 1,500 warriors was waiting to receive him. On September 5 the British gunners opened fire on the fleet at anchor in the river and after an artillery duel of an hour's duration the boats retreated down river to tie up presently at the St. Louis levee. The American loss in the engagement was trifling, but Taylor felt that his strength was inadequate to the task of destroying the Sauk town, and the British cannon rendered his position untenable. Both American and British commanders united in affirming that it was the British artillery which decided the contest. This consisted principally of Sergeant Keating's threepounder which had already won the battle of Prairie du Chien. That one gun worked by one artilleryman should decide the fate of two campaigns and two battles is a feat remarkable enough to deserve commemoration.[2] No further effort was made by the Americans to recover Prairie du Chien and the attempt upon Mackinac had failed disastrously. Until the summer of 1815 the Lake Michigan country remained completely under British control.

In the end American diplomacy accomplished brilliantly what American arms had signally failed to achieve. The progress of events in the European theatre of war had eliminated many of the original causes of discord between Britain and the United States and a common war weariness had disposed both governments to minimize others. The diplomats assembled at Ghent in 1814 and after prolonged discussion agreement on terms of peace was reached on December 24. The British diplomats had come to the peace table intent on erecting a permanent barrier between Canada and the United States in the Northwest by compelling the latter to renounce its sovereignty over the country between the Ohio and the lakes and forever dedicating the region thus surrendered to the Indian tribes inhabiting it. But the American representatives firmly declined even to consider any cession of territory and in the end peace was made on the simple principle of a return to the status which had existed at the beginning of the war.

It still remained to make peace with the Indian tribes and to effect mutual evacuations of conquered territory. In the summer of 1815 Fort Malden was restored to the British, who themselves retired from Wisconsin and Mackinac to establish a new center of control on Drummond Island, adjoining the mouth of the St. Marys River. During the same summer two U. S. commissions, one sitting at Spring Wells near Detroit, the other at Portage des Sioux near the mouth of the Illinois River, entered into more than a score of treaties with the western Indians. All were short and their provisions were practically identical, reciting that whereas the contracting parties had been at war they were now to be at peace and all acts of hostility committed by either party were mutually forgiven and forgotten.

But the British influence over the tribes was still powerful, while that of the Americans west of Lake Michigan was as yet slight. Although peace had nominally been restored, it yet remained to establish effective control over the northwestern tribes, and this involved the placing of garrisons at strategic centers along the highways of trade and travel.

Before the close of the summer of 1815 the government determined not only to establish garrisons at Chicago and Green Bay but to occupy Prairie du Chien and to erect a new fort at Rock Island and another near the Falls of St. Anthony. Colonel John Miller of the Third U. S. Infantry at Detroit was directed to occupy Mackinac and to him was committed the duty of supervising the garrisoning of Green Bay and Chicago.

Two companies of troops were assigned to the latter place and early in June they sailed from Detroit aboard the schooner *General Wayne*. The vessel reached Chicago on July 4, 1816, and the work of building the new fort was at once begun. Besides the soldiers, pit sawyers and other workmen had been brought from Detroit. A grove of pine trees near the lake shore four miles north of the river mouth was selected, and the logs were rolled into the lake and rafted down to the fort site. Although parties of Indians hung around, no trouble was encountered save from their begging and thievery. A few months later Major Stephen H. Long of the engineer department of the army visited Chicago. He reported that the construction of the fort had been pushed with commendable industry and would probably be completed during the following season.

Colonel Miller sailed from Detroit in time to reach Mackinac July 14. There he encountered reports that the natives were preparing to oppose the establishment of the fort at Green Bay and this induced him to go there himself with as powerful a force as he could muster. It comprised a detachment of artillery, four companies of infantry and two of riflemen, in all several hundred troops. The expedition sailed from Mackinac in four vessels on July 26 and three days later was off the entrance to Green Bay. Its waters were an unknown sea to the military, and Augustin Grignon, a Green Bay trader who chanced to be at Mackinac, was engaged to pilot the fleet. The *Washington*, of 100 tons burden, was the largest ship, her consorts ranging downward in size to the *Amelia*, a mere sloop. With the attitude of original discoverers, the invaders proceeded to give names to the more important islands encountered on the voyage up the bay. Ancient Potawatomi Island, where they tarried several days, was renamed Washington in honor of the flagship, while another prominent island was given the name of Lieutenant Colonel Chambers, the first commandant of the new fort.

The site selected, after an inspection of the river bank for several miles, was on the west bank of the river where stood the ruins of ancient Fort Edward Augustus, abandoned by Lieutenant Gorrell in 1763. Colonel Miller soon returned to Mackinac, leaving Colonel Chambers with five companies of troops, numbering about 300 men, to construct and command the fort. It consisted of a high stockade of pickets with a bastion at each angle in which a cannon was mounted. Not until several years later when a sawmill had been erected was the work completed.

While the expeditions were being prepared at Detroit for the occupation of Green Bay and Chicago, another assembled at St. Louis to establish American control on the upper Mississippi. Fort Armstrong was established on Rock Island within a few miles of the principal village of the belligerent Sauk and Foxes, while on June 16 a force of troops arrived at Prairie du Chien and began the erection of Fort Crawford. Three years later Fort Snelling was established at the mouth of the Minnesota River in the heart of the Sioux country. American authority was at last supreme around Lake Michigan.

[1] *Notes on the Ancestry of Major Wm. Roe Van Voorhis* (New York, 1881), 144-145.
[2] For the remarkable work of Sergeant Keating see M. M. Quaife, "A Forgotten Hero of Rock Island," in *Journal of the Illinois State Historical Society*, XXIII, 652-63 (January 1931).

Chapter 13

Sturgeon Boats

For thousands of years no progress was made in methods of transportation. The horse on land and the wind at sea had been harnessed for travel before the dawn of recorded history, and until the nineteenth century no substitute for them had been found. The discovery of the power of steam in the eighteenth century was soon followed by its application to travel on land and water, and the steamboat and the iron horse, both created less than a century and a half ago, made the rapid settlement of interior America possible.

The first successful steamboat in the history of the world, the *Clermont,* was placed on the Hudson River by Robert Fulton in 1807. Four years later the *New Orleans* was built at Pittsburgh for use on the lower Mississippi, and from about 1818 on more boats were added rapidly until by 1834 over 200 were plying the western rivers. Their introduction upon the Great Lakes came later, since the country there could not be settled until a practicable highway connecting it with the Atlantic seaboard should be provided. With the completion of the Erie Canal in 1825 this lack was supplied, and soon a flood of settlers began pouring westward across New York into the country around and beyond Lake Erie.

Well in advance of this development, however, a group of New York and Albany promoters had built at Black Rock the first steamboat on the Upper Lakes. The *Walk-in-the-Water,* as the pioneer ship was called, was completed in August 1818 and was designed to run between Black Rock and Detroit. In more ways than one, the *Walk-in-the-Water* marked an advance in the art of steamboat design and construction. Although considerable progress had been made in the decade after the launching of the *Clermont,* all the earlier ships were river boats, and not until 1817 when the *Ontario* was launched at Ogdensburg was any experience gained in constructing vessels for use on water subject to a swell. On her maiden voyage the

135

Ontario disclosed faults of construction which threatened to wreck the ship and compelled her immediate withdrawal from navigation until they could be corrected.

The *Walk-in-the-Water,* however, launched only a year later, proved herself an immediate engineering and financial success. Anyone who today would venture to sea in such a vessel would deserve the attention of a psychiatrist, but in 1818 the ship was undoubtedly the finest and safest steamboat in the world. The storms encountered by vessels on the Great Lakes are as violent as any on the ocean; yet here the *Walk-in-the-Water* and her successors were making voyages on regular schedule for twenty years before any steamship crossed the Atlantic; and here was gained, in large part, the knowledge and experience by which steam navigation on the ocean was made possible.

The new marvel was about 140 feet long and 32 feet wide, with a displacement of 330 tons.[1] Her hull had a depth of 8½ feet, and her engine, placed in the open amidships, was geared to two 16-foot paddle wheels. A single, tall smokestack towered rakishly aloft, while even loftier were the two masts, equipped with sails to supplement the power of the engine. This sturdy creation outlasted the ship itself and two later vessels in which it was successively placed. A committee of the Detroit Lyceum, appointed to report upon the *Walk-in-the-Water* after her maiden voyage to Detroit, pronounced her, save for one possible exception still under construction, the finest steamboat "in America or the world." Undoubtedly she was the fastest, yet like the early-day automobile, her engine was almost pitifully unequal to the performance of the tasks she faced. At Black Rock, the "horned breeze"—a dozen yokes of oxen pulling on a long towrope attached to the ship—had long been employed to assist the sailing ships up the Niagara into the open lake. Through her entire career on the lakes the *Walk-in-the-Water* was compelled to invoke the same sturdy ox power to assist her progress from Black Rock into Lake Erie.

Yet the new ship was so much better than any before her that her advent initiated a new era in lake transportation. Her maiden voyage to Detroit was made in forty-four hours and ten minutes of actual sailing, although stopovers en route lengthened the time consumed to four days. This was a vast improvement over the uncertainties of travel by sailboats, which were subject to so many delays that no pretense of maintaining a schedule could be made.[2] At first the sailing schedules of the *Walk-in-the-Water* provided for a round trip between Black Rock and Detroit every two weeks, but before the second season was ended this had been reduced to a single week. On the maiden voyage, made in August 1818, ninety-four passengers disembarked at Detroit. The arrival had been expectantly awaited for some time, and red men and white alike turned out en masse to view the wonder as the vessel steamed majestically up the Detroit. Oddly enough, Chief Walk-in-the-Water, for whom the ship was named, had died two months before, too soon to comprehend the honor conferred upon him. His fellow red men living along the river had been informed in advance of the strange boat which their Great White Father was sending to visit them, drawn through the rivers and lakes by sturgeon.[3] Since seeing is believing, their wondering whoops and exclamations of surprise—*Ta-i-Yah-Niche*—as the ship moved past, revealed their conviction of the truth of the explanation their white friends had given them. Their wonderment was hardly greater than the satisfaction exhibited by Detroit's only journalist over the fact that the city had now been brought within seven days' travel of New York.

For several seasons the sturgeon ship remained the only steamboat on the Upper Lakes, performing regularly her Black Rock-Detroit run, save for an occasional departure upon an excursion to Mackinac and Green Bay. The first of these trips was made in June 1819 when the ship sailed from Detroit on an eight-day tour to Mackinac, carrying sixty passengers and a cargo of supplies for the American Fur Company.[4]

A year later, the *Walk-in-the-Water* paid two visits to Mackinac, one in June, the other in August. On the first of these occasions her passenger list included General Alexander Macomb, the hero of Plattsburg, Ramsay Crooks of the American Fur Company, Dr. William Beaumont, whose studies of the human digestive processes have rendered his name immortal, and Reverend Jedediah Morse, "father" of American geography and father, also, of the inventor of the electric telegraph. On returning to Detroit the gratified passengers published a testimonial reciting the attractions of the voyage and commending it to eastern "gentlemen and ladies," while Dr. Morse affirmed that the sturgeon ship had brought Mackinac within fifteen days' travel from Boston.

In 1821 the *Walk-in-the-Water* ventured into Lake Michigan for the first time, having engaged to transport to Green Bay a detachment of soldiers bound for the Upper Country. This time the passengers numbered 200, among them being many army officers, and the round trip from Detroit consumed thirteen days.

Despite such performances, the engines of the sturgeon ship had more than once proved incapable of breasting the gales she encountered on the lakes. The final failure came on October 31, 1821, when for the last time the "horned breeze" hauled her from Black Rock up the Niagara into Lake Erie. A vicious gale was already gathering, and before many miles had been passed it burst in fury upon the doomed ship. Unable to proceed and in momentary peril of swamping, Captain Rogers turned his ship about in hope of regaining the shelter of Black Rock. He was compelled to cast anchor off Buffalo Creek, however, where the night was passed with anchors dragging and water pouring into the vessel's hull through the seams opened by the pounding seas. Toward dawn, as a last resort, the cables were cut and the *Walk-in-the-Water* was driven on the shore, a crushed and broken hulk. The terror-stricken passengers all escaped with their lives, to be sheltered and clothed by the villagers who had discovered the plight of the ship.

Despite her sorry ending, the *Walk-in-the-Water* had proved a profitable investment for her owners, who salvaged her engine and placed it in the new ship they proceeded to build. The *Superior* had a long career on the Upper Lakes, where for several years she remained the only steamboat. Her regular run was from Buffalo to Detroit, but like the *Walk-in-the-Water* she made occasional journeys into Lake Huron and Lake Michigan. In 1820 Governor Cass had negotiated a treaty with the Chippewa at Sault Ste. Marie by which the United States obtained title to a strip of land adjoining the rapids, on which to build a fort. The erection of Fort Brady followed in 1822, and one of the *Superior's* first errands was to transport thither 250 soldiers of the Second U. S. Infantry, sent to begin the new work. But the vessel drew too much water to permit her to pass the limestone bar at the foot of Lake George, and the soldiers were compelled to complete the voyage in open bateaux. Although the *Superior* was the first steamboat ever to enter the St. Marys River, the distinction of being the first to reach the Sault was reserved for the *Henry Clay* five years later.

The Erie Canal was completed in 1825, and the next season witnessed no less than six steamboats on the Buffalo-Detroit run, where one had sufficed until now. The Lake Erie Steamboat Company, owner of the *Walk-in-the-Water* and the *Superior,* now built the *Henry Clay, Niagara* and *William Penn,* while the *Enterprise* and the *Pioneer* were built by rival operators. Until after the Black Hawk War of 1832, none of these steamers ran regularly beyond Detroit. Occasional excursions as far as Mackinac and Green Bay continued to be made, however, and the accommodations offered to travelers continued to improve—at least on paper. For the season of 1829 the Lake Erie Steamboat Line advertised the installation of numerous improvements both for the comfort of the passengers and to "give the Boats greater speed and force." It was also announced that it was "in contemplation" to send a vessel to Green Bay during the summer, and in case this were done, due advance notice of the departure would be given. The company was still operating only the four little vessels of 1826, but in 1830 two more were added. This season, too, the negotiation of an Indian treaty at Green Bay caused the sending of two ships to that place, the first to carry the government officers and other passengers there, the second to return them to Detroit and civilization.

Comparison of the splendors set forth in the advertisements with the sober realities of such a journey is made possible by the narrative of a sprightly New England girl who in the summer of 1830 became the bride of John H. Kinzie, Indian agent at Fort Winnebago, Wisconsin, and accompanied her husband to her new western home.[5] At Detroit the couple took passage for Green Bay on the *Henry Clay,* congratulating themselves upon their good fortune in being spared the voyage in one of the tiny schooners of the period which ordinarily supplied the only means of travel to Lake Michigan. Conveyed to the dock in a French cart, the traveler was delighted with the fittings of the ladies' cabin, which seemed "the very climax of comfort and convenience." And so they proved, for the first twenty-four hours. Then, off Thunder Bay arose such a tempest as had frightened the passengers on La Salle's *Griffin* in 1679. The pitching and rolling of the boat and the consequent seasickness were borne philosophically, since for these discomforts the travelers were prepared; but a new one quickly appeared. The rain, falling in torrents, "made its way through every seam and pore of deck or moulding. Down the stairway, through the joints and crevices, it came, saturating first the carpet, then the bedding," until the ladies were driven to seek refuge in the men's cabin.

Here they were safe for a brief space, but soon the seams above opened and down upon their heads poured such a flood that even umbrellas were an insufficient protection; and nothing was left but to take to their berths, where they remained until the ship docked at Mackinac. Across Lake Michigan the storm resumed its sway, flooding the cabins as a matter of course, and continuing until the *Henry Clay* grounded hard and fast on the "flats" three miles below Green Bay. They took to an open boat and continued the trip "in wind, rain, and darkness," to arrive drenched and shivering at the only inn, which was already so crowded with guests that there was no room for the new arrivals.

Save for such infrequent voyages to Green Bay as those we have noted, the real beginning of steam transportation on Lake Michigan was brought about by the Black Hawk War of 1832. The early steamboats were wood burners, whose voracious boilers demanded frequent replenishing. As far west as Green Bay there were both harbors and settlements where firewood could be obtained, but at the south end of Lake Michigan there was neither. The Fort Dearborn garrison was removed to Green Bay in the spring of 1831, and the schooner sent from Detroit to transport its baggage could find anchorage only in the open lake, exposed to every storm that might arise.[6]

The story of the war has often been related, but never with adequate attention to the problems of transportation it involved. The mistake made by the War Department in abandoning Fort Dearborn was soon realized, and in March 1832, well in advance of the outbreak of hostilities, measures were being concerted to regarrison the post. Upon Major Henry Whiting at Detroit devolved the responsibility of procuring the needed supplies and transportation, and he reported that no steamboat could be obtained for the voyage save at an exorbitant price. "Indeed," he continued, "having no means of obtaining wood at the head of Lake Michigan, it would probably be out of the question."[7]

That it was not, however, was soon to be demonstrated. The troops at Fort Niagara were to be sent to Chicago, and on May 10 Whiting left Detroit for Buffalo, where he engaged a steamboat to convey them to Detroit. There they were to be transferred to a schooner which the steamboat would tow upriver into Lake Huron. This measure would save three or four weeks' time over making the entire voyage by sailing ship, and General Brady was insistent that the soldiers be sent on as swiftly as possible.

Meanwhile in Illinois the savages were conducting murderous raids upon the settlers, many of whom fled in panic to the tenantless walls of Fort Dearborn; from Detroit, General John R. Williams led a regiment of Michigan militia to the defense of Chicago until the regulars should arrive; at New Salem a tall young grocer's clerk named Abraham Lincoln enrolled in the local militia company to fight the redskins; and at Washington the War Department directed General Scott to assemble the garrisons of regular soldiers stationed along the Great Lakes and the Atlantic seaboard and conduct them to the seat of war beyond Lake Michigan.

General Scott promptly decided that only by steamboat could the troops be transported with the celerity the military situation demanded, and at Buffalo, Whiting, who had hurried eastward to join Scott, learned to the General's satisfaction that the steamboat owners would undertake the service although they still looked upon the proposed voyage to Chicago as wholly an experiment.

In all, four ships were engaged, the *Henry Clay, Sheldon Thompson, Superior* and *William Penn,* and the two first-named vessels reached Detroit the night of July 4, bringing respectively seven and six companies of soldiers; the *Superior* and the *Penn* arrived with additional companies during the next few days.

A large part of the oncoming army, however, was destined never to reach Chicago nor to engage an Indian in combat. Aboard the

Henry Clay was a soldier stricken with the Asiatic cholera. From Europe, where it had prevailed for many weeks, the scourge had crossed the ocean to Quebec in early June. From here it passed inland to Montreal and thence southward to Albany and New York. Eleven deaths had occurred at the latter place by July 4; in the two weeks ending July 28 there were more than 1,400. A month later the epidemic had practically run its course in New York and meanwhile was sweeping westward and southward across the country.

Brought to the lakes by Scott's soldiers, the cholera reached Detroit almost as soon as it struck New York. The sick man on the *Henry Clay* died in a few hours and new seizures quickly followed. To save Detroit from the epidemic, General Scott removed the *Henry Clay* to near-by Belle Isle, where after being serviced with medicines and other supplies by a small boat engaged for this purpose it sailed for Mackinac under orders to remain at Bois Blanc Island if the disease continued to spread. By the time the vessel reached Fort Gratiot at the entrance of Lake Huron so many of Colonel Twiggs' command were dead or dying that the crew refused to continue the voyage. Before the ship returned to Detroit, however, Colonel Twiggs disembarked his men, several hundred in number; casting discipline to the winds, they fled like panic-stricken animals anywhere to escape the clutches of their dreadful foe. Two-thirds of the entire command quickly vanished, and Colonel Twiggs sent a large number of young officers, fresh from West Point, back to Detroit on the *Clay,* having no need for their further service.

While Colonel Twiggs' detachment was thus undergoing disruption, the *Superior* and *William Penn* had reached Detroit, loaded with additional companies of soldiers, and those on the *Sheldon Thompson* had passed northward into Lake Huron. On the *Superior* the epidemic was already at work and the crew was in a mutinous state; however, the captain was persuaded to proceed as far as Lake Huron, towing a schooner along in which to continue the journey to Chicago. For a week or more chaos reigned. The *Thompson* like the *Clay* returned to Detroit, where an effort was made toward dispatching some of the troops by land to Chicago, but the demoralization of the soldiers rendered such a move impossible. Colonel Twiggs reported that scarce half a dozen men of his command were fit for duty, while the new recruits had dispersed to the last man. At Fort Gratiot, Major Point was begging for medical aid, but none could be sent since all the physicians at Detroit were busy combating the ravages of the epidemic among the civilian population. It subsided almost as rapidly as it had struck, and we leave the further story of events at Detroit to follow the *Sheldon Thompson* on her voyage to Chicago.

Before setting out for the West, General Scott, who was aboard the ship, had obtained some instruction concerning the character and treatment of the disease. No fatalities occurred until after the vessel entered Lake Michigan, when the epidemic broke out with deadly violence. The only surgeon on board became panic-stricken, drank a bottle of wine and took to bed where, to quote the disgusted commander's comment, he "ought to have died." In this emergency, Scott himself turned surgeon, applying as best he could the instruction he had received in New York. His principal effort was directed toward preventing a general panic, and from beginning to end of the epidemic he set an example to his men by exhibiting no sign of fear concerning it. Long afterward he told John Wentworth, mayor of early Chicago, that although he had often been in the midst of suffering and peril, he had never felt his entire helplessness as he did upon the lakes in the midst of the Asiatic cholera. "Sentinels were of no use in warning of the enemy's approach. He could not storm his works, fortify against him, nor cut his own way out, nor make terms of capitulation. There was no respect for a flag of truce, and his men were falling upon all sides from an enemy in his very midst."[8]

The *Sheldon Thompson* reached Chicago on July 10. On the two-day voyage up Lake Michigan sixteen soldiers had died and two bodies had been thrown overboard. By the twelfth, when an express left Chicago for Detroit, there were seventy-seven cases and twenty-five deaths. In the absence of a harbor the ship was compelled to anchor in the open lake and the troops were taken ashore in small boats. During the night which elapsed between the arrival at Chicago and the unloading of the soldiers, three more men died and were thrown overboard. Years later the captain of the ship recalled that their forms were plainly visible through the clear water, and to escape the gruesome sight the anchor was weighed and the vessel shifted to another location.

Ashore the troops occupying Fort Dearborn were moved to an open camp near by and the fort was converted into a general hospital for the men of Scott's stricken command. Here, as earlier at Fort Gratiot, the epidemic raged violently for several days, with 200 cases admitted to the hospital and almost one-third of them terminating fatally. One intelligent victim who recovered left a graphic account of his seizure while serving as officer of the day on the *Thompson*.

"I had scarcely got through my task [superintending the landing of the sick soldiers], when I was thrown down on the deck almost as suddenly as if shot. As I was working on the lower deck I felt my legs growing stiff from my knees downward. I went on the upper deck and walked violently to keep up the circulation of the blood. I felt suddenly a rush of blood from the feet upwards, and as it rose my veins grew cold, and my blood curdled . . . my legs and hands were cramped with violent pain."[9]

By her tragic voyage the *Sheldon Thompson* had achieved the distinction of being the first steamboat ever to visit the head of Lake Michigan, and July 10, the date of her arrival at Chicago, should be treasured in local memory. On the fifteenth she began the return voyage to Detroit and at Mackinac met the *William Penn* outward bound with several companies of soldiers which the *Thompson* had left behind at Fort Gratiot. Since these had gone through the epidemic, there were no further seizures among those who had survived to embark on the *Penn*. The remnants of Colonel Twiggs' command, besides those of other companies, were still scattered from Detroit to Port Huron, while two companies under Major Thompson had begun the overland march from Detroit to Chicago on July 17. Through some mismanagement at Buffalo, most of the stores required for the army had been left behind. They were embarked belatedly on several schooners which in addition to being becalmed in Lake St. Clair had much difficulty in ascending the river into Lake Huron. After some delay Major Whiting succeeded in hiring a steamboat, which he sent to "sweep the river" and assist the schooners into the lake. Three of them entered it on the seventeenth and spread their wings for Chicago, while a fourth schooner followed a few days later. At Chicago, meanwhile, Scott's soldiers were in urgent need of provisions and medicines, and to insure them a supply of the latter until the schooners should arrive Whiting dispatched a "faithful young man" overland from Detroit carrying enough cholera antidotes to dose 200 patients for fifteen days.

The perplexities of the harassed commander at Chicago are vividly depicted in the report which Whiting at Detroit made to his superior on July 22. A letter was sent by Scott the morning of July 18, "imploring" that the troops and supplies left behind be sent on. As yet but one detachment had arrived and the men were all either sick or engaged in caring for the sick. Scott could not know when writing this letter that the *William Penn* with four companies of troops aboard was fast nearing Chicago; or that the stores so urgently needed were aboard the schooners now afloat somewhere on Lake Huron; or that Whiting now had 200 tents at Detroit, which he was trying to engage some small schooner to take on, although fearful that such a vessel would not be able "to make the long stretch of Lake Michigan."

By the end of July the troops who had survived the ravages of the epidemic at Detroit and Fort Gratiot were again ready for active service, but the Secretary of War, who was now in Detroit, was unwilling to expose them further to the hazard of an outbreak of cholera on shipboard. Preparations for marching them overland to Chicago were under way when an express from that place reached Detroit bringing news of the arrival of the *William Penn* with four companies of soldiers, none of whom had fallen sick during the voyage. Returning, the *Penn* had put in at the mouth of the St. Joseph for wood, and, encountering Major Thompson's detachment which was marching overland from Detroit, had taken it aboard for conveyance across the lake to Chicago. At about the same time three of the schooners arrived with their badly needed cargoes, and with reports of a "lucky" voyage.

General Scott now set out, accompanied only by his staff, for the field of warfare in northwestern Illinois, leaving orders for Colonel Eustis to follow him with as many troops as should be able to move by the third of August. As far as present-day Beloit they followed an ancient Indian trail from Chicago; the track across the prairie sod made by the heavy army wagons was shortly turned into a highway by the incoming settlers and for a generation or more was called the Army Trail.

For the country around Lake Michigan the Black Hawk War was like the bursting of a dam which has long impounded the waters of some great river. The Erie Canal and the steamboat had made the region accessible; fear of the red man and his title to the soil were now eradicated. The operations of the armies brought to several thousand soldiers firsthand acquaintance with the entrancing wilderness west of Lake Michigan; and the East was flooded with newspaper articles reciting the attractions of the newly discovered paradise. The peopling of the country both east and west of Lake Michigan followed with a rush. The steamboats which pioneered the way to Chicago in 1832 brought more than a few sick soldiers and an epidemic of cholera. For Lake Michigan itself and for all the country adjoining they ushered a new age into being.

---

[1] The figures given by different authorities, as often with early steamboats, vary slightly. The ones here stated are approximately correct.

[2] Mrs. John H. Kinzie relates the experience of a relative who sailed from Detroit in June and reached Chicago in September, three months later. See her *Wau-Bun, The "Early Day" in the North-West*, edited by the present writer (Chicago, 1932), 3-4. In 1816 the fleet which conveyed the troops from Mackinac to Green Bay consumed seventeen days on the voyage.

[3] The sturgeon, then common in the Detroit and adjacent waters, attained a length of several feet.

[4] Detroit *Gazette*, July 16, 1819.

[5] *Wau-Bun*, pp. xix-xxii and 3-6.

[6] For an amusing account of the trials attending its loading see Mrs. Kinzie's *Wau-Bun*, 345-349.

[7] Letter of Whiting to General Jesup, Detroit, March 23, 1832, preserved in Henry Whiting Papers, Detroit Public Library. Much of the material in the following pages has been gleaned from this collection.

[8] John Wentworth, *Early Chicago*, 37. (Fergus Historical Series, No. 16, Chicago, 1881).

[9] Letter from Fort Dearborn, July 12, printed in Niles *Register*, August 11, 1832

Chapter 14

Admiral of the Lakes

Iₙ ᴛʜᴇ heart of the Detroit water front stands an ancient warehouse whose massive interior timbers bespeak the methods of a bygone age. On its exterior wall one still may read the name "Nᴇᴡʙᴇʀʀʏ ᴀɴᴅ Cᴏᴍᴘᴀɴʏ." Both building and sign are well started upon their second century of existence, and their enduring quality reflects admirably the sturdy character of the forgotten merchant who made history on the lakes a century and a quarter ago.

Although Oliver Newberry never lived in Chicago, his name deserves high rank on any list of that city's founders. In advance of all others he visioned its future commercial possibilities, and for a quarter of a century he worked more effectively than anyone else to promote its contacts with the outside world. He pioneered the city's vast packing and grain-exporting businesses, providing not only the meat and grain but the ships which carried them to their eastern market. He established the first steamboat service between Chicago and the East and exerted his influence to promote the building of harbors and other internal improvements. Yet today the monumental and many-volumed history of Chicago promoted by her great university contains but a single incidental mention of the man whom his contemporaries fondly called the Admiral of the Lakes.

Newberry was born at Windsor, Connecticut, in 1789. At the age of fifteen he migrated with his parents to Oneida County, New York, where several years later he enlisted as a soldier in the War of 1812. During his term of military service he was stationed for a time at Buffalo village, which had recently been ravaged and burned by the British, and in 1816 he returned to start a humble store there. He soon had occasion to make a journey to Detroit, crossing the southern Ontario wilderness on foot with a heavy pack on his back. Detroit, too, had suffered terribly in the recent war, but Newberry was sufficiently impressed in 1820 by its future business prospects to make it his permanent home.

Beginning humbly in rented quarters, he steadily progressed to a position of recognized civic and business leadership. Although he possessed few social graces and was never a good mixer, he was highly respected for his business integrity and shrewdness. His iron will was matched by a violent temper which led him on occasion to pour a torrent of invective upon anyone unlucky enough to become the object of his wrath. Despite his wealth he was untidy in dress, and his clothes, although of good quality, were commonly worn until they became threadbare. Usually he wore a tall hat, at first of beaver but in later years of silk, which served the double purpose of headdress and office. In it, each morning he would stow the papers he anticipated would be wanted during the day, and when he removed it in search of a particular paper all were likely to spill upon the ground to be patiently gathered up and returned to their singular filing case. In cold weather he usually wore a long French capote of blue broadcloth. Below it could be seen a pair of baggy gray trousers which in wet weather were tucked inside heavy cowhide boots. A confirmed bachelor, he cared nothing for social or domestic interests, devoting his entire time and energy to his business concerns.

Although these began humbly enough, they became steadily more complex and extensive. In addition to conducting the retail store, Newberry soon became engaged in the commission and forwarding trade and in furnishing supplies on government contract to the several army posts around the lakes. These activities involved heavy charges for transportation, and since freight rates were high, in 1825 he had a small sloop of fifty-four tons built for him at St. Clair, Michigan, and named it the *Pilot*. Besides carrying his own goods he began picking up the freight of others in want of transportation. Since the little *Pilot* quickly proved inadequate to his needs, he added other vessels until he presently found himself the owner of the largest fleet on the Upper Lakes. Several of the ships were built at St. Clair and one or two at other places, but soon after 1830 he converted the United States Arsenal property at the foot of Wayne Street in Detroit into a shipyard and this became the center of further operations.

Although Newberry had enjoyed but meager schooling, he was fond of christening his ships with historic names. One of them, a 107-ton schooner built in 1828 and dubbed the *Napoleon,* was long familiar to dwellers around Lake Michigan, and an early Chicagoan who fairly deserves the title of that city's first author lamented "that this great name should be used in the feminine gender." Piling Ossa on Pelion, however, Newberry years later built a fine brig which he named the *Napoleon II.* Other vessels bore such names as *Austerlitz, Marengo, Lodi, Jena, Marshal Ney* and *Prince Eugene.* This glorification of the exploits of the Corsican conqueror irritated Angus McIntosh, agent of the British Hudson's Bay Company at Windsor, who proceeded to import shipbuilders from Scotland to build a larger and more imposing ship than any Newberry possessed. When it was launched McIntosh named it the *Duke of Wellington,* in honor of Napoleon's conqueror. But the Admiral laughed last when subsequently he lured his rival's imported shipwrights away from their employer to build another vessel for him.

To facilitate the performance of his government contracts, Newberry stationed agents at the several army posts, and he himself made frequent journeys around Lake Huron and Lake Michigan to oversee his varied business interests. When the great rush of western immigration began in the early thirties the commission and forwarding business became both extensive and profitable. Newberry, already a veteran operator of ships and stores around Lake Michigan, now undertook the establishment of his own docks and warehouses at the several ports, and at the same time he built new and larger ships to meet the increasing demand for transportation of freight and passengers. The stores and commission houses, run either by employees or local partners, provided cargoes for his ships and these, in turn, advanced the conduct of their own operations. In effect, he had invented the chain-store idea a generation in advance of his time.

His contracts for supplying Fort Dearborn early drew his attention to Chicago, and in 1828 he sent John S. C. Hogan from Detroit to Chicago to look after his business there. Hogan proceeded to become a local fixture, marrying the daughter of the first postmaster and himself becoming the second. In 1831, George W. Dole became Newberry's Chicago agent and somewhat later his local partner in the commission and forwarding business. The inrush of settlers and soldiers in 1832 soon consumed the available stock of food and the demand for additional supplies became urgent. To meet it Dole opened a slaughterhouse, meanwhile sending agents into the surrounding country to purchase cattle and hogs and drive them into Chicago. The supply of meat soon exceeded the local demand and in April 1833 Newberry and Dole shipped to the Admiral at Detroit, on his own vessel, the *Napoleon,* 287 barrels of beef, 14 of tallow and 152 hides.[1] Until now no goods had ever been exported from Chicago save such products of the forest and wilderness as furs and maple sugar. The shipment on the *Napoleon* marks the beginning of the vast export trade in the fruits of civilized industry which was presently to win for the city the distinction of being the world's foremost provision market.

George W. Dole, Newberry's Chicago partner, was a man of energy and ability, and for many years the firm played a leading role in the city's business life. In 1839 it made the first considerable shipment of grain ever exported from Chicago, sending 3,678 bushels of wheat in Newberry's ship, the *Oceola,* to Buffalo.[2] The wheat was bought direct from the farmers' wagons on the land side of the warehouse and hoisted by rope and pulley, propelled by hand, or "Irish" power, to the upper story. It was loaded on the ship on the waterside through a spout which ran from the upper story to the deck, where it was emptied into four-bushel boxes, which were carried, again by "Irish" power, to the hold.

For several years Chicago enjoyed a wild boom, with immigrants flocking to the place while as yet there was no adequate local supply of produce to sustain them. The autumn of 1835 saw the season of navigation close with only a small stock of flour on hand for consumption during the ensuing winter. To heighten the prospect of famine Charles Chapman, a local speculator, bought up all the available supply, planning to resell it to the townsmen at an exorbitant price. But one of the Admiral's ships now appeared off the mouth of the river loaded with a cargo of flour. The speculator hurried to the Newberry and Dole warehouse, offering fifteen dollars a barrel for the entire cargo and anticipating reselling it at twice the purchase price. But Dole declined to deal with him, and rationed the cargo to families and other local consumers at hardly more than half the price at which he had declined to sell to Chapman. Although Mr. Newberry was not present to dictate this course of action to his junior partner, it was quite in harmony with his entire business career.

In 1833 the Admiral built at his Detroit shipyard a vessel long notable on the lakes, which he named the *Michigan*. Until now he had owned and operated only sailing ships; the *Michigan,* which at once became the Queen of the Lakes, marked his entry upon the field of steamboat operation. The new leviathan had a deck 156 feet long and an extreme width of 53 feet. She had two lofty smokestacks and three masts. Her cabins provided forty-eight berths for "gentlemen" and sixty for ladies, besides a dining cabin richly paneled and gilded. Instead of a single engine she had two, more powerful than those of any rival ship. They were low-pressure, walking-beam engines, and each was independently connected to its own shaft and paddle wheel.

This arrangement was entirely new and it seems never to have been imitated in any later ship. In calm weather the *Michigan* performed beautifully; but when gales bore down, tossing the water in tempestuous seas, one paddle wheel, deeply immersed, would be laboring with great difficulty while the other, lifted above the surface, would spin "like lightning." At such times the ship would stagger from side to side like a drunken sailor, shivering from keel to topmast, to the vast dismay of everyone on board.

In short the plan of having two engines each separately geared to its own side wheel did not prove a happy one. Yet the ship long retained her popularity with the public, probably for the excellent reason that travel on her competitors was productive of even greater trials. Completed late in 1833, the *Michigan* was placed on the Buffalo-Detroit run, but she continued the custom established long since by the *Walk-in-the-Water* of making occasional trips to Lake Huron and Lake Michigan, and two such excursions were advertised for the season of 1834. On the second, made in August, the entire circuit of Lake Michigan was covered, with stops at Chicago, St. Joseph and Grand River. Save for the army-chartered steamers of 1832 this was the first visit ever made by a steamboat to the head of Lake Michigan.

Until the season of 1837 there was no regular steamboat service between the East and Chicago, although in 1836, as in earlier years, occasional voyages were made to the head of Lake Michigan. On June 13, 1836, the "splendid steam packet" *Daniel Webster* sailed from Detroit for Lake Michigan, touching at Green Bay, Milwaukee,

Root River (now Racine), Chicago, Michigan City, New Buffalo, St. Joseph and Grand River. Apparently this voyage was looked upon as an excursion, since no freight was accepted for transportation. The same month the *Commodore Perry* made a similar journey from Buffalo around Lake Michigan, and in July the *James Madison* sailed from Buffalo for Lake Michigan and Chicago.[3]

At the opening of navigation in 1837 announcement was made that the steam packet *Pennsylvania* would leave Buffalo, "ice permitting," on May 1 for Green Bay and Chicago and would continue making such trips throughout the season, of which due advance notice would be given. At the same time it was announced that the *Michigan,* running regularly between Detroit and Buffalo, would make four voyages during the season to and around Lake Michigan, and definite dates for these voyages were advertised. Thus to the Admiral belongs the distinction of pioneering the first regular steamboat service to the head of Lake Michigan.

During the ensuing winter and spring Newberry built at Detroit a finer ship than any yet seen on the lakes, which he christened the *Illinois.* For a little space of time she outdistanced all competitors. She was 205 feet long, her tonnage was 756 and her powerful low-pressure engine was capable of driving her from Buffalo to Chicago in five days' time. When first launched late in the summer of 1838 she was placed on the Buffalo-Detroit run, but with the opening of navigation in 1839 this was extended to Chicago and a sailing schedule calling for round trips every fifteen days was advertised. The *Illinois,* the finest ship ever built by Newberry, long remained popular with the traveling public; her seaworthiness was unquestioned and her cabins and staterooms were loaded with an awe-inspiring quantity of gilt and other decorations.

The master of the *Illinois,* Captain Chesley Blake, was a salt-water sailor who had long been employed by Newberry as a ship captain. He was a man of gigantic stature, with a foghorn voice, a disposition far from meek and a wealth of profanity rivaling the vocabulary of the army in Flanders. He had numerous clashes with his employer from which he more than once emerged triumphant, repelling the Admiral's outbursts of invective with even louder shouts. When, as happened occasionally, Newberry was a passenger on his ship the doughty captain tolerated no interference by his employer. On one such voyage on the *Illinois,* homeward bound from Chicago to Detroit, Newberry was in a fussy mood and several times criticized the captain's management of the ship. At Mackinac Newberry went ashore and Captain Blake improved the opportunity to depart for Detroit, leaving the angry owner behind on the beach.

The Admiral's extensive business interests involved him in numerous enterprises aside from his shipping activities. He was a heavy stockholder in the Detroit and St. Joseph Railway (now the Michigan Central) and for many years was a member of its board of directors. He was a constant patron of banks and was particularly intimate with the Bank of Michigan. In the era of wildcat banking each issuing institution sent its bills as far away from home as possible, hoping they would never return for redemption, while rival banks sometimes endeavored to embarrass a competitor by collecting a quantity of its bills and turning them in for specie. A bank in Milwaukee had developed a habit of thus harassing the Bank of Michigan, and Newberry determined to put an end to it. In a trip around the lakes he procured as many bills of the offending institution as possible and on reaching Milwaukee produced $40,000 in currency from his carpetbag, for which he demanded immediate payment in cash. A heart-to-heart discussion behind the scenes followed, ending in the promise by the bank's officials to discontinue their obnoxious habit in consideration of the Admiral's refraining from pressing his demand for immediate redemption of the bills he held.

At Detroit, Newberry came to be regarded as a financial trouble shooter for the community, and on more than one occasion he came to the relief of distressed associates. In 1835 the city government itself became distressed through nonpayment of taxes and the disinclination of the banks to lend their funds with no assurance as to the date of repayment. In this dilemma the officials asked Newberry if he would lend the city $50,000 on its faith and credit. "Of course," was the answer; "when do you want it?" The matter dragged along until November, by which time the city was in need of $100,000, and this sum "Uncle Oliver" cheerfully supplied.

On another occasion the commandant at Mackinac sent an earnest appeal to Detroit for provisions to see the garrison through the winter, the government contractor having failed for some reason to provide them. Although it was mid-December and the season of navigation had been closed for a month, when this appeal was brought to Newberry he agreed to transport the supplies if it were humanly possible. The *Napoleon* was brought from her winter berth and with two veteran captains on board was dispatched upon her perilous voyage. The supplies were delivered and the *Napoleon* returned in safety to her winter quarters on the day after Christmas.

In 1838 the Patriot War opened, creating almost as much turmoil in Detroit as in Canada itself. A citizen-guard was enrolled to patrol the water front to prevent border raids and other violations of neutrality. While thus employed, one of the guards observed a man, poorly clad, approach the woodpile on the Newberry wharf, where he tied up with a rope as much cordwood as he could carry and started away with it. The guard quietly followed him to the door of a poor house on the outskirts of town, where he threw down his burden. The officer now stepped up and ordered him to pick up the load and carry it back to the wharf, which the culprit quietly did and was then allowed to go his way. A few days later the guard related the incident to Newberry, expecting to be commended for his zeal. But "Uncle Oliver" merely said, "You meant to do the right thing, but I wish you had minded your own business and let the man alone. These are hard times for poor people, and he must have been in want. I have plenty, and never would have suffered if you had let him keep the wood, and his children would have been happy for a little while in the morning."

Before the invention of the steam whistle the arrival and departure of vessels was heralded by ringing a bell or discharging a cannon. One day at Chicago a cannon which had been dumped into the river after the Fort Dearborn massacre of 1812 was dredged up. Newberry obtained possession of it and mounted it on the forward deck of the *Illinois,* where for a time it gave notice of the ship's approach to port. Political feelings ran high a century ago and the Admiral was an ardent Whig. In the presidential campaign of 1840 a great Democratic celebration was planned and the surrender of the cannon was demanded on the plea that it had merely been lent to Newberry. To circumvent this demand the cannon was hoisted after dark to the upper deck of the Newberry and Dole warehouse where it was buried in a bin of wheat until after the election. Meanwhile, Newberry had a huge pennant made for the *Illinois,* over forty feet long, on which the letters of the Whig party slogan had been sewn.

The twenty-year period which opened in 1833 marks the heyday of passenger travel on the Upper Lakes. On May 21, 1852, the Michigan Central Railroad ran its first train into Chicago a single day in advance of its bitter rival, the Michigan Southern. Two years later, in January 1854, the Great Western Railway, operating from Buffalo across southern Ontario, ran its first train into Windsor. For the first time an all-rail connection between New York and Chicago was established, and less than a year later a second through route from the East was established by the completion of the Michigan Southern road between Buffalo and Toledo. Before the opening of the railroads the water routes to the West were vastly cheaper and more expeditious than travel by land. Now the situation was suddenly reversed, and immigrants to the western country quickly shifted from the lake steamers to the railroads. A quarter of a century sufficed to span the quick rise and the even swifter decline of passenger travel on the Upper Lakes.

A pleasant picture of travel conditions toward the close of the period under review has been preserved for us in the letters of Thurlow Weed, the renowned New York politician, who came west apparently for the first time in 1847 to attend the River and Harbor Convention at Chicago.[4] At Buffalo the traveler embarked on the *Empire,* a "mammoth" steamer built at Cleveland three years before, which had an engine of 500 horsepower and a dining cabin 230 feet long. To the surprise of the easterner, he found her appointments as luxurious as those of the "splendid" Hudson River steamers with which he was familiar. Most of the passengers were delegates who like Weed himself were going to Chicago to attend the convention, and among them he found numerous acquaintances. On reaching Detroit the traveler was amazed to discover that he had made the journey from Albany in fifty-one hours, the shortest time, he was told, it had ever been performed.

At Detroit a "council of steam" was held by the ship's officers, at which the decision was reached to attempt the passage of the St. Clair Flats by night, an exploit which in the general absence of channel guides was seldom undertaken. Bets were made that the attempt would not succeed, which proved to be the case, since at a point in the channel where "two stakes" had disappeared the great ship ran hard aground and remained in this condition until morning.

Being a newspaperman on the alert for information, the diarist discovered that the *Empire* consumed 600 cords of wood, the product of over ten acres of heavy timber, on a single voyage from Buffalo to Chicago. At a point on the St. Clair River 106 cords were taken on board to feed the hungry boilers on the further journey to Mackinac. At St. Clair the passengers marveled over the gigantic framework of a steamer under construction, which on completion would become for a brief season the new "Leviathan of the Lakes."

July 4 found the *Empire* in the middle of Lake Michigan, and the day and the place conspired to provoke the tourist to some reflections upon the magnitude and the future prospects of the nation which had been founded seventy-one years before. The last and most memorable of these meditations deserves the attention of the reader.

"Here are a succession of mighty lakes, emptying themselves one into another, until, nearly 3,000 miles from their head, their waters mingle with those of the Atlantic, and upon the shores of these lakes is an extent of country capable of supporting and destined to receive, in the course of a half a century, at least *a quarter of a million inhabitants.*"

How inadequately the immediate future of the region could be foreseen by one of the shrewdest men alive is suggested by the fact that much less than half a century later the city of Chicago alone numbered more than a million souls.

At the close of the convention Weed embarked on the *St. Louis* for the return journey to Buffalo. Although the ship, a much smaller vessel than the *Empire,* was crowded to capacity, the trip proved even pleasanter than the outward voyage had been. Soon after the departure from Chicago a committee representing the passengers waited upon the captain with the request that instead of sailing directly to Buffalo they might make a tour to points of interest upon the lakes. The captain replied that the ship would take them anywhere and remain as long as they might desire for a daily charge of two dollars per passenger. Among the places visited were the Green Bay Islands and Sault Ste. Marie. At Mackinac a day's stopover made possible a leisurely inspection of the storied island, while the fishing enthusiasts were taken on a side excursion to Carp River, where trout were said to be plentiful. Although it was a wonderful place for fish, the fish were not in their places; or if they were, they were too wise to rise to the bait of eastern greenhorns. At nightfall the forty anglers rejoined their fellows, exhibiting few fish, but with faces swollen and blood-smeared from the attacks of mosquitoes and flies, which, unlike the trout, had "bitten magnificently" throughout the day.

The reader who now follows the story of these carefree excursionists cannot help but marvel over the extent and variety of the table fare they enjoyed. Breakfast was served from seven to eleven in the morning, the individual passenger partaking of the meal when he pleased. At noon lunch was served; at half past two dinner. Tea followed at seven and at ten o'clock the supper table was spread; and all the while the fare was as abundant and extensive in the midst of the wilderness as it could have been if the resources of New York City's Fulton Street market were at hand every morning. Although the distance from Buffalo to Chicago was 1,054 miles, the side excursions taken lengthened the return voyage to 1,500 and all this, meals and travel included, at the price of two dollars a day for each passenger. For once the reader of 1944 is compelled to emit a sigh for the good old times when Chicago and Milwaukee were villages, and harbors around Lake Michigan were still but visions of the distant future.

----

1 The invoice is printed in A. T. Andreas, *History of Cook County* (Chicago, 1884), 321. Slightly different figures are given by George B. Catlin (ms. notes in Burton Historical Collection) and by Bessie L. Pierce, *History of Chicago* (Chicago, 1937), I, 137. It is, of course, possible that the *Napoleon* conveyed only a part of the shipment.

2 Charles Walker had made the first shipment of wheat, amounting to 78 bushels, from Chicago to Buffalo in 1838.

3 Advertisements and sailing notices in Detroit *Daily Advertizer.*

4 The letters were written by Weed to his paper, the Albany *Evening Journal.* They are reprinted, somewhat abridged in J. B. Mansfield, *History of the Great Lakes* (Chicago, 1899), I, 209-219.

Chapter 15

Wind Against Steam

THE building of Fulton's *Clermont* in 1807 marked the beginning of a new era in transportation by water, yet the sailing ship did not lightly abandon the field to its power-driven rival. For more than half a century the steamboats themselves were equipped with sails to supplement the power of their engines, while for still another generation the sailing ships remained an important factor in the commerce of the Great Lakes. Toward the close of the nineteenth century, however, their number decreased rapidly and the opening decades of the twentieth marked the practically complete triumph of steam over sail.[1]

Judged by modern standards the early steamboats were almost incredibly weak and crude. They possessed, however, the one tremendous advantage of freedom from dependence upon the whims of the winds and the ability to maintain their schedules with a high degree of regularity. This advantage was so important that wherever they were placed in service they promptly obtained a monopoly of passenger travel.

But the sailing ships retained certain advantages which explain their persistence on the lakes for almost a century after the introduction of the steamboat. Foremost among these was their lower cost both of construction and of operation. The steamboats were equipped with machinery which was expensive to install and to operate. This consumed a great deal of space which on the sailing ship could be devoted to cargo, while the great quantity of fuel demanded by the wood-burning engines consumed even more. The steamboat excelled in speed, the sailing ship in economy of operation. The obvious result followed: the steamboat found its chief field of usefulness on main lines of travel where traffic could be secured in volume of a character important enough to justify the rates it must charge. The westward migration of the thirties and forties supplied this need, and made possible the rapid increase of steamboats in number and size during the period.[2]

THE CHANGES OF HALF A CENTURY

View of Manitowoc River in 1887 and in 1932. In the later picture the vessels from left to right are the *Arizona, Carolina, Grand Haven* and the whaleback *Christopher Columbus*, laid up by the economic depression.

THE LIGHTHOUSE AT ST. JAMES

This lighthouse, one of many on the lake, guards the entrance to the harbor of St. James on Big Beaver Island.

A SCHOONER OF THE '70's

The *J. B. Newland,* built at Manitowoc in 1870, is of oak, 149 feet long, with a gross tonnage of 157.

The sailing ships, on the contrary, represented but a small capital investment. The winds that propelled them cost nothing and the crews required to operate them were relatively small and inexpensive. Free from dependence upon supplies of fuel, they could navigate wherever winds and water ran and could afford to follow the byways of trade and travel where the volume of traffic was insufficient to justify the maintenance of steamboat service. They could also compete successfully with the steamboat for the carriage of such staples as grain and lumber on the main highway between Chicago and Buffalo. Since sailing ships had been in use for centuries, little room remained for improvement in the art of building and operating them. Unlike them, the steamboat was a new and revolutionary creation, which was destined to undergo a rapid evolution in response to the changing demands of commerce and the improvement of the builder's art. An important share of this progress was achieved by the shipbuilders of the Upper Lakes.

Like the beginnings of the automobile industry of the twentieth century, the infancy of the steamboat was marked by uncertainty and experimentation. Only through trial and error could the problem of the best type of machinery be solved. In the process engines of such different kinds were developed that the experienced observer could readily identify an approaching vessel when to the unpracticed eye it was but dimly visible on the horizon, and at night by the sounds of the revolving wheels or of the escaping exhaust steam. On all the earlier ships the engines were equipped with walking beams which projected high above the cabin and to which the proud owners sometimes attached the figure of a galloping horse that alternately rose and plunged forward in tune with the motions of the walking beam itself. Other ships had a square engine which also projected above the cabin, but instead of the walking beam it had a vertically moving crosshead, with swinging connecting rods on each side running to the cranks on the paddle-wheel shaft. These, when in motion, resembled the action of "a pair of crutches under a lame man." Still others were propelled by horizontal engines on the main deck, over which the cabin extended uninterrupted the length of the vessel, affording greater space for passengers and for the exercise of the builder's ingenuity in arranging and decorating it.

Competition in the carrying trade of the lakes was keen through-out the period under review and for some years the number of steamboats in operation grew rapidly.[3] A petition to Congress, pre-pared in November 1839 and signed by a majority of the owners and captains of ships then running, stated that there were fifty steam-boats on the Upper Lakes, and estimated that they had carried 200,000 passengers during the season then closing.[4] Almost all of these ships and all but a minor fraction of the volume of passenger traffic was the development of less than half a dozen years. Although the number of vessels continued to increase during the following decade, the larger increase in carrying capacity was accomplished by the process of replacing the older ships by new and ever larger ones.

Rivalry between the shipbuilders was acute, and the period of supremacy of each successive "Queen of the Lakes" was correspond-ingly brief. The leadership in size and magnificence of fittings was firmly grasped by the *Michigan,* built at Detroit by Oliver New-berry in 1833, and two Detroit ships, the *Plymouth Rock* and the *Western World,* jointly held it when the era ended a quarter of a century later. Both in size and in lavishness of equipment the *Michigan* for several years surpassed all other ships on the lakes.[5] In 1838 Newberry built a new and larger ship, which he named the *Illinois,* to which the title of "Leviathan of the Inland Seas" now passed. Although she proved to be a popular and successful vessel, she did not long retain her title, for in the same year the *Great Western* was launched by a rival builder at Huron, Ohio. Although the new ship was shorter than the *Illinois,* she was of considerably greater beam and of slightly larger tonnage.[6] She was the first lake vessel to be built with an upper deck cabin, and many anticipated that she would be topheavy and unsafe in a severe gale. These antici-pations quickly proved to be unfounded, and the *Great Western* was so successful that her design was widely imitated, introducing a revolution in ship construction. The addition of the upper cabin per-mitted the one on the main deck to be devoted entirely to freight and steerage, with consequent increase in cargo capacity. So obvious were the advantages of the new design that it was generally followed in new ship construction, and the upper works of many ships already in operation were revamped by the addition of an upper cabin.

About this time a far more revolutionary development in steamboat construction was introduced to the lakes through the genius of a Swedish engineer. John Ericsson, a man of amazing originality, is probably best known to popular fame as the designer of the *Monitor,* victor in the first battle between ironclads in the Civil War. Of more enduring importance was his development almost thirty years earlier of the screw propeller to replace the paddle wheels in ocean and lake navigation. His earlier work on this invention was done in England, where he wished to apply it to naval vessels. The government was deaf to his overtures, however, and in 1839 he brought his invention to America, where its value was quickly recognized.

In 1841 the *Vandalia,* of 138 tons, was built on Lake Ontario, where the obvious advantages of her new form of propulsion aroused instant admiration. Her compact machinery, weighing but fifteen tons, was entirely out of sight, and only a small smokestack astern revealed that she was equipped with steam power at all. Ten cords of wood were sufficient to drive her engines an entire day, in happy contrast with the cumbersome engines and paddle wheels of the side-wheelers with their ravenous appetite for fuel. In 1842 the *Vandalia* was taken through the Welland Canal into Lake Erie, where her example proved so popular that in the following year alone seven more propellers were built on the lakes, while by 1850 half a hundred were in operation.

The early propellers were small ships, making no pretension to the title of leviathan. Commonly they were 150 feet or less in length with a tonnage ranging from 150 to 300. Although they were equipped to carry passengers, their chief advantage over the side-wheelers lay in their economy of operation in transporting freight. The initial investment in them was small while the compactness of their machinery and their economy of fuel consumption gave them a relatively large cargo capacity. By 1844 there were ten propellers engaged in the Chicago trade and within another year or two more propellers than side-wheelers were being built. Gradually, too, their size was increased until by 1845 propellers of 350 tons were constructed.

The *Hercules,* which was built at Buffalo in 1843 and became widely known in the following years, will serve as an illustration of early propeller construction. She was 137 feet long and her tonnage was 273, about as large as the *William Penn* or the *Henry Clay* of the middle twenties. She had fourteen staterooms, each six feet square, with space available for forty-six more berths for passengers. Her engine, six feet square and weighing but fifteen tons, left almost the entire hull available for the storage of productive cargo. Although built and outfitted "superbly," the entire cost of this ship was but $20,000. Ten cords of wood, costing $17, would run her engines for a day, in contrast with fifty cords required by one of the larger side-wheelers. Yet on one occasion the *Hercules* made the run from Chicago to Buffalo in six days, bringing a cargo of 1,200 barrels of flour besides additional unspecified merchandise.

Although the propellers cut deeply into the trade and profits of the side-wheelers, it was chiefly the railroads which drove them into oblivion by robbing them of their profitable passenger trade. Until the middle fifties new ships of ever larger size continued to be built, the climax being reached when a railroad itself entered the shipping field.

This was the Michigan Central, whose construction was begun at Detroit in the middle 1830's. A year or two later the young commonwealth of Michigan, fired by the valor of ignorance, undertook the construction of three parallel lines of railroads across the Lower Michigan Peninsula. The Central road had reached Kalamazoo when the state, sick of its undertaking, reconveyed it to private ownership under whose vigorous management it was extended to Chicago in the spring of 1852. Meanwhile the Michigan Southern Railroad, starting from Toledo, entered Chicago one day later than the rival line, and presently established connections eastward with the Lake Shore and New York Central by which a through route was opened from the Hudson and New York City to Chicago.

The response of the Michigan Central to this development was prompt and characteristic. From the time the road was returned to private ownership it had competed vigorously for a share of the traffic from the East, establishing a line of steamboats between Buffalo and Monroe in 1848 to divert to itself as much traffic as possible from the Buffalo-Chicago all-water route. The next year it added to its fleet two new ships, the *Atlantic* and the *Mayflower,* which were larger than any yet seen on the lakes. Wonders for a day, their period of glory soon faded. Both ships were fitted with the largest and best types of boilers of their time, and the *Atlantic* promptly established a new speed record of 16½ hours for the Buffalo-Detroit run. The *Mayflower,* of 1,354 tons, was both the largest and the finest ship on the Lakes. Her 85 staterooms could accommodate 300 passengers, while the steerage had room for 300 to 500 more.

Both ships were destined to a tragic end. For the *Atlantic* this came on August 20, 1852, when she collided with the propeller *Ogdensburg* off Long Point, sinking in a few minutes with a loss of more than 100 lives.[7] The *Mayflower* lasted two years longer, being wrecked in a fog off Point Pelee in the autumn of 1854.

Meanwhile bigger ships were being constructed, and in 1854 the railroad climaxed the end of an era by placing in service the sister ships, *Plymouth Rock* and *Western World.* They were 348 feet long, of 2,000 tons burden[8] and were built at a cost of $250,000 each. In size, speed and luxury of equipment they outclassed all rivals.[9]

But the pitcher had gone to the well once too often. The completion of the Great Western Railroad from Buffalo to Windsor in 1854 left Lake Erie enclosed on both sides by parallel roads of iron. Passenger travel rapidly turned from the steamboats to the railroads, and the very size and splendor of the *Plymouth Rock* and the *Western World* hastened their impending doom. Too expensive to operate with the diminishing volume of traffic, they were tied up, along with the *Mississippi,* after only three years of service. For several years they lay unused at their Detroit docks. Eventually they were sold to purchasers who placed the engines in ships designed for the oriental service and converted their hulls into prosaic dry docks at Buffalo, Cleveland and Bay City. Almost forty years passed before their equals were again seen on the lakes and until the end of the century old men continued to recall nostalgically their departed glory.

In the absence of official records our best indication of the increase of traffic on Lake Michigan during the thirties and forties is obtained from the record kept by the Secretary of the Association of Steamboat Operators.[10] In 1833 the earnings by steamboats on business done with Lake Michigan ports amounted to $4,355; in 1834 it increased to $6,272 and in 1841 to $226,352. The number of steamboats employed on the lakes in 1840 was 48, varying in size from 150 to 750 tons and constructed at a cost of $2,200,000.

The number of sailing vessels on the Upper Lakes in 1841 was estimated by the secretary at 250. These varied in size from 30 to 350 tons, the largest being an old steamboat converted into a sailing ship. The larger ships were employed in carrying freight the whole length of the lakes, while the smaller ships were confined to shorter runs. Their cost ranged from $1,000 to $14,000 with an estimated average of $5,000, barely one-ninth the average cost of a steamboat.

In 1845 the same authority reported 60 steamboats, having a total tonnage of 23,000, and 270 sailing ships, with a tonnage of 53,000, on the Upper Lakes. In addition there were 7 steamboats and about 100 sailing ships on Lake Ontario, most of which operated "to the extreme end of Lake Michigan transporting large amounts of both freight and passengers."

Although the railroads had a disastrous effect upon the passenger traffic on the lakes, the extension of new lines westward from Chicago and Milwaukee in the fifties and sixties produced an ever-increasing volume of freight which demanded water transportation, a volume materially reinforced by the opening of the Illinois and Michigan Canal in 1848 and the Sault Lock in 1855. By 1860 there were, on all the lakes, 1,459 ships, of which 1,122 were sailing vessels and 335 were steamers and propellers. Eight years later, in 1868, there were 1,855 sailing vessels, with a tonnage of 293,978. From this date onward the number steadily decreased, falling below 1,000 for the first time in 1897. Twenty-five years later (1922) there were but 86, and in 1941 there were left but 6 schooners and 6 schooner barges. The century-old conflict between wind and steam had ended in the complete triumph of the latter.

It remains to notice the amazing developments of the last half century which were chiefly made possible by the substitution of ships of iron and steel for vessels built of wood. From the dawn of civilization until the closing years of the eighteenth century no iron ship had ever been built, and the idea that such a vessel could be made to float was greeted with derision. In 1787, however, a venturesome Englishman put it to the test of actual demonstration. "Yesterday my iron boat was launched," he wrote. "It answered all my expectations and has convinced the unbelievers who were 999 in a thousand. It will be only a nine-days' wonder, and then will be like Columbus's egg."

But the inventor was far too sanguine, for the shipbuilders of Britain declined for another half century to follow the example he had set. Although a few small iron ships were built for river service, not until a compensating arrangement for the compasses used on iron ships had been devised would navigators trust themselves in such a vessel on the ocean.

This was accomplished in 1839, and the building of the *Great Britain,* the first iron ship ever designed for ocean service, followed in due course. She was launched in 1843 and made the first transatlantic crossing two years later. She was one of the largest ships ever built down to this time and her construction introduced a new era in the art of shipbuilding.[11] The production of steel by the Bessemer process in 1858 made possible an even greater advance. Although the actual change from wood to iron and steel was gradual, the foundation had been laid for a sweeping revolution in waterborne trade and travel.

Meanwhile the first iron ships were promptly launched for service on the Great Lakes. In 1817 the British and American governments had agreed to limit their naval armament on the lakes to a single vessel of 100 tons or less, armed with one 18-pound gun, on Lake Champlain, Lake Ontario and the Upper Lakes. Rebellion broke out in Canada in the late thirties, however, and under the stress of this situation the British sent several armed ships to the Great Lakes. American public opinion became alarmed over the situation and the fortification bill enacted by Congress in 1841 authorized the President to construct armed vessels on the lakes at his discretion.

Construction of the 500-ton iron steamer *Michigan* was begun at Pittsburgh in 1842. The ship was built in sections, which were transported overland to Erie, where they were assembled and the vessel was launched in 1844. The *Great Britain* had not yet crossed the ocean, and the *Michigan* was America's first iron warship, if not the first in the world. She was equipped with two 8-inch guns and four 32-pounders, and her building was in plain contravention of the Convention of 1817. It was justified on the ground that Great Britain had first violated the Convention. In the expressive words of

Senator Allen of Ohio, spoken in public debate in 1841, the British already had armed steamers on Lake Erie and he thought "armed steamers were necessary to watch armed steamers."

The *Michigan* remained in service for three-quarters of a century, and for almost twenty years she was the only iron ship on the Upper Lakes. Her association with the assassination of King Strang in 1856 is related in a subsequent chapter. Numerous officers who later attained high rank in the U. S. Navy served on the *Michigan,* whose greatest period of usefulness fell in the years of the Civil War. In 1905 her name was assigned to a great new ocean battleship, and the old "Iron Ship" became known henceforth as the *Wolverine.* When her period of usefulness was at last outlived she was returned to Erie, where since 1923 she has lain quietly in the bay, exposed to the ravages of decay and vandalism.[12]

The first iron ship designed for commercial service on the lakes was the *Merchant,* which was launched at Buffalo in 1862. Six years later the iron ship *Philadelphia* was also launched at Buffalo. Her career ended on November 7, 1893, when she collided with the *Albany* in a heavy fog off Pointe aux Barques in Lake Huron, sending both ships to the bottom. Although several more iron ships were built during the early seventies, the wooden ship era continued until the end of the century, when the operation of several factors conspired to bring it to its close.

Chiefly these were the diminishing supply of oak for ship timbers and the steadily increasing quantity of goods which clamored for transportation; added to these was the third factor that beyond a certain size wooden ships could not profitably be built or operated. The only limit upon the size of ships of iron or steel was the capacity of the harbors and the connecting river channels to float them.

As the century neared its close fewer wooden ships were built, while the forces of advancing age and economic disadvantage combined to retire ever more of those already in service. The introduction of the steam barge, followed by the system of towing in use during the closing decades of the century, delayed but could not defeat the process. Large vessels proved themselves cheaper cargo carriers than small ones, forcing a rapid reduction in the rates charged for transporting freight. Under the influence of this competition the sailing ships either retired to the oblivion which awaits all man-made creations or, shorn of their ancient glory, were transformed into barges towed, sometimes as many as half a dozen in a row, by a steam barge or tug.

The employment of steel in shipbuilding was gradual, proceeding faster on the ocean than on the lakes. The first steel-built ocean liner was launched in 1879, and a year later ten percent of all British steamers under construction were being built of steel. By 1890 the proportion had increased to ninety-six percent, and so far as British builders were concerned the wooden ship era was facing its end.

On the Great Lakes the granddaddy of all bulk freighters was the iron ship *Onoko,* launched at Cleveland in 1882. With a gross tonnage of 2,164, she would be insignificant today, yet few ships have matched the series of cargo records she established. For ten of her first sixteen seasons she held the record for carrying the largest cargoes on the lakes, and with the freight rates which then prevailed she earned enough money "to load her down."

The first steel ship built for lake service was the *Spokane,* which was launched in 1886. With a tonnage of 2,357 and a length of 249½ feet, she was but slightly larger than the *Onoko.* But from this time onward the lake freighters increased steadily in size. The year 1906 saw the advent of the 600-foot ship and builders were confident that no engineering difficulties prevented the building of 1,000-foot vessels. But the lapse of another generation has brought only ships of 640 feet, since the capacity of the channels rather than the architectural skill of the builders is the factor which limits their size.

The one economic reason for the maintenance of these great ships is their ability to transport freight as rapidly and as cheaply as possible. This involves, of course, not merely the size of the cargo, but the number of cargoes carried in a season. To keep the freighters in motion on their water highways as much of the time as possible and to delay them in port as little as possible is therefore a prime economic consideration. Although records are established and broken with gratifying frequency, the recital of a few of the latest ones available may prove instructive.

With the advent of World War II the success or failure of our country's cause depended in large degree upon her steel-producing capacity, and the freighters which transport the ore from the mines of Lake Superior to the mill centers of Lake Erie and Lake Michigan bore an indispensable share in the maintenance of our fighting men throughout the world. New and longer freighters were rushed to completion, therefore, and a new and vastly larger lock was constructed to facilitate their passage through the bottleneck at the Sault. A few figures picture eloquently the results. Prior to 1940 the record (in round numbers) of iron ore transported in a single season was 65,000,000 gross tons. For 1941 the figure rose to 80,000,000 and for 1942 to 92,000,000 gross tons. For all bulk commodities taken together, the record prior to 1940 was 138,000,000 net tons; for 1941 this rose to 169,000,000 and for 1942 to 178,000,000 net tons.[13]

To turn to individual cargo performances, the *Fred G. Hartwell* in 1929 delivered 15,696 tons of soft coal at Duluth. The nearest approach to this record was made by the same ship in July 1943 with a cargo of 15,597 tons.[14] A record for Lake Michigan was established September 3, 1918, when 15,160 tons of soft coal were loaded at Toledo for delivery at Gary. Only one day later the *D. G. Kerr* loaded 15,532¾ tons at the same dock for delivery at Gary, establishing a record which still stood as recently as July 1942.

Moved by the ambition to construct a ship both longer and wider than any bulk freighter in existence, a Canadian builder launched the steamer *Lemoyne* in 1926. Over the years that have since elapsed she has proved a notable gatherer of cargo records, establishing no less than three new ones in a nine-day period in 1942. At the close of navigation in 1943 several of her records for carrying coal and grain still remained unbroken. Her supremacy as an ore carrier promptly vanished, however. The Pittsburgh Steamship Company in 1942 built five great ore carriers, each with an over-all length of 639¾ feet. These ships are longer by almost 100 feet than the greatest ocean ore ships and tankers, although the latter, by reason of greater depth and wider beam, possess a considerably greater cargo capacity than their inland rivals. Three of the new ships quickly established cargo records in excess of 18,000 gross tons (20,000 net tons) of ore, shipped from Lake Superior to Lake Erie ports.[15]

Between the loading by "Irish" hand power of the first considerable shipment of grain from Chicago in 1839 and the loading and discharge of the immense cargoes carried by the lake freighters a century later lies a gulf that is wide indeed. On a single day in July 1943 the nine ore-loading docks on the Upper Lakes provided the ore carriers with 567,000 gross tons of ore. The estimated capacity of seventeen leading Lower Lake ports to discharge ore cargoes was over 470,000 tons for a day of ten hours.[16]

For the season of 1941, the nine ore-loading docks made it their primary object to provide cargoes for the greatest possible number of vessels, rather than to achieve fast individual loading records. The close of the season revealed that the average vessel detention at all but one of the docks ranged from 20.4 to 35 minutes per 1,000 tons of ore loaded. Individual performances included the loading of a vessel at Superior with 12,414 tons in 1 hour and 40 minutes; another, with 9,000 gross tons in 1 hour and 10 minutes. At Marquette on May 13, 1941, the *Pam Schneider* entered port, received a cargo of 5,874 tons of ore and departed on her return journey 45 minutes later.[17] Even more impressive was the record established at Superior on October 12, 1942, when the *Frontenac* received 12,593 gross tons of ore with only 65 minutes' total detention in port.[18]

It takes longer to discharge a cargo than it does to load it, and the time required to discharge one cargo and take on another affords a better indication of the total period of detention of a ship in port between voyages. On July 9, 1931, at Conneaut the *William B. Schiller* unloaded over 10,000 tons of ore and loaded more than 11,000 of soft coal, totaling 23,074 tons of cargo, in 7 hours and 40 minutes. On the Upper Lakes the *Homer D. Williams* on September 26, 1939, discharged a cargo of limestone and took on one of iron ore, the two totaling 24,416 gross tons, in 9 hours, 35 minutes' actual operating time.[19] The latest record reported for unloading ore alone was established at Conneaut on June 8, 1943, when 14,275 tons of ore were discharged from the *D. G. Kerr* in 2 hours and 45 minutes, an hourly rate of 5,191 tons.[20]

So the unending race against time and expense continues, and on its outcome depends the welfare and prosperity of uncounted millions of people. When the great drab ships shuttle in constant procession from end to end of the lakes, fires glow in the steel mills and labor is everywhere in demand; when they lie idly at anchor despair and industrial stagnation grip the heart of the nation. Before the little town of Amherstburg in 1941 passed 29,770 vessels, the largest number witnessed by any spot on the globe. Since the season of navigation lasted but 262 days, the average daily passages numbered 114, or a vessel every 12½ minutes throughout the entire season.

---

[1] A few sailing ships still remain on the lakes. On January 1, 1941, there were seven on Michigan, Huron and Erie, and five on Lake Superior. U. S. Dept. of Commerce, *Merchant Marine Statistics,* 1941, p. 21.

[2] Until after 1840, when the country west of Lake Michigan began producing a surplus of farm products for export, the steamboats were further handicapped by their inability to obtain cargoes for their eastbound voyages.

[3] "There are Steam Boats now running on the waters of Lake Erie almost without number," wrote John Mullett of Detroit to Sylvester Sibley in April 1834. "The new steamboat *Michigan* as yet stands to the head of the list in point of size, splendour, and speed; altho the *Webster,* a new boat belonging to Buffalo bid[s] fair as respects speed to become quite a rival of the *Michigan."* The letter continues with notices of other vessels built or building and concludes with the forecast that the whole number of steamboats on Lake Erie and "vicinity" the coming season will be about thirty. Ms. in Burton Historical Collection, Detroit Public Library.

[4] Sen. Doc. 270, 26 Cong., 1 Sess., March 10, 1840. The petition was signed by the owners of thirty-one steamboats and by ship captains representing two more.

[5] Precise tonnage figures for the early steamboats are not easily determined. We have followed the official description printed by the U. S. Bureau of Navigation whenever available (*Merchant Steam Vessels of the United States, 1807 to 1856,* Washington, 1931). These figures frequently vary somewhat from statements contained in sailing schedules and other contemporary notices, while many steamboats known to have existed are not included in the compilation of the Bureau. The tonnage of the *Michigan* is there given as 473. Oddly enough, the old *Superior,* built in 1822 as successor to the *Walk-in-the-Water* and with a tonnage of 346, was second in size to the *Michigan.*

[6] James C. Mills, *Our Inland Seas* (Chicago, 1910), 117-118.

[7] Although the precise number is uncertain, it is commonly fixed at 131. An eyewitness report of the disaster is printed by Mills, *Our Inland Seas,* 143.

[8] More precisely, the *Plymouth Rock* registered 1,991 tons, the *Western World* 2,002. At this time there were but few ships under United States registry on the ocean of larger size. The U. S. Bureau of Navigation lists but fourteen having a tonnage in excess of 2,000; eight of the number listed were of less than 2,200 tons and were thus but little larger than the *Western World* and *Plymouth Rock.*

[9] Several ships built in 1853 were fairly close rivals in size; these were the *Queen of the West,* 1,851 tons, the *Mississippi,* 1,829 tons, and the *Crescent City,* 1,746 tons. The *Mississippi* was soon added to the Michigan Central fleet.

[10] For it, see James L. Barton, *Letter to the Hon. Robert McClelland . . . in Relation to the Value and Importance of the Commerce of the Great Western Lakes* (Buffalo, 1846).

[11] The *Great Britain* was 322 feet long, 50½ feet beam, and her tonnage was 3,618. On the subject of the early iron ships see S. C. Gilfillian, *Inventing the Ship* (Chicago, 1935) and E. K. Chatterton, *Steamships and their Story* (London, 1910).

[12] For the fuller story of the *Michigan* see M. M. Quaife's "The Iron Ship," *Burton Historical Collection Leaflet,* VII, 17-32. Public interest in the ship was aroused anew in the winter of 1944 when President Roosevelt countered a proposal to salvage the metal she contained by expressing a wish that she might be preserved as a historic memorial.

[13] Lake Carriers' Association *Bulletin,* May 1943.

[14] The depth of the channel, which in turn is governed by the lake levels from year to year, is a factor which helps to explain the length of time many of these individual cargo records have stood unbroken.

[15] Lake Carriers' Association *Bulletin,* issues for July 1942 and July 1943.

[16] Lake Carriers' Association *Bulletin,* September 1943.

[17] Lake Carriers' Association, *Annual Report for 1941,* 103-105.

[18] Lake Carriers' Association *Bulletin,* June 1943.

[19] Lake Carriers' Association, *Annual Report for 1940,* 96-97.

[20] Detroit *News,* June 10, 1943.

Part II

TALK OF MANY THINGS

Chapter 16

Beaver Skins and Queens

THE first white men who came to Lake Michigan found the natives of the Wisconsin and Michigan forests still living in the Stone Age. Although their mode of life was hard and rude they had mastered their environment and were economically self-sustaining. Before their astonished eyes the newcomers dangled a wide variety of goods whose superiority to their own rude products was instantly apparent. In particular, they displayed implements of iron—needles, fishhooks, hatchets, traps and guns—whose possession convinced the wondering red men that their visitors must be celestial beings. "Thou art a God," exclaimed the Green Bay Potawatomi to Perrot, the early Wisconsin trader, "because thou bringest us the gift of iron. Praised be the sun which has instructed thee and sent thee to us."

So at a single bound the Indian passed from the Stone to the Iron Age, a transformation which the people of Europe had taken thousands of years to effect. But the white trader was no god nor was he a philanthropic Santa Claus, and for the goods he offered he demanded a satisfactory exchange. Practically the only thing the Indian could offer was the skins of wild animals which thronged the American forests. The furs the trader chiefly desired belonged to the various members of the weasel family—above all, the beaver, which formerly abounded in almost every American river and lake. Before the white men came the Indian had hunted wild animals principally for food or to satisfy his own modest needs in the way of clothing and shelter. Now he abandoned his native arts to become dependent upon the white trader for the things essential to his continued existence. To procure them he became a professional hunter and trapper, and the skins he obtained were carried to London and Paris and Amsterdam, there to be fashioned into garments which the fine ladies of Europe coveted no less than the Indian squaws the trinkets and blankets, or the warriors the hatchets and traps received in exchange for them.

Such was the basis of the Indian trade over which wars were waged, dynasties rose and fell and the course of American history was shaped. There is a widespread but largely erroneous impression that the trader commonly imposed grossly upon the Indian. There were, of course, many dishonest traders, but there were also many honorable ones, and when the red man's brain was not befuddled by liquor he was not easily deceived or overreached. His standard of desires and values differed widely from those of the white man, of course, leading him often to pay exorbitant prices for things which the latter valued lightly; but such exchanges were not fraudulent, since each party to the transaction obtained the things he wanted at prices he was willing to pay. As in civilized life, many traders commanded the confidence and affection of those with whom they dealt; while those who resorted to dishonesty often found to their sorrow that the red man had an effective way of evening the account.

In order to trade people must come together, and in the earlier years of New France the natives of the Upper Lakes traveled hundreds of miles by canoe down the Ottawa and the St. Lawrence to Three Rivers or Montreal, where in a kind of annual fair they exchanged their furs for the goods they desired. Beginning about the year 1660, the traders swarmed over the western wilderness, and although the government tried to limit the trade to certain licensed individuals, its profits and attractions were so great that large numbers of colonists slipped away from their homes to engage in an outlaw trade in defiance of governmental regulations and edicts. An outlaw has excellent reasons for not advertising his activities to the world, but it is a moral certainty that the *coureurs de bois,* or outlaw forest runners, traced out almost every waterway and visited every Indian village in advance of the officials and missionaries whom we are wont to regard as the first explorers.

Although the King of England succeeded the ruler of France as Lord of the Great Lakes, and the latter in turn gave place to the new American Government, the fur trade continued to be conducted in much the same way to the end of the wilderness period. The bateau and the Mackinac boat were the vehicles of transportation in almost universal use, although on the Great Lakes themselves sailing vessels were also utilized in the British and American periods. The French-Canadian voyageur, as unprogressive as the red man himself, performed most of the hard physical labor with a cheerfulness which defied the appalling hardships he was compelled to undergo.

The Mackinac boat, employed throughout the interior of the continent, was but an overgrown development of the red man's birch-bark canoe. Although sizes varied, the larger boats were thirty feet or more long and six or seven feet wide at the middle, tapering to a point at either end. Upon a framework of slender cedar ribs, terminating in gunwales which were kept apart by slender bars of the same wood, layers of birch bark were fastened, sewed together with roots and their joints cemented by applying a gummy substance. Such a boat could be carried around rapids and across portages by four men, yet it would sustain a cargo of four tons. Apart from the crew of seven or eight men and their baggage, this would consist of materials for repairing leaks in the fragile boat, perhaps 1,000 pounds of provisions, and sixty or more packs of skins weighing ninety pounds each. On the outward voyages, instead of skins the cargo consisted of kegs of liquor and bales and packages of merchandise for the coming winter's trade. At the approach of night or of a storm on the lake the voyageurs were ready to leap overboard on an instant's warning to carry the boat and its contents ashore. When weather conditions permitted, a sail, supported by a small mast amidships, reinforced the brawny arms of the paddlers in propelling the vessel.

The bateau, of sturdier construction than the Mackinac boat, served the same general purpose and was manned by about the same crew. Like the Mackinac boat it had a mast and a sail which was used to aid the rowers whenever the weather permitted.[1]

The journal of Peter Pond, which has been mentioned in an earlier chapter, preserves some entrancing pictures of the wild life of the Northwest a century and three-quarters ago. In the years 1773 and 1774 Pond conducted two expeditions from Mackinac across Wisconsin and up the Mississippi to the interior of Minnesota, the first one comprising twelve large canoes manned by about a hundred men.

Here is his description of the first part of the voyage, as far as Green Bay:

"In Sept. I Had my Small fleet Readey to Cross Lake Michegan. On my Way to Grean Bay at the Mouth of fox river I Engaged Nine Clarkes for Differant Parts of the Northan and Westarn Countrey, and Beaing Mand we Imbarkt and Crost the Lake without Seaing an Indan or Eney Person Except our one. In three or four Days we arive at the Mouth of the Bay which is two or three Mile Brod. In the Mouth is Some Islands which we follow in Crossing to the South West Sid and then follow ye Shore to ye Bottom which is Seventey Miles whare the fox River Empteys into the Bay. We weant a Short Distans up the River whare is a small french village and thare Incampt for two Days. This Land is Exalent. The Inhabitans Rase fine Corn and Sum Artickels for farmmaley youse in there Gardens. They Have Sum trad with ye Indans which Pas that way. On the North Part of this Bay is a small Villag of Indans Cald the Mannomaneas [Menominee] who Live by Hunting Cheafley. Thay have another Resois—the Bottom of the Bay Produces a Large Quantity of Wilde Rice which they Geather in Sept for food. I Ort to have Menshand that the french at ye Villeg whare we Incampt Rase fine black Cattel and Horses with Sum Swine."

On a high bank of the Minnesota River the party constructed comfortable houses to serve as their headquarters for the winter. The trade proved profitable and Pond again returned to Minnesota the following year. But a war between the Sioux and the Chippewa now broke out and to restore peace the commandant of Mackinac ordered all the traders to persuade the Indians of their respective areas to accompany them back for a grand powwow and peace council. On the return to Mackinac in the spring of 1774, therefore, Pond was attended by a great concourse of traders and natives.

"We desended the fox River to the Botam of Greane Bay, and thare joined the Hole of ye Canoes Bound to Macena. The way ther was fair and Pleasant. we all Proseaded together acoss Lake Misheagan. At the end of two days we all apeard on the Lake about five Miles from Macenac, and Approacht in Order. We had flags on the Masts of our Canoes—Eavery Chefe his flock. My Canoes Beaing the

Largest in that Part of the Cuntrey and haveing a large Younion flage I Histed it and when within a Mile and a half I took ye lead and ye Indans followed close behind. The flag in the fort was histed—ye Cannon of the Garrison Began to Play Smartly—the shore was Lind with People of all Sorts, who Seat up such a Crey and hooping which Seat the Tribes in the fleat a Going to that Degrea that you Could not Hear a Parson Speak. At Length we Reacht ye Shore and the Cannon Seasd. I then toock my Partey to the Commander who treated us verey Well. I seat with them an Our and Related the afare and what I had Dun and what Past Dureing the Winter. After Interreduseing the Chefe I Went to my one House whare I found a number of Old frends with whom I spent the the Remainder of the Day."

The peace council was held by the commandant and was followed by several days of feasting and general whoopee. "Britening the Chane of frindship in a Veray Deasant Way" and vowing eternal friendship, Chippewa and Sioux scattered to their distant homes, while Pond, like Alexander Henry, presently transferred his operations to the then unknown Canadian Northwest. Here he performed notable services as explorer and map maker, and eventually returned to New England to live out his closing years in poverty and want.

Half a century later than Pond, Gurdon S. Hubbard, another New Englander, came out to Mackinac to enter upon the Indian trade as a clerk for the American Fur Company. This was in 1818 when he was barely sixteen years of age. After spending a decade and a half in the Indian trade Hubbard settled in infant Chicago, where for half a century longer he remained a prominent and useful citizen. His autobiography, dictated toward the close of his life, supplies the clearest description ever written of the way the fur trade was conducted around Lake Michigan.

The American Fur Company was in its heyday in Hubbard's time, and under the vigorous rule of John Jacob Astor was fast monopolizing the Indian trade of the entire western country. To Mackinac Island, the entrepôt of the huge enterprise, each springtime hundreds of traders and voyageurs from a thousand miles around directed their canoes. For a few weeks, while the prosaic details of checking in the annual harvest of skins and outfitting the traders for another year in the wilderness were accomplished, the island hummed with life and activity. Then the trading brigades departed for their winter stations, the thousands of red visitors scattered to their wilderness homes, and Mackinac slumbered until the return of another springtime.

Although the control of the vast business centered in New York, many of the goods and most of the men who were engaged in it came from Lower Canada. In the spring of 1818 a dozen clerks and a hundred voyageurs were being recruited at Montreal for the service of the company and young Hubbard entered upon a five-year engagement as a clerk. Early in May the new recruits left Lachine in a fleet of a dozen bateaux for their two months' journey to distant Mackinac. Each of the voyageurs was provided with a single blanket, and pea soup and salt pork were their only food. Their beds were the bare ground under the open heavens, save in stormy weather when a tarpaulin was spread to shelter them from the rain. They breakfasted at dawn and from then until sundown worked continuously save for an hour's rest at noon and an occasional pipe-smoke pause during the day. The heavily laden boats were forced up the swift St. Lawrence only by the hardest toil, especially in the numerous rapids where the crews of several boats concentrated their efforts upon a single one. While two men remained in the boat to keep its head to the current and seven or eight more pushed and pulled in the water, the rest toiled ashore, pulling on a rope attached to the bow.

From all this toil, the clerks were exempt. They messed with the commander of the brigade and had a thin mattress to sleep on and a tent for a shelter at night. Besides the pork and pea soup of the voyageurs they were supplied such delicacies as tea, sugar and hard bread; and they whiled away the time spent by the voyageurs in the rapids with rambles along the shore.

A month of such progress brought the expedition to Toronto, then a village of a few hundred inhabitants. Here the leader decided to transport the boats by ox team to Lake Simcoe and from there proceed by way of Lake Nipissing and French River to Georgian Bay. From here onward the journey was easy, and at length, seven weeks out of Montreal, the brigade arrived at Goose Island, within sight of the craggy heights of Mackinac. The lake was too rough to permit the crossing, however, and the men improved the twenty-four-hour delay to shave and wash and change to their best clothes, in readiness to make an imposing entry to the island capital.

The annual assemblage of traders and Indians was in progress, and while the red man made interminable high jinks the traders pushed the work of sorting and repacking their furs for shipment to New York. Grading the skins was expert work, since they varied much in quality and coloring and the price they brought was determined by these factors. For marten alone, no less than fourteen grades existed, running from "extra fine dark" and "number one dark" down to "good," "out of season," "inferior," "damaged" and "worthless." Save for bears, where a distinction was made between *he* and *she,* and where nine different grades were distinguished, none of the other skins ran to more than four grades. Both the grading and the counting were closely watched by the leaders of the outfits. Success or failure for the year depended upon the way this work was performed, and frequent disputes over the value and grading of the skins ensued.

Hubbard's first task was to assist in counting the skins. All were counted twice, independently, the first count being entered in a book which Hubbard did not see. If his count agreed with this record, the skins were pressed and sent to the shipping room; if the two counts disagreed he was required to make a third count, and if there was still a discrepancy another person was called in to count them again. The working day was from five in the morning until seven at night. All the time a stooping position was required.

Several score voyageurs, who were generally experienced hands, were detailed to assist in handling the skins for counting; another group comprised a wood-chopping gang; and still another was busy "lyeing" and drying the corn which was a staple of the voyageur's diet. They were drafted for these various fatigue duties only once in four years, being free the remaining seasons to spend the summer in loafing and carousals. In the Indian country their daily ration was a pint of hulled corn and two or three ounces of tallow, eked out on Sunday with some flour for pancakes. Far from revolting from this scanty fare, they jeered at the new men, who on the outward voyage from Montreal had been fed on pork and peas, dubbing them "pork-

eaters," and assuring them that before another summer they would
be thankful to have even corn and tallow to eat.

With their annual returns in and accounted for, the traders began
organizing their crews and preparing their outfits for their return to
winter quarters. The Lake of the Woods Brigade, having the farthest
to go, departed first, followed in due order by the other northern outfits, the Illinois and Wabash River brigades, and by those destined
for the shores of Lake Huron and Lake Michigan. In all cases the
procedure was much the same. Everyone on the island gathered at
the harbor, the voyageurs struck up some favorite boating song and
amid the farewell shouts and cheers of the multitude on shore the
boats glided away upon their distant journeys.

Hubbard was assigned to the Illinois River Brigade, numbering a
dozen boats and about 100 men. The brigade left Mackinac in early
September and twenty days were consumed in the journey to Chicago. When aided by a favoring wind, the boats hoisted a small
square sail and with its help the rowers could travel about seventy
miles in a day. Whenever the wind was wrong or the lake was
stormy, shelter was sought in some creek mouth. If such a haven
were lacking they unloaded the boats and hauled them up on shore
beyond the reach of the surf; the goods were covered with tarpaulin
and the men rested or engaged in rude sports until favoring winds
made it possible to resume the voyage.

The end of September found the brigade at the mouth of the
Calumet, where much of the night was passed in preparations for an
imposing entry to Chicago. At dawn the voyage was resumed, with
flags flying and the men in their holiday attire, while their oars kept
time to a rollicking boat song. Apart from the Fort Dearborn garrison, Chicago then comprised a few civilian traders and their employees, the latter usually French Canadians with Indian wives and
half-breed families. Fort Dearborn, evacuated and destroyed in 1812,
had been rebuilt and regarrisoned in 1816, and soon after the traders
had made their camp on the north bank of the river the officers paid
them a visit.

Several days were spent repairing the boats and then the journey
to the Illinois was resumed. From Chicago the brigade ascended the

South Branch of the river to about the point where Damen Avenue crosses it, the site of Father Marquette's camp of 1675. Here a day was spent in preparation for the dreaded passage through Mud Lake. This loathsome spot was a swampy depression in the prairie which in dry weather contained no water and in wet seasons drained both westward into the Des Plaines and eastward into the South Branch. Only in very wet seasons did it contain water enough to float an empty boat, while the mud to which it owed its name was very deep and around it grew a wall of grass and wild rice taller than a man and so dense and rank that it was almost impossible to penetrate it.

From the South Branch the empty boats were pulled up the channel leading into Mud Lake. In places where there was a hard bottom and absence of water they were placed on short rollers and in this way were propelled along until the lake was reached. Here mud, thick and deep, was encountered, but only at rare intervals was there any water. Four men remained in the boat while seven or eight more waded in the mud alongside. The former were equipped with boat poles, to the ends of which forked branches of trees had been fastened. By pushing with these against the hummocks while the men outside lifted and shoved, they jerked the boat along. The men in the mud frequently sank to their waists and at times had to cling to the sides of the boat to save themselves from being completely engulfed. Their limbs were covered with bloodsuckers which caused intense agony for several days, and sleep at night was impossible because of the swarms of mosquitoes which assailed them.

Three days of such toil sufficed to bring them to the outlet into the Des Plaines, where hard ground was again reached. The trip down the Des Plaines and the Illinois to the mouth of Fox River required almost three weeks more of arduous toil. There were frequent portages where the goods were carried on the backs of the voyageurs while the lightened boats were pushed ahead on rollers or placed on poles and dragged over rocks and shoals. In such fashion, year after year the downward journey to navigable water on the Illinois was made, until 1824 when Hubbard was placed in charge of the Illinois River posts. He then adopted a plan which he had vainly urged upon his predecessor of transporting the goods from Chicago to the Indian hunting grounds on pack horses, the boats being scuttled, meanwhile, in the swamp to insure their safety until they should be needed for the return voyage to Mackinac, laden with furs, the following spring.

Until this plan was adopted, the annual journey up the Illinois and the Des Plaines to the Chicago was attended by difficulties hardly less formidable than those which marked the downward journey in the autumn. To ascend the Des Plaines at all, advantage must be taken of the brief spring flood, when the river was a roaring torrent. From Starved Rock as far as Cache Island the boats advanced at the rate of seven or eight miles a day with the men frequently wading in the icy water to propel them against the swift current. The remainder of the journey to Chicago was easy, as the entire countryside was flooded, and the boats sailed across it without regard to the course of the river channel or the limits of Mud Lake.

The first season Hubbard was assigned to a post on the Illinois at the mouth of Bureau Creek, just outside modern Hennepin. Here the men built a rude log hut in which to pass the winter and Hubbard had the good fortune to make chums of two Indian boys of his own age. They taught him their language and their lore of hunting and trapping. He learned how to distinguish the tracks of the different animals and whether they were walking slow or fast or running. He also learned to know the marks made on tree trunks by such animals as raccoons and panthers, and although his companions had many a joke over his awkwardness and lack of skill, he gained from them an indispensable wilderness schooling.

During his life as a trader his outer dress was a capote or buckskin hunting shirt confined at the waist by a sash or buckskin belt in which he carried a knife and sheath, a tomahawk and a tobacco pouch made of mink or otter skin. Besides tobacco it contained a flint and steel, together with a piece of dry punk with which to strike a spark when a fire was needed. Under the outer garment he wore a calico shirt, breechcloth and buckskin leggings; his feet were protected by "neips"— square pieces of blanket cloth folded over—encased in moccasins. He usually went bareheaded, and his hair was left uncut; when traveling in winter he carried, and sometimes wore, a blanket. Thus equipped, he often went on long journeys to the Indian hunting camps, walking at times fifty miles or more in a day. The vigorous outdoor life he led soon developed him into a powerful man, to whom his Indian friends gave the name of "Papamatabe"—the Swift Walker.

Early in March 1819 the leader of the Illinois Brigade began collecting his men and furs from their scattered stations in readiness for the return journey to Mackinac, and together the thirteen bateaux made the usual toilsome ascent of the Illinois and the Des Plaines to Chicago. Here several days were spent in camp, where the Wrigley and Tribune towers now point heavenward, repairing the boats in preparation for the more serious task of coasting around Lake Michigan. Late in April this journey was begun, and since there was no particular hurry it was conducted in leisurely fashion. At the St. Joseph, where a pause of several days was made, the brigade was joined by the traders who had wintered on that river. At Grand River the entire party, now numbering 150 men or more, again encamped for several days in order to witness the Feast of the Dead which the Indians of western Michigan had assembled to celebrate.

One evening the traders were told that the next morning a drama of primitive justice would be staged. The autumn before in a drunken quarrel an Indian had killed a son of the chief of the Manistee band, and the killer was to deliver himself in the morning to suffer the penalty for his crime. He was a Canadian Indian who had married a girl of the Michigan band and had thus become a member of it. At the time of the killing he was the father of several children and was very poor, having nothing but a few traps and his meager wearing apparel.

According to Indian law his life would be taken for his crime unless he could ransom it by paying the family of the dead man a suitable quantity of furs or other articles of value, and if he failed to present himself for sacrifice his wife's brothers would be held responsible for his crime. Having nothing of his own, he secretly departed with his family by night for the headwaters of the Muskegon where he had trapped before, hoping to obtain by his winter's efforts enough beaver and other skins to satisfy the chief whose son he had killed. Before leaving he told one of his wife's brothers of his plan and where he could be found in case it should become necessary to return and deliver himself up for punishment.

After burying the murdered man, the chief took counsel with his remaining sons, who, knowing the offender was too poor to pay their demands, determined upon his death. Unable to find him, however, they demanded that his wife's brothers satisfy their claim. All but the one to whom he had confided his plan believed he had fled for refuge to his Canadian relatives, but this one offered to find and bring him back or, failing, give his own life instead.

The journey was long and difficult, and with no landmarks to go by he knew only that the murderer was somewhere on the head-waters of the Muskegon. Meanwhile the winter had proved unusually severe and the spring had been marked by great floods. The bears had remained in their dens and the beaver, marten and mink had not been found, so that instead of accumulating a store of furs the hunter had barely succeeded in preserving his family from starvation. In this situation nothing remained but to pay his tribal obligation and when found by his brother-in-law and informed of the chief's demand, he readily agreed to return with his family to the mouth of Grand River during the Feast of the Dead to undergo the penalty in store for him.

Today Grand Haven is one of Lake Michigan's pleasantest east coast resorts, peopled each summer by thousands of city dwellers in search of health-giving rest and recreation. Somewhere within its borders the drama whose setting we have sketched was about to be enacted. Soon after sunrise the news spread through the camp that the culprit was approaching. The chief with his family took his place in a hollow between two sand dunes, while the traders, together with the Indians, took station on the adjoining hillsides to witness the affair.

Presently was heard the monotonous thump of an Indian drum, followed by the mournful voice of the hunter chanting his own death song and followed by his wife and children in single file, slowly marching toward the place selected for his execution. Reaching the spot, he placed the drum on the ground, while the squaw and her children seated themselves on mats which had been placed for them. Addressing the chief, the doomed man said: "In a drunken moment I stabbed your son, provoked to it by his accusing me of being a coward and calling me an old woman. I fled to the marshes at the head of the Muskegon, hoping the Great Spirit would favor me in the hunt, so that I could pay you for your lost son. I was not successful. Here is the knife with which I killed him; by it I wish to die. Save my wife and children. I am done."

The chief accepted the knife and handing it to his oldest son said, "Kill him." Not a murmur was heard from the victim or from his wife and children, nor was any word spoken by the crowd of witnesses. Only the singing of the birds, indifferent to human tragedies, broke the stillness of the spring morning. Every eye was fastened upon the victim, who stood motionless, calmly eying his executioner. The latter advanced and, placing his hand upon the victim's shoulder, plunged the knife into his breast to the handle. For a brief space he stood erect, the blood gushing from the wound; then his knees began to quake, his eyes and face assumed an expression of death, and he sank upon the sand.

The wife and children sat quietly, making no sound until life was extinct, when they threw themselves upon the body with cries and lamentations. The chief and his family sat motionless for some time, apparently regretting what had been done. Then he arose and approaching the body said: "Woman, stop weeping. Your husband was a brave man, and like a brave, was not afraid to die as the rules of our nation demand. We adopt you and your children in the place of my son; our lodges are open to you; live with any of us; you shall have our protection and love."

"Che-qui-ock"—it is right—exclaimed the assembled Indians, and the tragedy was ended.

---

1 For a description of the Mackinac boat see Henry R. Schoolcraft, *Narrative Journal of Travels through the Northwestern Regions of the United States . . . in the Year 1820* (Albany, 1821), 67-70. Much information about the bateau is supplied by Gurdon S. Hubbard, *Autobiography* (Chicago, 1888); reprinted in Lakeside Classics Series (Chicago, 1911).

Chapter 17

Forest Dwellers

IN ITS primitive state the country around Lake Michigan afforded an alluring home to wild life. Almost every variety native to North America from the ponderous buffalo and the clumsy moose to the industrious beaver and the lowly muskrat filled the forests and prairies. The lakes and streams were alive with waterfowl, prairie chickens abounded in the grass lands and the whir of the partridge was heard from every forest glade. The cheery call of bobwhite echoed from the open fields, and in spring and autumn uncounted thousands of swans, cranes, geese and ducks passing on their aerial flight filled the sky with their strident clamor.

Some of these varieties are still abundant, but most, with depleted numbers, maintain a precarious hold on existence, while others have vanished altogether and the very memory of them has faded from the public mind. As the settlement of the country proceeded, the native environment underwent a radical change. The forests were cut down, the prairies were fenced and plowed, marshes and streams dwindled or vanished altogether and the wild life faded away. In large part this was inevitable, since cities do not flourish in the wilderness nor can cultivated farms and virgin prairies exist in the same space. But the process was intensified by the forces of insensate greed and reckless waste, and often the birthright of coming generations was sacrificed for the sake of immediate individual gain. Too late the public awoke to a realization of the loss that was taking place and tardy measures were instituted for the more careful conservation of such natural resources of scenic beauty and wild life as still remained.

A variety of reasons exist to explain the persistence of some species in close contact with civilization and the speedy fading away of others. The moose and the elk once ranged over Michigan and Wisconsin and both long since vanished from these states. Today a few elk are preserved on state game farms and similar private preserves, but none is to be found at large and efforts to re-establish both elk and moose have met with but slight success.

186

Quite otherwise has been the story of the deer. Although never extinguished, their number had become sadly diminished at the time laws were passed for their protection, accompanied by a powerful public sentiment against violation. Thus protected, the number of deer has rapidly increased in all the cutover areas of Michigan and Wisconsin, its only limit, apparently, being the one fixed by the extent of their available food supply. In Michigan in quite recent years deer have been introduced in certain southerly counties, with consequences not entirely happy. Although the animals show no lack of ability to thrive and multiply, the farmers whose growing crops they invade and over whose highest fences they leap with ease resent their depredations and protest against the measures passed for their protection.

A citizen of Iowa once published a book devoted to the proposition that the buffalo had never lived in that state, although the animal had once ranged over its entire extent and had withdrawn from it hardly two generations before the volume was written. So, too, the memory of the buffalo's presence around Lake Michigan has long since perished. Yet the early French explorers found the huge animal in large numbers on the prairies of Indiana and Illinois and its northward range undoubtedly included the unforested areas of southern Wisconsin and Michigan. There were few prairies at Detroit, wrote Cadillac in 1702, but fifteen leagues distant at the entrance to Lake Erie boundless prairies, stretching away a hundred leagues, began. "It is there," he continued, "that these mighty oxen, which are covered with wool, find food in abundance."[1] The familiar name for the site of Fort St. Joseph at Niles was *Parc aux Vaches,* meaning the cow (or buffalo) pasture, and the name given by the French to Fox River of northern Illinois and southern Wisconsin was *Boeuf,* or Buffalo River.

Although no record of buffalo on the actual site of Chicago has been found, as with Detroit they dwelt in abundance a few miles away. When Father Marquette was spending the winter of 1674-1675 there, he was befriended by two outlaw traders who were living, the priest recorded, eighteen leagues distant, "in a fine place for hunting cattle, deer, and turkeys." In connection with all these early reports it should be noted that the French called the buffalo wild cattle or oxen. The companions of La Salle on their first visit to Illinois found buffalo horns in amazing numbers along the Kankakee, although they encountered no live animals, since the savages had set fire to the countryside and driven them all away. Father Hennepin's narrative supplies us with a detailed description of the native method of hunting them. He also explains *Pimetoui,* the native name for Lake Peoria, as meaning "a place where there is an abundance of fat beasts"; and the Dutch illustrator of his book, who never saw America, has provided a diverting picture of a buffalo bull standing amid palm trees and other curious vegetation.

In 1687 the young nephew of Henry de Tonty, the Sieur Deliette, joined his uncle in Illinois, where he remained for many years, four of them at Chicago, and his *Memoir* supplies the best description of primitive Illinois ever written. At Mount Jolliet on the Des Plaines, he records, "one commonly comes upon the buffalo." On his first buffalo hunt, although the young Frenchman fled in terror from the huge beasts, the Indians whom he was accompanying killed 120 of them. A few days later Deliette chanced upon a calf stretched on the ground and gasping from exhaustion and succeeded in killing it. Although the savages told him it was not worth shooting since calves were never fat, they celebrated his exploit by holding a feast in which they thanked the Master of Life for enabling him to kill his first wild game.

The most interesting animal of the region was the clownish black bear, found everywhere in the forests which hemmed Lake Michigan. The red men regarded him with superstitious reverence as their relative and "grandmother," and although they did not hesitate to kill him when in need of food, they sought to appease his spirit with elaborate apologies to the dead carcass.[1] A bear hunt was a great event to them, to be undertaken with much preparatory ceremony. Although the pioneer settlers shared none of the red man's superstitions about the animal they looked upon a bear hunt as a neighborhood frolic which they would cheerfully postpone all other duties to engage in.

Encounters with bears filled a prominent place in the memories of the pioneers, and practically every community had its stock of bear stories which commonly did not suffer in the process of retelling. Some of the tales which formerly circulated in one central Wisconsin neighborhood about "the old man with the fur coat" have fortunately been collected in print.[2]

"Sleek and amiable in the autumn, he crawled into the hollow of a tree or crevice in the rocks for his winter's nap. The roaring of the winter wind and the drifting of the crystal snow were unheeded by him as he slept until nature awoke in the spring.

"When he emerged from his hibernating season he was a lean, hungry specimen with a gnawing appetite ready for any unwary bug, ant or small game that chanced to fall in his way. He was often forced to the extremity of making a meal on tender roots or other vegetable matter found on a sunny hillside or along an inland stream. In the fall he grew fat on berries, nuts, honey, and other foods he found in the richly stocked storehouse of nature. During the summer months he was apt to be lean and shaggy and less good-natured than at other seasons of the year.

"In pioneer days the bear hunt was a diversion sought by the youths now grizzled by the procession of the years. Among the quartzite hills, where deer to this day dwell, and in the woody wilderness almost without limitations beyond, the bear found a more or less secluded habitat. But when he ventured into some near-by cornfield or pig-sty the entire neighborhood was set in commotion. Not only was there cheer in the chase, but a savory roast to refresh and a garment of fur to keep away the cold as a reward of the effort."

One autumn day a farmer, Ira Palmer, with his sons was hard at work in his field, while near by their Celtic neighbor, Patrick Knelley, was also toiling. Unknown to them, the day before, the Risley boys had come upon a bear, and early that morning a band of neighbors with their dogs had started in pursuit of it. The chase proved long and wearisome and the afternoon had arrived with bruin still eluding his pursuers. Quite without design he took a course which led him across an open field in plain view of the industrious plowmen. All ceased work at once, and while Knelley mounted a horse and galloped madly homeward for his gun, the Palmers kept excited watch of the movements of the bear. Wearied by his long retreat, that gentleman leisurely ambled toward the highway, where he calmly squatted in a small pool of water which lay beside it. Just at this juncture Patrick came back with his gun, and rushing up to the pond fired the old fowling piece at the half-submerged bear.

"The result was astounding. With the elasticity of a rubber ball, the enraged animal bounded from the water and charged at his tormentor. The battle was on! Terrified at the turn affairs had taken, the Irishman gave a despairing glance at his companions, who had remained at a safe distance. The bear was all but upon him. As the animal rose on his haunches, Patrick struck out with the butt end of his gun. The weapon parted, and man and beast clinched in a mighty embrace. Over they rolled, now in the road, now in the water. When the posse which had followed the bear's trail during the morning came upon the scene the picture that met their astonished eyes resembled a kaleidoscopic mixture of man, mud and beast. No one dared shoot for fear of injury to Knelley, and not one among the onlookers cared to risk his life by breaking in upon the combatants. It was a thrilling moment. At last the opportune instant arrived. Risley raised his gun, a report echoed through the valley, and bruin released his hold.

"Breathless, hatless, tattered and dripping, the son of Erin emerged from the pool amid the shouts of the spectators. Before anyone could utter a word the sputtering, blood-stained Irishman cried out between gasps:

" 'He's mine! He's mine! Begorra he's mine!'

"The problem of ownership in this case was an interesting question for pioneer jurisprudence. The matter, it is said, was finally adjusted by Risley taking the pelt and Knelley the carcass."

However interesting he might be, "the old man with the fur coat" was too combative and too fond of the farmers' hogs and calves to make him an agreeable neighbor. The jingle,

> "I'm not afraid of anyone
> They're all afraid of me
> I only have to show my teeth
> To make them turn and flee,"

was too true for comfort, and as fast as the country filled with settlers the doom of the bear was sealed. In the cutover areas of northern Michigan and Wisconsin a few of his number still survive, but sad experience has made him so shy of humankind that he is only rarely encountered.

In the autumn of 1845 a young sportsman from the East paid a visit to a friend who had settled at Saginaw. Tiring of inactivity, he

THE GREAT LAKES NAVAL STATION

At Great Lakes, 1,000 miles from the ocean, the greatest naval training station in the world is maintained. The view shows one phase of the physical hardening program for students.

THE ADMINISTRATION BUILDING AT GREAT LAKES

GREAT LAKES NAVAL STATION COLOR GUARD

The color guard marches in review on Ross Field, with Administration Building in background.

undertook a ten-day jaunt across the central Michigan wilderness to the logging camp of another friend on the Muskegon River, and his subsequent record of the excursion affords a fascinating picture of the profusion of wild life which crowded the Michigan forests before its destruction at the hands of the settler had begun.[3]

"I do not think there was an hour of daylight on the trip when squirrels were not too numerous to be counted, while pigeons were a constant quantity from start to finish. Grouse in the thickets and quail in the high oak openings, or small prairies, with droves of wild turkeys among heavy timber, were met with almost hourly, and there was scarcely a day on which I could not have had a standing shot at a bear. But the most interesting point about the game ... was the marvelous abundance of deer. They were everywhere, on all sorts of ground and among all varieties of timber; very tame they were, too, often stopping to look at the stranger, offering easy shots at short range, and finally going off quite leisurely."

One novel experience was an encounter with an animal originally tame which had developed into "the wickedest and most formidable looking" beast the sportsman had ever met. He had seated himself at the foot of a small oak tree to rest, after emerging from a long struggle over low, marshy ground, when the creature appeared among the bushes a short distance away.

"It looked like a hog, but stood too high on its legs; and how would such a beast get there anyhow? Nearer and nearer he came, and at last walked out into an open spot less than twenty yards distant. It was a wild hog of the ugliest and largest description; tall as a yearling, with an unnaturally large head, and dangerous looking tusks, that curved above his savage snout like small horns. There was promise of magnificent power in his immense shoulders, while flanks and hams were disproportionately light. He came out to the open leisurely munching his acorns, or amusing himself by ploughing deep furrows with his nose, and not until within ten yards did he appear to note the presence of a stranger. Suddenly he raised his head and became rigid as though frozen to stone; he was taking an observation. For a few seconds he remained immovable, then his bristles became erect, and with a deep, guttural noise, he commenced hitching himself along in my direction, sidewise. My hair raised, and in an instant I was on my feet with the cocked rifle to my shoulder—meaning to shoot before his charge, and then make good time up the tree. But there was no need. As I sprang to my feet he sprang for the hazel bushes, and went tearing through them with the speed of a deer, keeping up a succession of snorts and grunts that could be heard long after he had passed out of sight. I am not subject to buck fever, and was disgusted to find myself so badly 'rattled' that I could scarcely handle the rifle. At first I was provoked at myself for not getting a good ready and shooting him in the head, as he came out of the bushes; but it was better to let him live. He was not carnivorous, or a beast of prey, and ugly as he was, certainly looked better alive than he would as a porcine corpse. No doubt he relished his acorns as well as though he had been less ugly, and he was a savage power in the forest. Bears love pork, even as a darky loves 'possum; and the fact that he was picking up a comfortable living in that wilderness, is presumptive evidence that he was a match for the largest bear, or he would have been eaten long before. . . ."

More abundant even than the four-footed animals were the flocks of wild fowl and other feathered life which filled the sky or blackened the marshes and prairies. One of the most beautiful as well as useful of these native birds was the quail, whose cheery "bobwhite" echoed from every roadside and meadow. Its ancient abundance is recorded in the Old Testament, for the children of Israel in their wanderings feasted upon its tender flesh. Despite the efforts made in recent decades by conservation officials to protect it, the quail seems doomed to follow the pathway already taken by the great auk and the passenger pigeon to complete extinction.

> "Shrill and shy from the dark they cry,
> Faintly from over the hill,
> Out of the gray where shadows lie,
> Out of the gold where sheaves are high,
> Covey to covey, call and reply,
> Plaintively, shy and shrill."

Another splendid game bird which formerly crowded all the prairies of the Middle West was the prairie chicken. When the Prince of Wales (later King Edward VII) visited America in 1861 the high-light of his entire tour was the brief period of quail and chicken shooting he enjoyed at Dwight, Illinois, a short distance south of Chicago. Everywhere greeted by enthusiastic crowds (at Detroit they were so tumultuous as to threaten his safety and actually to push some of his entourage into the river), the prince thoroughly enjoyed the brief respite from listening to interminable speeches and dancing with the daughters of countless ambitious dowagers which his short excursion to the prairies afforded. One would seek far for a clearer description of the virgin Illinois prairie than the one drawn by the special correspondent of the London *Times* who accompanied the royal party.[4]

Incidentally, we owe to the same writer a good description of the now forgotten prairie wolf hunts of pioneer Illinois. The settlers would assemble on horseback at dawn around a circle forty miles in diameter and advance toward its center, driving before them the wild game thus entrapped. As the circle contracted the surrounding line of hunters became steadily denser. The deer and other animals were permitted to escape at will, but the hunters, who were armed only with clubs, were merciless to the wolves, which were condemned to wholesale slaughter.

As recently as three-quarters of a century ago the passenger pigeon was still to be found around Lake Michigan in numbers which stag-ger ordinary human credulity. Barely a quarter of a century sufficed for their complete destruction. Although the original range of the pigeon embraced most of the United States east of the Great Plains, it was found in the Middle West in greatest numbers and here it finally perished.

One ardent admirer of the beautiful bird who lived to regret its disappearance was Simon Pokagon, chief of the Southern Michigan Potawatomi. He writes:

"It was proverbial with our fathers, that if the Great Spirit in his wisdom could have created a more elegant bird in plumage, form, and movement, He never did. When a young man I have stood for hours admiring the movements of these birds, I have seen them fly in unbroken lines from the horizon, one line succeeding another from morning until night, moving their unbroken columns like an army of trained soldiers pushing to the front, while detached bodies of these birds appeared in different parts of the heavens, pressing forward in haste, like raw recruits preparing for battle. At other times I have seen them move in one unbroken column for hours across the sky, like some great river, ever varying in hue; and as the mighty stream, sweeping on at sixty miles an hour, reached some deep valley, it would pour its living mass headlong down hundreds of feet, sounding as though a whirlwind was abroad in the land. I have stood by the grandest waterfall of America and regarded the descending torrents in wonder and astonishment, yet never have my astonishment, wonder, and admiration been so stirred as when I have witnessed these birds drop from their course like meteors from heaven."[5]

Another contemporary observer wrote:[6]

"Those who were not living in the days of passenger pigeons cannot visualize the wonderful phenomenon they presented. The birds traveled in flocks of countless millions over the Midwest. One of the fondest recollections of my boyhood is that of visiting their nesting grounds, close to my home in LaCrosse County, in 1876. It was in the spring, when the farmers were sowing grain, that the pigeons began coming and no one at first seemed to sense what was taking place. The constant passing of the flocks of millions was a mystery, until the report came that the birds were nesting in the Oxbow, an area several thousand acres in extent, so named from a bend in Black River, forming a sort of peninsula covered with jack pine. . . .

"Our visit to the nesting grounds occurred as the young birds (squabs) were about to leave their nests. Scarcely a tree could be seen but contained from ten to fifty nests, according to its size and branches. We knocked the young fledglings out of their nests with long poles, their weak and untried wings failing to carry them beyond our reach, and gathering them up alive, put them into our wagon racks, made and fitted especially for the purpose. People came from far and near with every sort of conveyance to haul the young birds away and indulge their passion for killing upon the old birds, which also were slaughtered by the thousands. I shall never forget that day, and the memory of it brings a sting of conscience as I realize that the magnificent passenger pigeon is gone forever and that not one of these birds is left in all the world."

A profusion of other testimonies to the overwhelming numbers of the passenger pigeons might readily be supplied. John James Audubon, the noted naturalist, who was a careful observer, undertook to estimate the number of birds in a typical flight. Assuming a column a mile in width ("far below the average size") passing steadily overhead for three hours, flying at the rate of a mile a minute, and allowing two pigeons to the square yard, he reached the result of 1,150,-000,000 birds; and with each pigeon in need of half a pint of food daily, such a flock would consume 8,712,000 bushels of food each day. Alexander Wilson, who also observed the birds along the Ohio River, by a similar calculation arrived at the figure of 2,230,000,000 pigeons, requiring daily 17,424,000 bushels of food.

The figures given suggest the reason for the characteristic migrations to which the pigeon owed its name. These were not occasioned by changes in the weather, but wholly by the need for a fresh supply of food. The pigeons fed chiefly on forest "mast"—beechnuts, acorns, etc.—and as long as this remained adequate they might nest in a given locality for years in succession. When it failed for any reason, they set out in search of a new nesting place, flying so rapidly and powerfully that a migration of several hundred miles might be made in a single day. When a nesting place had been once selected, the supply of food available close by would soon become exhausted, necessitating daily flights of a hundred miles or more from which they returned each night to the roosting ground.

Although the white man for decades indulged in wholesale slaughter of the passenger pigeon, the reason for its utter disappearance in the final quarter of the nineteenth century remains still unsolved. The destruction carried on was insensate and disgusting to contemplate and there seems no present profit to be derived from repeating its sickening details. Perhaps as vivid an illustration of its character as any that may be found is afforded by Audubon's story of two Kentucky pioneers, who drove 300 hogs to the roosting ground a distance of 100 miles, there to fatten upon the pigeons which were to be slaughtered.

The same observer, in 1805, noted schooner loads of pigeons brought to the wharf at New York City to be sold for one cent apiece, while twenty-five years later they were so abundant in the markets of the same city that "piles of them meet the eye in every direction." Eventually a class of "pigeoners" developed, professional hunters who interchanged information about the movements of the flocks and followed them up to slaughter for market. A single hunter might take 200 dozen or more birds in a day, and the efforts of the professionals were supplemented by all the settlers for miles around.

Yet Audubon was convinced by more than thirty years of observation, having in view their rapidity of natural increase, that nothing save "the gradual diminution of our forests" would accomplish a decrease in their vast numbers. Chief Pokagon, writing after the event, in 1895, bitterly blamed the white hunter for the destruction, calculating that in thirty years of the greatest slaughter 23,000,000 birds had been sent to market. Both men were wrong in their calculations. The destruction of the forests of Michigan, Wisconsin and Minnesota had only well begun in 1880, when the last great flight of pigeons ever witnessed had become one with history; while Alexander Wilson's estimate of over two billion birds in a single flight discloses the inadequacy of Chief Pokagon's calculation that the marketing of less than one million yearly could have any appreciable effect in hastening their extermination as a species.

For whatever reason, barely half a century after Audubon's forecast of the survival of the pigeons while the forests remained, their destruction had been accomplished. As might be expected, observers differ somewhat in fixing the time of their disappearance, but there is general agreement upon the fact that they were never seen in considerable numbers after the close of the seventies. Chief Pokagon fixes upon the spring of 1880 as the time and Benzie County, Michigan, as the place of their last known nesting. Another observer states that "prior to 1881" they were a common bird of passage throughout southern Michigan and nested commonly in the northern part. In the spring of 1881 they did not return and from that time were seen but rarely. Another witness is still more definite. "There are no wild pigeons in Iosco County, nor have there been any here since April 1, 1880." On that day, the reporter continues, vast numbers of pigeons passed overhead and although it was Sunday the whole town of Tawas turned out to kill them. "Since that day there have been no pigeons here."

The presence of a few birds continued to be reported (probably often erroneously) from time to time for a decade or more longer. Since about 1900 even such reports have ceased. The last known survivor of all the uncounted billions died of old age in the Cincinnati Zoological Garden, September 1, 1914. It was then twenty-nine years old, having been hatched from an original flock procured from Michigan in 1879.

1 For interesting accounts of Indian bear hunts and the subsequent ceremonies see *Alexander Henry's Travels and Adventures*, Chap. XVII; and Emma H. Blair, *Indian Tribes of the Upper Mississippi Valley* (Cleveland, 1911), I, 126-132. The ancient superstitions concerning the bear still persist among the Ottawa and Chippewa of Michigan and Wisconsin.

2 Harry E. Cole, *Baraboo Bear Tales* (Baraboo, 1915).

3 George W. Sears ("Nessmuk"), *Woodcraft* (New York, 1884), Chap. VIII. Reprinted in *Michigan History Magazine*, XV, 634-644.

4 N. A. Woods, *The Prince of Wales in Canada and the United States* (London, 1861), Chap. 15.

5 *The Chautauquan*, XXII, 202.

6 Willis E. Barber, in M. M. Quaife, *Wisconsin, Its History and Its People* (Chicago, 1924), II, 382-383.

Chapter 18

Cream City Birth Pangs

MILWAUKEE and Chicago have many things in common. Both are great industrial centers on the west shore of Lake Michigan; rivers divide both into three "sides"—North, South and West; both are ancient Indian village sites and early fur-trade centers; both retain their Indian names, whose meaning no man certainly knows; both are inhabited by a congeries of peoples drawn from many nations and races.

Of Milwaukee this last was always true. Our first description of the place was written by Father St. Cosme in 1698: "This is a River where there is a Village which has been a large one, consisting of Mascouten, Reynards, and some Poux. We stayed there two days, partly because of the wind [on the lake] and partly to recruit our people a little, because there is an abundance of Duck and teal in the river."

Already, it will be noted, Chicago had a north shore rival, although it is necessary to add that after sampling its attractions the travelers resumed their journey to the southern metropolis. Eighty years later, in 1779, Captain Robertson of His Royal Majesty's sloop *Felicity* found the Milwaukeeans "a mixed Tribe of different nations," and in 1817, U. S. Indian Agent Bowyer affirmed that they were "composed of renigadoes from all the tribes about them, viz., the Saques, Foxes, Chippewas, Menominees, Winnebagoes, and Potawatomies." Since the total population numbered only 300 warriors and their families, the mixture was pretty complete.

Today, as of old, the people who dwell around Milwaukee Bay are a mixture distilled from many nations, and still the townsmen disagree volubly among themselves upon almost every social and political issue that arises. In the World War of 1914-1918 it was widely feared that only the presence of the United States Army would restrain the disloyal activities of Milwaukee's Germanic citizens; especially was it feared that the day of the universal draft registration would be attended by bloodshed and rioting. No troops were sent, and no outbreak occurred, and General Charles King who, although himself of purest Yankee descent, knew his fellow townsmen, had the satisfaction of reporting to his military superior at Chicago about four o'clock in the morning: "Registration completed in Milwaukee County without disorder save for a fist-fight at one enrolling-booth between two young fellows of Germanic descent who both insisted on being first in line."

Such contentions are old stuff in Milwaukee. As long ago as 1779 Major De Peyster, the British commandant at Mackinac, described the townsmen as "a horrid set of refractory Indians," and uttered threats of dire chastisement to be inflicted upon them.[1] This meant, of course, that they had been won over to the rebel cause by the blandishments of George Rogers Clark, who had invaded the French Illinois towns and to whose banner the natives as far north as Milwaukee had flocked. This same autumn the spokesmen of King George aboard the *Felicity* vainly endeavored to win back the disgruntled Milwaukee chiefs "by fair means or foul." A generation later, in the War of 1812, although most of the natives of Wisconsin sided with the British against the Americans, some of the Milwaukeeans did not, and the spectacle was repeated, the King's agent denouncing them as a set of "imposters," unworthy to share the royal bounty.

Wherever the Indian went the white trader followed, and it may reasonably be assumed that traders resided at Milwaukee more or less regularly throughout the French period. We have specific mention of this in 1743 and again in 1762, when a band of natives from "Milwaky" visited the commandant at Green Bay to make "great complaint of the trader amongst them."[2]

The name of this trader is unknown, but two years later we come upon one who lived many years at Milwaukee. The Pontiac War began in 1763 and Wisconsin, as usual, was the scene of divided counsels. Two English traders were murdered and plots were formed to do away with several more.[3] A Frenchman who exerted his influence to save them was St. Pierre of Milwaukee. We have no knowledge of his earlier history, but it is a reasonable surmise that he belonged to the well-known Canadian family of Le Gardeur St. Pierre. Jean Paul Le Gardeur was a grandson of Jean Nicolet, the discoverer of Lake

Michigan, and a well-known explorer and army officer. His son, Jacques Le Gardeur, Sieur de St. Pierre, was long active in the North- west as trader, explorer and army officer. In 1753 he was sent to the upper Ohio where he received the young Virginian, George Wash- ington, who had been sent by Governor Dinwiddie of Virginia to demand that the French withdraw from the Ohio country. Although he treated Washington with utmost courtesy, he repelled the Gov- ernor's demand with vigor, and the message he sent back in answer to it is a model of military dignity and firmness.[4]

Our information concerning the Milwaukee trader is fragmentary, but it suffices to fix upon him the distinction of being the first known white resident of the place. He was living there in 1766 when he dispatched a canoeload of corn to Mackinac and in 1774 when he again sent two canoes to that place. Presumably he was still there when John Askin sent the *Archange* to Green Bay and Milwaukee in 1778 "in search of corn." He was still there in 1779, when the *Felicity* visited Milwaukee, and Joseph St. Pierre, who may have been a son or other relative, was there in 1800 and in 1807. In 1839 an aged Indian pointed out the site of St. Pierre's house at the corner of Fifth and Chestnut Streets. Evidently he was a long-time resident of Mil- waukee, and until information not now available shall come to light he must continue to bear the distinction of being the great city's first known white inhabitant.[5]

There were, of course, other traders in Wisconsin in the closing decades of the eighteenth century, some of whom settled at Mil- waukee. In 1925 the Milwaukee Old Settlers' Club unveiled in Mitchell Park a bronze tablet with inscription: "On this site the first permanent fur trader Jacques Vieau in 1795 built his cabin, the first house in Milwaukee." When the present writer ventured to observe that existing documentary evidence indicated that Vieau was neither the first "permanent" trader nor his cabin the first house at Mil- waukee, the Old Settlers rallied to the defense of their tablet, and a spokesman for the club prepared and read before it a fourteen-page argument in support of the statements concerning Vieau and his house.[6]

Yet the contemporary proof of their inaccuracy is readily available. Quite apart from St. Pierre, whose long residence at Milwaukee beginning as early as 1764 has been noted, there were others with a better claim than Vieau to the title of first resident trader.

One of them was Francis Laframboise, whose brother Alexis began trading at Milwaukee in 1784 or 1785. Somewhat later Alexis placed Francis in charge at Milwaukee and himself remained at Mackinac where he died, a prominent citizen and a captain of militia, April 2, 1800. Francis lived with a Potawatomi wife by whom he had several half-breed children. He is also reputed to have been unsuccessful in trade and largely on these grounds, apparently, the local historians have passed him by in their search for the first Milwaukee settler.[7] In 1800, however, he mortgaged his property at Milwaukee to Joseph Laframboise of Mackinac, who may have been his brother. The list included a lot of ground, one acre square, two houses, a store, a milk-house, stable and a barn. It also included six horses, four oxen, three cows, a colt, and "other property" unitemized.[8] Although this inventory is less impressive than the list of property which the Chicago trader, Point Sable, sold this same year to Jean Lalime, it completely disposes of the idea that Laframboise was a mere blanketed squaw man living in a bark tepee or dugout.

Half a dozen years later, John Kinzie of Chicago purchased from Laframboise several head of livestock. Soon afterward Joseph Laframboise died, and Claude Laframboise, as his administrator, made a demand upon Kinzie for payment for the livestock or for their immediate surrender on the ground that the animals sold to him were identical with the ones mortgaged to Joseph in 1800. Kinzie promptly engaged a lawyer and began collecting affidavits from other Milwaukeeans in support of the contention that the animals he had purchased were not the ones which Francis Laframboise had mortgaged.

Our only interest in the ancient dispute lies in the incidental light the correspondence sheds upon the Milwaukee community of 150 years ago. One of the letters written by Francis Laframboise shows that he was still living in 1807 and that he had been selling a considerable amount of livestock not long before. Other Milwaukeeans of the year 1800 who testified concerning the property of Francis were Joseph St. Pierre and Antoine Le Clair. The old-age recollections of Antoine Le Clair, Jr., written long afterward, tell us much about his father, the signer of Kinzie's affidavit.[9] According to his son, he removed from St. Joseph to Milwaukee in 1800 and from Milwaukee to Peoria in 1809. In 1802 Joseph Laframboise removed from Mackinac to Milwaukee where he became Le Clair's competitor in trade.

"He and Le Clair kept Mackinac blankets, ammunition, cheap and coarse calicoes, cloths, tobacco, pipes, knives, awls, needles, and vermillion paint, but no liquor. These articles were exchanged for furs and peltries, which Le Clair took to Detroit and sold for goods, while Laframboise took his furs and peltries to Mackinac. Le Clair would go to Detroit in the spring, select his goods, and about the month of May a small sailing vessel would leave Detroit with his purchases and those of William Burnett stationed at the mouth of the St. Joseph, and John Kinzie and Robert Forsyth at Chicago, and deliver them. The same vessel probably brought goods for the Mackinac traders. Thus were matters of transit managed on upper Lake Michigan from about 1800 to 1809."

Le Clair further remembered Joseph Laframboise as "a fine worthy man" who left Milwaukee and returned to Mackinac about the year 1807; the date of this removal must have been considerably earlier, however, for he was killed en route to his station on Grand River in the autumn of 1806. Of him and his wife, Madeline Marcot, an Ottawa woman, Mrs. Elizabeth Baird has left a charming characterization.[10] He was a very devout man and especially careful in his observance of the Angelus.

"Out in the Indian country, timed by his watch, he was as faithful in this discharge of duty as elsewhere. Whenever in any town when the bells of his church rang out . . . at six in the morning, at noon, and at six in the evening, he and his family paid reverent heed to it. Madame Laframboise, his widow, maintained this custom as long as she lived, and it was very impressive. The moment the *Angelus* sounded she would drop her work, make the sign of the cross, and with bowed head and crossed hands would say the short prayers, which did not last much longer than the solemn ringing of the bells.

"In 1809 Laframboise left Mackinac with his wife and baby boy (his daughter being at Montreal at school) for his usual wintering place on the upper part of Grand River in Michigan. They traveled in Mackinac boats, or bateaux. There were two boats with a crew of six men to each. They were also accompanied by their servants—old Angélique, a slave, and her son, Louizon—all whom made a large party. At the last encampment before reaching Grand River, Laframboise, while kneeling in his tent one night, saying his prayers, was shot dead by an Indian who had previously asked for liquor and had been refused. The widowed wife, knowing that she was nearer Grand River than her own home, journeyed on, taking the remains of her husband with her, and had them buried at the only town in that vicinity, which was near the entrance of the river—the present Grand Haven, Michigan.[11]

"The heroic woman then proceeded to her husband's station, where she remained until spring, trading with the Indians. Upon returning to Mackinac she secured a trader's license and continued to pursue the Indian trade for many years. Although she always retained the Indian costume, she had obtained a ready command of the French language, and when past middle age she learned to read. She sent her children to Montreal to be educated, and the eldest, Josette, a graceful and beautiful girl, in 1817 married Captain Benjamin K. Pierce of the U. S. Army, elder brother of a future President of the United States. After the wedding, which the mother and aunt of the bride attended in full Indian costume, Captain Pierce took his wife to his quarters in the fort, while Mrs. Laframboise departed upon her usual winter trading sojourn."

The romance was of short duration, for Mrs. Pierce died in 1821. She was interred on her mother's plot of ground and beside her was placed her young son, Langdon Pierce. To preserve the graves intact the bereaved mother of Mrs. Pierce offered the land for a church site.[12] The offer was accepted and a few years later the old church was removed to the new site, to be subsequently replaced by old Ste. Anne's which still remains in use. In the Pierce family genealogy, a volume of 367 pages, one finds the one-line record, "Benjamin K., b. Aug. 29, 1790; m. —— La Flambau," followed by entries of similar brevity for the Captain's second and third wives.

We return to Jacques Vieau, who according to the confused family memories related by his sons first came to Milwaukee in 1795.[13] He had married Angélique Le Roy of Green Bay, daughter of Joseph Le Roy and a Potawatomi woman, and by her or another consort he had a dozen children. Obviously all of them were mixed bloods, and several of them were born at Milwaukee during Vieau's sojourns there as a trader. These continued more or less regularly for many years, although throughout the entire period he maintained his permanent home at Green Bay, where the remainder of his children were born. According to Andrew Vieau's story, about the year 1797 or 1798 the fur company by which he was employed sent him to winter at the Wisconsin Portage for two or three seasons; a contemporary invoice of merchandise sent into the Indian country from Mackinac in 1808 discloses that this year he was sent to Green Bay, and another clerk, P. J. Lacroix, was stationed at Milwaukee.[14] That Vieau traded at Milwaukee more or less regularly over a long period of years beginning toward the close of the eighteenth century is clear; but nothing in the record supports the contention that his was the first house or that he was the first "permanent" trader there.

More interesting, however, is the fact that Vieau was instrumental in bringing to Milwaukee the man whom all unite in regarding as the "father" of the modern city. This was Solomon Juneau, a native of Lower Canada, who in 1816 came out to Mackinac as a clerk for the American Fur Company. There he was detailed as Vieau's assistant and in 1818 was sent to Milwaukee. He had already married Vieau's daughter Josette, and he soon purchased his father-in-law's interests at Milwaukee. Like Vieau, however, Juneau continued for a decade and a half to maintain his home at Green Bay. Before long Vieau again began trading at Milwaukee, thus becoming a rival of his son-in-law. About the year 1836 Vieau, now an old man,[15] once more retired to live at his home in Green Bay.

Solomon Juneau was a splendid figure physically, six feet four inches tall, with dark curly hair, fine features and an engaging manner. Like Gurdon S. Hubbard of early Chicago fame, he possessed the ability to make the transition from the primitive Indian trade to the world of Yankee industrial civilization, although it was his good fortune to be materially aided in this connection by Morgan L. Martin, his shrewd Yankee partner. Until 1831 Juneau remained the typical French trader of the wilderness era. Sensing its fast-approaching end, apparently, he now began to master the English language and took the steps necessary to become an American citizen. Two years later the tide of American settlement reached Lake Michigan, and it required no great discernment to perceive that an important city must develop on the west shore of the lake. This same year the boom which is still continuing struck Chicago, and Martin perceived that the opportunity was ripe to found another city at Milwaukee. He presented his project to Juneau, who supplied his land preemption, and the two men became equal partners in the enterprise. The Indian title to the land was not quieted until 1835, when they platted a town site and offered the lots in it for sale.

The most hectic land boom the western country ever experienced was at its flood and the success of the enterprise was foreordained. Already the overflow of speculators from Chicago was beginning to spill northward along the lake shore and Juneau afforded all possible encouragement to those who came to Milwaukee. He gave (with Martin) a site for the courthouse, for a lighthouse, for the Catholic Cathedral, and the Protestant Milwaukee Female College. Although his suddenly acquired fortune largely vanished in the panic of 1837, he continued to be regarded as a leading citizen of the new metropolis. He became its first postmaster, and despite his French-Canadian background, when the city was incorporated in 1846 he was elected its first mayor. A better illustration of the magic whereby America transforms her alien-born of whatever breed into enterprising, enthusiastic citizens would be difficult to find, and Milwaukee does well to honor the memory of her founder.

In 1852 Juneau, at the insistence of his wife, left Milwaukee to found the new town of Theresa in Dodge County, which he named in honor of his mother. When he died four years later his remains were returned to Milwaukee for burial, with six Menominee chiefs serving as his pallbearers. Many years later Morgan L. Martin, his partner in the real-estate promotion, paid him this striking tribute:

"[We] were joint owners of the original plat of Milwaukee. We never made any written memorandum of the terms of our partnership, and on account of his residence on the spot he took the principal management of our joint interest for more than three years. At the close, accounts were adjusted and property valued at hundreds of thousands divided, with as little difficulty as you would settle a trifling store bill."[16]

Relations have always been close between Milwaukee and Chicago. Today it is but a two-hour run by auto or train between the two cities, and Chicago daily papers are on sale on the streets of Milwaukee almost as soon as they are in Chicago. In the primitive period the great trail running from Green Bay to Chicago and around the south end of Lake Michigan brought Milwaukee within relatively easy contact with both these cities, while all lake traffic between the Straits of Mackinac and Chicago found Milwaukee an easy port of call.

It naturally followed that visitors to either place were likely to call at the other en route, as did the Seminary priests on their journey from Canada to the lower Mississippi in 1698. In the Fox Wars of a generation later Chicago was more than once the rendezvous of detachments of warriors and Frenchmen proceeding westward to attack the Foxes in Wisconsin. In 1803, when Captain Whistler came from Detroit to Chicago to establish Fort Dearborn, Thomas G. Anderson, a Milwaukee trader, "thought it his duty" to pay a neighborly call upon the newcomers, and mounting his horse made the hundred-mile ride to Chicago to do so.

These are but random illustrations of the relations between the two places. Both Chicago and Milwaukee were within the trade orbit of Mackinac and Detroit and both whites and Indians rather easily migrated from one place to the other. The prolific Laframboise family was represented at Chicago as well as at Milwaukee and Mackinac. Some members of the family were inmates of the household of John Kinzie, the Chicago trader, and when Kinzie in the spring of 1812 killed Jean Lalime in a personal affray he fled to Milwaukee for refuge. A little later this same summer, on the eve of the Chicago Massacre, three members of the local militia company which Captain Heald had organized deserted to Milwaukee. Evidently they were either French or mixed bloods who felt safer among the Indians than they did at Chicago among the whites.

[1] *Wisconsin Historical Collections*, XVIII, 384.
[2] Journal of Lieutenant Gorrell, in *Wisconsin Historical Collections*, Vol. I.
[3] *Wisconsin Historical Collections*, XVIII, 267-268.

[4] For the career of Le Gardeur see *Bulletin Recherches Historiques,* V, 233-236.

[5] For the presence of St. Pierre at Milwaukee in 1766 see John Porteous, "Journal from Schenectady to Mackinac, 1765-67," ms. in Detroit Public Library; for his presence in 1774, see *The John Askin Papers,* I, 52. On the visit of the *Archange* to Milwaukee in 1778, see *Ibid.,* 75, 91, 99.

[6] *Jacques Vieau and his House,* paper read before the Old Settlers' Club of Milwaukee County, December 6, 1925, by K. K. Kennan.

[7] See Kennan, 12-14, who supposes that Alexis "simply made annual excursions from his home in Mackinac with a stock of trinkets and goods which he exchanged for furs"; and that Francis "had some sort of structure . . . more in the nature of a bark hut or dugout than anything which could properly be called a house."

[8] For this and succeeding statements I have drawn upon the correspondence and papers relating to the dispute between Claude LaFramboise and John Kinzie in 1807 over the legal title to certain livestock which Kinzie had recently purchased from Francis Laframboise. These documents are preserved among the Solomon Sibley Papers in the Burton Historical Collection, Detroit Public Library.

[9] Printed in *Wisconsin Historical Collections,* XI, 238-242.

[10] For her story see *Wisconsin Historical Collections,* XIV, 17-64.

[11] Laframboise was killed in the autumn of 1806 instead of 1809 as here stated. The date is established by a comparison of Mrs. Baird's narrative with statements in letter of Claude Laframboise to John Kinzie, June 11, 1807, and letter of George Schindler to Solomon Sibley, July 9, 1807, mss. in Burton Historical Collection, Detroit Public Library.

[12] Rev. A. I. Rezek, *History of the Diocese of Sault Ste. Marie and Marquette* (Houghton, 1907), II, 177-178.

[13] One son was born in 1815 (perhaps 1818) and the other in 1820, hence they had no personal knowledge of the date of their father's first coming to Milwaukee; their statements upon matters concerning which they should have had accurate knowledge are so contradictory that no reliance can be placed on the statement that their father came to Milwaukee in 1795. Andrew said he was born in 1815 but Peter (himself born in 1820) said 1818 was the correct year. Andrew affirmed that their mother was "about 105 years" old at the time of her death in 1862. This would have made her 63 when Peter was born in 1820, and she had another child subsequent to Peter. Andrew stated that his father was born in 1757 and a page later fixed the date at 1751; while Buck, the historian of early Milwaukee, believes that 1767 was the correct year. Andrew stated that his father had twelve children, while Peter said there were thirteen. The latter supposed his father came to Milwaukee from Montreal about 1776, and Andrew fixed the year as 1793. It seems obvious that no dependence can be placed upon the accuracy of such old-age memories as these, yet it is to them that we owe most of whatever knowledge we possess concerning the career of Jacques Vieau. For their narratives see *Wisconsin Historical Collections,* XI, 218-233 and XV, 458-469.

[14] Mss. among Solomon Sibley Papers, Burton Historical Collection, Detroit Public Library.

[15] Peter Vieau says "then 74 years old," thereby giving us 1762 as still another birth year for his father.

[16] Martin's narrative, in *Wisconsin Historical Collections,* XI, 406. See also Edwin S. Mack's monograph on the founding of Milwaukee in Wisconsin Historical Society, *Proceedings* for 1906, 194-207.

Chapter 19

The Mystery of the "Southerly Bend"

At OLD Chillicothe in the autumn of 1802 the constitutional fathers of Ohio were engaged in their task of framing a government for the new state when into their midst strolled an ancient hunter, clad in garments of buckskin and carrying a long Kentucky rifle. The state makers were themselves frontiersmen who saw nothing remarkable in the old man's appearance, but when he began to talk they listened with rapt attention. He had come from the wilds of Lake Michigan and he warned the legislators to watch their step, for the maps they were using were all wrong and the great lake really extended many miles farther south than the map makers had led them to believe.

To understand their concern over this information we must examine the Ordinance of 1787, enacted by Congress for the government of the territory northwest of the Ohio River. The close of the Revolution had left the new nation in possesion of a vast colonial domain stretching from the Alleghenies to the Mississippi and from the Great Lakes to Spanish Florida. As yet it was chiefly a wilderness, but already settlers had begun pouring into it, particularly in the area lying south of the Ohio. Hardly had the colonies gained their national independence, therefore, when they were forced to consider the problem of how they should govern their own colonial domain. The solution they reached is one of the happiest political discoveries ever made. Instead of holding the people of the new country in a state of permanent colonial dependence they would establish and administer temporary governments over them, with the promise that as soon as the country was sufficiently settled new states would be organized and admitted to the Union as full and equal partners of the original thirteen.

The enactment of the Ordinance of 1787 marks the first application of this policy. It created a single territorial government for the entire Northwest Territory; but looking to the future it provided that not less than three states nor more than five should ultimately be organized, guaranteeing that each should be admitted to the Union upon attaining a free white population of 60,000 persons. If only three states were created their boundaries were to be approximately the same as those of present-day Ohio, Indiana and Illinois, projected northward to Canada. But Congress might, at its future discretion, form either one or two additional states "in that part of the said territory lying north of an east and west line drawn through the southerly bend or extreme of Lake Michigan."

Having in view the contemporary state of ignorance of the geography of the western country, one can only admire the hardihood of the Congress of 1787 in thus making detailed provision for its division into future states. But legislators have ever acted in this fashion, leaving to future generations the burden of correcting their blunders as best they may. The provisions we have recited planted the seeds of vast future turmoil whose issue altered for all coming time the geographical and political complexion of every one of the states of the Old Northwest, inducing one careful historian to ponder whether the ancient hunter at Chillicothe may not have been "the evil one himself."

In every generation one looks to the map makers for geographical information. The map of British North America made by John Mitchell and published at London in 1755 exerted a compelling influence for almost a century. It was used as the basis for the boundary decisions in the discussions attending the making of the treaty of peace of 1783 and either it or other maps made like it undoubtedly provided the geographical ideas entertained by the authors of the Ordinance of 1787. But the old hunter had learned that the maps of Lake Michigan were grossly inaccurate, since the lake actually extended fifty miles or more farther south than they commonly represented. It followed that a line drawn eastward through its "southerly bend" might not strike Lake Erie at all, but fall instead to the south of that body of water.

This consideration explains the concern of the constitution makers over the old hunter's information. They naturally desired that Ohio should extend to Lake Erie, and they were further concerned to have within their state the mouth of the Maumee River and the site of the great city which would one day arise there. Since no one really knew whether the "Ordinance Line" would intersect the west end of Lake Erie or fall below it, they proceeded to insert in the boundary clauses of the new constitution a proviso to the effect that if the Ordinance Line should prove to fall south of the mouth of the Maumee, then with the consent of Congress the northern boundary of the state should be a straight line drawn from the southerly extreme of Lake Michigan to the northeast cape of Maumee Bay.

Thus one of the articles of compact declared in 1787 to be "forever unalterable, unless by common consent" was calmly marked for destruction within fifteen years, without consulting the wishes of the people of future Michigan and Wisconsin. As it turned out, over thirty years passed before the issue was finally settled, years marked by a succession of political errors and vain efforts to remedy them which left a permanent mark upon all five states of the Old Northwest. By a curious perversity of fate, Congress never formally admitted Ohio to the Union, and to this day there is no agreement among scholars upon the birth date of the state. Hence the effort of the Ohio convention to repeal an important provision of the Ordinance of 1787, to which that state owed its very existence, passed for the moment unnoticed. But in January 1805 Congress created Michigan Territory with the Ordinance Line as its southern boundary, thereby rejecting, at least by implication, the boundary proviso of the Ohio constitution. At Maumee Rapids was an ancient French-British trading center to which a considerable number of American families were added in the years following 1796. This community was a natural commercial and geographical outpost of Detroit, and it was separated from southern Ohio by a wide wilderness as well as by the Indian ownership of the country stretching southward to the Greenville Treaty line. Quite as a matter of course, therefore, it was treated as belonging to Michigan Territory and was so governed for over a third of a century.

With the close of the War of 1812 the issue of the disputed boundary, hitherto purely academic, sprang to life. For several years the attention of all Ohioans had been directed northward, and thousands of soldiers had served in the campaigns for the defense of the state and the recovery of Michigan Territory, which had been lost to the British in the summer of 1812. Even before the war began, Congress on May 20, 1812, had authorized the President to have the northern and western boundaries of Ohio surveyed and marked in accordance with the Ohio Enabling Act of April 30, 1802, but the advent of hostilities had compelled the postponement of the task. With the war ended, this cause for delay was removed, and in August 1816 the Commissioner of the General Land Office directed that the work be undertaken.

The surveyor, William Harris, was an Ohioan and instead of running and marking the Ordinance Line, as the Act of 1812 and the instructions of his superior directed, with calm contempt for his commission he surveyed the line demanded by the Ohio constitutional proviso of 1802 and reported his performance both to his official superior and to the Governor of Ohio. Thereupon the Ohio Legislature made haste to "ratify" the Harris line as the northern boundary of the state.

Even before this the initial rape of Michigan's southern border had been perpetrated by Indiana, which became a state in 1816. The bill authorizing her to frame a state constitution was first introduced on January 5, 1816, and it became a law on April 13. Between these two dates, in the course of its passage through Congress the clause fixing the Ordinance Line of 1787 as the northern boundary of the state was quietly altered to "an east and west line drawn through a point ten miles north of the southern extreme of Lake Michigan." This extension deprived Michigan of about 1,100 square miles of her best soil, together with such future cities as Elkhart, South Bend and Michigan City and the lake shore from Gary eastward to the present Michigan line. Even so, Indiana's partisans were disappointed, for they had tried to fix the boundary at 42 degrees, some eighteen miles still farther north. Had this been done, Michigan would have lost 1,800 more square miles of territory, comprising the larger portion of present-day Berrien, Cass, St. Joseph and Branch Counties.

It may be doubted whether anyone in Michigan even heard of Indiana's raid upon her territory before the passage of the law of April 13, 1816. Had it been otherwise, the territory, without a spokesman in Congress and still reeling from the blows dealt her in the late war, was in no condition to make effective protest. But when the report of the Harris survey of the Ohio boundary became known, the governor and judges of Michigan promptly addressed an eloquent protest to Congress against the impending aggression; in doing so they made formal record of their nonacquiescence in the success of the Indiana raid.

This memorial stirred the Secretary of the Treasury to order the re-marking of the Ohio boundary in compliance with the Act of 1812, and this was done by Surveyor John Fulton in the summer of 1818. His survey of the Ordinance Line placed it five miles south of the Harris line at the Indiana boundary and eight miles south of it at the Lake Erie end. The intervening tract of some 468 square miles, known ever since as the "Toledo Strip," was thus marked out as the area in controversy, and it now became clear that the Ordinance Line intersected Lake Erie, as Ohio had feared, east of the mouth of the Maumee.

Reports of both surveys were transmitted to Congress, where the matter rested until the summer of 1832. Meanwhile the settlement of southern Michigan and northern Ohio was progressing rapidly, and the latter state, encouraged by the example of New York, was embarking upon a program of canal construction, one of whose leading features was a waterway running from Lake Erie by way of the Maumee and Miami Rivers to the Ohio. This improvement would insure the development of an important city at the mouth of the Maumee, and the prevalent economic ideas made intolerable to Ohioans the prospect that the city their enterprise was to create should belong to another state.

To the people of Michigan the issue seemed equally clear and vital. The population and the agricultural resources of the territory were chiefly confined to its southern end and to lose the Toledo strip would mean a material curtailment of both. Moreover it had been guaranteed to Michigan in the most solemn language known to political science, and since the first establishment of the territory she had exercised jurisdiction over it. If political guarantees had any meaning, her right to it was as clear as to the city of Detroit itself.

About this time, too, came an assault upon her borders from another direction. Following the admission of Illinois to the Union in 1818 the territory to the northward which we now know as Wisconsin was attached to Michigan. This union was regarded as temporary, however, and as early as 1824 agitation for the organization of a new territory west of Lake Michigan was begun. In 1828 the House Committee on Territories gave its approval to the measure, but the citizens of Detroit interposed an effective veto since the boundary clauses of the bill had been drawn to include in the new territory Mackinac and the Sault, which had belonged to Michigan Territory since its organization in 1805.

Faced thus with threats of dismemberment on all sides, Michigan's leaders rallied to the defense, and one of the last acts of Governor Cass before entering President Jackson's cabinet in 1831 was to submit a message to the Territorial Legislature reviewing the history of the several boundary issues and making formal official record of Michigan's opposition to the raids in progress. By 1832 the voters were demanding admission to statehood, which Ohio's representatives in Congress strenuously opposed until the troublesome boundary issue should be determined to their satisfaction.

At this juncture of affairs the twenty-two-year-old Governor of Michigan, Stevens T. Mason, initiated a new and revolutionary course of action. Addressing the Territorial Legislature on September 1, 1834, he urged that the territory abandon the role of suppliant, and after having established by a census her possession of the 60,000 inhabitants which entitled her to statehood, organize a state government, elect senators and representatives in Congress and demand admission to the Union as a matter of right.

This program was executed in the course of the following year. The census, promptly ordered by the Legislature, disclosed a population of over 85,000 in the counties east of Lake Michigan. With this fact established, a constitutional convention was called to meet at Detroit in May 1835. Since its members knew they were engaged in a revolutionary procedure they stated their case in the document in language which breathed the spirit of 1776. In October the voters approved their work by an overwhelming majority (6,299 votes to 1,359), a complete set of state officials was elected and the new state government went into peaceable operation.

The fact that the revolution was accomplished during the administration of President Jackson, who in 1832 had crushed the incipient rebellion in South Carolina, detracts nothing from the boldness of the proceeding. Although the President sought to stay its progress by dismissing Governor Mason from office and appointing John S. Horner of Virginia to replace him, he made no real effort to support the authority of that luckless official, who upon reaching Michigan was publicly jeered at, rotten-egged and for the rest completely ignored.

So ingloriously after thirty-one years of activity Michigan Territory winked out of existence. In its stead had come into being a state *de facto,* which had authority then and ever since recognized by the people of Michigan, but its legality was denied and its existence ignored by the national government. Under its authority taxes were levied, justice was administered and civil contracts were made and enforced. The situation was anomalous and could not last, but for almost a year and a half Michigan continued as a state *out of the Union,* while her people pursued their daily vocations as peaceably and securely as ever before or since.

Some solution of the impasse, for which the cowardice of earlier Congresses was primarily responsible, must evidently be found. Although the issue at stake was vital to the welfare of three great commonwealths a spirit of levity characteristic of American public life tempered the determination with which the conflict was waged. The ultimate victory of Ohio was foreordained. A sovereign state of a million population, she carried a weight at the ballot box and at Washington by which puny Michigan, a dependent territory one-tenth as populous, could not fail to be overborne. To Ohio's own influence was added also, as the struggle progressed, the votes of Indiana and Illinois, whose northern boundaries had also been established in disregard of the Ordinance Line. Although both Michigan and Ohio summoned their militia to arms and the two governors led their respective armies to the tented field, no fighting ensued nor was any seriously intended. We refrain, therefore, from dwelling upon the comic opera aspects of the Toledo War, to save our space for the statement of its substantial results.

In February 1835 the Ohio Legislature passed an act extending the boundaries of the three adjacent counties to the Harris line and appointing commissioners to run and re-mark it. Michigan replied with an act providing heavy penalties for any infringement upon her territory. Governor Mason led a Michigan army to Toledo and Governor Lucas an Ohio army to Perrysburg. President Jackson dispatched a peace delegation to pour oil on the troubled waters and in general exerted his influence to prevent the commission of actual violence. Supported by the sober good sense of the warring factions, these measures proved successful and the further conduct of the controversy was transferred from the armed frontier to the halls of Congress at Washington.

There a long debate ensued which terminated in a characteristic political compromise. The election of 1836 was close at hand, and whatever the abstract merit of Michigan's cause might be, not even President Jackson could afford to antagonize the voters of Ohio, Indiana and Illinois. On April 2, 1836, therefore, an act was passed for the admission of Michigan to the Union, conditional upon her prior assent, by a convention of delegates elected for the purpose, to the state boundaries which the act prescribed.

To one unaccustomed to practical American politics, these were sufficiently surprising. On the south, Indiana was to retain her existing boundary, while Ohio was to be given the Harris line, running to the north cape of Maumee Bay, for which she had all along contended. To Michigan, as a recompense for the rape thus inflicted upon her, was tossed unasked and undesired that portion of the Upper Peninsula extending westward from the meridian of Mackinac to the present Wisconsin boundary.

Thus was demonstrated anew the principle that in democratic America might at the ballot box makes right. But the people of Michigan still remained unreconciled to the demonstration. The state legislature made due provision for a "Convention of Assent" to meet at Ann Arbor on September 26. It met, rejected the proffered boundaries by a decisive vote and adjourned, leaving matters thus at a complete stalemate.

But it is the business of rulers to govern and of politicians to gain offices. A whole school of the latter, thirsting for the sweets of office, was eagerly awaiting the attainment of statehood to gain its ends. A few Democratic party leaders assumed the authority to convoke a second "Convention of Assent" at Ann Arbor on December 14, 1836. It met and although wholly without legal status promptly "assented" to the act of Congress. President Jackson, eager for any peaceable exit from his difficulties, with a straight face reported to Congress that Michigan had complied with the terms of its conditional act of admission, and on January 26, 1837, that commonwealth became a state *in the Union.*

But the discord unloosed by the story which the ancient hunter related to the constitutional fathers of Ohio in 1802 was far from ended.

Youngest of all the states of the Old Northwest is Wisconsin, and the reader will not have failed to note that the sop of the Upper Peninsula thrown to Michigan in imagined recompense for the loss of the Toledo Strip was given her at the expense of the future commonwealth west of Lake Michigan. More significant than this, however, was the spoliation Wisconsin had already undergone at the south, when the state of Illinois was admitted. Her enabling act for admission was modeled upon the Indiana act of 1816 and since that state had obtained an extension northward of ten miles beyond the Ordinance Line of 1787, the Illinois bill, as it was first introduced, provided for a like extension. Although all Illinois contained but a handful of white inhabitants, and these were concentrated at the extreme southern end of the state, her delegate in Congress procured an amendment which fixed the northern boundary at the line of 42° 30′.

This was sixty-one miles north of the Ordinance Line, and fifty-one north of the ten-mile extension as first proposed. In justification of this fresh flouting of the "forever unalterable" Ordinance, it was argued that with only an outlet on the Mississippi Illinois would become tied to the south, commercially as well as sentimentally; with an extensive Lake Michigan coast line she would establish commercial and other relations with New York and the eastern states. Although this reasoning sounded convincing, it utterly failed to foresee that the introduction of the iron horse, already close at hand, would go far to nullify all the arguments based upon a water-borne transportation economy.

Since there was no one to protest the Illinois grab, it was consummated as easily as that of Indiana two years earlier. By it, 8,000 square miles of farmland, embracing practically fourteen Illinois counties, were added to that state at the expense of Wisconsin. Within the area are such cities as Freeport, Galena, Rockford, Elgin and Waukegan; above all others in importance is, of course, Chicago and its adjoining suburbs. Today more than half the population and probably a larger proportion of the wealth of the entire state lies within the sixty-one-mile northern belt which would have belonged to Wisconsin if the Ordinance Line of 1787 had been preserved inviolate.

The protest of Wisconsin, although belated, made up in vigor what it lacked in promptness. Wisconsin Territory was set off from Michigan in the summer of 1836 and within two years Governor Dodge was urging the legislature to provide for a popular referendum on statehood. The electorate proved indifferent, however, and for several years nothing was done, although Governor Doty, Dodge's successor, persistently advocated the statehood question. With it, too, he included the demand for the restoration of Wisconsin's "original" boundaries, by which he meant the areas lost to Illinois in 1818 and to Michigan in 1837. No one really cared about the northern area, however, which was a distant and supposedly worthless wilderness. The fourteen Illinois counties, close at hand and already the seat of thriving towns and settlements, were another matter. In December 1843 Governor Doty devoted almost all of his annual message to the legislature to an argument in favor of statehood and the reclaiming of the "original boundaries." The right of the people to form a state government without awaiting permission from Congress was asserted, and the authority of that body to refuse admission on the score of unsatisfactory state boundaries was denied. *"A state out of the Union,"* observed the governor, "has as good a right to her established boundaries as a state in it," and a large part of the message was devoted to a demonstration of Wisconsin's supposed right to the Michigan Upper Peninsula and northern Illinois.

This appeal met an enthusiastic reception in the legislature. A long report on the boundaries was made to the council by Moses Strong, wherein that enthusiastic exponent of advanced democracy fairly outdid the language of Governor Doty in asserting the rights and grievances of the territory as against the tyranny of Congress. That body, unmindful of its duty to preserve the integrity of infant Wisconsin, had at various times alienated vast sections of her territory to Illinois, Michigan and Great Britain. Wisconsin's right to form a state government and resume control of the territory of which she had been despoiled was unquestionable. But the probable consequences of such action must be considered; none of the usurping powers would be disposed tamely to yield possession of the areas they had filched from Wisconsin. The people "at the very outset of [their] political existence [would] find [them]selves involved in a controversy of the most serious character with the states of Illinois and Michigan and the kingdom of Great Britain." The probability that the United States would come to the aid of Wisconsin in such a struggle was admitted to be slight.

From this seeming grave of defeated hopes the budding politician drew forth a shining consolation prize. Although Congress could not restore to Wisconsin her despoiled territory, it was still within the power of that body to make *atonement* for the wrongs it had perpetrated against the helpless territory. This might suitably take the shape of providing such internal improvements as the people of Wisconsin fancied but were themselves unable or unwilling to pay for. Harbors at Milwaukee, Racine and other lake ports, a railroad across the territory from Lake Michigan to the Mississippi, canals and the improvement of rivers for navigation were the works modestly suggested.

The outcome of the labored argument was the dispatch of a memorial to Congress from the Wisconsin legislature which surely is as strange a document as any ever presented to that august body. It summed up the arguments and conclusions we have surveyed, and presented the demand for *atonement* in the form of an ultimatum but thinly veiled. Congress was called upon "to do justice, while yet it is not too late, to a people who have hitherto been weak and unprotected, but who are rapidly rising to giant greatness, and who at no distant day will show to the world that they lack neither the disposition nor the ability to protect themselves." If, unhappily, Congress should prove deaf to this appeal for justice, "or refuse to atone for the wrongs they have done us," let it beware of the consequences, for

"Wisconsin will never peaceably submit to so gross a violation of her rights, and after she has done all to obtain a peaceable redress of her wrongs which reason demands, and shall have failed, she will resort to every other means in her power to protect and preserve her rights," for "whatever the sacrifice *the integrity of her boundaries must be observed.*"

The governors of Ohio and Michigan a decade earlier had led their armies to the Toledo Strip to do battle for the area in dispute. The politicians of Wisconsin, however, exhausted their belligerency in oratorical blasts of east wind. When the ineffectiveness of these methods became apparent, resort was had to the normal procedure by which the territorial delegate to Congress asked permission to introduce an enabling act for Wisconsin. The bill was introduced in the House of Representatives in January 1846 and was adopted by that body with but little discussion on June 9. The following day, however, Rockwell of Connecticut moved its reconsideration, stating that the Wisconsin delegate had inserted in it, without the knowledge of the House, provisions which that body would never knowingly grant. The objectionable matter pertained to the old issue of boundaries. Against the ineffectual opposition of Delegate Martin the bill was reconsidered and the obnoxious clauses were stricken out. It was passed by the Senate without further amendment and became a law early in August. In the entire course of its passage through Congress the only issue raised was over the boundary question; on this, that body squelched the aspirations of the territory as ruthlessly as the similar aspirations of Michigan had been denied a decade earlier.

Before statehood was finally achieved Wisconsin underwent another marked curtailment of her borders, involving still another violation of the "unalterable" compacts of 1787. According to that document "not less than three nor more than five states" should be created from the Northwest Territory. But the Wisconsin Enabling Act limited the state on the northwest to the St. Louis and St. Croix rivers, giving to future Minnesota the extensive portion of that state which lies east of the Mississippi River.

Whether the numerous violations of the boundary clauses of the Ordinance of 1787 we have described were necessary or desirable would furnish food for endless discussion. That they materially altered, whether for good or ill, the complexion of all the states of the Old Northwest, however, leaves no room for debate. But for them, Michigan would today possess the rich southern zone which includes such industrial centers as Michigan City, South Bend and Toledo, while on the north she would lack the relatively barren and unprosperous area embracing most of the Michigan Upper Peninsula. Indiana would have no harbor on Lake Michigan nor any of the busy industrial centers which stretch westward from Elkhart and South Bend to Gary and the Illinois line. Breath-taking indeed would be Wisconsin's domain, embracing St. Paul and Duluth, the entire southern shore of Lake Superior as far east as the meridian of Mackinac, and on the south the Lake Michigan shore as far as Gary, with corresponding curtailment of the states of Illinois and Minnesota. Perhaps it is just as well that the old hunter, if not the "evil one himself," opened at Chillicothe another Pandora's box of discord over the real position of Lake Michigan's "southerly bend."

Chapter 20

The Tread of Pioneers

***

WHEN, in the thirties, the dweller on the Atlantic seaboard began to listen to the call of the West, the choice of route and of time for making the journey were questions anxiously debated. An article published by the enterprising editor of the *Illinois Monthly Magazine* in November 1831 provided many valuable "hints" for the benefit of prospective immigrants to that state. Although it was written with particular reference to the southern half of Illinois, then the only settled portion of the state, much of the information given applied with equal force to western travel in general.

Most of the conditions described have long since passed away and only by an active effort can the reader now visualize them. The season of the year for making the journey, we learn, would depend upon the mode of conveyance adopted. In the springtime, all *natural* roads west of the mountains were bad from the time the ground thawed until warm weather; as for *artificial* roads, these were so infrequent in the West that the traveler should leave them wholly out of account when planning his journey. In the spring season the rivers were full, the bottom lands were drowned and travel in any direction was impeded or rendered wholly impossible by high water; and the traveler by land at this season must expect to wade through mire and water knee-deep or, "peradventure," even deeper.

These same conditions, however, made the spring the best season for travel by water. The streams were now swollen, rocks and snags were buried deep beneath the surface and the steamboat could glide from place to place, ascending small rivers and finding its way to points far removed from the ordinary channels of navigation.

The autumn, on the other hand, was the season for land travel. Then there was ordinarily but little rain and the weather was mild and steady. The roads became hard and good and many of the smaller streams became entirely dry, while others could be forded with ease and safety. This was the season of abundance, also, when crops were ripe and cattle fat and food cheaply and easily procured.

Those who proposed to come west by water, therefore, should plan to make the journey in the spring, while travelers who elected to come by land should set out in September. Both winter and summer were objectionable on account of the extremes of the weather. With good taverns to be found only on main roads and in the large villages, the traveler must be prepared to encounter hardships to which his life in the East had not accustomed him. At times, long stages must be made; the night's shelter might be a one-room cabin filled to overflowing, or no house at all with consequent exposure to the weather. At best the journey would prove a drain upon the traveler's energy and vitality, and if made under the conditions either of winter or of midsummer this strain would be needlessly increased.

Our immediate interest, however, is in the tide of settlement which poured into the upper Northwest. The War of 1812, like every such conflict, produced widespread changes both in the nation and in the lives of individuals. Five hundred thousand men, from a total population of barely 8,000,000, had enlisted in the army for shorter or longer periods. Necessarily their employment was interrupted, their businesses suffered and attachment to their homes was weakened. After the war a severe business depression ensued, further unsettling the lives of thousands. The natural result followed: the flow of westward migration, long since established, swelled to floodtide proportions. Until the late 1820's, however, but little of it was directed toward the upper Northwest which was still almost entirely inaccessible to the ordinary emigrant.

Two important developments were now to hasten the end of this isolation. In 1818 the *Walk-in-the-Water*, the first steamer on the Upper Lakes, was put into service between Black Rock and Detroit, marking the beginning of a relatively dependable means of transportation on the water. In 1825 the Erie Canal was opened and with solemn ceremonial the water of Lake Erie was wedded to the Atlantic in New York Harbor. The economic and social consequences of the two developments were revolutionary in their scope. The wealth of the Northwest, poured into the lap of New York, fixed

MODERN MILWAUKEE

This air view shows today's Milwaukee, the great industrial center which grew from the Indian village described by St. Cosme in 1698.

DADDY OF ALL TYPEWRITERS

C. L. Sholes's first patent for a typewriter was granted June 23, 1868. This machine, now in the Smithsonian Institution, was patented twenty-one days later.

THE LONG HOUSE AT CERESCO

This was the last and best building of the Phalanx, erected about 1849-1850, and succeeding the original Long House.

that city as the metropolis of America, and compelled her seaboard rivals—Boston, Philadelphia, Baltimore and Charleston—to embark upon a feverish race for railroad connections with the interior to retain for themselves a share of the inland commerce. Meanwhile, from New England and the northeastern states as well as from Europe a stream of emigration, pouring westward by the canal and the Great Lakes, rapidly peopled the northern portions of Ohio, Indiana and Illinois, as well as the southern sections of Michigan and Wisconsin.

Although the northwestern wilderness proved an irresistible lure to homeseekers, they paid heavily in toil, privations and hardships for the new homes they obtained. Save for the beautiful oak openings of southern Michigan and the intermittent prairies of Illinois and southern Wisconsin, practically the entire country was densely forested and the work of clearing the land was exceedingly arduous. Broadly speaking, the generation of original settlers gave their lives to the task of transforming the wilderness into cultivated homes to serve as a heritage for their successors.[1]

Regardless of economic or social station, all who came to the Northwest must travel either by land or by water. Emigrants from Europe, New England and New York commonly crossed New York by way of the Erie Canal, or by land along the parallel route of the Genesee Pike to Buffalo. Here they could either embark on a lake vessel for Detroit or other western port, or they could continue to journey overland along the south shore of Lake Erie. Arrived at its western end they might debark at Monroe or Detroit to begin their journey inland or the voyage might be continued around the lakes to Milwaukee or Chicago. The journey by water was relatively easy, although it was not devoid of hardships; while the flimsy lake steamers with their puny engines exposed their passengers to appalling risks—from the elements in case of storm, from fire and from boiler explosions at all times. Then, as always, the traveler possessed of means could purchase certain comforts denied to the poorer emigrant, but no money whatever could purchase avoidance of the fundamental hardships which the vehicles and the highways of the time imposed.

All who came west by land must encounter the hazards of the dreaded Black Swamp at the western end of Lake Erie.[2] Whether in the Black Swamp or elsewhere, the need for passable highways was urgent and practically all Westerners were enthusiastic supporters of the governmental policy of internal improvements. The military disasters suffered in the War of 1812 had taught the government the bitter lesson that it could not defend the western country in the absence of highways over which to move its armies. In 1824 Congress appropriated money for the survey of roads of national importance, and the President allocated one-third of the entire sum to surveying a military highway connecting Detroit, the military center of the Northwest, with Fort Dearborn at Chicago. Thus was born the famed Chicago Road, which followed the general course of the ancient Indian trail, running southwestward by way of Ypsilanti, Coldwater and White Pigeon to the south end of Lake Michigan. The actual survey was begun at Detroit in 1825 and the work of improvement was prosecuted for several years. By 1830 a stage service ran from Detroit as far west as Tecumseh. In 1832 it was extended to Niles and in September 1833 to Chicago.

But standards of highway excellence are purely relative, and the reader must not hastily assume that from this time onward travelers between Detroit and Chicago could complete their journey on any definite schedule, or without danger to life and limb. A young man who journeyed westward from his native New Hampshire in the autumn of 1836 to become a distinguished citizen of Chicago has left us a moving recital of the hardships he encountered.[3]

He wrote to his sister:

"We set out from Detroit on Thursday about noon in a snow storm, or rather, what is worse, half snow and half rain, and only went twelve miles that P.M. such was the bad state of the roads. Not a stone, but all mud and clay and beyond description bad. Never in all my life before did I see such roads. We had no coach, but a long and narrow cart with seats in it. The next morning we set out at 3 o'clock and such was the condition of the roads that we had to go afoot for twelve miles. We had gone about 2 miles when the driver called after us and said his carriage had broken down. There we were, up to the top of our boots in the mud, and what to do we knew not, but at length we espied a log cabin not far distant and we went to it and awakened the inhabitants. There we remained until daylight, when I flung my valise over my shoulder and set out with the other passengers and we had got over the twelve miles and we were taking dinner, when the cart came up. We here jumped in and never stopped for rest until we arrived at Michigan City upon the southeast corner of Lake Michigan, upon the northern boundary of the State of Indiana. To describe to you the roads, sometimes as beautiful as man could wish; sometimes bad enough to have been created by the infernal devil himself, the different landscapes, the various manners of the inhabitants, the flat and rolling prairies, the living of the people, the Indians, or even my own feelings after riding from Friday morn at 3 o'clock to Monday at 9 P.M., I have not time. I could sleep none; if I fell asleep it was only to bump my head against the coach (for we had coaches at different times for about one-fourth of the way) or to risk falling out of the cart. . . . If I left the stage I could get aboard no other as they were always full, never being allowed to take but eight passengers.

"Three of us left [at Michigan City] and went to bed. Never before did I realize the advantages of sleep. In the morning we arose with spirits as buoyant as ever determined to foot it for the other sixty miles. We found a wagon and three men going to Chicago and we put our baggage aboard and kept up with them. We went twenty miles that day to what is called the Beach House, a log cabin 9 miles from any other habitation, close to the Lake Shore. One room was the Ladies cabin and Ladies lodging room and the other was the Bar Room or gentlemen's lodging room. In that small room, *only* 23 lodged that night. The beds were fixed in the manner of births [*sic*] on board a steamboat, one above another—3 tiers."

They arrived in Chicago on Thursday at noon six days out of Detroit, after walking the remainder of the way. Even so the traveler congratulated himself for having chosen the overland route. At the Beach House he overheard talk about a compass and other wreckage coming ashore and next day, a few miles farther on, he came upon a large schooner "that had been washed on shore with her whole crew" and completely wrecked. "Could I but rehearse to some of the people [at home]," he continues, "the sufferings, trials, and misfortunes that I have witnessed a hundred times over in emigrants, they would remain at home and be willing to dig hard for even a competency. One generation can never reap the advantages of Emigration, and why put oneself to such trouble to get away from society, meetings, and schools in order that children may come up wealthy in ignorance?"

Seven years later in 1843, although the railroad was now running as far as Jackson, the hazards of travel, at least in winter, had been little reduced. Two Detroit citizens who departed on the cars bound for Chicago on the morning of January 2 reached their destination on the evening of the sixth.[4] In the five days of travel they had undergone a variety of toils and discomforts no less harrowing than the traveler of 1836 had experienced. Although their train reached Ann Arbor at 2:00 P.M. on Monday, it consumed five hours going the next seven and one-half miles. Here it ceased progress altogether and the handful of passengers, after a considerable delay, were fortunate to obtain a sleigh which carried them on to Dexter.

"At 10 o'clock we sat down to Dinner as mean and miserable as could well be imagined. We [had] a hungry dog along, and we could not coax him to partake. This was the first we [had] had to eat since breakfast at 7 in the morning till 10 at night. Went to bed and cold as it was without any fire the Major declared it fairly . . . produced an unpleasant odour. I wrapt myself entirely in my Blanket and slept fair. Breakfast at the same place and manner. The cars had made their way up and at 11 o'clock we started again. Some 8 or 10 men had gone ahead 3 hours previous to shovel off the track. We concluded that the train from Jackson would meet us soon and they having cleared the track we should get to Jackson in good season. So we put out and kept going until 3 o'clock P.M. and got 10 miles. We then got a sleigh and went to Jackson some 22 miles the coldest day this year. We got to Jackson about 7-½ P.M. Took dinner about 8 o'clock P.M. and nothing to eat since breakfast again. Found the stage about starting so we got aboard. Got to the first station about 12 o'clock at night and found the stage from there had started some 2 hours before we arrived and we could not go on untill next night—a little 7 by 9 shanty dirty and no beds all full. After awhile a couple of *loafers deadheads* as they are termed got up to take the stage back to Jackson and we had the privilege of occupying the one they left for the rest of the night. So Maj[or] and myself went up [to] a small room with 3 beds in it—2 put in each of the 2 beds—the one we were to occupy stood under the roof so that it rested on the foot of the bed—the sheets etc looked as if they might have been used for floor cloths or Dusters for 6 months—however we got along by putting our buffalo at the bottom and Blank[et] over us and slept quite comfortably. We staid there all Day and ate Breakfast and Dinner and it was what we call hard. We had fun sleighing to Michigan City and from there to this place we took wheels. Wednesday and Thursday night rode all night—yesterday it thawed and rained but the wind changed last night and it [is] quite cold."

For those immigrants who availed themselves of the water route, Buffalo was the great port of embarkation. Once afloat on the lakes most travelers going as far as Lake Michigan continued by water as far as Chicago. The voyage around Lake Huron and Lake Michigan was long and frequently stormy and many preferred to avoid it by landing at Detroit or Monroe and making their way by land across southern Michigan and northern Indiana. If this phase of the journey was begun at Detroit the traveler followed the great Chicago Road running southwestward around the head of Lake Michigan to Chicago. A variant of this route, opened in the thirties and known ever since as the Territorial Road, led through Ann Arbor, Jackson and Kalamazoo to St. Joseph on Lake Michigan.[5] On reaching St. Joseph, the traveler crossed the lake by schooner or (later) steamboat to Chicago; while those who followed the Chicago Road from Detroit to Niles sometimes abandoned it here in favor of a passage by boat down the St. Joseph and thence across the lake.

The rapidity with which white civilization spread over the virgin wilderness adjacent to Lake Michigan in the decades following 1830 is little short of incredible. As late as 1820, Michigan Territory, then including all of modern Wisconsin, had less than 9,000 white population. By 1830, this had increased to 31,689 with all but a handful of newcomers located in the southeastern counties of the Lower Michigan Peninsula. In 1840 Michigan alone, reduced to her present boundaries, had a population of 212,000; by 1850 this had increased to 397,000; and by 1860, to 749,000.

Turning to Wisconsin, the area included within the present state contained in 1836 somewhat less than 12,000 white persons; the U. S. Census of 1840 returned almost 31,000, that of 1850, 305,000, and of 1860, 775,000. The census returns for Indiana and Illinois do not disclose with like clarity the rush of settlers into the northern portion of these states, since their southern sections were settled much earlier than the northern and the figures for the total population do not differentiate between the two. In 1821, Governor Cass and Henry R. Schoolcraft, traveling from St. Louis up the Illinois River, encountered not a single white habitation between Peoria and Chicago; and save for a considerable influx of miners to the lead-mine region around Galena, northern Illinois was still practically uninhabited ten years later.[6]

Broadly speaking, the tide of settlement spread over southern Michigan and northern Illinois in the decade of the thirties, roaring onward over Wisconsin and across the Mississippi ten years later. The obvious accompaniment of this rapid filling up of Lake Michigan's imperial hinterland was an astonishing increase in the amount of travel and in the number of ships on the lake itself. Once more a resort to figures will help to give us a background to the story of this magical development.

In 1830 Chicago had no harbor nor any place in the U. S. Census returns. Harbor improvement and growth of population began together in 1833 and for many years the demand for shipping continued to outrun the capacity of new vessels built. As trade and travel increased, contemporary observers found the resources of the language inadequate to express their admiration and amazement over the spectacle of the flocks of freighters and passenger ships which vexed the blue waters of the lakes. For several years Chicago had no appreciable export trade and vessels eastward bound resorted to the sand of the lake shore for ballast. With the filling up of the back country, however, and the opening of radial highways giving it access to Chicago,[7] the process was begun which in less than a generation was to make the city the greatest provision market and one of the greatest ports on the globe. Ten years after the first export statistics were recorded at Chicago in 1836, 1,400 ships departed from the harbor in a single season; fifty years after the tragic arrival of the first steamboat in 1832, there were more than 26,000 arrivals and clearances of vessels, a number greatly exceeding the combined totals for New York, New Orleans and San Francisco.

An interesting glimpse of the throng of early travelers by lake boat is given us in the narrative of the New York editor, Charles Fenno Hoffman, who visited the western country in 1834.[8] Making a tour of the vessel, he encountered amidship "a group of emigrants collected around a stove, where an English mother nursing her infant, a child lying asleep upon a mastiff, and a long-bearded German smoking his meerschaum on the top of a pile of candle-boxes" were the only complete figures amid "an indefinite number of heads, arms, and legs lying about in the most whimsical confusion." Obviously these people were traveling as "deck passengers," supplying their own food and shelter in return for a very low rate of transportation. Proceeding, the observer came upon two "tolerable" cabins on either side of the ship just forward of the wheels, both of which were filled with emigrants more comfortably bestowed. The occupants at the bow of the ship were a horse and several dogs, and as they had been there several days (the ship had twice sought refuge in port from the storms) the place "might have been mistaken for either stable or kennel."

Ascending a ship stairway, Hoffman spent some time surveying the belongings of the emigrants with which it was crowded.

"They differed according to the origin of their owner. The effects of the Yankee were generally limited to a Dearborn wagon, a feather-bed, a saddle and bridle, and some knickknack in the way of a machine for shelling corn, hatchelling flax, or, for aught I know, manufacturing wooden nutmegs for family use. Those of the Englishman are far more numerous; for John Bull, when he wanders from home, would not only, like the roving Trojan, carry his household gods with him into strange lands, but even the fast-anchored isle itself, could he but cut it from its moorings. Whenever, therefore, you see an antique-fashioned looking glass, a decrepit bureau, and some tenderly-preserved old china, you will probably, upon looking further, have the whole house-keeping array of an honest Briton exposed to your view.

"But still further do the Swiss and Germans carry their love of family relics. Mark that quaint-looking wagon which lumbers up a dozen square feet of the deck. You may see a portrait of it among the illuminated letters of a vellum-bound edition of Virgil's Bucolics. It was taken from an Helvetian ancestor that transported Caesar's baggage into winter-quarters. What an indignity it is to overwhelm the triumphal chariot with the beds and ploughs, shovels, saddles, and sideboards, chairs, clocks, and carpets that fill its interior, and to hang those rusty pots and kettles, bakepans, frying pans, and saucepans, from candlesticks, old horse-shoes, and broken tobacco-pipes, like trophies of conquest over Time, along its racked and wheezing sides. That short man yonder, with square shoulders and a crooked pipe in his mouth, is the owner; he, with the woollen cap, that is just raising his blue cotton frock to thrust his hand into the fob of his serrivalleys. That man had probably not the slightest idea of the kind of country he was coming to. His eyes are but now just opening to his new condition; nor will he sacrifice a particle of his useless and expensive trumpery until they are completely open. That man has not yet a thought in common with the people of his new abode around him. He looks, indeed, as if he came from another planet. Visit him on his thriving farm ten years hence, and, except in the single point of language, you will find him (unless he has settled among a nest of his countrymen) at home among his neighbours, and happily conforming to their usages; while that clean-looking Englishman next to him will still be a stranger in the land."

---

[1] For vivid pictures of the experiences of two pioneer families, one in Michigan, the other in Illinois, see William Nowlin, *The Bark Covered House,* and Rebecca Burlend, *A True Picture of Emigration,* both edited by the present writer, in the *Lakeside Classics Series* (Chicago) in 1936 and 1937.

[2] The Black Swamp, about 4,000 square miles in area, comprised several present-day Ohio counties at the southwest corner of Lake Erie, extending from Sandusky Bay to the lower course of the Maumee. Heavily timbered and with an underlying clay foundation impervious to water, during much of the year the swamp resembled a shallow, muck-bottomed lake. Only in extreme cold weather, when it was solidly frozen over, could it be traveled with relative ease, and all who encountered it retained lifelong memories of its horrors. Today, the "swamp" presents a picture of fertile farms and prosperous homesteads as attractive as any in mid-America.

[3] Letter of John Wentworth, Chicago, November 9, 1836, printed in Chicago Historical Society *News Review,* October 1943.

[4] Letter of Samuel A. Hastings to Eurotas P. Hastings, Chicago, June 7, 1843, in Burton Historical Collection, Detroit Public Library.

[5] The two highways are approximately represented today by U. S. Highways 12 and 112.

[6] In 1823 Major Long's exploring expedition was delayed at Chicago a considerable length of time before a guide who could lead it across country to Prairie du Chien could be procured.

[7] For the story of the development of these highways see M. M. Quaife, *Chicago's Highways Old and New. From Indian Trail to Motor Road* (Chicago, 1923).

[8] Charles Fenno Hoffman, *A Winter in the West,* I, 103-109. The particular scenes described were witnessed by Hoffman while traveling from Cleveland to Detroit but the description applies no less to travel on Lake Michigan.

Chapter 21

Utopia—Nineteenth-Century Model

THE Wisconsin Constitution was fashioned a century ago in the heat of a great struggle between radical idealists and conservative standpatters, and so well was the work performed that although Wisconsin has been for a generation the synonym for political experiment and progress, the constitution still continues to satisfy the needs of the twentieth-century commonwealth.

One of the eloquent conservative leaders in the ancient struggle against radicalism was Marshall M. Strong of Racine, to whom "John Barleycorn" in March 1847 paid this tribute:

"How strange it seems, and yet how welcome, in these days of shallow quackery and raving demagogism to listen to a true man! . . . He it was that first dared to "appeal from Alexander drunk to Alexander sober"; he first by his manly stand rolled back the swelling flood of mad fanaticism that threatened to engulf us, and to him will chiefly belong the honor of saving our beloved Wisconsin from being converted into a Fourier phalanx—a playground for lunatics and idiots."[1]

Political movements are the expression in the field of government of those interests which happen to occupy for the time being a foremost place in the minds of the voters. The decade which witnessed the admission of Wisconsin to statehood was marked by a rash of social and economic experiments, which found political expression in the first Wisconsin Constitution of 1846; its decisive repudiation by the voters, despite the well-nigh universal desire for statehood, was chiefly due to the conviction on the part of the majority that it was time to put a check upon the zeal of the experimenters for transmuting their theories into the basic law of the land.

So we see that such problems as those of capital and labor or of production and distribution are not new. A century ago even as now, society was on the march both in Europe and America, and

1848, the very year of Wisconsin's admission to the Union, is still remembered as a year of revolution. Today such terms as "phalanx" and "Fourierism" mean little to the reader, but in 1847 they were as familiar as "Townsend Plan" or "New Deal" or "Share the Wealth" are now. Charles Fourier, the theorist who gave birth to these little-remembered terms, was a Frenchman who quite probably lived and died without ever hearing even the name of Wisconsin. But Albert Brisbane,[2] a keen-minded young American, became his ardent disciple, and in 1840 he published a book, *The Social Destiny of Man,* by which Fourier's theories concerning an ideal organization of society became known to American reformers and radicals.

One of the enthusiastic converts to the new gospel was Horace Greeley, famed editor of the New York *Tribune,* whose columns were freely devoted to expounding it. Under the influence of such advertising, scores of Fourierite colonies, or "phalanxes" were spawned. Most of them met early shipwreck on the hard rocks of reality and all save one have long since been forgotten. The one exception was the Brook Farm Community, established by a group of New England literati who hopefully aspired to settle the vexed problems of capital and labor and the scarcely less difficult one of what to do about domestic "servitude." Needless to say, they succeeded in neither; but the Brook Farmers were fluent talkers who enjoyed a grand time socially as long as their capital lasted.[3]

Pioneer Southport (now Kenosha) was a bit of Yankeedom transplanted into the Wisconsin wilderness. Here in 1842, in a village of half a thousand souls scarcely half a dozen years removed from the primeval forest, a general literary magazine was founded; here·was established Wisconsin's first free public school, and here was assembled a group of men and women whose plain living and high thinking need not suffer by comparison with the palmiest days of Puritan Massachusetts.[4] Obviously such a community would maintain a lyceum, wherein the members discussed such issues of philosophy or politics as were of current interest. On November 21, 1843, the subject of debate was, "Does the system of Fourier present a practicable plan for such a reorganization of society as will guard against our present social evils?" The interest aroused by the discussion led to repeated further debates in which the "merits" of the Fourierite system were explored. One of the participants in them was Warren Chase, a man of thirty, of New England birth and possessed of an inquiring mind. He became a convert to Fourierism, and when taunted by the question why he did not practice it he determined to do so.

From many points of view the enterprise, which soon became known as the Wisconsin Phalanx, was fortunate, but in none more so than in the character of its leader and the choice personnel of those who enlisted under his banner. Unlike many men of radical tendencies, Chase possessed a sober disposition and real executive ability, and no scandal, either sexual or financial, ever tainted the reputation of the colony which he dominated throughout the period of its existence.

The competence of the leader was never better displayed than in the choice of Ebenezer Childs of Green Bay, a shrewd and capable pioneer businessman, to select a suitable location for the home of the "Association." Thoroughly familiar with northeastern Wisconsin, he chose a fertile tract of land in Fond du Lac County which is today one of the garden spots of Wisconsin. The nearest settlement was then twenty miles distant and the acreage secured comprised some of the finest farming land in the state. Through it flowed a small stream, named by the colonists Crystal Creek, which afforded both adequate drainage and power for mills. Thus the Wisconsin Association avoided the mistake, frequently committed by other bands of visionaries, of attempting to create an Eden under the handicap of sterile soil and other economic disadvantages.

By the end of May 1844 an organization had been effected at Southport with a constitution and seventy-one members. Shares of stock were sold with a par value of $25, and those who joined became shareholders in a joint stock enterprise. Three trustees were appointed to assume the general direction of affairs and to hold title in the name of the subscribers to all the property of the association. The report of the committee on the selection of a site for the colony was approved, and the treasurer was authorized to enter the land in his own name and thereafter deed it to the trustees for the association. At this point occurred an exercise of that shrewdness for lack of which communistic enterprises have often failed to prosper. Distrusting for some reason the fidelity of the treasurer who had been chosen, Chase, by an arbitrary assumption of authority, contrived to send the money to Green Bay by private conveyance and have the land entered in the name of Michael Frank, a prominent citizen of Southport who was not identified with the movement. Less than six months later the association was calling upon the bondsmen of its treasurer to make good his obligations, which he was refusing to meet.

In all, 1,440 acres of land were purchased, and on May 20, 1844, the first band of colonists, comprising nineteen men and one boy, departed from Southport in wagons to begin the establishment of the new Utopia. They were furnished with a tent to serve as a temporary shelter until buildings could be erected, and with a supply of necessary tools and livestock. Of equal importance at least, they were earnest and industrious men of sober habits, well equipped both by character and by previous training for the work they were undertaking.

A letter[5] written by one of the band on May 27, 1844, the day on which the work of establishing the colony was begun, affords an excellent view not merely of the initial steps taken, but of the character of the settlers as well:

"After dinner the members met in the tent and proceeded to a regular organization. . . . A prayer was offered, expressing thanks for our safe protection and arrival, and invoking the Divine blessing for our future peace and prosperity. The list of resident members was called (nineteen in number) and they divided themselves into two series, viz., agricultural and mechanical (each appointing a foreman), with a miscellaneous group of laborers, under the supervision of the resident directors. . . . The stock consists of fifty-four head of cattle, large and small, including eight yoke of oxen and three span of horses. More men are expected during the week, and others are preparing to come this summer. Families will be here as [fast] as the building can be sufficiently advanced to accommodate them.

"A few words regarding the domain. There is a stream which, from its clearness, we have denominated Crystal Creek; it has sufficient fall and water supplied from springs for one or two mill seats. It runs over a bed of limestone, which abounds here and can be had convenient for fences and building. There is a good supply of timber and prairie. Every member is pleased with the location, and also the arrangement for business. Up to this time no discordant note has sounded in our company. We have begun without a debt, which is a source of great satisfaction to each member."

Probably no communistic experiment was ever entered upon under conditions more favorable for success than was this one—able leadership, excellent land, a fair supply of capital and a chosen body of workers familiar with the environment of the frontier. Eighty acres of wheat were sowed the first season, and in addition a considerable acreage was planted to corn, buckwheat, potatoes and other vegetables. The need of a sawmill for getting out lumber was imperative and the work of damming the creek and constructing a mill was undertaken, but the winter of 1844-1845 found it uncompleted. The construction of three buildings had been begun on the arrival of the first party, and by September these were far enough advanced to permit sending the tent back to Southport. But during the first year there was urgent need of lumber though the lack was overcome to some extent by the use of hay for covering. During the summer additional colonists arrived, comprising chiefly the families of those who had composed the advance party, and by autumn the total number had increased to eighty. The name Ceresco had been given the settlement by Chase, in honor of Ceres, the ancient goddess of growing vegetation.

On the whole the colony prospered, at least in a material way. The annual report issued in December 1845, the end of the second season, estimated the value of the property at $27,725.22. The noted long house (32 feet by 208 feet) had been built and twenty families were living in it. The sawmill was completed, and a schoolhouse, dining hall, grist mill, barns and other outbuildings had been erected. Throughout the life of the colony further material progress continued to be made, and economic failure, the rock on which so many communistic enterprises have foundered, was not a factor in the dissolution of the Ceresco experiment.

But the achievement of material well-being, though important, was not the sole end for which the organization had been created, and in the social and intellectual realms of life the application of Fourier's theories of "Association" met with but dubious success, despite the fact that the colonists seem to have comprised an unusually harmonious group of men and women. Although accused of irreligion by outsiders, the first group of colonists had included two lay preachers, the first meeting at Ceresco had been opened with prayer, and the annual report for 1846 stated that the study and adoption of the principles of the association led all reflecting minds to accept the principles of Christianity.

The colonists were total abstainers and strong liquor was neither used nor sold in the colony. The annual report for 1845 characterized "intoxication, lawsuits, quarreling, and profane swearing" as the four great evils afflicting the world, and declared the colony free from their presence, and that with a continuance of the present habits and character of its members it would always continue to be so.

It had been the design of the founders, without destroying the family, to have the colonists dwell in common as far as possible. Thus, the long house had a common reading or assembly room, while attached to it by a covered passage was a common dining hall and kitchen. But although food was abundant and so cheap that the average cost of good board during the year 1845 was only sixty-three cents a week, the number of families that patronized the common dining room steadily diminished until in 1848 every family was maintaining its own. This development was symptomatic of a far-reaching change that was proceeding in the attitude of the colonists toward their organization. In the beginning, the experiment had been entered upon with the zeal and enthusiasm characteristic of a movement which the participants hoped would revolutionize human society. Within a few years zeal and enthusiasm were conspicuous by their absence, and with the realization of such a state of mind dissolution of the colony was inevitable.

The provisions made concerning the relations of capital and labor were decidedly unusual. One of the most striking aspects of the theories of Fourier had been his supposed success in according to manual labor a dignified and prosperous station in society. At Ceresco was afforded the fairest opportunity that could be desired to put the theory to the pragmatic test. An annual appraisal of the property of the colony was made, and the increase was awarded one-fourth to capital and three-fourths to labor; the colonists were commonly the stockholders, yet it is interesting to observe that a feeling prevailed that the proportion awarded to capital was too high.

In November 1844 the board of directors classified all labor done in the colony in three groups: first, necessary labor, which included "digging and stoning wells, all work in water, labor necessarily requiring persons to be exposed to storms, mixing mortar, and tending masons"; second, useful labor, comprising "all mechanical and agricultural labor not comprised in other classes, washing, teaming, milking, taking care of stock, bookkeeping, and writing"; third, attractive labor, comprising "cooking, dining room work, ironing, domestic choring, gardening, horticulture, care of fowls and bees, and all necessary business of the board of directors." All work was credited by the bookkeeper in terms of hour units, and the colonist paid his obligations to the association from his accumulated store of labor credits. In computing these a scheme was adopted whereby work done in the three classes we have noted received credit in the ratio of 24, 20 and 15. Thus, it will be seen, no suitable premium was put upon skilled labor and no provision whatever was made for the professions. As for executive ability, it is sufficient to note that the talent of a director procured little more than half the reward accorded the man who mixed mortar.

It seems apparent, human nature being what it is, that such a plan could not long retain the support of its devotees, to say nothing of winning fresh converts from the outside world. By 1849 the Wisconsin Phalanx had run its course, and by common consent it was determined to dissolve the colony. The work of dissolution was carried out harmoniously, and many of the colonists remained in Ceresco as individual holders of tracts of land formerly belonging to the colony. All obligations of the colony were met, and enough remained to retire the stock at a small premium.

So the most successful test of the socialistic theories of Fourier ever made in America came to its untimely end. Despite an ideal location, a choice body of colonists and unusually capable leadership, the members preferred a return to the evils of ordinary society over a continuance of the Utopian state of Fourier's dreams. Unlike Brook

Farm Community the Wisconsin Phalanx had proved an economic and financial success but a complete social failure. Even Warren Chase, its ardent founder, was forced to conclude that it had "tried to live before its proper time and of course must die and be born again." The lapse of a hundred years has brought no indication of the fulfillment of the concluding prophecy.

At Sheboygan Falls, as at Southport, the theories of Fourier attracted deep attention, and as a result of the village discussions ten families agreed to join in the establishment of a Fourierite community at some point in Sheboygan County. Lacking both harmony of views and able leadership, however, the movement accomplished little. An initial schism developed over the choice of location for the colony, one faction favoring a site adjoining Lake Michigan, the other a location twenty miles inland from the lake. The lake shore experiment soon came to naught. The other group secured a tract of government land and with the designation of the Spring Farm Association carried on a co-operative enterprise for three years under the ambitious motto of "Union, Equal Rights, and Social Guarantees." But the colonists numbered a mere handful, their financial resources were insignificant and poverty and poor crops at length induced them to abandon the enterprise.

Waukesha County became the scene of two abortive co-operative colonies, both of which originated in England. The first was founded in 1843 by Thomas Hunt of London, a writer on the London *Chronicle,* who became an enthusiastic disciple of the communistic theories of Robert Owen. With about thirty followers Hunt located on Spring Lake in Waukesha County, where for three years the attempt to exemplify in practice the theories of Owen was continued. But the leader was a visionary and his followers were city men who knew nothing of the laborious calling of agriculture. In the circumstances, failure was inevitable.

The other Waukesha County communistic experiment was launched by a group of London mechanics who in 1843 organized themselves as the Utilitarian Association of United Interests. Each man paid the sum of twenty-five pounds sterling into the common fund. In the case of married men this membership fee secured the admission of their families. In May 1845 sixteen of the co-operators sailed from England to try their hand at farming on the Wisconsin frontier. The eight men of the company included a bookbinder, a plasterer, a wood turner, a tailor and a glover. One scans the list in vain, however, for any mention of a farmer. Upon reaching Milwaukee the colonists sent out a small delegation to search for land and 200 acres were purchased near Mukwonego. A portion of it was low and ill-drained, and before long practically every member of the colony was wrestling with fever and ague. In three years they admitted that they were "starved out" and abandoned the enterprise. The land was sold and the colonists scattered, some of them going to Milwaukee where in the pursuit of their accustomed trades they achieved a relative degree of prosperity.

Pioneer Wisconsin was likewise the scene of two co-operative experiments wherein the element of religion was a controlling motive. One of them was the community of St. Nazianz in Manitowoc County. The other was the holy city of Voree on the boundary between Racine and Walworth Counties.

The founder of St. Nazianz was a German priest, Father Ambrose Ochswald, who conceived the design of founding a Catholic co-operative community in America. The political turmoil in Germany following the Revolution of 1848 inclined many to listen with interest to such a proposal, and Father Ochswald set about the execution of his project. With characteristic thoroughness, he devoted two years to the study of medicine in order that he might heal the physical ills of his followers as well as attend to their spiritual wants. Wisconsin was selected as the destination of the colonists, and in May 1854, 113 of them assembled at Strassburg and from there began the long journey to the western shore of Lake Michigan. Reaching Milwaukee in August, the party took temporary lodging there while the leader looked for a suitable location for their future home. It was found in southwestern Manitowoc County, and hither Father Ochswald led an advance party of men toward the end of August to begin the work of establishing the new foundation. Their first work was to raise a rude cross, after which a small log church and a number of houses, likewise of logs, were erected. In the absence of oxen or other beasts of burden the men are said to have brought the logs to the buildings on their own backs.

The goal of Ochswald was the creation of a society which should be united both in religion and in material possessions, and scriptural authority for his plan was derived from certain passages of the New Testament.[6] To accommodate the unmarried members of the colony two convents were built, known respectively as the sisters' house and the brothers' house. Every adult member performed some kind of manual labor: while the sisters attended to household duties, the dairy and gardens, and made straw and knit goods, the men were busied at labor appropriate to their sex. The married members lived in the village near by, but they obtained all their supplies from the colony, and their interest in it was coequal with that of the celibate members.

Under the strong rule of Father Ochswald, St. Nazianz prospered for many years, being incidentally aided, no doubt, by the economic upheaval which attended the Civil War. The death of the leader left a gap which could scarcely be filled, and from 1870 on numerous difficulties beset the colony and led in time to a radical change in its character. Instead of the communal organization instituted by the founder, a joint-stock corporation was created under the name of the Roman Catholic Association of St. Nazianz. Beginning in 1874 married persons were denied admission to the association, and from 1896 on no new members were taken in. This was in pursuance of an arrangement previously made for transferring the property to the Catholic Society of our Divine Savior, the transfer to become complete with the death of all the members of the earlier association.

Stranger and more sensational than any of the foregoing is the story of the Mormon community of Voree founded by James J. Strang near Burlington in the middle forties. The founder was a bizarre character who grew to manhood in western New York, taught school, practiced law, edited a newspaper and founded a family, all before reaching the age of thirty. In 1843 he migrated to Burlington, where a brother-in-law who had preceded him had adopted the Mormon faith. The following winter Strang visited the Mormon capital of Nauvoo in western Illinois, where under the instruction of Prophet Joseph Smith he quickly became a Saint.

Smith was killed four months later by a Gentile mob and among the candidates competing for the succession to the vacant leadership was Strang, who produced a letter supposedly written to him by Smith nine days before his death foretelling that event and appointing Strang as his successor. Rival aspirants for the honor angrily denounced this as a hoax, and the letter, now in the possession of the present writer, seems to bear out this construction. But Strang further fortified his claim by announcing that at the very moment the letter was being written at Nauvoo he had been visited by an angel at Burlington bringing celestial confirmation of his appointment to lead the shepherdless church.

A year later the angel came again, this time with directions concerning certain holy records, inscribed in cipher, which were buried beneath the roots of an oak tree beside White River a mile or so out of Burlington. They were duly dug up by Strang's followers and were translated by him with the aid of Urim and Thummim, the transparent stones with whose help Joseph Smith had translated the Book of Mormon. Although all this hocus-pocus seems silly enough to the observer now, a century ago it sufficed to convince hundreds of gullible Saints of the truth of Strang's pretensions.

Both Prophet Smith and the angelic visitor had urged Strang to found a new holy city on the site where the plates had been found. To Voree—meaning Garden of Peace—as he named it, presently flocked as choice a collection of zealots and crackpots as any single community could well contain, and factionalism, quarreling and backsliding characterized the life of the holy city throughout its brief span of existence.

It had been founded as a religious community and most of its economic life centered about the fiscal and communistic enterprises of the church. At the April 1847 church conference Strang was made trustee in trust for the church and all lands were to be held in his name. The requirement to tithe constituted the fiscal foundation of the church, and provision for this had been made very early by a divine revelation to Strang. A later revelation of July 1, 1846, commanded the building of a temple and a "strong tower" at Voree, which should be "the beginning of the preparation whereby the poor may be exalted and the oppressed lifted up, and all my servants made equal in their temporal things." This revelation contained the first hint of the communistic organization which the leader was about to impose upon his followers under the name of the Order of Enoch, which was finally instituted in January 1848.

But the Saints came slowly into the order, despite all urgings of the Prophet. In August 1849, therefore, an additional divine inducement to enter upon the pleasures and profits of communism was held out to them. To Prophet Strang appeared no less a personage than his fellow prophet Elijah, bringing the news that God had determined to reward those Saints who had been faithful to him by giving them a dispensation to conduct baptisms for the dead at Voree "during their poverty," and until they should have time to build the temple. To the initiated the implications of this inducement were obvious enough. The founder of Mormonism had evolved from a puzzling scriptural text a doctrine by which faithful Saints, by undergoing baptism for their deceased relations, might procure for them all the advantages they might have gained had they themselves undergone baptism in life. But these baptisms must take place in the temple, secure from the gaze of the ungodly, and according to Elijah only those might enjoy the boon who belonged to the Order of Enoch and had paid their tithes. Thus the whole matter was under Strang's thumb; to compel the payment of tithes and membership in the communistic order he had brought to bear upon his followers a leverage as powerful as any ever devised.

The measures required to put the new ordinance into execution were taken at the church conference held shortly following the revelation; officials were appointed to administer and to record the baptisms and the assembled congregation adjourned to the river bank, where the Prophet initiated proceedings by redeeming "by revelation of God" the bodies of ex-President Polk, Lord Byron and Oliver Cromwell. George J. Adams, fellow member with Strang of the First Presidency of the Church, then proceeded to redeem the bodies of Napoleon Bonaparte, Samuel Adams and John Quincy Adams. President Polk had died a pious Methodist less than three months before; and never, it may safely be affirmed, did a single Wisconsin pasture contain such an assemblage of worthies as were collected on this occasion.

Despite such influences the Order of Enoch proved a dismal economic failure, and the Prophet presently quietly shelved it in favor of a new scheme for which like divine approval was affirmed. In the summer of 1846 he had obtained a revelation which disclosed "a land amidst wide waters" which was to be the future home of the Saints. The new holy land was Big Beaver Island at the northern end of Lake Michigan, of which Strang had gained some information on one of his eastern journeys. Settlement was begun here in 1847, and before the close of 1849 almost fifty Mormon families had settled around the shore of Paradise Bay to found the town of St. James.

Although the struggle to maintain themselves while establishing homes in the wilderness was a severe one, the eager brain of the Prophet had already hatched a new and startling development. Although Smith and other leaders at Nauvoo had dabbled with polygamy and spiritual wifery, Strang had until now sternly denounced these "abominations," cutting off from the church and assigning to perdition those Saints who ventured to indulge in them. In 1849, however, he obtained a new revelation of God's will commanding the establishment of polygamy, with Strang himself as the first exemplar of the new order; more surprising still, it was revealed that God was about to establish His Kingdom on earth, and that "His servant James" had been predestined from ancient times to serve as His Vicegerent and King.

Before the Kingdom could be set up a number of preparations must be made, but Strang determined to launch the new domestic order at once. The object of his first affection was Elvira Field, a charming girl of eighteen years, whose parents had been converted to Mormonism but had not "gathered" to the Beavers. To her came Strang's Prime Minister and co-President of the Church, George J. Adams, a broken-down actor of incredible vileness of mind and soul, with the message that the Prophet had received a new revelation commending the polygamous order in the kingdom about to be established and that to Elvira had been awarded the honor of becoming his first plural wife and his queen in the new Kingdom. All this must be kept secret for the present even from the girl's own parents. Strange as it may seem Elvira accepted the offer in all sincerity, and vanishing from the ken of her loved ones staked her entire future on the fantastic proposal disclosed to her by the Prophet's lecherous messenger. Half a year later her distracted family was still vainly seeking to learn what had become of her.

The winter of 1849-1850 was spent by Strang in the East "rolling up" converts for the church and lobbying at Washington for an exclusive grant of the Beaver Islands to his followers. Elvira accompanied him on the tour, dressed as a boy with hair shorn and posing as Charles J. Douglass, his nephew and secretary. If Strang really expected to conceal this fraud from his followers he was sadly disappointed. Even before the departure from Beaver Island there were scandalous whisperings concerning "Charley's" sex identity, and in Philadelphia and other eastern centers, sharp-eyed Saints fell to discussing his "anatomical peculiarities" in terms unfit for reproduction in print.

Meanwhile the elders of the church who had gone out on mission the year before were returning to the Beavers with the converts they had won, in readiness for the annual conference which had been set for early July. The new revelation, which the Prophet had already imparted in secret to a few chosen intimates, was now in readiness to be publicly proclaimed. God had committed to His Prophet a second holy record, inscribed as usual on metallic plates, and so precious that the ancient Jews had kept it in the Ark of the Covenant itself. Lost by them and to the world for thousands of years, it had now been miraculously disclosed to Strang, who at a subsequent date published it as *The Book of the Law of the Lord*. Unless this was another product of the Prophet's lively imagination it is the most important book ever printed, for it contains a comprehensive frame of government for his people who are to inherit the earth. No Old World tyrant ever wielded greater power over his subjects than the rural New York lawyer, speaking as God's mouthpiece, provided for himself in this volume.

On July 8, 1850, in the unfinished tabernacle beside the blue waters of Paradise Bay, hemmed in by a forest of everlasting green, the King of all the Earth was crowned. A section from *The Book of the Law* was read and the 400 awe-stricken spectators swore with uplifted hands to be God's people and to observe henceforth the laws His Prophet should reveal to them. Finally, the Prophet himself, clad in a bright red robe, was escorted to the platform, where Prime Minister Adams, the ham tragedian, acting as master of ceremonies, placed upon his brow a metal crown having a cluster of stars in front. Henceforth forever the Coronation Day was to be celebrated with feasting and sacrifices. To round out the work of organizing the Kingdom, before the day was over Strang emitted another revelation awarding "the Islands of the Great Lakes" as an inheritance to the Saints and delegating to the King the authority to apportion them.

"Forever" in this particular case proved to mean six years, for in 1856 the Prophet perished at the hands of assassins and the Kingdom was blotted out. To account for this disastrous issue of Strang's dreams we must take note of certain pertinent facts. Although he chose to describe the islands as "uninhabited" the Mormons were not the first to settle there. The adjoining waters were the resort of fishermen from all the surrounding area, while on Big Beaver itself a small settlement of Gentiles had been established on the north side of Paradise Bay. Eventually they were driven from the island by the Saints, but this triumph merely transferred the struggle to the wider field of the entire surrounding area. The hatred between Gentiles and Saints soon became so bitter that a state of intermittent civil war lasting for several years and marked by frequent outbursts of violence ensued. One of the more lurid incidents was the battle of Pine River, which might better be called the battle of Lake Michigan. Pine Lake is now Lake Charlevoix, and around its outlet, then known as Pine River, the city of Charlevoix has developed. Here in the summer of 1853 was a settlement of Gentile fishermen to which various renegade Saints had fled for refuge. So great was the hatred of the settlers for the Mormons that they had openly threatened to kill any process server from St. James who should venture among them.

The Saints returned their feeling with interest, and Strang's organ, the *Northern Islander,* characterized the settlers as "little else than a band of vagabonds and thieves" and asserted that "the sight of an officer of the law sets them all in a twitter." Mormon St. James was the seat of government of Emmet County, and on July 12, 1853, Sheriff Miller set out with fourteen men in two open boats for Pine River to summon certain of the fishermen whose names had been drawn for jury duty. The approaching boats could be seen far out in the lake by the fishermen, affording them ample time to prepare a hostile reception.

The Mormons landed on a narrow beach under a bluff which was covered with timber and bushes. The sheriff quickly explained his mission and his party was in the act of embarking for the return journey when a murderous fire was opened on it by a body of fishermen who had gathered on the bluff and on the beach below it. Six of the Mormons were shot, although none of the wounds proved fatal. Before them lay twenty-five miles of open water, while behind three boats crowded with angry fishermen were launched in hot pursuit. For about ten miles the desperate Saints, aided by a light wind, kept beyond range of their enemies. When the wind died down the Gentiles drew nearer and opened fire upon the laboring boats. These were riddled with bullets, and it seemed that all of the occupants would be slain until a vessel upbound from Buffalo to Chicago appeared in sight and in response to the frantic appeals of the Mormons took them all on board. The baffled pursuers now gave over the chase and returned to Pine River.

The year 1855 marked the zenith of Strang's regal career. For five years he had outridden every hostile storm. The number of his subjects was steadily increasing and settlers from Big Beaver were colonizing the mainland around Lake Charlevoix, while outposts of Mormonism were being established as far away as Drummond Island in Lake Huron. Despite this appearance of success, however, the Kingdom contained within itself the seeds of swift dissolution. Strang's autocratic rule had bred a hatred in the minds of some of his own followers which did not hesitate at assassination, and they improved the heritage of Gentile hostility which the years had developed to incite an avenging mob which overthrew the Kingdom and banished its subjects far and wide.

Dr. H. D. McCulloch, one of the few really capable members of the Kingdom, was the principal architect of the assassination, although the actual killers were two pitiful creatures named Thomas Bedford and Alexander Wentworth. To all of these men Strang's measures had given deep offense, and one of them, for committing an act of adultery, had been severely flogged. Through McCulloch's scheming the U. S. Steamer *Michigan* was induced to visit St. James, putting in on June 16 at the dock, which lay directly in front of his store. Within the store the assassins waited in readiness while an officer of the ship was sent to summon Strang to come on board, as the captain wished to see him. Complying, he had stepped upon the bridge leading to the pier when Bedford and Wentworth emerged from the store and coming up behind him shot him in the head. Two more bullets were fired into the body of the helpless man as he lay prostrate on the pier, after which the two murderers rushed aboard the steamer and begged the protection of her officers, which was readily granted. One hesitates to accuse the officers of a United States revenue cutter with complicity in a plot to assassinate an American citizen, yet all of the available evidence strongly supports such a conclusion. The sheriff was refused the custody of the murderers, who were borne away to Mackinac and there promptly given their liberty. A few days later they had the effrontery to return to St. James, again on the *Michigan,* where they attempted to arrest some of the Mormon leaders, threatening to take the Prophet "dead or alive."

Fearing that a subsequent raid would prove more successful, a number of the Mormon leaders took their departure from the island in advance of it. The dying Prophet himself was removed to Voree, where he breathed his last on July 9. Meanwhile Gentile mobs descended upon the Beavers and drove the leaderless and bewildered Saints into headlong and hopeless flight, while their houses and property became the spoil of the marauders.

So amid scenes of suffering and violence the Kingdom vanished from the earth. At Voree the body of the King reposed for three-quarters of a century in an unmarked grave whose site during much of the time was included within a cow yard. Scattered over the face of the country are a few zealots who still profess their belief in Strang's teachings and strive to preserve a semblance of his church organization. On the Beavers no Mormons have lived since the tragic summer of 1856; of all their works, only the names they gave—Saint James, Font Lake, Gennesaret, Galilee, the King's Highway—remain.

---

1 Madison *Wisconsin Argus,* March 9, 1847.
2 Father of Arthur Brisbane, the well-known twentieth-century journalist.
3 The Brook Farm was not founded as a Fourierite colony, but it was converted into one in 1845 through the influence of Brisbane.
4 Among the number was a young schoolteacher, Louis P. Harvey, who achieved subsequent fame as war governor of Wisconsin, and a young printer, C. Latham Sholes, whose invention of the typewriter has done more to emancipate womanhood from economic and social thralldom than all the reformers and politicians who can be named.
5 Printed in Wisconsin Historical Society, *Proceedings* for 1902, 200.
6 Book of Acts, IV:32-37.

Chapter 22

Perils of the Deep

I<small>F</small> L<small>AKE</small> M<small>ICHIGAN</small> were to be drained dry, a project seriously discussed a century ago, the hulks of scores of ships now entombed on the bottom would once more appear in view. With them would be found the skeletons of the hundreds of men and women who perished when they went down, and a wide variety of valuable cargo such as whisky, coal, lumber, gold, iron and copper.

The navigation of the Great Lakes is vastly safer today than it was a century or so ago, partly because of the improvement in the mechanical and shipbuilding arts which the century has witnessed, but equally, perhaps, because of the many safeguards in the way of lighthouses and buoys, coast guards and lake surveys, and, above all, the rigid licensing and inspection standards which all who sail the lakes must now pass. Yet despite all these things disaster and sudden death still companion the mariner on his voyage, to strike in ways totally unexpected and frequently unexplainable after they have happened.

A moving ballad of the olden time describes the fate of the *Julie Plante* which was lost, with all her crew, "on wan' dark night on Lac St. Clair." Although the *Julie Plante* was a humble wood scow, the terror and suffering of those who perished with her was no different from that endured by hundreds of others who died in larger and grander ships.

When the tempest began to rage the crew, according to the balladist, "got scar't an' run below." But:

> "De captenne walk on de front deck
> An' walk de hin' deck too—
> He call de crew from up de hole
> He call de cook also.
> De cook she's name was Rosie
> She came from Montreal,
> Was chambre maid on lumber **barge,**
> On de grande Lachine Canal."

The wind blew harder, from all directions at once, and Rosie in terror cried out to the captain, "W'at I shall do?" The anchor would not hold the scow, which continued to drift, and the crew could not abandon ship because the "skeef" had been lost.

> "De night was dark lak' wan' black cat,
>   De wave run high an' fas',
>   W'en de captenne tak' de Rosie girl
>   An' tie her to de mas'.
>   Den he also tak' de life preserve,
>   An' jump off on de lak',
>   An' say, 'Good-bye ma' Rosie dear,
>   I go drown for your sak'.'"

Next morning captain and Rosie, crew and vessel, all were lost.

> "For de win' she blow lak' hurricane
>   Bimeby she blow some more,
>   An' de scow bus' up on Lac St. Clair
>   Ten arpent[1] from de shore."

The minstrel concludes his poem with this bit of sage advice which no true sailor ever heeded:

> "Now all good wood scow sailor men
>   Tak' warning by dat storm
>   An' go an' marry some nice French girl
>   An' leev on wan' beeg farm.
>   De win' can blow lak' hurricane
>   An' s'pose she blow some more,
>   You can't get drown on Lac St. Clair
>   So long you stay on shore."

Salt-water sailors usually look down upon their Great Lakes cousins, but theirs is the valor of ignorance, for the navigation of the Inland Seas demands no less fortitude and probably greater skill than that of the oceans themselves. On the latter the peril from collisions and from shoals is commonly slight, save on entering and leaving port, when the service of a local pilot is engaged. On the lakes, the dangers of collisions and grounding are appallingly common. Tempests rage on oceans and lakes with equal violence but the ocean navigator can run before them indefinitely, while the lake captain is exposed to the dangers of a lee shore practically all the time; periodically, too, he is compelled to battle with ice blockades which on the ocean are seldom encountered.

Ordinarily, on the lakes as on the ocean, the disasters which occur are capable of rational explanation, yet great ships still leave port to vanish without a trace, their fate forever a mystery. A few years ago I listened to this story, told by a man of unquestioned character and veracity. While driving along a road near the upper end of Lake Huron on a quiet sunny day, his eye occasionally rested upon a small vessel calmly sailing along within easy eyesight. Perhaps five minutes had passed since his last look at it when, looking again, the lake was empty; the vessel had vanished, never to be seen or heard of again.

It seems impossible to explain such an occurrence save on the supposition that the ship suddenly turned turtle; but even this theory sheds no light on the question why it did so. In another disaster, also on Lake Huron, the tug *Frederick A. Lee* vanished from sight under the very gaze of First Officer Donald Mauts of the near-by ship *Munson*. The latter reached the spot within fifteen minutes to find only bits of wreckage and pieces of cabin furniture floating about. Evidently the *Lee* had sunk too suddenly for any of her crew to leap overboard, and the only plausible explanation that could be evolved was that mud might have been sucked into the boilers to cause an explosion which destroyed the vessel.[2]

Still other tragedies occur which are explainable although no less sudden. The greatest in all the history of the lakes, measured in terms of the number who perished, was the overturning of the *Eastland* at her Clark Street dock in the narrow Chicago River on July 24, 1915. Although more than 800 persons perished in a few minutes, no one was ever punished for the disaster, which was apparently occasioned by the failure of those in charge of the vessel to fill the water-ballast tanks before taking on a capacity load of excursionists. Lake tugs turn turtle far too often, although for different reasons than the *Eastland*. Thus the *Admiral* turned over, drowning her crew of fourteen men, while towing the tanker *Cleveco* in Lake Erie, December 2, 1942. Shortly afterward the *Cleveco* herself sank with her 24,000 barrels of oil for eastern war plants and her crew of eighteen.[3]

How such accidents happen is illustrated by the one which befell the *America,* 400 feet off the head of Belle Isle in the Detroit River in the night of October 21, 1941. The freighter *B. F. Jones* had grounded in a mud flat at this point and the *America* and two sister tugs were laboring to free her. "I gave the order for full speed ahead," reported Captain Damas. "I felt the power go in and we seemed to stand still for a few seconds. Then we shot ahead, just like a knife through the water. Then we turned over." Six men of the crew of thirteen were drowned, several of them while sleeping safely, as they had supposed, in their berths.[4]

The death of these men, surrounded by all the lifesaving resources of a great city, is pathetic enough, but what shall we think of the fate of the score of passengers and crew whose lives were snuffed out within five feet of safety in the wreck of the *City of Muskegon* on October 28, 1919? The ship had left Milwaukee the night before and while crossing the lake had encountered heavy seas. She fought her way through the raging billows until, with Muskegon harbor and safety at arm's reach, she was caught up in a heavy undertow and dashed violently upon the concrete pier. Here she held fast for a few seconds and then tore loose; her engines failed, her lights went out and she was soon pounded to pieces. Some of those on board leaped to safety on the pier. Others fell to their death between it and the ship, while still more, probably, were unable in the darkness to find their way on deck at all.

A lighthouse tender who chanced to have a pocket flashlight did what he could to light the dock for the fugitives. "But I couldn't hold it everywhere," he said, "and many still missed the dock."

"They will probably send me to hell," moaned Captain Miller, half-crazed by the disaster, "but what could I do? ... I gave the alarm and stuck to my post and saw the boat dashed to pieces."[5]

Although disasters continue to overtake lake shipping, one of their chief causes a century ago has been largely eliminated. When ships were built of wood and boilers of iron and both vessels and operators went uninspected and unlicensed, boiler explosions and fires were appallingly common. Charles Dickens, who voyaged on Lake Erie in 1842, records in his *American Notes* that the high-pressure engines of the ship made him feel "as if I had lodgings on the first floor of a powder mill."

Today boiler explosions and fires are infrequent,[6] but in their stead collisions have become far more frequent by reason of the increase in lake traffic, and tempests contine, as of old, to take their toll. One of the commonest causes of collisions is the prevalence of fogs which blind the navigator and sometimes defy the exertion of his utmost skill to avoid disaster. Other causes, of course, are the forces of wind and water which often swerve the vessel from its intended course or even wrest it entirely out of control of the pilot. In channels which are narrow or crowded with traffic, even a slight shift from the intended course may produce a collision or shipwreck. On June 15, 1943, three collisions occurred and two great ships were sunk in a single day. The new 621-foot ore carrier *Frank Armstrong,* engaged upon her second trip, was rammed in the St. Marys River by the freighter *Goderich;* the *George M. Humphrey,* a 12,000-ton ore ship, was sunk in sixty or seventy feet of water off Old Fort Mackinac Point; and the *Brewster,* a grain ship carrying 90,000 bushels of Lend-Lease wheat to England, was sunk near Walpole Island in the St. Clair River. The vessel lay on her side in thirty-five feet of water and the swelling of her cargo soon buckled her plates.

The narrow margin by which appalling tragedies are sometimes averted was thrillingly illustrated in June 1936 when death lightly brushed more than 1,500 Detroit excursionists on the steamer *Tashmoo.* Homeward bound in the Sugar Island Channel of the Detroit River, the busiest waterway in the world, the vessel struck a rock. The crew stuck to their posts although the water in the engine room swirled to the stokers' waists and the band played on for the hundreds of dancing passengers while Captain McAlpine raced against wholesale death for the nearest dock. In ten minutes he reached Amherstburg, where the ship soon sank beside the dock in twenty-five feet of water. One can only theorize over the presence of such a rock in a channel thronged with ships. "It is my opinion," said Captain McAlpine, "that a dredging crew, to save time, had dumped rock in the channel sometime earlier in the night."[7]

An awesome tragedy which left no survivors occurred on Simmons Reef, a few miles northwest of Beaver Island, on New Year's Day, 1927. Seven weeks earlier, on November 8, the tanker *J. Oswald Boyd,* laden with 900,000 gallons of gasoline, had grounded there, and when the rescuing tugs proved unable to set her free they took off her crew of nineteen men. The vessel lay in water so shallow that few salvage ships could reach her, leaving her cargo free spoil for anyone daring enough to appropriate it. For some time the Beaver Island fishermen visited the *Boyd* in their motorboats, shutting off their motors on approaching, since a coating of oil covered the water around the ship. Then the salvage rights were purchased by the Beaver Island Transit Company and the small steamer *Marold* was dispatched to remove the cargo.

The *Marold,* operated by eighty-three-year-old Captain Hill and a crew of four, was a World War I submarine chaser which had been equipped with cabins for passengers and placed on the Charlevoix-Beaver Island run. About sundown of the short New Year's Day observers forty miles distant noted the flames which billowed heavenward from the *Boyd,* whose huge cargo had exploded, blowing the *Marold* and her crew to eternity together. When next day a coastguard vessel visited the scene, it found the pilothouse and top deck of the *Marold* blown on the deck of the tanker; the steamer herself had vanished, and two more residents of Beaver Island had escaped perishing with her crew only because they had overslept on New Year's morning when the *Marold* left St. James.

Although no mystery attends the fate of Chicago's storied "Christmas ship," the *Rouse Simmons,* her loss is worth relating for its human interest. The *Simmons* was a three-masted schooner whose owner for years had brought from the northland to the Chicago River a cargo of Christmas trees for the city trade. On November 25, 1913, the vessel set sail from Thompson Harbor near Manistique for Chicago on her annual voyage of Yuletide cheer. Just two weeks before, the great storm of November 9 had ravaged all the lakes and another gale was rising as the *Simmons* left port. But time was pressing if the cargo was to be in Chicago in time for the Christmas trade, and the captain courageously put to sea in the face of the gale. At dawn of the twenty-sixth the *Simmons* was sighted off Sturgeon Bay by the

Coast Guard with distress signals flying, but even the lifesavers were unable to put to sea in the storm that was raging. However, they reported to the Coast Guard Station at Kewaunee the plight of the *Simmons* and the lifesaving crew there went out in search of her. A blinding snowstorm was now raging, obscuring the vision, and for a long time they found nothing. In a momentary lull of the storm, however, the ship was seen, hull coated with ice and with sails in tatters. Then the storm curtain closed down once more and the *Rouse Simmons* was never seen again.[8] A bottle washed ashore on the beach at Sheboygan contained this note, signed by Captain Schuneman: "Everybody good-bye. I guess we are through. Leaking bad. Endwald and Stede fell overboard Thursday. God help us."

Probably the most constant single cause of disasters on Lake Michigan throughout the centuries has been the tempests which often develop suddenly and rage with appalling fury. The Indian canoe was always at their mercy, and legends are not wanting of large-scale tragedies which resulted when fleets of canoes ventured too far from land. At one time the Wisconsin Winnebago, at war with the Foxes on the Michigan side of the lake, sent an army of 500 braves against them, but a tempest arising, they perished to the last man. "Their enemies were moved by this disaster," the chronicle continues, "and said that the gods ought to be satisfied with so many punishments; so they ceased making war on those who remained."[9]

The absence of natural harbors made the navigation of Lake Michigan particularly hazardous for the early mariner. From Green Bay and the Manitous southward there was not a single place of refuge, so that vessels were compelled to anchor in the open lake to receive and discharge passengers and cargo and in case of storm to flee 200 miles or more before shelter could be found.

The story of the loss of the *Hercules* illustrates the peril to which all ships which ventured into Lake Michigan were exposed. The little schooner sailed from Chicago homeward bound to Detroit on the evening of October 2, 1818. On the morning of the third, one of the worst gales the oldest inhabitant could remember developed and raged for two days. No tidings of the *Hercules* came to the anxious watchers at Chicago until on October 9 a party of Indians from

KING BENJAMIN PURNELL

Photograph reproduced from *The Book of Wisdom. The Flying Roll, Book 2*, published by The House of David at Benton Harbor. The resemblance to conventional depictions of Jesus Christ is not wholly accidental.

Courtesy of the Benton Harbor News-Palladium

THE HOUSE OF DAVID BASEBALL TEAM

The flowing tresses were worn in pursuance of King Benjamin's religious teaching. The absence of whiskers is probably due to the youth of the players.

Grand River arrived, bringing with them some objects they had picked up along the shore at the south end of the lake. Among them was a scale which belonged to Lieutenant Eveleth, a promising young West Pointer attached to the Engineer Corps of the Army, who was returning on the *Hercules* from a tour of observation of the military defenses in the Northwest. A rescue party dispatched from Fort Dearborn returned three days later with the report that they had found the lake shore near what is now Michigan City strewn with fragments of the ship for a distance of twelve or fifteen miles. Only one body had been found and that in an unrecognizable condition. The hull of the ship had vanished completely, although portions of the masts had blown ashore. Before the arrival of the searching party the neighboring Potawatomi Indians had appropriated and carried off every article of value which had come ashore.[10]

One of the seamen on the *Hercules* was a young Vermonter named Luke Sherwin, who had recently come to the lakes, and who a few weeks before her destruction had proudly written his brother in Vermont, "I am now a sailor," adding that when the season of navigation closed he might accompany a friend upon a journey to New Orleans.[11] A few weeks later his corpse was battered to nothingness amid the breakers which dashed themselves upon the shore at the head of Lake Michigan.

The fate of those aboard the *Hercules* is still braved by all who embark upon the Inland Seas, despite all the improved resources of modern scientific and mechanical skill. The tempest of November 9, 1913, in which a dozen vessels and over two hundred lives were lost, remains the greatest destruction of life and property by a single storm. But almost a century earlier, in November 1842, when Great Lakes shipping was still in its infancy, about a hundred lives were lost and almost fifty vessels wrecked in a single tempest. Eighteen ships were wrecked on the north shore of Lake Erie alone and many more on the shores of Michigan and Ontario.[12] Again in 1869 a three-day tempest raged from November 16 to 19. Almost a hundred vessels were driven ashore or foundered, and thirty-five of them were total losses.

That the strength of the gale still laughs to scorn the puny devices of men is illustrated by a storm, described in the press as the greatest of a decade, which broke over Lake Michigan on November 11-12, 1940. Several great freighters were lost or driven ashore and over sixty lives were reported lost. Off Pentwater the pulpwood carrier *Novadoc,* running between Chicago and Fort William, went aground, its back broken by the fury of the November gale; all but two of its crew of nineteen men were saved from impending death by the small fishing tug *Three Brothers,* which braved the stormy sea to bring them ashore.

The rescue gave rise to a curious dispute. Although the captain of the tug was blazoned in the press of the nation as a hero deserving of the Congressional Medal, the local Coast Guard sourly denounced him as a mere glory-seeker who had ignored the unwritten law of the sea by refusing to come to their aid when asked to help in launching the coast-guard boat, which was making ready to succor the crew of the stranded ship.

The storm meanwhile, unmindful of such bickering, rushed eastward across Michigan to overturn great steel radio towers at Detroit, blow in scores of plate-glass windows and whip the Detroit River into a fury of tossing whitecaps. While it was raging, the 445-foot freighter *George Ingalls* cast off from its dock at Iron Street, bound down river with a cargo of automobiles for Cleveland, only to be driven half a mile upstream and within a hundred yards of the Belle Isle bridge before control of the vessel could be regained.[13]

Among the most distressing tragedies ever enacted on Lake Michigan were the destruction of the *Phoenix* by fire in 1847 and the *Lady Elgin* by collision in 1860. In both cases scenes of horror which could scarcely be excelled were relieved by displays of heroism which thrill the heart of the reader even after the lapse of a century.

The *Phoenix* was a propeller of 302 tons, built in 1845, which plied between Buffalo and Chicago. On November 11, 1847, she began her westward run, heavily laden with merchandise consigned to Chicago and with a capacity load of passengers, almost all of them emigrants from Holland coming to join relatives and friends who had already found homes in Michigan or other states of the Middle West. The route of the *Phoenix,* like that of most other ships, ran down the Wisconsin shore of Lake Michigan, since there were no important towns on the eastern coast. Leaving Manitowoc in stormy weather after midnight of November 21, the vessel strained under her load and the firemen fed her boilers furiously. About four o'clock in the morning smoke began pouring from the engine room and the alarm of fire was given.[14] Although a bucket brigade was formed, it soon became apparent that efforts to subdue the fire were vain and the vessel's two small lifeboats were launched with forty-three passengers and crew, all of whom reached the shore in safety.

Left behind on the doomed *Phoenix* were some 200 souls, including passengers and crew, most of them the Dutch emigrants who were hopefully nearing the end of their 4,000-mile pilgrimage. Two hours passed by, while the fire continued to rage and they desperately awaited the return of the lifeboats or the arrival of other rescuers. They came, but too late. Many of the passengers had sought refuge from the fire and smoke by retreating to the rigging, where they perished one by one as the flames mounted the tarred ropes and fired the sails. Others leaped into the lake, to sink at once in the icy water or to cling precariously to pieces of floating wreckage from which they eventually slipped to their watery graves; some remained on their floats and perished from the cold.

Meanwhile at near-by Sheboygan the alarm had been given and the work of rescue was set in motion. The lifeboat of the schooner *Liberty* was manned and started for the scene, followed by many small boats launched by civilians, while the propeller *Delaware,* which chanced to be in the harbor, began raising steam to join in the work. As it turned out she arrived first, about seven o'clock, to find but three persons, all men, still alive. Two hundred had perished in the flames or in the icy water.

Amid the murky hell of the burning *Phoenix* looms forever the heroic figure of David Blish, a Southport merchant. Only thirty-three years of age and the father of four small children, he had every reason to wish to live, yet he cheerfully gave his life to ease the agony of a crowd of alien immigrants. Offered a place in one of the lifeboats, he declined, preferring "to take my chances with the rest," and while the boats were being loaded he stood at the gangplank to prevent them from swamping. During the voyage he had made friends with the Hollanders, paying particular attention to the children, and in their last agony he did not fail them. One story represents that when the fire was far advanced he took in his arms a lost and terror-stricken little girl, shielding her body from the flames by interposing his own. So he moved through the inferno, a veritable angel of mercy; at the end he contrived to launch a little raft and with two children still in his arms clung to it until overcome by the cold. "Greater love hath no man than this."

Fortunately for those who found places in the lifeboats the lake was now calm after the storm which had prevailed. Although an effort had been made not to swamp the boats, they were loaded to capacity, and some who had plunged into the water endeavored to cling to them. One woman thus held on all the way to shore. Another passenger, a girl who had got her hands on one of the boats, was forcibly thrust off and sent to her death by those inside. In such an extremity necessity knows no other law. The second boat was launched with only one oar and had to be sculled all the way to shore. It dipped a good deal of water and the Hollanders baled this out with their wooden shoes.

Although there was no wholesale absence of discipline on the part of the crew, only three of whom manned each of the lifeboats, it is significant of the changing standards of the sea which have since come about that among them were the captain and the first mate of the *Phoenix*. Today such officers remain with their ship, while "women and children first" is the universal rule.

Strange as it may seem, the tragedy of the *Lady Elgin* in the night of September 7-8, 1860, was brought about by the dispute between North and South over the issue of Negro slavery. In the prevailing fashion of the time Milwaukee's Irish ward, appropriately known as the "Bloody Third," had a military company called the Union Guards. All Wisconsin had been shaken to its depths by the controversy over the Glover slave rescue, and the state authorities, not excepting the Supreme Court, openly defied the efforts of the Federal Government to enforce the obnoxious Fugitive Slave Law. But the Bloody Third was Democratic to a man and when Governor Randall, a states-rights Republican, asked the captain of the Union Guards what he would do if called upon to assist in enforcing the edicts of the state courts in opposition to the Federal authority, he answered that he would stand by the flag of the United States. The Adjutant General of the state now deprived the soldiers of their arms and disbanded the company. Thereupon the Bloody Third boys determined to buy their own equipment, and on September 6, accompanied by friends and relatives to the number of several hundred, they engaged the *Lady Elgin* for an excursion to Chicago to attend a Democratic rally, hoping to realize enough money to rearm the company.[15]

When the speech making and carousing was ended the *Lady Elgin* departed on the return journey to Milwaukee, late in the night of September 7. The distance between the two cities is about a hundred miles and one-fourth of it had been covered when fate bore down upon the merrymakers in the shape of the Chicago-bound lumber hooker *Augusta*. A storm had arisen and the *Lady Elgin* was steaming northward against the wind. The *Augusta,* a schooner, was sailing east by south, with the wind and under heavy sail. Although the *Lady Elgin's* lights were clearly seen at a considerable distance, no effort was made to change the *Augusta's* course until the ships were almost together. Then the captain called "Hard up!" but still the course was not altered,[16] and she crashed the *Lady Elgin* amidship, tearing a great hole in her side and inflicting some damage upon herself. A minute or so later the two ships drew apart and the *Augusta* continued on her way to Chicago, her captain making no effort to learn the extent of the damage he had inflicted, or to stand by the stricken steamboat.[17]

Within fifteen minutes the engine fell through the ship and the hull soon followed it to the bottom, while the hurricane deck and perhaps more of the upper works were torn loose and floated free. Two small boats containing twenty-one persons had been launched and both reached shore, although four of the passengers in one of them were drowned en route.

Thus the vast majority of the 400 persons aboard the *Lady Elgin* either went down with her or were thrown into the lake, where many succeeded in gaining pieces of wreckage for support. About two score got to the hurricane deck, where Captain Wilson did his utmost to direct and encourage them. Close to the shore it ran aground on a sand bar and broke up, and those whom it had carried almost to safety were lost in the boiling waves.

Meanwhile from Winnetka, Evanston and other adjacent points

the townsmen crowded to the lake shore to gaze helplessly upon the scores of men and women drifting inland to their death in the raging surf. In this way hours passed and reporters even had time to come from Chicago to witness the death struggles of scores of victims. Among the onlookers, however, was one brave youth, a student of Northwestern University, who in addition to being a good swimmer possessed a dauntless soul. When he perceived that the passengers drifting helplessly ashore were too weak to make their way through the surf unaided, he plunged into the water and seeking out a drowning woman managed to bring her to land. Again and again he returned for others, until he was overcome by his exertions and by exposure to the chilly lake. Wrapped in blankets he was standing by a fire which had been built when he saw a man drifting in, apparently holding another person in his grasp. Inspired by the sight, he determined upon one last effort, and two more victims, who proved to be husband and wife, were torn from the angry water.

In all the noble youth entered the water sixteen times, to bring back seventeen persons who were about to perish; and sinking at last in exhaustion and delirium he repeated over and over the question, "Did I do my best?" Although no monument preserves the memory of David Blish, the hero who perished with the *Phoenix,* a grateful university has inscribed a suitable bronze tablet as a memorial to heroic Edward Spencer.

The story of the *Lady Elgin* had a curious aftermath which is worth relating. Terrible indeed was the grief of Milwaukee's Bloody Third, which had furnished most of the 300 victims. Almost every family mourned its dead and all without exception sorrowed for friends and neighbors. The youth and beauty of the entire community had been almost completely destroyed.

While the survivors mourned, they nourished their wrath. Months later the hated *Augusta* came into Milwaukee to lay up for the winter and to be disguised by her owners with a coat of black paint and a new name. When the Third Ward learned about it murmurs of protest swelled to imprecations and a movement was started to mob and burn the ship. To avoid such a fate the owners hastily sailed the *Augusta*—renamed the *Colonel Cook*—out of the harbor and started her on her way to the broad Atlantic. After years of wandering as a tramp she returned once more to the Upper Lakes. Captain Humphrey, who had rescued her from the Irish mob, had taken his wife and little daughter to sea with him. He presently returned to Milwaukee and the lakes; years passed, and the little girl had become a woman and the wife of a lake captain, when one day in Marquette harbor her husband called to her to come and meet an old friend. Responding to the summons, she looked down upon a little schooner close at hand, "a ragged waif of a ship, with the paint cracking off, and sadly needing overhauling." It was the *Colonel Cook*.

But the years had done their work. The forgotten skeletons of the bold lads and bonny lassies of the old Bloody Third were scattered over the lake bottom off Waukegan, 300 feet deep, and the grief of parents and friends had been assuaged by time's healing hand. The old lumber hooker might even have resumed her hated name and no one would have uttered an imprecation or raised a hand in anger.

---

[1] The word *arpent*, as used here, means a distance of a little less than 200 feet. See Explanatory Note, page 369.

[2] Detroit *Free Press*, November 15, 1936.

[3] Detroit *News*, December 2 and 4, 1942.

[4] Detroit *News*, October 23, 1941.

[5] Detroit *Free Press*, October 29, 1919, and October 15, 1939.

[6] A newer cause of explosions proceeds from the carrying of gasoline in tankers. On August 9, 1941, the Canadian tanker *Transiter* blew up in the River Rouge at Detroit five minutes after leaving her dock with a cargo of 600,000 gallons of gasoline aboard. Two of the seventeen persons aboard perished, a deck hand and the captain's wife. Detroit *Free Press*, August 9 and 13, 1941.

[7] Detroit *News*, June 19, 1936. While this chapter was being prepared the death of brave Captain McAlpine at Windsor, January 1, 1944, was reported. Detroit *News*, January 4, 1944.

[8] Dana T. Bowen, *Lore of the Lakes* (Daytona Beach, 1940), 170-171.

[9] Narrative of Bacqueville de la Pothrie, originally published in Paris in 1722; translation in *Wisconsin Historical Collections*, XVI, 3-5.

[10] Letter of Captain Daniel Baker, October 13, 1818, to General Alexander Macomb, printed in Detroit *Gazette*, November 13, 1818.

[11] The letter is preserved in the Burton Historical Collection, Detroit Public Library.

[12] J. B. Mansfield, *History of the Great Lakes*, I, 638.

[13] Detroit *News*, November 12 and 13 and December 5, 1940; *Free Press*, December 1, 1940.

[14] The best account of the loss of the *Phoenix* is William O. Van Eyck, "The Story of the Propeller *Phoenix*," in *Wisconsin Magazine of History*, VII, 281-300.

[15] H. J. Desmond, "Early Irish Settlers in Milwaukee," in *Wisconsin Magazine of History*, XIII, 373; Frances M. Stover, "The Schooner that Sunk the Lady Elgin," *Ibid.*, VII, 35; M. M. Quaife, *Wisconsin*, II, 222-223.

[16] The first mate testified that the vessel steered "pretty wild," and would not answer her helm readily.

[17] For accounts of the disaster I have drawn upon the *Illustrated London News*, September 29, 1860; Mansfield, *History of the Great Lakes*, I, 683-687; Stover, "The Schooner that Sunk the Lady Elgin," *Wisconsin Magazine of History*, VII, 30-40; J. S. Currey, *Chicago; Its History and Its Builders* (Chicago, 1912), II, 336-339.

Chapter 23

The King of Benton Harbor

WHERE La Salle in 1679 built Fort Miami on the bluff overlooking the mouth of the St. Joseph River now lies the city of St. Joseph and close at hand on the eastern bank of the river is Benton Harbor. St. Joseph is the older community and Benton Harbor the larger and wealthier one. To the fact that in earlier years there was much jealousy between the two is due their wholly illogical separate municipal existence. Both are resort towns and in recent years they have united to promote the May-time Blossom Festival which attracts thousands of visitors. At Benton Harbor is one of the largest fruit markets in America, attended by buyers from hundreds of miles around; and here, too, is the Israelite House of David, whose story will demand our further attention.

It begins with Joanna Southcott, an Englishwoman of humble station, who late in life, in 1792, suddenly adopted the role of a prophet. Before her death in 1814 she had attracted 100,000 followers to her standard and had issued dozens of religious publications. In 1813, when well past sixty, she announced that on October 29, 1814, she would become the mother of Shiloh,[1] by immaculate conception. Instead, when the appointed time arrived she went into a trance and presently died.

Joanna was the founder of the cult of the seven angelic Messengers,[2] of whom she was herself the first. The others followed in due course, ending with the seventh, King Ben of Benton Harbor. The fifth Messenger was John Wroe, who claimed the divine distinction in 1822 and died in 1863. Although he was undoubtedly insane, he was exceedingly active and he introduced important modifications of the faith. Among them were the practice of circumcision, the wearing of hair and beard uncut and the doctrine of the necessity of cleansing of the blood. With him, too, began the long succession of accusations of immorality, including the now familiar charge of wholesale misconduct with young girls. Over these charges his following split into two factions; those who seceded followed the leadership of John Ward and continued to be known as Southcottites, while the faction which adhered to Wroe became known as Wroeites.

Although Wroe was illiterate, he dictated extensive messages to his "scribes," to be subsequently published in many volumes. He made several visits to Australia and America and won followers in both these lands. He fixed the beginning of the millennium in 1863, and when he died suddenly on February 5 of that year, his followers confidently anticipated his bodily resurrection.

The sixth Messenger was James J. Jazreel, who led the flock until his death in the early eighties. In 1888 Michael Mills became a convert to the cult, and for several years supported himself by proselyting for the faith and by selling copies of its sacred writings. The most important of these was a thick 800-page book of sermons, published by Jazreel for the edification of the Gentiles. It was called *The Flying Roll,* and from it his followers were popularly known as "Flying Rollers."

In 1891 Mills proclaimed himself to be the long-expected seventh Angel, and establishing a "God-House" in Detroit, presently succeeded in attracting eighty or a hundred followers to the colony. For a short time the Flying Rollers aroused only mild curiosity as they went about the streets in somber garb and with unkempt flowing hair. But curiosity was transformed to antipathy when reports presently became noised about that the habits of Prince Mike and his followers were such as to make the colony a menace to the morals of the community.

The public wrath exploded when Mrs. Mills entered suit for a divorce from her husband and in doing so preferred accusations of the practice of gross immorality at the God-House. Not only was Prince Mike maintaining a forty-nine-year-old "spiritual affinity," in the person of Eliza Courts, but he was also guilty of misconduct with several young girls whom he had induced to live at the house. Mike and his affinity were both arrested and Eliza's plea that she be permitted to occupy the same cell with him was rudely denied. At the same time several of the girls were taken into protective custody for holding as material witnesses.

One of them was Bernice Bickle, a child of fifteen years, whose parents in Toronto were zealous adherents of the cult. Mike had met her at her uncle's home in Sarnia in the autumn of 1891 and on returning to Detroit he had promptly obtained a revelation identifying her as the tenth "God-Head," who was to exemplify the virtue of "Obedience" in the God-House. In response to this information Bernice was brought to Detroit in December by her mother and entrusted to the tender mercies of the lecherous Angel, who promptly undertook by the employment of religious arguments to persuade her to submit to his desires. But "Obedience" proved herself unexpectedly chaste and stubborn, resisting for some weeks all of Mike's blandishments and provoking him to the threat that if she did not soon submit she would be in her grave. In February he accomplished his purpose and henceforth Bernice was the newest member of the harem of young girls inhabiting the God-House.

Haled before the Court to answer to the charges that had been prepared, Mike refused to plead or to employ an attorney, saying only that God would protect him. A few days later, however, one of the ablest lawyers of Detroit voluntarily undertook his cause and in the ensuing trial labored valiantly to defend him. So great was the popular indignation against him in Detroit that a change of venue to Washtenaw County was granted and the trial opened at Ann Arbor on June 14. Seldom has the staid university city been more deeply stirred. As in the earlier hearings at Detroit, the courtroom was packed to its capacity and overflow crowds thronged the corridors and the lawn outside the building; to afford moral support to the girl witnesses, a formidable body of matrons occupied the front benches of the courtroom throughout the entire trial.

But three state witnesses were called to seal the doom of the now-fallen angel. Bernice Bickle bravely recited her pitiful story, which was substantially repeated by two more girl victims of Prince Mike's lust. Although Bernice's father and mother had come from Toronto to repudiate their own daughter and affirm their faith in the purity of her seducer, it took the jury but a few minutes to arrive at a verdict of "guilty," and the judge promptly sentenced him to five years' imprisonment, the maximum penalty allowed by the law. The crowded courtroom broke forth in a demonstration of wild applause which the court officials made no effort to repress.

One of Prince Mike's followers who notably failed to profit by the lesson of his downfall was a young Kentucky hillbilly named Benjamin Franklin Purnell. In 1877 at the ripe age of sixteen he had married Angelina Brown, but the responsibilities of marriage added nothing to his cares; while Angelina continued to live with her parents, Ben "visited around." At the end of a couple of years a daughter was born and he came "home" for a time. Several more months passed in idleness, and when Angelina at length suggested that he find some employment to support his wife and child, he remarked that he thought he would go visiting again and wandered out of her life forever. Fifty years later she testified in court that he had never provided as much as a single dollar for her support.

Although Ben was a stranger to humdrum work, he was not wholly unenterprising. Soon after he deserted his wife and baby he entered upon an illicit union with Mary Stollard, who lived a few miles away in the next county. At this time Ben was about nineteen years of age and Mary was two years younger. They presently appeared before a justice of the peace in Aberdeen, Ohio, and underwent the odd procedure of formally acknowledging themselves as man and wife. A couple of years later Ben applied for a divorce from Angelina and wrote her that she was "free." Without bothering to confirm the information she subsequently married again; but since Ben neglected to prosecute his suit to a decree, both Angelina's union and his own with Mary Stollard remained bigamous to the end of their respective lives.

Such was the background of the future King and Queen of the House of David. Although their life for many years was obscure, from Mary's testimony in court years later, eked out by other sources of information, we are able to reconstruct it to some extent. They moved about from place to place, living for a time at Richmond, Indiana, where Ben actually worked at broom making and other odd jobs. During these years, also, he obtained a copy of *The Flying Roll* and its teaching determined his further vocation in life. In January 1892 he joined Prince Mike's colony in Detroit and before long attained the dignity of a "Pillar" in that bizarre community.[3] Here they resided for the next three years, engaging, in common with other colonists, upon missionary tours, exhorting and peddling *The*

Flying Roll from door to door wherever purchasers could be found.

Years later Elizabeth Kester remembered that Ben, on one occasion, proposed that a group of the colonists should "swap wives" temporarily, adding that she saw nothing immoral in his conduct. Considering the standards which Prince Mike himself had exemplified, this is not surprising, but Ben presently committed an offense which even this community of crackpots would not tolerate. Not content with the station he had achieved in it, he conceived the design of wresting the leadership of the cult from Prince Mike. After that unfortunate Angel was committed to the penitentiary his affinity, Eliza Courts, had assumed the title of Princess Michael and administered the colony in his stead. Thus matters went along until the spring of 1895, when "at cockcrowing" of the morning of March 12 the "graft" or spirit of the Lord "lit" upon Benjamin, who now proclaimed himself the true seventh angelic Messenger and Prince Mike as an imposter.

At the moment of the annunciation Ben bellowed so loud that the commotion he created was heard in the neighboring houses, and when somewhat later he called a meeting to announce his new dignity, one of the flock argued that since God speaks in a still small voice it could not have been the spirit of the Lord which had descended upon Ben.

The sequel disclosed that he had estimated too lightly the influence of the Princess Michael, who retained firm control over the cult. For his treason to Mike, he was dismissed from his office of Pillar and driven from the colony; with Mary and their small daughter he set out upon another preaching tour which took him to her old home and his own in eastern Kentucky.

During the next few years the couple wandered about from place to place, equipped with a pushcart which contained their meager belongings, preaching and hawking copies of their sacred literature as opportunity offered. Fortune at length smiled faintly upon them when an Ohio farmer gave them shelter for a year, and the smile broadened perceptibly when Silas Mooney, a truck gardener of Fostoria, afforded them a haven in his home for another year. Thereafter the devotion of Mooney and his wife Cora to Ben and Mary never faltered, and to the end of Ben's life they remained his devoted and more or less important subjects.

Ere now, Ben had begun to compose his first and most fundamental sacred writing, the *Star of Bethlehem,* and with $1,200 supplied by Ben Pelton, it was printed at Ashland in 1902.[4] Meanwhile the zealots who were attracted to his standard surrendered enough of their means to enable him to procure a building for a tabernacle. In it, on one occasion, he announced that at a future meeting the Holy Ghost would designate the "Virgin" of the flock by placing a visible symbol upon the head of the woman for whom this honor was reserved. Oddly enough, at the appointed time the symbol was seen on the head of Mrs. Mooney, who was certainly no virgin although she was Ben's benefactor in the flesh.

At Fostoria, as at Detroit and other places, hostile criticisms of the new sect soon began to circulate. They were intensified by a distressing tragedy which occurred in February 1903. Hettie Purnell, now sixteen years of age, obtained employment in a plant devoted to making explosives for Fourth of July noisemaking canes. On her first day of work an explosion occurred by which she and seven other workers were killed. Although years later Ben spoke feelingly of the death of his daughter, his conduct at the time was callous. Hettie's death was conclusive proof that she had been disobedient to the faith and the parents refused to admit the burned and disfigured remains to their home or to assume any responsibility for their burial.[5] Hettie was given a Christian burial by considerate townsmen whose liking for the strange sect in their midst was not increased by this exhibition of parental inhumanity.

It mattered little to Benjamin, however, for opportunity was already beckoning him to a greener pasture. At Benton Harbor, Michigan, there had long been a local group of Flying Rollers. Its most prominent members were two brothers, Louis and Albert Baushke, who had achieved wealth and local prominence as carriage makers. The prospect of wealth was like manna in the wilderness to Ben, who opened a correspondence with the two brothers which resulted in an understanding that Ben and Mary were to remove from Fostoria to Benton Harbor. In March 1903, only a month after Hettie's death, they entrained for the new Promised Land.[6] With them went Silas and Cora Mooney and their young son, besides two other zealots, and these seven pilgrims comprised the original "ingathering" to the new religious center.

For King Ben and his bigamous consort the hegira to Benton Harbor marked the dawn of a new era. Prosperity smiled upon them and their days of poverty and obscurity were gone forever. Prince Mike and his Princess had long since left the country, and there was no one to dispute Ben's angelic pretensions which the local cult members cheerfully swallowed. To them he was Shiloh, Immanuel, Gabriel, the younger brother of Christ, the seventh angelic Messenger and the King of the Israelites. Under the influence of his teaching, ably supplemented by the blandishments of the bands of proselyters sent out on tours over the country, believers flocked rapidly to the New Jerusalem at Benton Harbor, and since all who came were required to surrender their property to the King his wealth and power kept step with their numbers.

Something approaching a master stroke was perpetrated in 1904 when Ben himself crossed the Pacific to Australia, intent upon taking over the many Wroeite disciples who dwelt in the land "down under." Although his progress was attended by tumults and brawls, many of the faithful accepted his claims and leaving their native land forever accompanied him in a body to distant Benton Harbor. The party, eighty-five in number, returned through the Indian Ocean and the Mediterranean Sea, the only notable incidents of the voyage being a row with members of the crew over the paucity of tips they received and the picking of Ben's pocket by a degraded Gentile who secured nothing for his pains.

Before long the following Ben attracted to Benton Harbor numbered several hundred persons. In the beginning they were sheltered in scattered dwelling houses, but the sorry experience of Prince Mike at Detroit had disclosed some of the dangers arising from too close contact between Israelites and Gentiles, while amid such surroundings the communal life Ben preached could be realized only in part. Accordingly a tract of land outside the city was procured for the colony and a building called the Ark was erected for its accommodation. Larger and better buildings soon followed, to which such names as Shiloh, Jerusalem, Bethlehem and the Diamond House were given. Other structures to serve the various needs of the community were erected as circumstances permitted, but increasing numbers long taxed the available living accommodations and the colonists were crowded together in quarters which in some cases sadly lacked the ordinary conveniences of civilized life.

Meanwhile they were dressed in the simplest clothing and fed on a vegetarian diet which knew nothing of luxury. They were strangers alike to privacy and to the joys of family life, and their living quarters were frequently shifted, without explanation or prior notice, at the convenience or whim of the King. That some who had surrendered their property, their homes and their freedom in exchange for such an existence should sooner or later entertain thoughts of rebellion is less strange than that hundreds endured their lot uncomplainingly and with no hope of relief through the unending years.

Those who chose might leave the colony, of course, but on entering it they had surrendered whatever property they owned to the King and had deprived themselves of any claim upon him for its return or for recompense. In actual practice, seceders were commonly provided with a railroad ticket to their intended destination or to one arbitrarily determined for them by the King, and in addition a small amount of cash, like convicts discharged from the penitentiary. Illustrative of this procedure is the testimony of Emil Rosetta, whose parents had surrendered over $10,000 worth of property upon joining the colony. Emil was then a sturdy youth of nineteen. Upon withdrawing ten years later, he received a parting gift of $10. "I received a dollar a year," he testified. "For ten years' work I got $10."

In short, the economic status of the colonists was no better than that of the ante-bellum Negro slave, while in certain respects their social condition was even worse. King Ben was an enlightened and usually a kindly master; so too was St. Clare, the owner of Uncle Tom. The Negro could be sold down river, but until he was, he commonly enjoyed the possession of a cabin in which he lived with his wife and children. King Ben usually dispersed the members of a family, and on occasions when husband and wife were left together the marital relation was sternly prohibited. When the whim seized him he also performed marriages wholesale, without asking the prior desire or choice of his subjects; and having done so, sternly prohibited them from the enjoyment of normal human relations.

Long in advance of Hitler or Mussolini, he devised a system of espionage and control at which Judge Fead, after listening to 15,000 pages of testimony, could only express his amazement. Upon joining the colony each member submitted a written life confession to the King. Thereafter monthly written confessions were required, in which, in addition to reporting upon his own conduct the subject was required to report every instance of misconduct of word or deed by others which he had observed. These reports were collected by the "sweepers"[7] and carefully read, and although the contents were generally trivial, everything deemed desirable for the King to know was brought to his personal attention.

By such methods King Ben maintained his despotic authority over subjects whose minds were drugged from the beginning by their acceptance of the teaching that he was their divinely appointed ruler, through whom alone they could escape the death which awaits all mankind. Illustrative of the extent to which this control extended is the case of Ruth Wade. She was an exceptionally high-spirited girl whom Ben first debauched and then peremptorily married to a man whom she had not chosen or desired, after which he sent them out together upon an extended missionary tour, while still requiring them to observe the "virgin law." When, after months of such close association, Ruth ventured to kiss her young husband she quickly repented of her supposed sin and loyally reported it in her next monthly confession. Upon her return to Benton Harbor she was rebuked in public meeting by Ben for this act of "lust," and ostracized by her girl companions—"all because I had looked up to you as God and made my confession trusting you with it," as she wrote in a later letter to Queen Mary, when the scales had fallen from her eyes.

Coming to Benton Harbor a forty-two-year-old failure in life, in twenty years King Ben accumulated property amounting in value, according to various estimates, to several million dollars. In part, this remarkable achievement was undoubtedly due to his own shrewdness and administrative ability. In larger measure, however, his financial success was the result of factors inherent in the community he developed. Only those who were more than ordinarily religious and sober-minded were attracted to it. To them habits of thrift and industry were second nature and they led extremely simple lives wherein no trace of luxury or vanity was tolerated. They eschewed meat, liquor and tobacco as a matter of religious principle, and in almost a quarter of a century no single member of the colony, save only its licentious leader, ever indulged in conduct which required the attention of the police. Even the little children were productive workers, since Ben regarded education as worse than useless, and wasted neither time nor money upon it.[8] In fact practically everyone worked, and save for satisfying the requirements of bare existence no one received any pay for his toil.

With all these advantages, and located in an agricultural Eden, the colony could hardly have failed to prosper. Yet Ben added other striking sources of income which evidence his possession of both enterprise and imagination. The twin cities lie directly across the lake from Chicago and in the pre-automobile age they were the great city's nearest and most popular summer resort, reached by a pleasant voyage for a round-trip fare of fifty cents. Summer resorters are avid for amusement, and to accommodate the thousands who thronged to Benton Harbor Ben established a small-scale Coney Island, whose busiest and most profitable day fell on Sunday.[9] Although no figures are available it has been stated that as many as 200,000 persons patronized the park in a single season. Whatever the number, since the Benjaminites did all the work and even manufactured the engines and other equipment of the miniature railroad, the park was a constant source of profit to the King.

Two other enterprises which advertised the colony were the band and the baseball teams which toured the country for decades. The bewhiskered ball players, in particular, proved a great attraction to the baseball-minded public whose attendance was rewarded with a rare display of athletic skill. An observer who witnessed a game played in 1923 with a smart semipro team from Chicago racily describes the slaughter of the latter to the tune of 30 or 40 to 0. At that, it was the House of David's second team which committed the massacre, the first team being absent on a tour on which they had won fifteen of the first sixteen games played.[10]

The regularity with which the long-haired boys mowed down their opponents induced the suspicion that some of them were Gentiles in disguise who had been hired to bolster the Israelite team with their athletic skill. At one time a pitcher named Mooney was a great gate attraction, in part because of his prowess but still more because of his reputed offer of a position with the Chicago Cubs. Mooney went stale, however, and was unable to pitch for a time. The Israelites, nothing daunted, quietly replaced him with one of their own members, who was advertised to the public as the real Mooney. In circles less concerned with the problem of personal salvation, such a substitute is known as a ringer.

Deceptions such as this were of slight importance, but from the foundation of the colony Ben was secretly addicted to a practice which threatened to involve both colony and King in one common ruin. Although no one knew better than he the reason for Prince Mike's downfall at Detroit, the knowledge did not deter him from embarking upon a course of wholesale immorality with his youthful female subjects. There is no present need to enter upon a detailed recital of his exploits, but whoever examines the thousands of pages of testimony upon his conduct must be convinced, as was the court, that until practically the end of his life he was engaged in illicit relations with a large number of young girls.

Upon Prince Mike the heavy hand of the law descended promptly, and the reader will naturally ask how King Ben could carry on the same practices with impunity for practically a quarter of a century. The answer involves several factors which must be pointed out. Prince Mike was unwise enough to settle in the midst of a large city and his following never attained numbers or wealth sufficient to enable it to influence public sentiment or to exert political pressure upon public officials. King Ben located his kingdom outside a small city and he quickly achieved wealth and numbers of followers sufficient to exert a powerful influence over both local public opinion and the agencies of law enforcement. The disinclination to shoot Santa Claus is universal and the people of Benton Harbor were disposed to look tolerantly upon the leader who was bringing wealth and increased business activity to the community.

In another respect Ben was merely fortunate. It was Prince Mike's own wife who rebelled against the humiliation of sharing his bed with a harem and loosed the shafts of public indignation upon him. Unless Queen Mary was incredibly moronic, a thing which no one has ever suggested, she could not possibly have been ignorant of Ben's extensive immorality. Yet for more than twenty years she viewed it with complacency and according to some witnesses even actively abetted it.

Yet the question still persists how numbers of normally decent individuals could be induced to participate for years in practices which the moral judgment of mankind deems abhorrent. The answer lies in the well-nigh incredible sway which the King exercised over the minds of his subjects. Their redeemer and lord, he was incapable of doing wrong. When he seemed, judged by ordinary human standards, to be committing an evil act, they believed he was doing it merely to test their faith. The consequence followed that men and women normally sane would refuse to credit the evidence of their own senses. Thus a double standard of truthtelling and of morals was inculcated, under which cult members were permitted to deceive the Gentile world with a clear conscience and a straight face.

The perverted doctrine, apparently originated by John Wroe, of the necessity of cleansing the blood, which could be accomplished through sexual intercourse, proved a potent aid to the King's evil designs. The young girls whom he corrupted were always immature. Some of them were born in the colony and others had been brought to it at a tender age. Necessarily they knew little of the Gentile world outside which was constantly pictured to them as a horrifying thing; while within the colony they were constantly subjected to the teaching that they owed implicit obedience to Ben. "They brought us up to the House of David," Ruth Wade, who had come to the colony as a young girl, testified. "The band was playing and Benjamin came out all dressed in white, and we walked through the archway and I thought I was going right into the gates of Paradise." When, subsequently, she entertained doubts of the purity of his conduct and went to her mother with them she was told that everything Benjamin said was right and holy and to doubt him was to be damned. Thus rebuked, she did not confide in her mother when subsequently she fell victim to his lust and she still continued to look up to him as to God.

When suits were started and investigations threatened, Ben resorted to several characteristic measures of defense. One of these was to procure the mass signing of depositions by the girls of the colony denying that they had been intimate with him. Allied to this was the spiriting away to places of concealment of the girls whose testimony might prove damaging. As for Ben himself, he had one unfailing resort from danger—he ran away or went into hiding within the colony.[11] To facilitate such escapes, warning signals were arranged and secret retreats were constructed.

In 1910, when charges of immorality were advanced, the first of the series of group marriages was resorted to and at the same time Benjamin conveniently disappeared for a season. In 1914 when Moses Clark sued Ben for having debauched his wife some years before when she was a girl member of the colony, he took refuge in Canada and another mass marriage ceremony was staged. In 1919 when similar charges were made by Isabelle Pritchard and her daughters, another blanket affidavit, signed by fifty female cult members and testifying to Benjamin's purity of conduct, was prepared. All prior disappearing exploits were dwarfed to insignificance, however, by Ben's final achievement of concealing himself in the colony for almost four years while the baffled representatives of the law conducted a vain search for him.

The King's last public appearance was at a Christmas reception in 1922. Thereafter years passed while the colonists continued their placid pursuits, none of them caring to ask or discuss the whereabouts of their absent master. During 1923 the sheriff twice raided the colony in search of King Ben, without positive result. Three years later, on the night of November 16, 1926, a detachment of state police, guided by Bessie Daniels, a disgruntled former cult member, broke down the doors of the Diamond House with axes and rushing upstairs halted the flight of an emaciated old man, garbed only in nightcap and underwear, whom Bessie identified as King Ben. In the confusion one woman fled to the basement and escaped. Three others, clad only in nightgowns, were captured. One of the captives was Myrtle Tulk, a member of the King's inner circle of confidants and long his personal attendant. The two remaining were attractive young members of the cult, whose presence in Ben's secret retreat could only be accounted for on the ground that they were there to gratify his urge for feminine society.

For King Ben the end of indulgence in earthy recreation had arrived. Dressed by Myrtle Tulk, he was conveyed to the county jail, whose doors had long been yawning for him. An action to abate the colony as a public nuisance and to remove Ben and Queen Mary from all further connection with it was instituted in due course by the attorney general of Michigan. An exhaustive investigation, conducted in the summer of 1927, involving the examination of scores of witnesses and the production of thousands of pages of testimony, concluded with the issuance of a decree for the appointment of a receiver and the exclusion of Ben and Mary from the further conduct of the colony's affairs.

Meanwhile Ben was called before the bar of a greater judge than any mundane court could provide. On December 16, 1927, only five weeks after Judge Fead's decision declaring the colony a public nuisance had been rendered, the King, reduced to a mere shadow of his former husky self and weighing less than a hundred pounds, breathed his last. The wasted body was embalmed by his followers and, consigned to a magnificent casket, was placed in the Diamond House, where it remains, awaiting whatever resurrection the future holds in store.

Unlike King Strang's earlier kingdom at the Beavers, which toppled to headlong ruin when its creator was slain, Ben's colony still continues to thrive, although in modified form. Following his death the court order for its dissolution was rescinded by the Supreme Court, which sensibly reasoned that a higher power had abated the nuisance by removing Ben from the earthly scene. During the King's later years H. T. Dewhirst, a former local judge of California, had joined the colony, where he soon acquired a commanding influence. Self-confident and aggressive, he gradually usurped the authority formerly wielded by Francis Thorpe, who had long served as Ben's secretary and executive agent.

Although the outsider, lacking authoritative means of securing information, can only tentatively survey the scene, it seems apparent that Dewhirst utilized the long illness and seclusion of the King to make himself *de facto* ruler of the colony and that Mary and Thorpe, whose positions and influence were alike being undermined by the newcomer, joined in opposition to him and endeavored themselves to grasp the power which was slipping from the hands of the dying monarch. In the struggle they were completely outgeneraled by their shrewder and more worldly opponent, who was a graduate of the school of practical mundane politics. Some light upon the palace revolution that was waged behind the scenes was revealed by Benjamin, whose testimony in his trial disclosed his discovery that Mary was disloyal, and that he had been nursing a scorpion in his bosom.[12]

Whatever the truth may have been concerning the matter, the death of the King left Dewhirst in complete possession of the colony, with Mary and Thorpe outside the breastworks. He had the office and its records, the loyalty of the office staff of workers, the vault containing the treasure, and all of the buildings and other physical property. Although Mary claimed to have the support of a majority of the colonists, ugly charges were bandied that the judge was seeking to dragoon them to his support by depriving them of food and other necessities of life.[13]

Eventually Mary, unwilling or unable to continue the legal fight, accepted such terms as she could get and in 1930 the House of David was rent in twain. Dewhirst retained the original colony site with all its improvements, including the amusement park, the cash and jewels and even the body of the man who for almost fifty years had been Mary's life partner. To her went various farms and the hotel in Benton Harbor; she also retained (or continued to maintain) the baseball team. Deprived of shelter for herself and her followers, she moved down the road a few rods and began the erection of a new set of buildings, humbler in size and architecture than those from which she had been ousted. The stranger who visits the scene might readily assume the two sets of buildings to be parts of a single organization. But an invisible barrier, Alpine in altitude, separates the two colonies, and the followers of each profess a complete disdain for the existence and activities of the rival group. To Mary's followers the Dewhirst adherents are "Danites," or rebels against God; since one can prove anything by drawing upon the allegorical and frequently unintelligible writings of Benjamin they have no difficulty in identifying Judge Dewhirst with Dan, a judge in Israel who coveted the head rulership and like Lucifer proceeded to usurp it. To distinguish her own faction from those of her rival, Mary calls it

"The Israelite House of David as reorganized by Mary Purnell," or more briefly "the City of David"; and in utterances of recent years the effort is made to place her on a par with Benjamin as coauthor of his writings and the woman divinely appointed to complete his work.

Since the split-up, both leaders have exhibited marked ability in the management of their respective affairs. The enterprises of Judge Dewhirst have been more spectacular but the ability displayed by Queen Mary has been no less substantial. A recent investigator reports that her followers appear more contented and that they are well-clothed, hard-working people. The Dewhirst adherents have tended to become more worldly-minded, as evidenced by their "smoking cigarets and sprinkling their talk with cussing." Queen Mary conducts farming operations and runs the hotel and a tourist camp. The judge has developed a large fruit-freezing plant in Benton Harbor, a cannery and greenhouses, and has established, a few miles outside the city on the main highway to Chicago, one of the most imposing tourist lodges to be found east of California. Associated with it is a surprisingly good night club, where hard liquors and other divertisements abound.

Freed from the incubus of King Ben's sexual vagaries and exhibiting the sober industry which has always characterized the rank and file of the Benjaminites, they enjoy the respect and good will of their Gentile neighbors. But the era of proselyting died with King Ben. Neither organization sends out missionaries and neither displays any great desire to obtain new adherents.[14] Meanwhile the years pass and the arrival of the millennium, which Ben originally fixed for July 21, 1906, still stubbornly lags, while the beards of the "little people" have turned from their original black or red to white, and one by one their bodies are silently carted away to be deposited in the ever lengthening rows which adorn the local cemetery. Save to the eye of faith, the early end of the "ingathering" so hopefully begun four decades ago seems inevitable.

---

[1] See Genesis, 49:10: "The scepter shall not depart from Judah, nor a lawgiver from between his feet, until Shiloh come; and unto him shall the gathering of the people be." Although theologians advance varying interpretations of the passage, to Joanna's followers Shiloh meant the Messiah, or Christ.

[2] Based on Revelation, 10:7.

[3] The "Pillars" were a group of officials who, subject to the leadership of the angelic Messenger, supervised the affairs of the cult.

[4] Judge Fead, who had a copy of the book before him, states that it was printed at Fostoria; but Mary testified that it was printed at Ashland. Ben, in his rambling autobiography printed in *The Ball of Fire,* made the same statement:

> "*The Star of Bethlehem* was printed at Ashland, Ohio. We often talked our experiences to the family with whom we were stopping. And there came a time that we went up to Ashland to see about our printing; and preaching on the way; and she went along and saw many of those things fulfilled. . . . At Ashland they had got the money for the printing of the *Star* before hand; and we had trouble in getting it finished; and on this trip we entered their printing office and boarded with them, and rather against their will, until the work was well on the way."

[5] This conduct, abhorrent to Gentile minds, was a necessary consequence of the church teaching on the subject of bodily immortality. Since the "elect" are to live forever, provided they keep the faith, the fact of death automatically establishes their disobedience. At Benton Harbor a wife was not permitted even to see her husband who had just expired, while a young girl who touched her dead mother's body was deemed unclean.

[6] The two Baushke families turned over their fortune of about $100,000 to Ben, the first gift of any considerable size he received.

[7] The "sweepers" were assistants of the King who executed his orders for shifting the quarters of inmates, collecting the confessions, and other routine matters. In effect they were a standing body of investigators for Ben, to whom they reported whatever they learned which was deemed amiss. *A Book of Rules,* published for the guidance of the colonists in their everyday relations, contained these orders, among others:

> "Anything seen out of the way (that is of the Jew or Gentile), report to officers at once if it be worth notice, so that they can be watched—this is the duty of all.
> "And it is furthermore the indispenable and holy duty of any and all to make reports . . . and anything contrary is disobedience and disgrace to the most high calling. Anyone concealing evils and misdoings is a partaker of the same and an enemy; and such reporting must be made to Mary and Benjamin only—no talking about it to each other."

[8] "Dung more useful [than education]," he wrote. "Dung can be put on ground and do something." Ben's own son, Coy Purnell, was reared in complete illiteracy.

[9] The Israelites professed to believe in the Sabbath, but with the aid of the biblical verse which says that a thousand years are but a day in the Lord's sight, they were able to postpone its observance some 6,000 years.

[10] Webb Waldron, *We Explore the Great Lakes* (New York, 1923), Chap. 18.

[11] As usual, scriptural warrant for such evasions of the law were not lacking. Verses cited to show that Jesus had set the example for Ben of fleeing from his enemies include Matthew 2:14-15; John 8:59; John 12:36; John 7:10; Luke 4:29-30.

[12] "Scorpion" is a favorite epithet in the colony to characterize traitors and backsliders. The King, however, expressed his confidence that Mary had not been guilty of "carnal" misconduct. Since she was almost seventy years of age, this seems reasonable enough.

[13] The royal treasury was believed by Mary's faction to be fabulously rich, consisting of bales of thousand-dollar bills and quantities of diamonds and other jewels. Quite possibly its richness was greatly overestimated. Cora Mooney, who had been a trusted adherent of Ben since the Fostoria days, affirmed that he liked to keep his cash in thousand-dollar bills, and that he was saving it up for use in some future anticipated emergency. On the matter of food, Mary charged that although her followers outnumbered the opposition they were being given but ten percent of the total amount distributed.

[14] Disagreeing in all things else, for some reason unknown to the writer the two have united in suppressing *The Star of Bethlehem,* the first and most fundamental of Ben's sacred writings. Efforts to purchase it are met with the response that Gentiles are unable to understand it and copies are available only to persons who have already mastered the other sacred writings.

Part III

ALL AROUND THE COAST

Chapter 24

From Waugoshance to Sleeping Bear

FROM Petoskey and Little Traverse Bay to New Buffalo, a distance of 300 miles, Lake Michigan's eastern coast is hemmed with orchards of apples, peaches, plums and cherries, interspersed with berry fields reddened by the sun of midsummer and vineyards purple in autumn. Annually in springtime the orchards burst forth in an orgy of scented bloom whose gorgeous display draws motorists by thousands from the cities and towns within driving range. In the autumn they are again lured from their homes to view the parade of colors—dull red, bright yellow, burnished gold and flaming scarlet—which the beeches and maples, oaks and birches of the north woods don to bid farewell to the declining year.

Scientific explanation of the East Coast Fruit Belt is the fact that the vast reservoir of water we call Lake Michigan is less susceptible to changes of temperature than is the surrounding land. Centuries in advance of the modern heat engineer, it was air-conditioning the west winds which blew over it, absorbing their extremes of summer heat and winter cold and giving the east coast the freedom from freezing temperatures in late spring and early autumn which the successful cultivation of orchard and small fruits requires.

Although the lake breeze accounts for the existence of the Fruit Belt, the particular varieties cultivated vary more or less from north to south and even between different localities lying in the same general latitude. Peaches and grapes, in whose production Michigan ranks third among the states of the Union,[1] are chiefly confined to the southerly half of the lake coast, while apple and cherry orchards flourish throughout its entire extent. Two southern counties, Berrien and Van Buren, alone account for five-sixths of the state's grape production. Berrien is also the banner apple county, although Oceana, halfway up the coast, is a close second, and Leelanau, Mason and Grand Traverse, lying well to the north, all produce tremendous quantities of apples.

More cherries are raised in Michigan than anywhere else in America, and Traverse City is the world capital of cherryland. Yet Berrien County, far to the south, presses close upon Grand Traverse, and cherry orchards are a familiar sight throughout the entire extent of the Fruit Belt. Apple orchards were developed extensively in the Traverse Bay area a generation in advance of cherries. Toward the close of the nineteenth century, however, the adaptability of the region for cherry culture was established, and the planting of the vast orchards of the present day followed in due course.

Point Waugoshance, a narrow sandy peninsula which juts westward into the lake, bounds the east coast at its northern end. Here in early June 1763 Alexander Henry and several companions in misery, survivors of the massacre of Fort Michilimackinac, were rescued from their captors who were conducting them to the Beaver Islands, where they were to be boiled and eaten. A few miles down the coast from Waugoshance lies the Indian settlement known in recent decades as Cross Village. Anciently it was called L'Arbre Croche, or the Crooked Tree. Here a Jesuit mission was established in 1742 and it was largely the civilizing influence exerted by the missionary that kept the Ottawa from joining the Confederacy of Pontiac against the English twenty years later.

Cross Village is probably the oldest settlement of continuous occupancy in the state of Michigan.[2] Through the primitive period it was a center of Indian trade, and during much of the time it was a convenient source of supply for the corn needed to feed the voyageurs. Here Captain Etherington was given safe shelter for several weeks following the massacre of Michilimackinac in 1763, and from here, augmented by the garrison from Green Bay and attended by an escort of friendly Ottawa from L'Arbre Croche, he set out for Montreal on July 18. The Indian wife of John Askin, long a prominent merchant of Mackinac and Detroit, seems to have been a resident of L'Arbre Croche, and here the oldest son, John Askin, Jr., was born, probably in 1762. Educated by his father and reared in the ways of civilization, he was long an agent in the British Indian Department at Fort St. Joseph and other places, and he figured prominently in the capture of Mackinac from the Americans at the opening of the War of 1812.

The proximity of L'Arbre Croche to Mackinac insured the loyalty of the Ottawa to Great Britain throughout the period of revolutionary warfare. From time to time they embarked upon expeditions against the "Rebels" which led them to points as distant as the Hudson River Valley and the French Illinois. Of one such undertaking we have an interesting record. In a council held at L'Arbre Croche on July 4, 1779, Major De Peyster, the Commandant of Mackinac and rhymster friend of Robert Burns, delivered a long harangue to the chiefs which he subsequently turned into English verse. Filled with Indian terms and technical allusions, it would be largely meaningless but for the footnote explanations which the author throughtfully supplies. If not the earliest poem composed on the shores of Lake Michigan, it is certainly one of the most curious.

Following the American occupation of Mackinac in 1796 the L'Arbre Croche Ottawa gradually came under American influence. Although the Jesuit mission had long since been discontinued, they retained their interest in the Catholic faith. In 1802 when a Protestant missionary from New England, the Reverend David Bacon, visited Mackinac, intent upon establishing himself at L'Arbre Croche, they firmly vetoed the design. Said their head chief to Bacon:

"My father, we think the Great Spirit did not put us on the earth to learn such things as the white people learn. If he had thought it proper, he would have taught us such things when he put us here. My father, we cannot live together so as to attend to these things like the white people. The Great Spirit has given them cattle and everything about them that they want to live upon. If they are hungry they have only to go into their yard and kill an animal. But he gave us no such things. When we are hungry we have to go away and hunt to get something to eat. If we set out in the morning we may have to run all day to find something and we sometimes have to go without."

Convinced that he would never be permitted to carry on his work at L'Arbre Croche, Bacon was meditating a permanent establishment on Mackinac Island to which he hoped to attract an increasing number of the natives. In this, too, he met with insuperable obstacles, and before long he abandoned both the local field and missionary work altogether. A son, Leonard, born at Detroit in 1802, during the temporary sojourn of the parents there, became in the succeeding generation one of America's most noted preachers.

Today the very name of L'Arbre Croche is forgotten. Cross Village, the northernmost hamlet of Lake Michigan's eastern shore, is a small settlement of Ottawa and Chippewa, whose most conspicuous building is an attractive little church. Along the shore line southward to Little Traverse Bay runs the most beautiful driveway in Michigan, bowered in maples and beeches, through which one catches occasional glimpses of the blue waters of Lake Michigan and the distant Beaver Islands. Save for Green Bay, Little Traverse and Grand Traverse Bays are the two principal indentations around the thousand-mile shore line of Lake Michigan. All this east coast region is Vacation Land, crowded each summer with dwellers from midwest cities and from the heated southland, many of whom have developed luxurious country estates. Leopold and Loeb, whose murder of little Bobby Franks stirred the nation in 1924, passed many boyhood summers on one such estate near Charlevoix before they began their permanent residence within the grim walls of Joliet Penitentiary. All of the advantages which wealth and education could bestow availed nothing to restrain them from their evil course, bringing ruin upon themselves and unspeakable grief and suffering upon their own and their victim's families.

Just outside Petoskey on a wooded elevation which overlooks Little Traverse Bay is Bay View Assembly, where since 1876 the Methodist Church has maintained a summer Chautauqua. The physical equipment includes a fine auditorium, facilities for golf and other sports and several hundred cottages built on the terraced slope above the beautiful bay. Instruction of college grade in music and the liberal arts is given throughout the summer by a faculty of capable teachers, while a profusion of concerts and addresses by leaders of national prominence are provided for the enjoyment of the general public.

The names of Little Traverse and Grand Traverse Bays preserve the memory of the French voyageurs of bygone centuries who coasted the lake shore in canoes and Mackinac boats in pursuit of the Indian trade. Instead of making the long detour around the shore line of these bays, they shortened their journey and its toil by crossing from headland to headland. The shorter crossing they called *la petite traverse* and the longer one *la grande traverse,* names which today, in rough translation, are applied to Little Traverse and Grand Traverse Bays, as well as to Grand Traverse County and Traverse City.

Charlevoix County and the city of Charlevoix, which lie a few miles south of Little Traverse Bay, derive their names from the noted eighteenth-century Jesuit historian and explorer who in 1719 was commissioned by King Louis XV to make a report upon the French colonies in North America. He devoted almost three years to this mission, journeying by open canoe up the St. Lawrence and through the Great Lakes. From St. Joseph at the south end of Lake Michigan he crossed to the Kankakee River and followed that stream and the Illinois to the Mississippi and the latter to the Gulf of Mexico, reaching New Orleans early in 1722. His valuable *Journal Historique* supplies our only traveler's description of interior America in the first quarter of the eighteenth century.

Lake Charlevoix was called Pine Lake by the early American settlers of the region. It is one of Michigan's largest interior lakes and its extensive shores are lined with orchards, summer cottages and camps. At its eastern end is Boyne City and on its southerly arm East Jordan, ancient lumbering centers now chiefly devoted to the entertainment of resorters. About a mile from Lake Michigan, Lake Charlevoix empties through a short passageway into Round Lake, which in its turn empties by another short outlet into Lake Michigan. Three-quarters of a century ago Round Lake was transformed by government engineers into the harbor of Charlevoix, and while the lumbering era lasted it was the scene of much activity. In more recent years the commerce of the place has vanished and the beautiful harbor shelters only pleasure boats.

An interesting development of the last two decades around the northerly half of the lake is the smelt runs which occur each spring in the rivers emptying into Lake Michigan. The smelt is a tiny fish of shining silvery color which grows to a length of four to ten inches.

They were first planted in Lake Michigan a generation ago in the hope that they might serve as a food supply for larger existing species. For a decade or more they throve unseen in the waters of the great lake until in the early twenties, to the amazement of the local populace, they began making the runs for which the adjacent rivers are now famous.

The smelt run only at night, crowding the streams from bank to bank with their well-nigh incredible numbers. Quick to capitalize the attraction, the merchants of Beulah in 1925 proclaimed a Smelt Festival, a custom imitated at East Jordan and several other places as the smelt invaded successive rivers. In anticipation of the event electric lights are strung along the river bank, which is crowded by thousands of smelters who have come from Chicago, Detroit and points even more remote than these. Equipped with buckets, wash tubs, sacks, dip nets and other paraphernalia appropriate to the occasion they eagerly await the announcement that the run is on. Then for fifteen or thirty minutes they frantically dip for fish, which they thrust into the receptacles they have brought along or dump in piles upon the bank; after this the lights are turned off and a breathing period ensues until the frantic scramble is resumed.

No American festival would be complete without its "queen" and other kindred diversions, which the local promoters do not neglect to supply. At East Jordan, for example, a Smelters' Parade, banquet and ball are held; a King of Smelts is crowned, his royal proclamation read and a display of fireworks is witnessed. Both on Lake Charlevoix and Crystal Lake winter fishing for smelt has become popular. Hundreds of fishing huts are hauled out on the ice to create a temporary town, called Smeltania, for which a mayor, city manager and traffic officers are appointed. To supply the demand which the presence of hundreds of persons creates, grocery and other stores spring into being as if by magic.[3]

Grand Traverse Bay, over thirty miles deep and almost half as wide, is divided into two arms by sliverlike Old Mission Peninsula, at whose outer tip Old Mission Light, lying exactly midway between the North Pole and the Equator, safeguards the shipping that enters the bay. Between it and the base of the peninsula where Traverse City has grown up lie almost continuous cherry orchards, comprising

THE GARY WORKS OF THE CARNEGIE-ILLINOIS STEEL CORPORATION

TULIP TIME IN HOLLAND

TRADITIONAL SWEEPING OF STREETS AT TULIP TIME FESTIVAL

what is claimed to be the densest concentration of cherry trees in America.

Traverse City, metropolis of the bay country, was founded in the late 1840's as a lumbering town, and today it is chiefly noted as a resort and orchard center. To harvest the annual crop requires the labor of hundreds of pickers, large numbers of whom are city dwellers who welcome the opportunity to combine a summer outing with paid employment amid pleasant surroundings at labor for which no great degree of skill is demanded. Each summer the city turns the harvest season into a carnival by staging a Cherry Festival, to which nation-wide attention is attracted by the device of sending a "queen" to Washington on the mission of presenting a huge cherry pie to the President.

The Leelanau County Peninsula thrusts northward, fingerlike, between Lake Michigan and Grand Traverse Bay. It is bounded on three sides by water, and it contains numerous inland lakes in addition, the largest and most notable being Glen and Leelanau lakes. The former is proudly acclaimed by local dwellers as the third most beautiful lake in the world. Perhaps their modesty in conceding that two others outrank it is deserving of commendation. But they admit that the county contains "the world's largest cherry orchard" and the largest sand dunes in America.

Most noted of the sand dunes is Sleeping Bear. Although it may not be the largest in America, it is easily one of the most notable on Lake Michigan and the charming legend which explains its name is deserving of remembrance. It is a "live" or moving dune, bare of vegetation save for a small clump of stunted trees at its summit, which rises steeply several hundred feet above the lake. The westerly winds which blow almost constantly here drive the dune inland at the rate of several feet a year, burying the forest in its pathway and uncovering the gaunt skeletons of trees ages old on its rearward side. The prevailing air currents make it an ideal site for glider flights, and before the present World War began glider enthusiasts from all parts of the country resorted here to practice their sport.

The narrative of Gurdon S. Hubbard, who visited the Sleeping Bear as a young fur-trade employee in 1822, discloses that its appearance has changed but little since that time. Indian legend relates that there was once a terrible forest fire on the Wisconsin side of the lake, which drove all the animals into the water. Among them were a mother bear and her two cubs who, to escape the flames, struck out for the Michigan shore. They swam for several days, but the cubs became confused in the smoke and before reaching the land their strength gave out. The mother bear, on landing, paced the shore for days, calling in vain for her children, until at length she too become exhausted and fell asleep. There she still lies, looking out upon the lake, and to reward her devotion the Great Spirit has created North and South Manitou Islands where the cubs sank from sight. Here they remain to this day, as any doubter of the legend may readily convince himself.

The Manitous are the southerly extension of the archipelago which includes the Fox and Beaver Island groups. South Manitou has a fine harbor, which in recent years has frequently been utilized as the base for the annual maneuvers of the ships of the Great Lakes Naval Reserve. In an earlier generation it was a highly prized port of safety for vessels menaced by the heavy gales which blow on Lake Michigan. Along with Big Beaver, the Manitous were favorite fueling stations for steamboats in the era of wood-burning engines. To provide the fuel, woodcutters were engaged to live on the islands, and since no one else did, they led a lonely existence. Sentimental Margaret Fuller, who toured the lakes in 1843 expecting to find exemplified in the western wilderness the ideal way of life, was shocked by their slovenly dwellings and unkempt persons. "I had thought of such a position, from its mixture of profound solitude with service to the great world, as possessing an ideal beauty," she sorrowfully recorded. A shrewder observer than Margaret was Thurlow Weed, who came along four years later. Under no illusions concerning the ideal life of the wilderness, he confined his comments to the absence of animal life on the Manitous. There were neither animals nor birds and even reptiles were seldom seen; in the absence of all these, even the mosquitoes, "finding no one to torment, come not to the Manitou Island."

The Beaver Islands, in French the *Isles du Castor,* were known to the earliest white explorers of Lake Michigan, to whom they afforded a convenient way station on the passage from Mackinac to Green Bay. Big Beaver, thirteen miles long and from three to six miles wide, is much the largest island of Lake Michigan. Others in the group have such names as High, Garden, Trout, Squaw, Gull, Hog and Whiskey. Around them lie the best fishing grounds in Lake Michigan, and fishing is the principal occupation of the islanders, most of whom live at St. James, a quaint Irish fishing village which hugs the curving shore of beautiful Paradise Bay.

A mail boat runs daily throughout the season of navigation between St. James and Charlevoix. In winter the islanders are almost completely shut off from contact with the mainland, although airplanes have made such contact possible in more recent years. To serve their medical needs the state subsidizes the lone resident physician. Several small lakes dot the interior of the island, where a limited amount of farming is carried on. Although the climate is obviously ideal for fruit raising, the islanders confine their labors almost wholly to fishing, the annual harvest of which has sadly diminished in recent decades.

High Island, third largest in the group, attained much notoriety two or three decades ago as the imagined penal colony maintained by King Benjamin Purnell for the disposition of his disobedient subjects in the kingdom at Benton Harbor. Lurid tales of the hard life of those who were consigned to exile here gained currency in the city press, to be repeated even in such an official publication as the Michigan volume of the American Guide Series, written and published under the authority of the United States Government. Sole kernel of truth behind these fantasies seems to have been the fact that King Ben purchased, and for some years exploited, the timber right on a portion of the island. He may also have employed it at times as a convenient hide-out for subjects whose presence was desired by the government as witnesses in suits charging the King with immorality, but the imaginary penal colony with its hundreds of heart-broken "exiles" pining away the weary years until death should come to their relief had no material existence.[4]

---

1 Statistics of production are based on reports for the year 1939.

2 Precisely where, along the coast extending northward from Little Traverse Bay, the Indian town was located at different periods is difficult to determine. Jonas Shawanesse, an Ottawa resident of Harbor Springs, states that L'Arbre Croche was at or near present-

day Seven Mile Point, well to the south of Cross Village, giving as the reason that Cross Village is exposed to the cold northerly winds from across the lake, while L'Arbre Croche, with its southerly exposure, is a more sheltered location. He further gives the Ottawa name for Cross Village as *Nimawatigoing;* or "Place of the Cross"; and the name for L'Arbre Croche as *Waganokse,* or Crooked Tree. Interview, January 14, 1944.

[3] From the beginning of the smelt runs in the early twenties until the spring of 1942 the number of smelt steadily increased until millions of pounds were being taken each year and fishermen and conservationists began to fear they would crowd other species of fish from the lake. Like the army of Sennacherib, however, they were suddenly destroyed by some unknown agency, millions of fish being washed up on the shores of Lake Michigan and Lake Huron in the autumn of 1942. There were no smelt runs nor smelt festivals in the spring of 1943 nor any Smeltania—"largest city on ice in the world"—on Lake Charlevoix in the winter of 1943-1944. No smelt were found in the stomachs of lake trout in the summer of 1943, and none was caught by fishermen during the winter of 1943-1944. Why they perished remains (as of mid-February 1944) a complete mystery. Only in Lake Crystal, which is separated from Lake Michigan by a dam, over which fish may escape into Lake Michigan, but from which none can return into the smaller lake, have the smelt survived the epidemic. It was here (at Beulah) that the first smelt run occurred two decades ago. Information supplied by Michigan State Department of Conservation, Feb. 21, 1944.

[4] *Michigan. A Guide to the Wolverine State* (New York, 1941), page 605.

Chapter 25

Along the Dutch Coast

THE early history of practically all of Lake Michigan's East Coast settlements is identified with the rise and decline of the lumbering industry, and subject to variations of local detail the story of one might be made to serve for all the rest.

Beginning of settlement was made at Traverse City, for example, in 1847, when an Illinois farmer named Boardman obtained title to a tract of land at the mouth of what has ever since been called Boardman River. A small sawmill was built the same season, but the enterprise met with only limited success. Meanwhile at Chicago three enterprising young men operating under the firm name of Hannah Lay and Company established a retail lumberyard at the corner of Jackson and Canal Streets, buying their stock from ships arriving in the harbor. In 1851 they decided to establish their own sawmill, and a preliminary investigation having disclosed the presence of 100,000,000 feet of standing pine in the little Boardman Valley available for purchase from the government, the Boardman property was purchased. The new firm pushed its operations with unusual zeal and efficiency and to the end of the lumbering era it dominated the commercial life of Traverse City.

Far more important were the lumbering activities which centered at Manistee and Muskegon. At both places important rivers enter Lake Michigan through lakes which required only the dredging and protection of the entrance to provide roomy land-locked harbors, ideally suited for the handling of logs and the development of sawmills. Both towns were noted Sawdust Cities during the lumber boom; both descended at its close to the depths of stagnation and despair, from which in recent decades Manistee has made a moderate, and Muskegon a sensational, recovery.

Life in the Sawdust Cities had much in common with that of a gold-rush town. A characteristic story of early Manistee concerns the longing of the millworkers and lumberjacks for the companionship of women. At length a townsman returned from a visit to Chicago accompanied by two young women. The exciting news spread rapidly through the settlement, and while the fair visitors were being conveyed from the schooner in rowboats to the shore, the entire population flocked to the landing place to view the spectacle. Even the night workers, sound asleep in their boardinghouse, were informed of the arrival and all without exception sprang from their beds to rush to the scene of enchantment.

Manistee preserves also its stories of the uproarious conduct of the lumberjacks, particularly on Sundays when the mills were closed or on their return from a winter of labor in the woods. Heavy drinking and free-for-all fighting were commonplace at such times, while any citizen venturesome enough to appear on the streets wearing a silk hat or a boiled shirt was likely to be quickly separated from both by the fun-loving roisterers. On one occasion death claimed a man called "Mexico" whose life had been notoriously violent. There being no minister at hand to conduct the funeral, a layman assumed charge and announced a hymn which began:

> Brother, thou wert mild and lovely,
> Gentle as the summer breeze,
> Pleasant as the air of evening
> When it blows among the trees.

The fire which devastated Chicago in October 1871 had its more dreadful counterpart in the forests of Wisconsin and Michigan. The season had been excessively hot and dry, vegetation had been scorched by the sun and the leaves of the trees were shriveled from lack of moisture. On Sunday and Monday, October 8 and 9, the days when Chicago was burning, the forests along the east coast from South Haven northward were ablaze. The town of Holland was burned, and South Haven, Muskegon and other places were saved only by the desperate efforts of the townsmen. At Manistee these availed nothing and the night and day of October 8-9 witnessed the destruction of the city. Recovery from this setback proved rapid, however, and the mills which crowded the busy shore line of Lake Manistee roared on without cessation until the end of the century, when one by one they became forever silent. Today an economy based on agriculture and on salt and other manufactures supports a population one-half as large as that of the Sawdust City of the roaring nineties.

The story of Ludington at the mouth of Pere Marquette River is in striking contrast to the usual Sawdust City saga. Here Father Marquette breathed his last in 1675 and although changes in the location of the river mouth have intervened to render the precise site of his martyrdom uncertain, his memory is still venerated around Lake Michigan. Whether his influence or that of James Ludington be responsible, Ludington's lumbering era was a period of relative calm and respectability. Ludington was a notably successful Milwaukee capitalist who in 1859 acquired a small sawmill and a quantity of pineland at the mouth of the river. In 1867 he platted a town site, and two years later sold his interests for half a million dollars to the Pere Marquette Lumber Company.

If not a saint like Father Marquette, Ludington was a high-minded businessman, with a genuine interest in the moral welfare of the town he created. "Never a public enterprise was started of advantage to the place," wrote the local historian years later, "but that Mr. Ludington's draft for a liberal sum was received as a gift." In 1868 when a report was spread that a saloon was to be opened, he publicly stated that it was untrue, and that "so long as I can control the matter I will not allow a liquor saloon to live in the village that bears my name." To maintain this control he had inserted in all deeds to town lots the condition that no liquors were to be sold on the premises. By contrast, at Manistee open barrels of whisky were placed in the streets, into which passers-by who were reluctant to imbibe were sometimes thrust headfirst by the merry loggers.

The Muskegon is the most important river of northern Michigan and three-quarters of a century ago it was one of the world's foremost logging streams. In the primitive period its valley was the habitat of beaver, bear, otter, mink, lynx and other fur-bearing animals. From an early period, therefore, it was resorted to by traders. In 1779 when Captain Samuel Robertson of His Majesty's sloop *Felicity* cruised around Lake Michigan in search of supplies of corn, the Muskegon was one of his most important calling places. A

Negro whom Robertson calls "Black Peter" was then the local trader, and others of his color whose trading station seems to have been farther up the lake had recently passed the Muskegon in a small vessel en route to Mackinac with a considerable quantity of corn.

With this brief glimpse of their activities Black Peter and his sable companions recede into the obscurity of the past, leaving unsolved the mystery of their origin and how, at a time when Negro slavery prevailed everywhere in America, they came to be engaged in their hazardous wilderness calling. But young Gurdon S. Hubbard, who forty years later wintered on the Muskegon, has left us a clear picture of the experiences he underwent. Although he was only seventeen years of age and had spent but a single year in the fur trade he was given the command of a party consisting of three Frenchmen, which was sent to winter sixty miles up the Muskegon, somewhere in the vicinity of what is now Big Rapids.

On the journey from Mackinac they were frequently detained by bad weather and finally reached Muskegon Lake in early December to find it frozen over and further progress by canoe impossible. Hubbard thereupon established his winter quarters in an abandoned hut which some earlier trader had occupied, and sent his three men, loaded with as large an assortment of goods as they could carry, inland in search of the Indians, while he remained alone to guard the canoeload of goods until they should return.

The days passed into weeks, and having little to do and little to eat Hubbard experimented with the Indian method, described by Alexander Henry, of spearing fish through a hole in the ice to which they were lured by a small decoy made in the image of a fish. At first his efforts proved unsuccessful, but believing that he could do anything an Indian could he persevered, and before long was able to spear as many fish as he could use.

Thus an entire month passed while the lonely boy, torn with anxiety over the prolonged absence of his men, was reduced to the companionship of an equally lonely wolf which came each night to devour the remnants of the fish he threw out. "I could see him through the cracks of my house, and could easily have shot him," he wrote, "but he was my only companion and I lay awake at night awaiting his coming."

We have not space to continue the story of his adventures with the wilderness, wild animals and Indians throughout the remainder of the winter, or of his subsequent long career as one of Chicago's prominent citizens. Seventeen years after his winter sojourn on the Muskegon another youth named Martin Ryerson, sixteen years of age, came there as an Indian trader. The surge of settlers beyond Lake Michigan was now swelling to flood tide, and the cities and homesteads they were founding developed a ravenous appetite for lumber. Young Ryerson had the foresight to acquire title to extensive holdings of pine timber and within a few years he laid the foundation of the great fortune he eventually came to possess. Like Hubbard, he presently became one of Chicago's leading businessmen; his son, also named Martin, who died in 1932, was one of the city's foremost philanthropists, playing a leading role in the development of such institutions as the University of Chicago, the Field Museum and the Art Institute. Thus the wealth derived from the pine forests of the Muskegon was transmuted to promote the cultural advancement of Chicago and the nation.

A single generation of furious destruction spanned the rise and fall of Muskegon as a Sawdust Metropolis. Large-scale lumbering operations on the Muskegon began about the close of the Civil War; they rose in a crescendo of intensity during the early eighties and sank with sickening rapidity in the following decade. For thirty years the city rode the crest of a fabulous prosperity; at its peak there were forty millionaires who vied with each other in displays of wealth. "It was magnificent while it lasted," writes the local historian, "but the intoxication of wealth blinded everyone to the consequences. Muskegon was drunk with a frenzy of destruction and there was little thought of the future. Get rich quick . . . was the watchword of the time."[1]

An earlier chronicler thought it probable that Muskegon would presently be producing one billion feet of lumber in a season— enough to house a city of 125,000 souls. Its nearest approach to this goal was in 1887 when 665,000,000 feet of lumber and 520,000,000 shingles were produced. Ten years later these numbers had dwindled to less than 25,000,000 and 42,000,000 respectively.

The effect of this decline upon the city was distressing. A sharp decrease in population, a silent water front, vacant houses and stores, unkempt streets and a desperate citizenry limned the story of Muskegon's decay. Sadder still and more enduring were the consequences for the state of Michigan. To quote again the local scribe:

"The finest white pine and hardwood forest in the world is now a man-made desert of fire-blasted stumps and slashings. The Muskegon River, once choked with timber as far as the eye could see, is empty.... There are rotting piles and moss-covered wharves where once echoed the busy refrain of forty-seven giant sawmills, adding night and day to the vast board pile surrounding Muskegon lake."

Although the state of Michigan still struggles vainly to repair the consequences arising from the destruction of its forests, upon Muskegon a new prosperity, more substantial than the Sawdust City ever knew, has dawned. The busy whir of the machines in dozens of factories has replaced the shrill clamor of the saws in the forty-seven great lumber mills of a pioneer generation. Included among them are such diverse enterprises as one of America's foremost makers of gasoline engines, a leading maker of office filing devices, and the largest manufacturer of billiard tables and bowling alleys.

Muskegon is the burial place and near-by Lake Harbor was for many years the home of Jonathan Walker, the Man with the Branded Hand. Walker was a Massachusetts sea captain and an ardent antislavery advocate who in 1844 endeavored to run several slaves to freedom in the Bahama Islands. The undertaking failed, and Walker, taken captive, was conveyed in irons to Pensacola, where he was placed in jail with his legs confined in heavy shackles and his body fastened by a stout chain to a large ringbolt fixed in the wall.

After months of confinement he was tried in the Federal court and, besides other penalties, was sentenced to have the letters SS, signifying Slave Stealer, burned in the palm of his right hand with a red-hot branding iron. The sentence was carried out, with the natural result that the brutality inflicted on Captain Walker stirred the opponents of slavery to intensify their agitation. The poet Whittier celebrated the affair in his stirring poem, "The Branded Hand," written in 1846. One of its verses is inscribed on Walker's monument, which was erected after his death in 1878:

Then lift that manly right hand,
Bold plowman of the wave,
Its branded palm shall prophesy
Salvation to the Slave.
Hold up its fire-wrought language,
That whoso reads may feel
His heart swell strong within him,
His sinews changed to steel.

On another base of the monument an open hand is displayed, showing the letters burned into the palm.[2]

Thirty miles southward from Muskegon may be seen a cluster of place names which seem to have been imported directly from the land of windmills and wooden shoes. Such indeed is the fact, for here where Black River loses itself in Black Lake a valiant Dutch dominie a century ago established a colony which has long since become the foremost center of Dutch influence and culture in America; and the colonists sought to preserve the memory of their homeland by giving to the towns they founded in the west Michigan wilderness such names as Holland, Zeeland, Vriesland, Graafchap and Overisel.

Enterprising Dutch colonists gained a foothold along the Hudson River early in the seventeenth century, and in doing so they neatly separated New England from the English colonies to the southward. In 1664 an English fleet remedied the situation by seizing New Amsterdam, which became henceforth the colony of New York. For practically 200 years after this seizure Dutch migration to North America ceased, to be renewed only in the middle of the nineteenth century.

Animating causes of the new migration were the persecution to which dissenters from the established church in Holland were subjected and a severe economic depression which gripped the Netherlands about the same time. Most of the dissenters were humble folk, poor in worldly goods, whose misery was intensified by the disabilities and imprisonment imposed upon them by a stern and unsympathetic government.

Thus harassed, they began, like the Pilgrims of an earlier century, to dream of a haven from poverty and oppression in the lands beyond the sea. Their first choice was fixed upon the rich colony of Java, since they wished to retain their national allegiance and culture. But for the stupid refusal of an inept and short-sighted government, the easy conquest of Java by the Japanese in World War II might never have been effected. Barred from the Orient, the Dutch dissenters determined to remove in a body to America, where they hoped not merely to enjoy religious liberty but through common association and effort to preserve their native culture and improve their economic condition.

Leader of the migration was the Reverend Albertus Van Raalte, a man small in stature but "mighty in words and deeds." To his shrewd common sense and capacity for leadership much of the subsequent success of the colony was due. With about fifty followers, he landed at New York in mid-November 1846 after an ocean voyage of forty-seven days. America was a vast country, and the colonists had no clear idea where they would find a home in it, although they had some tentative idea of settling in Wisconsin Territory.

Arrived at Detroit, however, the advent of winter, together with an offer of employment for the men in a shipyard on the St. Clair, combined to influence their further movements. While the men went to work to obtain support for the winter, Dominie Van Raalte pushed the search for a suitable location for his colony. In this he was afforded all possible advice and hospitality by Governor Cass and other officials and citizens, and this aid the colonists were ever afterward eager to acknowledge.

Thus guided, Van Raalte journeyed overland in late December to Allegan, where he was welcomed by John R. Kellogg, a pioneer of that settlement. In company with Kellogg and an Indian guide he prospected the Black River Valley, until he came on the last day of the year to Black Lake, where a Presbyterian Indian mission had been established some years before. Convinced that this was the best possible site for his colony, he now returned to Detroit. Here, in a conference attended by numerous leading citizens, his selection was approved by the general judgment of the group. Reassembling his band of followers, Van Raalte again set out across Michigan, this time in midwinter, for Black Lake. At Allegan a pause of several days ensued while provisions were gathered and preparations made for the final stage of the journey. Then, leaving the children and all but one of the women at Allegan to be brought on when shelters were in readiness, with an ox team to draw their supplies and with the one woman to serve as cook, the men pushed on to the appointed site.

Some Yankee workmen who had been engaged at Allegan soon followed them, and under their expert direction the Dutchmen began to master such pioneer crafts as chopping down trees, building loghouses and laying out roads through the forest. Two sheds, sixteen by thirty feet in size and roofed with brush, were the first buildings in which the women and children, brought on from Allegan, were presently housed.

Such was the beginning, a century ago, of the beautiful and prosperous city of Holland. Additional shiploads of colonists soon arrived to add their numbers and strength to the settlement, and the immigration thus begun continued for many years. For half a century past the number of natives of Holland in Michigan has remained fairly constant at about 30,000. The number of persons of Dutch blood and descent is, of course, many times this figure.

The first winter was a severe one, and before a year had passed the land of promise had become the land of death for many of the colonists. Money was scarce and provisions were scarcer, and by early spring it became apparent that the quantity of land cleared would not provide food enough for the second winter. Men were sent to seek and cultivate every abandoned Indian camp site for miles around, and the crops raised on them were carried home, sometimes for a dozen miles or more, on the backs of the settlers.

In the absence of a regularly established local government, the colonists held voluntary town meetings in which affairs of public interest were discussed and determined. Personal disputes were adjudicated, roads and bridges built, a school and a church were organized and conditions of labor and wages regulated. A community store was established and a 100-ton schooner was purchased to transport new settlers from Buffalo and other lake ports. As at Pilgrim Plymouth, however, communistic undertakings did not prosper. The "colony" store proved a dismal failure and the schooner was disposed of after a single season.

The newcomers soon overran the limits of the parent settlement and began establishing others in the adjacent region. Colonists from

Zeeland founded the town of Zeeland in July 1847, while other groups gave the names of their own homelands to Vriesland, Graafchap and Overisel. Scarcity of capital and the lack of established industries led many of the colonists to seek employment in the neighboring Yankee communities and this expansion continues. Today the Dutch comprise an important part of numerous east coast cities and counties. Holland still remains almost solidly Dutch, and they comprise larger or smaller elements of Muskegon, Grand Haven, Grand Rapids, Kalamazoo and other west Michigan cities.

As rural dwellers they have spread over half a dozen counties occupying the rich central portion of the East Coast Fruit Belt. There is much low-lying muck land in western Michigan, but the Dutch have had centuries of experience in coping with such an environment. By industrious toil they have converted the deep muck soil into truck farms of amazing fertility. Kalamazoo is the celery capital of America, and the Dutch have made it so. It is also the market center for more than half the peppermint oil of the world, in the production of which the Dutch play a major part.

Grand Rapids, the metropolis of western Michigan, has more residents of Dutch descent than any other city in the country. Reflecting the frugal Dutch influence, in 1930 Grand Rapids held second place in home ownership among American cities of over 100,000 population. It is America's furniture capital, to which the world turns for designs in furniture as it does to Paris for styles in gowns. Here are the largest furniture factories in the world and here are provided great exhibit halls for the annual fair which is attended by dealers from all over the country.

Although Holland is still but a small city, it has become the foremost center of Dutch cultural influence in America, as has already been noted. Religion, morality and education were the three basic conditions which the New England author of the Ordinance of 1787 enumerated as "necessary to good government and the happiness of mankind." Nowhere else in America are they held in higher honor than among the descendants of the Dutch settlers of western Michigan. Dominie Van Raalte was insistent upon the provision of the means of education for his followers. "This is my Anchor of Hope for this people in the future," he said of Holland Academy which was established in 1851. Fifteen years later the Academy became Hope College, from which, although still but a small institution, an astonishing number of preachers, missionaries, physicians and other professional workers have gone forth to lives of usefulness around the world.[3]

Two unique agencies established at Holland in recent years are the Netherlands Museum and the annual *Tulpen Feest* or Tulip Festival. The museum seeks to preserve and spread information concerning the Dutch contribution to American life, as well as to develop a better understanding between the Netherlands and the United States. A national repository, it contains exhibits of Dutch costumes, works of art and of utility, models of the ships which brought the pioneers to America, ancient Bibles and textbooks and typical Dutch household interiors.

The annual Tulip Festival is one of America's most colorful and informative exhibitions of historical pageantry. It originated in 1929 when Miss Lida Rogers, teacher of biology in the local high school, stressed in a lecture the possibilities of a flower festival. From this seed was developed the folk festival which annually attracts more than half a million visitors to Holland. In preparation for their coming no less than 3,000,000 tulip bulbs are planted in the tulip lanes and on the near-by farms. The "tulip lanes" are literally lanes of tulips, planted along the curbs of certain streets for a distance of several miles.

The opening day of the festival is featured by the ceremonial scrubbing of the streets. At an appointed hour the mayor and city council, clad in gowns of bygone days, solemnly parade through the town and as the result of their inspection a trumpet blast announces the decision that the streets must be scrubbed. In response to this summons men swarm forth with pails of water, using the old carry yoke, while women in wooden shoes and characteristic Dutch dress vigorously scrub the pavements with brushes and brooms.

With the scrubbing completed the *Klompen* (wooden shoe) dancers appear. These are 200 or more high school girls, half of them dressed as Dutch boys and half as Dutch girls and trained in the folk dances of their ancestors. The dances are repeated daily. On one evening of the festival a musical event of unusual quality and importance is staged. A pageant, *Tulip Time,* depicting both the history of the city and the history of the tulip, is repeated each year.

The festival has, of course, a commercial aspect which the thrifty Dutch burghers do not wholly ignore. Yet it is characteristic of their sturdy idealism that on Sunday, which might readily draw the largest attendance of the entire week, all the exhibits are closed and no activities take place save a program of psalm singing in beautiful Hope College Chapel and an appropriate evening service in one of the city churches. How a city of 15,000 can accommodate forty times as many visitors in a single week seems to call for some explanation. Many, of course, come from western Michigan and drive home for the night. For the rest, the townsmen throw open their homes and to supplement the hotels and public rooming houses, several ships of the Chicago, Duluth and Georgian Bay Steamship Line which have their winter quarters at Holland are utilized as hostelries during the week. Actual checks have established that the city cares for about 15,000 visitors nightly throughout the festival. If Detroit were to care for 2,000,000 or Chicago for 4,000,000 each night, it would constitute a comparable achievement.

Despite all the sentiment and pageantry, however, there is no thought of divided allegiance, and better Americans than the Dutch of Michigan are found nowhere. As long ago as the Civil War, from a total population of 4,000 they contributed 400 soldiers to the Union Army, of whom 399 had been born across the sea. Although in some of the homes which still contain original emigrants the Dutch language is spoken, it is not taught in the schools, and to the rising generation it is an unknown tongue. In most of the churches the services are conducted solely in English and even the very word "Dutch" has been dropped from their name, which is now simply "The Reformed Church of America." A few of the churches, however, continue to hold one service in Dutch, usually in the afternoon, for the convenience of recent immigrants and the survivors of an earlier generation who for obvious reasons cling to their mother tongue.

[1] Centennial edition of Muskegon *Chronicle*, July 10, 1937, p. 6.

[2] Frank E. Kittredge, *The Man with the Branded Hand* (Rochester, 1899).

[3] Student enrollment for 1941-1942, the last prewar year, was 555. As of 1938 the college had graduated 523 preachers, 127 missionaries, foreign and domestic, 73 college and theological professors, 120 physicians and 53 chemists and biologists. Data supplied by W. C. Wichers, Director, The Netherlands Museum, Holland.

Chapter 26

Duneland

WIND and wave have conspired for ages past to create the dunes which border the southern and eastern coasts of Lake Michigan. In the chapter that follows, however, we will direct particular attention to the southern coast of the lake, stretching eastward from the Illinois-Indiana state line. Here at the front door of America's second city the forces of nature have created a strangely beautiful world, endowed with a wealth of floral and faunal life. Visitors from across the ocean who toured America a century ago were aroused to a state of ecstasy by the wild beauty of the dunes, but only in recent decades have those who live nearest them begun to appreciate their charms, and only belatedly, in response to the urgings of a group of enlightened nature-lovers, has the state of Indiana insured the preservation of a small fragment of the dunes for public use and enjoyment by setting aside a few thousand acres of them as the Dunes State Park.

One of the advocates of such a measure whose enthusiasm has won for him the title of "Apostle of the Dunes" has effectively expressed his sense of their challenging beauty in these lines:[1]

"Magic are the Dunes where they meet the sea—the sea that bore them. There is an ocean-like grandeur in the broad stretches of beaches; the waves, chasing one another in madness, pitch high; the west wind roars and the sand blizzard rules; seagulls fill the air like giant snowflakes. Then the Dune country is in its making, and a grand drama is enacted on those Indiana shores.

"Spring, when dogwood and shadbush vie with each other in garlanding hills and valleys; when violets and columbine cover the forest floor with a carpet for fairies only to tread upon; when seas of lupines invade the Dune meadows, and the love songs of mating birds fill the air!

"Summer, in deep green, with shadows refreshed by cooling breezes from the lake!

"Autumn, when the Dune partakes of every ray in the rainbow; when sand-cherries set the beaches aflame; and the sand and wind-beaten pines look at it all in amazement, reflected in the turquoise sea.

"Winter, in its white mantle of snow, a fairy-land marked by the footprints of its native inhabitants."

In former geologic ages the surface of Lake Michigan was much higher than it is at present, and its area was correspondingly larger. Along its shore the winds and waves combined to create dunes which today, owing to the subsequent lowering of the lake level, lie inland a considerable distance from its shore; and between them and the dunes which line the present lake shore extends an expanse of timbered sand hills and intervening hollows and marshes.

There are "live" or shifting dunes and "dead" or fixed dunes. "Dead" dunes are those which have become covered wholly or in part by vegetation. This tends to prevent the wind from blowing away the sand of which the dune is composed and thus to preserve it as a more or less permanent feature of the landscape. "Live" dunes are entirely devoid of vegetal covering and the winds are constantly at work shifting their form and location. The prevailing winds in the Great Lakes area blow from the west and northwest and the dunes are driven inland, toward the south and the east. They advance remorselessly, filling the marshes and smothering the forests in their pathway; on the rearward side forests long since buried are once more brought to view. On occasion the air currents are reversed, and instead of building up hills, conical amphitheaters are hollowed out. Formations of this type are known by the expressive name of "blowouts."

Before the white man came to despoil them the dunes were covered by a forest of white pine, which here reached its extreme southern range. As the pine was lumbered off, other trees, principally oak, frequently took its place. At times, however, the dunes thus denuded remained bare, being transposed into "live" or shifting dunes.

From time immemorial Duneland has been crisscrossed by important highways, and today several of the great trunk lines running from Chicago to the East traverse it. In primitive times an important

Indian trail ran southward from Green Bay around the head of the lake and thence onward to Detroit. Another, known in later years as the Great Sauk Trail, passed eastward from the Mississippi to the head of Lake Michigan where it united with the trail from the north. At Parc aux Vaches, near Niles, the Sauk Trail was intersected by another which ran southeastward to the important Indian center at the Maumee-Wabash Portage, where now is the city of Fort Wayne.

Over the Great Sauk Trail for unnumbered generations bands of red men trooped in single file, intent on missions of peace or of arms, until with the passage of time they had beaten a narrow pathway deep in the soil. From the time of the earliest French occupation the traders utilized it, La Salle being probably the first white man to come this way. Over it passed the earliest postmen in the Northwest, soldiers carrying the meager mails between the several army posts. Eventually, in the second quarter of the nineteenth century, the government transformed it into a military highway connecting Detroit and Chicago, and with the rush of settlement across southern Michigan it acquired its permanent name of the Chicago Road. It reached the shore of Lake Michigan at what is now Michigan City, where Trail Creek, called by the French Rivière du Chemin, entered the lake, and from here followed along the beach the remaining sixty miles to Chicago.

The character of the highway through this part of its route varied with changing weather conditions from a splendid boulevard to the most exhausting and tedious roadbed known to civilized travel. "While we kept at the water's edge," records an immigrant of 1834, "with gentle swells rolling in among the horses' feet, the wheels of our stage would hardly leave a mark on the wet sand, while fifty feet inland the dry sand was nearly impassible." "After a northwest storm," relates another pioneer, "when the sand was packed by the waves, the drive was just splendid, but when the sand was dry and loose it was just horrible. A good team would make the distance [from Michigan City to Chicago] in six hours when the way was all right, and it was a six day's good drive when the way was all wrong."

Apparently it was "all wrong" more often than all right, however, for before many years the stages abandoned the beach in favor of a route through Baillytown, Thornton and Blue Island. On both the older and the newer route the crossing of the Calumet River was a point of much concern to travelers. The river itself was unfordable, but upon entering the lake the sand borne along by the force of its current was deposited, creating a bar underneath the surface of the lake on which a driver who knew the way could pass around the mouth of the stream. Since the location of the bar was continually shifting, however, and since in any event strangers could not be familiar with it, the excursion into the waters of Lake Michigan was always an adventure of uncertain outcome.

One such passage made in the spring of 1835 by a youth of nineteen remained a vivid memory for more than half a century. The narrator had fallen in with a Virginian en route to Illinois who had a covered wagon which contained, in addition to material goods, his wife and numerous daughters. They had never seen a large body of water before and they gladly accepted our pioneer's offer of assistance in passing the mouth of the Calumet. His own wagon, drawn by oxen, was first driven successfully over the dangerous course. When he undertook to pilot the Virginian's wagon, however, the terrified women begged him to draw nearer in shore. In attempting to comply he precipitated them into the very danger they were seeking to avoid, for the bar was formed at the point where the current of the river lost its force, and the course of safety lay well out in the lake away from the mouth of the stream. Veering in too close, the wheels sank in the softer sand near the river and wagon and freight were stalled. Into the water to his armpits plunged the guide, an extra yoke of oxen was attached, and the wagon with its cargo of panic-stricken women was safely drawn to the shore.

When the stage road was moved inland from the lake shore, about the year 1837, it crossed the Calumet on a bridge of such wondrous construction that the memory of its passage was stamped indelibly on the minds of the pioneers. The structure was over sixty rods long, and was made of poles throughout. Cribs were built of poles for the piers, poles were used for stringers, and small poles and split timbers were laid across these to form the floor. One pioneer, familiar with the subaqueous lake passage around the mouth of the river, had far more fear of the "ever-to-be-remembered-by-those-who-crossed-it" bridge. The effect produced upon travelers by their first sight of it is sufficiently indicated by the simple statement that they commonly walked across it, rather than ride over it in the vehicle.

On one occasion a woman with a child came along and just before reaching the bridge encountered a nest of hornets. The maddened horses dashed over the crazy structure at full speed, while the woman, unable to check them, in some way managed to place her child on the bottom of the wagon, and pressing it down with her feet to save it from being jolted overboard, clung grimly to the reins throughout her perilous ride. To the chronicler it seemed that a special providence had intervened to save the two from destruction.

One who traveled the Chicago Road a century ago with soul attuned to the beauties of Nature was the celebrated Englishwoman, Harriet Martineau. Her first sight of Lake Michigan, from atop a dune at Michigan City, filled her with emotions too moving for utterance.[2]

"The sun was going down. We watched the sunset, not remembering that the refraction above the fresh waters would probably cause some remarkable appearance. We looked at one another in amazement at what we saw. First, there were three gay, inverted rainbows between the water and the sun, then hidden behind a little streak of cloud. Then the sun emerged from behind this only cloud, urn-shaped; a glistening, golden urn. Then it changed, rather suddenly, to an enormous golden acorn. Then it was quickly narrowed and elongated till it was like the shaft of a golden pillar; and thus it went down square. Long after its disappearance, a lustrous, deep crimson dome, seemingly solid, rested steadily on the heaving waters. An inexperienced navigator might be pardoned for making all sail towards it; it looked so real."

Leaving Michigan City, a ride of several miles brought the traveler again to the lake shore, through an expanse of sand "so extensive, hot, and dazzling as to realize very fairly one's conceptions of the Great Desert."

The narrator continues:

"I walked on ahead of the whole party till I had lost sight of them behind some low sand-hills. Other such hills hid the lake from me; and, indeed, I did not know how near it was. I had plowed my way through the ankle-deep sand till I was very much heated, and turned in hope of meeting a breath of wind. At the moment, the cavalcade came slowly into view from behind the hills; the laboring horses, the listless walkers, and smoothly rolling vehicles, all painted absolutely black against the dazzling sand. It was as good as being in Arabia."

At Niles the party had debated whether to continue by stage around the lake to Chicago or to embark on the new steamer *Delaware* for the voyage across. The decision to stick to the land trip found confirmation when on the following day, with the stage winding in and out among the sand hills, the passengers were called to alight and run up a bank to see a wreck.

"It was the wreck of the *Delaware*—the steamer in which it had been a question whether we should not proceed from Niles to Chicago. She had a singular twist in her middle, where she was nearly broken in two. Her passengers stood up to the neck in water for twenty-four hours before they were taken off; a worse inconvenience than any we had suffered in coming the other way. The first thing the passengers from the *Delaware* did, when they had dried and warmed themselves on shore, was to sign a letter to the Captain, which appeared in all the neighboring newspapers, thanking him for the great comfort they had enjoyed on his vessel."

The dunes are forever associated with man's conquest of the air, for they were the scene in 1896 and 1897 of Octave Chanute's notable experiments. Chanute was a famous builder of bridges and a keen investigator of aerial problems. Thirty years earlier the Lilienthal brothers of Germany had conducted a series of noteworthy gliding experiments in which one of them eventually lost his life. Chanute began his own experiments at a 95-foot dune just outside Miller, with a Lilienthal monoplane, but finding it both dangerous and inadequate he devised a five-plane glider having a rudder in the rear and with movable surfaces to maintain the center of gravity. Later he simplified this to a triplane, and eventually to a biplane, which would sustain a man of 175 pounds although the glider itself weighed but 23.

He was a keen observer of the flight of birds and would watch for hours the evolutions of the gulls and other large birds which frequented the dunes. Eventually he discovered from his observations of the sparrow the secret of how to bring an airplane to a safe landing.

In all, hundreds of flights were made from the dune he had selected as the site most favorable to his experiments. With the help of his assistants he would push the glider to the top of the dune and with a running start glide as far as possible toward the lake, which was a few hundred feet distant beyond an intervening sand ridge. Sometimes the glider would fail to surmount the ridge; at other times, it would pass over it and come down on the beach; while on still other efforts the plane would soar out over the lake some distance before falling, when a boat would be sent to rescue the bold experimenter. Finally, he was so seriously injured in a fall to the ground near the water's edge that the experiments were discontinued for good. By them Chanute had discovered the principle of the biplane, and when the conquest of the air was achieved a few years later by two younger men of Dayton, Ohio, it was with the biplane Chanute had developed, to which they added a motor and an improved rudder.[3]

Despite the heavy volume of traffic which traverses Duneland by rail and motor road, or passes in review before it by water, the dunes have long afforded a refuge to human derelicts who have fled from the busy world of strife and turmoil to the peace and quiet of the sand hills. For many years Earl H. Reed, a Chicago artist, haunted the dunes in search of refreshment for his soul and subjects for his brush, and to his sympathetic pen we owe a series of books which depict with rare insight and charm many of these pathetic characters.[4]

In a different spirit the Chicago newspapers a quarter of a century ago fastened temporary fame upon one of these strange figures whom they glamorized as "Diana of the Dunes." Who "Diana" really was, the reporters seem never to have discovered. She first came to public notice about the year 1916, when some fishermen observed a young woman who had become the occupant of an abandoned hut made of driftwood, and who had a habit of bathing nude in the lake. All this was nothing to marvel over, but "Diana's" refusal to submit to interviews and her evident avoidance of visitors generally afforded free scope to reportorial fancy. The tale was readily invented that she was a victim of disappointment in love, and the publicity inflicted upon her provoked many offers of marriage from the lunatic fringe of male humanity. Whether to escape such attentions or for some better reason she eventually accepted a mate who is reputed to have been a giant of a man and who lived with her in her sandy retreat until her death in 1922.

In recent decades the vast industrial development which centers at Chicago has pushed steadily eastward around the lake shore, overwhelming Duneland as it advances with a congeries of cities whose roaring furnaces and bellowing smokestacks redden the sky by night and blacken it by day. Crude oil piped from the plains of Texas and iron ore conveyed in freighters from the mines of Lake Superior converge upon the valley of the sluggish Calumet to create one of the foremost steel and refining centers in the world. So rapidly has the industrialization of this area proceeded that the figures one might present are outdated almost before they appear in print. Less than forty years ago the population of the Calumet region amounted to scarcely 20,000, with Hammond the only considerable town. Today the four contiguous cities of East Chicago, Whiting, Hammond and Gary have a combined population of several hundred thousand, which the establishment of each new factory or the expansion of one already existing continues to swell.

Climax of this development is Gary, wonder child of the U. S. Steel Corporation. Barely a generation ago this organization laid its plans for a new steel center at the head of Lake Michigan, where it quietly gained control of thousands of acres of sandbanks and swamps. In 1906 the actual work of developing the site was begun with all the resources of modern engineering science and the accumulated resources of the great corporation. Hills of sand were cut down, and intervening marshes were filled. The site selected for the new mill was built up to an average height of fifteen feet by pumping sand from the bed of the lake. Even the Calumet River had to be relocated and given a new mouth half a mile distant from its former outlet. A harbor was created by building huge breakwaters out into the lake and excavating a 23-foot-deep, 250-foot-wide canal for over a mile inland and providing a turning basin 750 feet in diameter.

With the immediate employment of hundreds of workmen and the prospective employment of thousands more, ambitious individuals intent upon profiting from the new development began flocking to the site. All this the company had foreseen, of course, and a subsidiary corporation had been devised to oversee the task of developing the city as yet unborn. Provision was made for broad streets and generous alleys, and for sewerage and water systems adequate to the needs of a city of 250,000 people. Space was reserved for parks and other civic uses and black dirt was brought in by trainloads from near-by Illinois to spread upon the waste of white sand with which nature had endowed the site.

By such methods a city of 100,000 souls was created in less than a quarter of a century where for uncounted ages the wilderness had reigned supreme. Today the sister cities of the sluggish Calumet basin comprise one of America's foremost centers for the production of the equipment needed to fight the battle for freedom from world dictatorship. Necessarily, however, as industry advances, primitive life and beauty disappear. Probably nowhere in the world can a more striking illustration of this truth be seen than in the cities of the Calumet.

[1] Jens Jensen, in Introduction to George A. Brennan, *The Wonders of the Dunes* (Indianapolis, 1923).

[2] *Society in America* (London, 1839), I, 335-345. Miss Martineau's visit was made in the autumn of 1836 when the settlements around the head of Lake Michigan were still in their early infancy.

[3] For years following his glider experiments Chanute was known to the natives of the region as "The Crazy Old Man of the Sand Dunes," and the stories they related concerning him did not suffer through retelling. Such has ever been the gulf separating the pathbreakers of science from the mass of commonplace humanity. His first wings, they affirmed, had been thatched with chicken feathers. A small boy who listened to these stories was deeply impressed by the spectacle of the "lonely old man" and of his efforts to fly. See Edwin W. Teale, *Dune Boy. The Early Years of a Naturalist* (New York, 1943), 118-119.

[4] *The Dune Country* (New York, 1916); *Sketches in Duneland* (New York, 1918); *Tales of a Vanishing River* (New York, 1920).

Chapter 27

Bay of the Stinking Water

WHEN Jean Nicolet in 1634 fared forth in quest of the "People of the Sea" he skirted the northern coast of Lake Michigan and came at its western end to the portion we know as Green Bay. As yet the French knew nothing of the extent and contour of the new-found lake and the map makers did not attempt to do more than indicate its lower or northern end. Since Nicolet had found the People of the Sea here, they called it the Lake of the Stinking Water and the "People" themselves, who proved to be the Wisconsin Winnebago, acquired the unlovely name of "Puants" or Stinkers. In succeeding decades the explorers acquired a fair conception of the contour of the lake, which they later called Illinois or Michigan; they continued, however, to call the Winnebago "Puants," and the bay on which they lived became the Bay of the Puants, or Bay of the Stinking Water.

Lake Michigan extends through more than four degrees of latitude, one-twentieth of the distance from the Equator to the Pole, and the climatic differences between its northern and southern coasts are marked. To the visitor from the south parts, however, familiar with its frequent cities and its highly developed countryside, the contrast of north and south in the realm of economic development seems even greater.

From St. Ignace to Escanaba at the opposite corner of the north coast is 150 miles as the state highway runs. Yet in all this distance there are only half a dozen insignificant hamlets and two towns of about 5,000 souls. Nor is the population of the region increasing appreciably. In the thirty years ending in 1940 the total increase for the counties which bound the shore line from the Straits of Mackinac to the Wisconsin state line, a distance of 200 miles, was barely 3,000.

Mackinac County, one of the four, is one of the oldest in Michigan. As originally established by Governor Cass in 1818, following the admission of Illinois to statehood and the consequent extension of

Michigan Territory westward to the Mississippi, the county was of vast extent, embracing most of modern Michigan together with extensive portions of northern Wisconsin and Minnesota. Today, oddly enough, no one really knows the legal name of the county, which has shrunk to a tiny fraction of its original extent. Governor Cass in 1818 named it Michilimackinac and no formal action changing the name has ever been taken, yet for a hundred years or more, both in legislative enactments and other official publications, the name has been spelled indifferently "Mackinaw" and "Mackinac." The county now is long and narrow, extending almost eighty miles from east to west. Fishing and the entertainment of resorters are the chief economic pursuits. Since 1940 the population of the county has undergone a sharp decrease, occasioned by the migration of its workers to wartime jobs in distant industrial centers.

St. Ignace, gateway to the Upper Peninsula, is the only considerable town. Car and auto ferries ply between it and Mackinaw City and the volume of traffic in recent years has given rise to a demand for a bridge across the Straits which would be several miles long and would cost a huge sum of money. Annually in summer thousands of tourists pour into the Upper Peninsula to recreate body and soul amid the pollen-free retreats of the quiet Northland. With the approach of autumn they return southward to be replaced by other thousands of deer hunters, eager to exchange for a brief space of time the conventions of city and feminine society for the carefree life of camp and forest.

Schoolcraft County, lying west of Mackinac, honors the memory of Henry R. Schoolcraft, industrious collector of Indian lore, to whom Longfellow was indebted for the legends incorporated in his poem, *Hiawatha*. Creator of the legends was the Chippewa tribe of Indians who ranged extensively along the shores of Lakes Superior, Michigan and Huron. The Upper Peninsula is sometimes called Hiawatha-land and the naming of one of its counties for Schoolcraft, who recorded the legends, is highly appropriate, although the Chippewa did not confine themselves to this immediate area.

The county, like all of the Upper Peninsula, is thinly inhabited. Explanation of the paucity of population in a country whose shores have been frequented by the white man for more than three centuries lies, of course, in the character of its natural resources. Originally these consisted in the iron and copper deposits and in the wealth of forests and fisheries which nature had abundantly provided. The copper mines adjoin Lake Superior and do not properly enter our story. Most of the iron ore also finds its way to market by way of Lake Superior although an important fraction finds outlet at Escanaba by freighters which ply Lake Michigan. There remain the lumber and the fisheries, but the short-sighted greed of an earlier generation despoiled the land of its trees and the water of its fish. Since the region is poorly adapted to agriculture the population is limited to the number which finds employment in the vanishing lumbering and fishing industries, and in the growing one of the entertainment of sportsmen and summer vacationers.

The fame of Rudyard Kipling is world-wide. Less advertised are the two Michigan villages which bear his name, Rudyard on the highway from St. Ignace to the Sault, and Kipling on Little Bay de Noc a few miles north of Escanaba. The two towns have nothing in common save for their names and their insignificance. Kipling, once the site of a charcoal iron furnace and a shipping point of some slight consequence, by 1940 had dwindled to a population of two-score souls. When its distinguished namesake was informed about his wilderness offspring he indited a somewhat jovial poem beginning:

> "Wise is the child who knows his sire"
> The ancient proverb ran
> But wiser far the man who knows
> How, when, and where his offspring grows
> For who the mischief would suppose
> I've sons in Michigan.

Delta County was so named a century ago because as first constituted it had the shape of an isosceles triangle. Today it is approximately square and the name has been shorn of its former significance. It surrounds Big and Little Bays de Noc, named for a tribe of Indians who vanished from earth so long ago that we have practically no real knowledge of them. The two bays are merely the northward portion of Green Bay. On Little Bay de Noc lie the cities of Gladstone and Escanaba, the latter the metropolis of the entire coast from

St. Ignace to Green Bay and since World War II began a point of national importance and interest. Originally a lumbering and fishing center, its excellent harbor made it the obvious port of a congeries of railway lines which spread fingerlike to tap the Menominee Iron Range of northern Wisconsin and the Upper Peninsula.

Here as early as 1864 was begun the development of great docks to which much of the ore from the nearer ranges is brought for shipment by lake carriers to the steel centers down Lake Michigan and Erie. The Achilles heel of American national defense is Sault Ste. Marie, which is closed entirely in winter and might be closed in summer by a hostile bomb judiciously dropped. After Pearl Harbor the government rushed thousands of soldiers to guard the vital locks, and pushed with furious haste the construction of the new and immensely greater General MacArthur Lock which was completed in 1943.

Lest the Sault gateway be blocked entirely, however, it was proposed to enlarge greatly the docking facilities at Escanaba and to increase the railroad equipment to permit the handling of a vastly greater tonnage of ore from the Lake Superior mines than had ever been transshipped there. This was distinctly a war measure, since the cost of moving bulk freight by rail so far outruns the cost by water that under normal conditions only the ore from the nearer Menominee Range could profitably be brought to Escanaba. As the war progressed, however, the steadily waning fortunes of the Axis powers and the difficulty of diverting the materials and labor to the new undertaking which the project called for led to its abandonment. Whether in some future hour of crisis the Sault may itself become a new Pearl Harbor, with resultant national disaster because the alternative route from the iron ranges to the mills has not been developed, only time and some later historian can tell.

Over a hundred miles long and from ten to twenty wide, Green Bay lies like a knapsack on the stalwart back of Lake Michigan. Dwarfed by the great extent of the parent body of water, its magnitude is appreciated by but few observers. Yet save for the Great Lakes themselves it is much the largest body of fresh water in the United States.

One of the tribes driven westward in the seventeenth century from

their earlier homeland was the Menominee. Nicolet encountered
them on the Menominee River in 1634 and here they remained for
over 200 years. In a treaty made with the government in 1831 they
claimed ownership of the country as far south as Milwaukee, but
several other tribes claimed much of the same territory. In 1854 they
were given a reservation on Wolf River, comprising a portion of
their ancient homeland, and here they still remain. They were loyal
to the British in the Pontiac War of 1763 and again sided actively
with them in the War of 1812. One of their principal chiefs was
Tomah, whose village was on the site of Green Bay City. When the
American troops arrived to establish Fort Howard in 1816, Colonel
Miller paid a visit to Tomah, hoping to win his friendship. When he
explained that he proposed to establish a fort, Tomah replied: "How
can we oppose your locating a council fire among us? You are too
strong for us. . . . You can choose any place you please for your fort,
and we shall not object."[1]

Menominee County, hemmed in between the bay and the lower
course of the Menominee River, had an odd and amusing origin. In
1861 Anson Bangs, a resident of Wisconsin who had married a Dutch
girl named Bleecher and who owned some property in the area, visited Lansing and induced the legislators to create the county and
name it in honor of his wife. If Bangs could spell her name correctly,
the lawmakers could not, and the county emerged from the legislative hopper with the name of "Bleeker." The actual settlers of the
district, however, were so incensed over Bangs's presumption that they
refused to organize the county until after they had themselves procured a new act in 1863 naming it Menominee.

At the mouth of the Menominee, separated by a state boundary line
and united by a fine bridge, lie the flourishing twin cities of Menominee, Michigan, and Marinette, Wisconsin. The location of Indian
villages here early attracted white traders to the site. If old-age recollections may be trusted it also attracted some black ones, for Augustin
Grignon relates that in 1790 or 1791 two Negroes from Mackinac
opened a trading house on the site of Marinette, "where St. Germain
was many years previously killed." To impress their red customers
the Negroes indulged in some sleight-of-hand displays, pretending
that they were medicine men and could converse with the spirit

world. Their act backfired, however, when some of the Indian children died and their superstitious elders conceived the Negroes to be responsible. A crowd of warriors attacked them in their trading house and both were slain in the melee that ensued.[2]

Marinette, whose name and memory the name of the city celebrates, was the offspring of an Indian mother and a French father, who herself lived successively with two white men and bore them numerous children. She died in 1863, supposedly seventy-two years of age. A kindly woman, she had been looked upon as a mother by all the Indians and early settlers, whom she was ever ready to help in time of need.

The Winnebago Indians whom Jean Nicolet visited in 1634 continued to reside in the Fox River Valley for more than 200 years, until they were finally expelled from their homeland by the white race toward the middle of the nineteenth century. One of the members of the expedition dispatched from Mackinac by Major Robert Rogers in 1766 to go in search of the mighty River "Oregon" and the Northwest Passage around America was Captain Jonathan Carver. Although he got no closer to the Pacific Coast than the Upper Mississippi and the shore of Lake Superior, he produced a book of *Travels* which is famous to the present day. At the entrance to Lake Winnebago Captain Carver came upon an interesting character in the person of a female chief, or "Queen," whose difficult Winnebago name has become transformed into the romantic English equivalent, "Glory-of-the-Morning." Royal blood ran in her veins, for she had inherited her office from her father, who had been head chief of the tribe. Although Carver found her "a very ancient woman, small in stature and not much distinguished by her dress from several young women that attended her," it suited his purpose to pay her every possible courtesy, to the manifest delight of her attendants.

To Wisconsin, some time before the middle of the century, had come a French army officer named Sabrevoir Decorah. Apparently he became fascinated by the wild life of the wilderness, for he abandoned his commission to engage in the Indian trade and in due time married the Indian Queen. Years passed, a daughter and two sons were growing up, when that destiny which frequently shapes our lives wrecked the domestic peace and happiness of Glory-of-the-Morning. Five thousand miles away across the Atlantic a greedy Prussian king coveted the territory of Austrian Maria Theresa, and in the effort to gratify his avarice deluged the world with blood and slaughter for a quarter of a century. Second of the two world wars that followed was the Seven Years' War of 1756-1763. France and England were drawn into it, and Sabrevoir Decorah was summoned back to the colors to aid in the defense of New France.

Glory-of-the-Morning, of course, remained in her Winnebago village and her sons elected to remain with her. In time they became chiefs of the tribe and their descendants are still numerous in Wisconsin. Decorah took the daughter with him to Canada and Glory-of-the-Morning never saw husband or child again. He was killed in the battle of Ste. Foye near Quebec in 1760; the child, given a Christian education, in due time became the wife of a Montreal merchant.

Unspeakable grief was thus inflicted upon the Wisconsin forest Queen by an Old World monarch miscalled "the Great" who certainly never heard of her existence. Her sad story was popularized in recent years by Professor William E. Leonard, a late brilliant member of the literary faculty of the University of Wisconsin, in a playlet which has repeatedly been presented by groups of amateur dramatists. The mills of the gods grind slowly, yet sooner or later they complete their round. The shade of Glory-of-the-Morning must have hovered solicitously over a company of Wisconsin soldiers a quarter century ago in which no less than thirty-five of her descendants had enrolled to do battle against imperial Germany. Although we lack specific information, it seems certain that their sons are performing a worthy part in the war upon the madman who today misrules the German people.

The Menominee River forms a portion of the Michigan-Wisconsin state boundary line, the determination of which grew out of an ancient quarrel and provoked a modern one. When Congress in 1836 dumped the Upper Peninsula into the lap of unwilling Michigan neither legislators nor anyone else had any accurate knowledge of the local geography. One of the maps consulted showed the Menominee and Montreal Rivers both rising in Lac Vieux Desert—Lake of the Abandoned Fields—and providing a practically straight continuous waterway from Lake Superior to Green Bay. So the boundary was made to run through Green Bay by the usual ship channel, up the middle of the Menominee or its nearest connecting tributary to the Lac Vieux Desert and thence down the Montreal River to Lake Superior.

But when, a few years later, Lieutenant Cram of the Topographical Engineers was sent to survey the boundary he made some surprising discoveries. The Menominee is filled with islands and no one can readily say where the middle of the river runs. Lac Vieux Desert empties into neither Menominee nor Montreal but instead into the southward-flowing Wisconsin; between it and the Montreal River intervenes a distance of sixty miles or more; and the Montreal itself is composed of two nearly equal affluents, an eastern and a western, which unite only a short distance from the entrance of the river into Lake Superior.

Here was a pretty set of geographical problems which defied the wit of Lieutenant Cram to reconcile. Unable to run the line as Congress had prescribed, he arbitrarily adopted the eastern branch of the Montreal as the main river and ran a straight line from its source to the middle of the Lac Vieux Desert. By this course Wisconsin gained over 800 square miles of territory which would have belonged to Michigan if the western branch of the Montreal had been adopted as the boundary. More important, although at the time wholly unknown, Wisconsin gained the rich iron deposits of the Montreal River area.

At the time no one objected to Lieutenant Cram's procedure, since no one really understood the geographical details involved in it. But in 1908, when Michigan framed a new constitution, her spokesmen realized the loss the state had suffered and the new document was drawn so as to include within the boundaries of Michigan the area it was contended she had wrongfully been deprived of. For good measure the line from Lake Michigan through Green Bay was redrawn so as to transfer Washington and Chambers Islands from the jurisdiction of Wisconsin to that of Michigan.

Years of discussion between the two states followed with Michigan's spokesmen repeatedly appealing for Wisconsin to join with her in an adjustment of the rival claims and Wisconsin steadily declining to consider such a course. Finally, in 1932 Michigan began suit in the U. S. Supreme Court against Wisconsin. More years passed, until on March 16, 1936, the last word on the boundary subject was pro-'nounced. On the consideration that Michigan had for many years acquiesced in Wisconsin's exercise of control over the area she belatedly claimed, the court declined to disturb this jurisdiction. However, the boundary through the Menominee River was clarified by assigning all the islands in the lower half of the river to one state and all in the upper half to the other. So exactly a century after Congress prescribed the boundary between Michigan and Wisconsin its final identity was established.

Two narrow fingerlike peninsulas, one jutting southward from the Upper Peninsula, the other northward from the Wisconsin mainland, with the gap between spanned by a chain of islands, set off Green Bay from the remainder of Lake Michigan. Big and Little Summer, St. Martin, Rock and Washington are the more important members of the island chain. Between Washington Island and the tip of the southern peninsula lies the passage named Death Door. An ancient tradition, documented as long ago as 1817,[3] relates that here a band of Potawatomi warriors perished while engaged in a foray against their Winnebago enemies. Perhaps a better explanation of the grim name might be found in the disasters which have overtaken mariners since the advent of the first white explorers. La Salle, it will be recalled, was marooned here by a tempest for several days in 1679 and the minds of modern dwellers of the region are filled with tales of shipwreck and disasters which the passing years have witnessed in the waters around Death Door.

Door County, which derives its name from the adjacent channel, and comprises all but the lower end of the peninsula, is one of the oddest counties in the United States. Here "south is north and north is south" climatically speaking, for the farther north one goes the more thoroughly air-conditioned by the surrounding mass of water does the tapering peninsula become, and the higher the mercury in the thermometer rises. When a cold wave develops, the temperature

at Sturgeon Bay near the base of the peninsula is likely to be half a
dozen degrees lower than at points forty miles or more farther north.
As a consequence, peaches and certain other fruits are grown more
successfully at the north end of the county than they are farther
south.

With more than 200 miles of irregular shore line and with a varied
and frequently rugged contour the peninsula presents frequent scenes
of breath-taking beauty. Of it a noted landscape architect a generation ago wrote: "Reminding one constantly of the coast of Maine, the
shore with its many graceful indentations is a never-ending delight.
... Almost at each step on the land, each boat's length on the water, a
new vista is opened, a new composition afforded."

The arrival of American garrisons west of Lake Michigan in the
summer of 1816 marked the beginning of a period of army rule which
lasted for many years. In the recent war both white and red inhabitants had been almost unanimously hostile to the United States, and
they viewed the arrival of the troops with corresponding dread and
antipathy. At Green Bay, says Miss Martin, healths still went round
the convivial board to the British king, and it was freely predicted
that the Americans would have a dangerous time replacing "the
best of governments." In such circumstances, remote from the centers
of civil authority, army rule was of necessity supreme, and it required
a strong hand to maintain the dignity and authority of the United
States. At its best, military rule bears hard on civilians, and when,
as sometimes happened, the commandants were disposed to abuse
their power, there was little to check their excesses.

In recent months the entire nation has been stirred by the report
of the slapping of a sick soldier by his commanding officer, under
the stress of front-line battle strain. How greatly the army has
changed since a century ago may be seen from the recital of some
of the happenings at Fort Howard and other posts west of Lake
Michigan. Drunkenness, both of officers and men, was almost universal; even so, we are startled to read of the treatment of Captain
Boardman at Fort Howard in 1828, whose superior had become
intoxicated and while in this condition had stolen a keg of oysters
from the warehouse of Judge Arndt. For the offense of incautiously

expressing his opinion of this conduct, Captain Boardman was court-martialed on charges of conduct unbecoming an officer and a gentleman and of disrespect to his commanding officer. On these charges he was convicted and sentenced to dismissal from the army, although President Adams intervened to save him from this disgrace.

Although the local historian does not identify the superior officer who figured in this tale, the commandant of Fort Howard in 1828 was Major David E. Twiggs. He ended a career of fifty-nine years in the army in 1861 when "for his treachery to the flag of his country" he was dismissed in disgrace. Although his ability was never questioned, he was heartily disliked for his tyrannical conduct toward both soldiers and civilians. While he was stationed at Green Bay his brutality so aroused the resentment of one of the soldiers that he determined to assassinate his commander. Stealing into his quarters, the would-be murderer attempted to shoot him through the head in his sleep; but the gun missed fire and Twiggs, awakened by the noise, sprang upon the soldier and knocked him senseless to the floor. Instead of preferring charges against the culprit, however, Twiggs placed him in confinement and subjected him to a long-continued course of mistreatment. "For many months," say the authors of *Historic Green Bay,* "daily torture was inflicted upon the unhappy assassin, who was purposely kept from trial in order that he might serve as an example to other unruly subordinates."

Another officer whose memory is still odorous in Wisconsin was Colonel Chambers, builder and first commandant of Fort Howard. However, in 1817 he was transferred to Fort Crawford at Prairie du Chien, and most of the stories of his misconduct are associated with that place. For several years after the fort was established the army officers treated the inhabitants as a conquered people, trying civilians by court-martial and subjecting them to unusual and ignominious punishments. Joseph Rolette, a prominent trader and citizen, was banished to an island by Chambers, where he was compelled to remain all winter.

While under the influence of liquor Chambers pursued a young girl with infamous motive and she sought refuge in the house of Jacques Menard. Menard reproached Chambers for his conduct, who thereupon ordered a file of soldiers to tie Menard up and give him twenty-five lashes. While this punishment was being prepared a young son of another well-known trader pleaded with Chambers so effectively that after a few blows had been inflicted upon Menard his further sentence was remitted.

In 1826 Chambers was dismissed from the army, on the charge, according to local tradition, of cutting off a soldier's ears. His later career is obscure, although the same tradition represents that he joined the Mexican army and fought against his former countrymen in the war of 1846-1848.

Fortunately for the good name of the army, not all officers were of the type of Twiggs and Chambers. Colonel John McNeil, who commanded Fort Howard in 1823-1824, was a thorough disciplinarian who at the same time was genuinely liked by both soldiers and citizens. He was a man of gigantic stature who enlisted in the militia at the age of thirteen and at eighteen commanded a company. His heroism was officially attested at Chippewa and at Lundy's Lane, and stories of his physical prowess are numerous. On one occasion while on recruiting duty he quelled an antiwar mob by tossing several of the rioters through the nearest window, after which the remainder turned in flight. On another, he was sent with a flag of truce to the British army. The mission concluded, he was about to return when the British officer begged permission to ask a personal question.

"Anything you please, sir," was the answer.

"Pray, sir, what is your height?"

"Six feet, six inches in my stockings, sir."

"And what is your weight?"

"About three hundred pounds," McNeil replied.

"Are there many men of your size in the American army?" asked the Britisher.

"I am ranked as a man of no uncommon stature; I am the youngest in my family, and the smallest of them all."

"Then may the Lord have mercy on the British army."

When Colonel McNeil came to Green Bay he found the garrison in a relaxed state of discipline and the condition of the fort in general far from ideal. He at once instituted a rigid discipline and began putting the fort in perfect order, much to the disgust of the officers and men whose easygoing life was suddenly ended. But they soon discovered that the stern soldier had another side to his character.

He had a large mess room erected and when winter closed in, it was found to be admirably adapted to the social gatherings which he encouraged the young officers to organize. Balls and theatricals followed, to which townsmen as well as officers' families were invited.

When the leaders of the French Revolution put their king and queen to death a century and a half ago there remained as a prisoner in the Temple the young son of the royal pair, who is known to history as Louis XVII. More commonly, perhaps, he is remembered as "the Lost Dauphin," for although he was undoubtedly done to death by his captors no report of his actual fate was ever made public. Thereby the world was given a mystery which remains unsolved and the way was opened for a succession of fraudulent pretenders to the identity of the murdered prince.

Incidentally, too, the way was opened for the development of an interesting chapter in the history of Lake Michigan. Living among the Oneida Indians of central New York about the year 1820 was an erratic quarter-breed teacher and preacher, Eleazer Williams, who entertained delusions of grandeur and, like the house painter of Austria, aspired to authority over his fellows. The tribes of New York were under increasing pressure from their white neighbors and the proposal was made to remove them to a new home in the unsettled West. Williams eagerly promoted the idea and he seems to have dreamed of becoming the ruler of a revived Iroquois confederacy to be established west of Lake Michigan.

Before the migration could be begun the consent of the Menominee and Winnebago Indians who were the owners of the country must be obtained. At a great council attended by hundreds of Indians held at Green Bay in the autumn of 1822 the Menominee agreed to permit the eastern Indians to settle in their territory, but the Winnebago firmly refused. Before departing for their autumn hunt, however, they staged an entertainment for their white and red visitors, concluding with a war dance of which an eyewitness has left this picture:

"The Winnebagoes at that time . . . were in all their perfection of savage wildness; two thousand of them, men and women, old and young, were massed in a circle, standing fifty deep; the whites, army officers, in the center ring and the warrior dancers, drummers, and singers in the center. Twenty of their most stalwart young warriors took their places with not a thread of clothing save the breechclout; but all painted in most gorgeous colors, and especially the faces, with circles of black, white, red, green, and blue around the eyes, giving the countenances expressions indescribably fierce and hideous, all armed with tomahawks, knives, and spears. At first the dance was slow, to measured time of the drum and song; for there were a hundred singers, with the voice of the drummer, both male and female—the latter prevailing above the former. Soon they began to wax warm, the countenances assumed unearthly expressions of fierceness; their tread shook the solid earth, and their yells at the end of each cadence rent the very heavens. None could endure the scene unmoved—unappalled."[4]

At the end of the dance the Winnebago made ready to leave and within an hour the last one had departed. Yet the consent obtained from the Menominee—promptly regretted by that tribe—made possible the removal of several hundred Oneida and other New York Indians to Wisconsin, where their descendants still reside. Interminable bickering with the Menominee, reinforced no doubt by Williams' own shiftiness and incompetence, prevented the attainment of his dream of dictating the affairs of an Indian confederacy in the Northwest.

Twenty-five years later, now an old and beaten man, Williams produced a new and more startling claim to royal rank. In brief, he was none other than the Lost Dauphin of France and this had been revealed to him by the Prince de Joinville, who in 1841 made a tour of America as far west as Green Bay. According to Williams the prince had summoned him to his hotel and there, after acquainting him with his true station in life, had invited him to sign a document formally renouncing his title to the throne of France; promising, in return, the provision by the French king of a princely establishment and the reservation to Williams of all the private property belonging to the royal family which had been confiscated during the revolution. But the poverty-stricken mendicant of the raw Wisconsin frontier virtuously answered that he could not think of sacrificing his honor, and thrust the proffered wealth and princely station aside.

For twelve years all this was kept a profound secret by Williams. Then an eastern magazine printed a story identifying the Lost

Dauphin with Williams, a book entitled *The Lost Prince* was published and the ballyhoo was on. Although the Prince de Joinville promptly repudiated the entire story of his supposed interview with Williams, the quarter-breed Iroquois conducted himself so plausibly that the formidable section of the American public which enjoys being bamboozled with fairy tales credited his preposterous claims, and even yet believers in them are occasionally encountered. As recently as 1937 Hollywood discovered his story and publicized it in the film *A King without a Crown*.

The "King" in question, who had virtuously refused wealth and a princely station in 1841, died seventeen years later in poverty and obscurity, in a cottage which had been erected for him in the period of his temporary fame.

"[The house] presented an object of cheerless desolation, without a mitigating ray of comfort or a genial spark of home light. His neatly finished rooms had neither carpets, curtains, nor furniture, save a scanty supply of broken chairs and invalid tables; boxes filled with books, the gifts of friends, lay stored away in corners; his dining table ... covered with the broken remains of former repasts, and his pantry and sleeping room disordered and filthy, left upon the visitor an impressive feeling of homeless solitude ... impossible to efface from the memory."[5]

The seventeenth-century explorers found many tribes of red men living around the bay and the observer today finds it a melting pot of racial and national groups. The first Icelandic settlement in America was made on Washington Island three-quarters of a century ago and descendants of the original settlers are still represented there. Ephraim, in the Door Peninsula, was founded as a religious colony by a group of Norwegian Moravians, in whose wake others of their countrymen soon followed.

About the same time the Belgians began coming to the region in such numbers that they now number many thousands spread over the counties of Brown, Kewaunee and Door. The firstcomers were attracted to Green Bay by the representation that here were people familiar with their own French tongue, and presently such place names as Riviere Rouge, La Misere, St. Sauveur, Luxemburg and

Brussels adorned the map of the bay area.[6] Not always, however, are such names bestowed by homesick emigrants in memory of their homeland. The towns of Sevastopol and Malakoff in Door County signify no Russian settlements but merely an interest in the news from the then recent Crimean War.

At Little Chute in southern Outagamie County is the principal settlement of Hollanders in Wisconsin, whose ancestors settled here in 1848. Leader of the colony was Father Van den Broek, who had come to America as a missionary and in 1839 had settled among the Indians at Little Chute. Several years later his red charges migrated to another location, and the missionary conceived the idea of replacing them with fellow countrymen from his native Holland. As the result of his efforts three shiploads of emigrants embarked at Amsterdam for the land of promise and after a voyage of fifty-five days landed at Boston.

Among the emigrants was a six-year-old boy, Chrysostom Ver Wyst, who in his turn became a missionary priest and in old age prepared a charming narrative describing the early years of the colony. His father was desperately poor, and the house of unhewed logs which the neighbors assisted him to raise was at best a sorry shelter. It had no floor, and when the wind was wrong the wretched wooden chimney smoked fearfully. In cold weather the inmates would be too warm in front while their backs were almost freezing. Four years of unremitting toil by the father and his two sons sufficed to clear thirty acres of land.

Father Ver Wyst later recalled:

"We had to work like beavers all the year round, and our only leisure was on Sunday afternoons. For the first two years we had no oxen, and we were compelled to plow with heavy grub-hoes. Oftentimes our wrists would ache from digging and working in the hard, rooty ground. It was hard, slavish work through the entire year. I remember seeing Father cut our grain with a sickle, such as was used 4,000 years ago."

But even this hard life had its compensations for there were occasional jollifications. One of them was held just before the Lenten fast. After Mass was over all would adjourn to the priest's house where the young folks danced until sundown. All decent women were expected to be at home before dark and there was never any dancing at night. There was also a guild or society at the head of which were a king and queen for the year. On the appointed day all the members would meet to shoot down a wooden bird mounted on a high pole. The lucky marksman who shot down the last piece of the bird would be proclaimed king, with the privilege of choosing his queen and receiving a large silver heart which he wore during the year in token of his dignity. Dancing and other jollification by the young folks filled out the remainder of the day.

Wild game was plentiful and the passenger pigeons could be seen "by millions." Occasionally a bear would raid a pigpen or hen roost, sometimes with unexpected consequences. One Sunday when the people were at church a big black animal came into the village in search of fresh pork. Mrs. Van Der Heide was at home, and aroused by the squeals of the family pigs she rushed out of the house just in time to see the bear making off with one of them. As he tried to pull the porker over a rail fence the housewife grabbed its hind feet and pulled with might and main, while the bear, growling fiercely across the fence, did likewise. It was a pitched battle for some little time until Mrs. Van der Heide called to her small son to come and beat the bear across the hind legs with a stick. The animal gave way before this attack and the housewife retained her pig. It profited the poor pig little, however; it would have been eaten by the bear, and it was so badly injured that it was promptly butchered and eaten by the family.[7]

[1] *Wisconsin Historical Collections*, III, 282.

[2] Augustin Grignon's Recollections, in *Wisconsin Historical Collections*, III, 265.

[3] Judge Samuel A. Storrow, "The Northwest in 1817," in *Wisconsin Historical Collections*, VI, 166. For a detailed statement of the tradition, garnished with modern trimmings, see H. R. Holand, *History of Door County Wisconsin* (Chicago, 1917), 38-40.

[4] Recollections of A. G. Ellis, *Wisconsin Historical Collections*, VII, 224-225.

[5] The literature concerning Eleazer Williams is voluminous and controversial. The authoritative exposure of his fraudulent claim is by William W. Wight, "Eleazer Williams—His Forerunners, Himself," *Parkman Club Publications*, No. 7 (Milwaukee, 1896).

[6] Xavier Martin, "The Belgians of Northeast Wisconsin," in *Wisconsin Historical Collections*, XIII, 375-396.

[7] For the story of the Dutch settlement of Little Chute and vicinity see Chrysostom A. Ver Wyst, "Reminiscences of a Pioneer Missionary," in Wisconsin Historical Society *Proceedings* for 1916, 148-185.

Chapter 28

Down the Green Bay Road

To THE Indian, as later to the white man, Green Bay and Chicago were places of importance and the two were, of course, connected by well-established trails. From Green Bay to Milwaukee there were two distinct trails, both of which the white man developed into important highways. One ran southeasterly to Manitowoc Rapids, from where it followed the general course of the lake shore, though keeping to the higher ground some distance inland from the beach. The other trail ran up the southern bank of Fox River as far as Wrightstown and skirted the eastern shore of Lake Winnebago to Fond du Lac at its southern end. From here it ran due south as far as Rubicon, in eastern Dodge County, where it turned southeastward through Menominee Falls to Milwaukee. Southward from Milwaukee the two trails, now united into one, kept inland from the lake shore some distance, coming in sight of it only at Grosse Pointe. At Racine and Kenosha it ran five miles inland from the beach and at Waukegan about three miles. Nearing Chicago, it again divided into two alternative trails, one veering inland to and down the Des Plaines, keeping to the divide between that stream and the North Branch of the Chicago for the last dozen or fifteen miles; the other trail kept along the height of land between the North Branch and the lake, terminating at the north bank of the river opposite Fort Dearborn.

A tragedy of peculiar sadness associated with the Green Bay Trail was the murder of Dr. William S. Madison near Manitowoc on May 12, 1821. He was the young surgeon at Fort Howard. About a year and a half earlier he had married a Kentucky girl, and the couple had lived together but a short time when he was ordered to rejoin his regiment at Fort Howard. Leaving the young wife at home, he had journeyed through the wilderness to Green Bay, where months later he received news of the birth of a son. At last he obtained a leave of absence for the express purpose of visiting his wife and child, and on May 11, 1821, he set out over the trail to Chicago in company with the mail carrier. On the afternoon of the following day they fell in with Ketaukah, an Indian, who followed along after the white men. Toward sundown when they were nearing Manitowoc Rapids, they came to a small ravine bordered with shrubbery. Here the mail carrier took the lead, followed by Dr. Madison, with Ketaukah in the rear. A gunshot rang out and the postman turned around to find Dr. Madison had been shot through the back, receiving a wound which he himself pronounced mortal. When a detail of soldiers arrived from Fort Howard, he was already dead.

His body was carried back to Green Bay and there interred with due military honors, while the young wife and the son he was never to see continued to await his arrival in distant Kentucky. Meanwhile Ketaukah was brought into the fort by the chief of his band. Transferred to Detroit by the soldiery, he was there sentenced to death and along with another Wisconsin Indian who had killed a trader near Green Bay was executed in a double hanging on December 27. The executions, which were public, were carried out in the county jail yard, on the site of Detroit's present downtown Public Library building. The murderers had conducted themselves with quiet dignity during their captivity, and they walked to their death in like fashion, little understanding the white man's bewildering judicial methods.[1]

Probably the first white men to utilize the Green Bay Trail were a forlorn band of fugitives from Iroquois rapine whom Tonty led northward from Chicago in the early winter of 1680.[2] Our earliest accounts of travel over it are the narratives of the mail carriers who before the coming of the settlers traversed the wilderness between Fort Howard and Fort Dearborn. At first this task was performed by a soldier detailed by one or other of the commandants. In summer, however, the mail was conveyed in sailing vessels and the townsmen might remain without news from the outside world for weeks in succession. The round trip, made overland in winter, might consume a month, and if the carrier did not arrive at the expected time it was assumed that he had become victim of some accident or of unfriendly Indians.

In June 1832 Congress provided for a post road between Chicago and Green Bay, and the improvement of the Indian trail was completed in 1834. "Improvement" is a relative term, however, and the reader must not hastily vision a broad cement highway of twentieth-century vintage. Andreas' *History of Chicago* states that stakes were driven and trees blazed along the line of the highway, and that as far north as Milwaukee the trees were cut down to a width of two rods and puncheon or log bridges were constructed over the otherwise "impassible" streams. But the proof of the pudding is in the eating. Horace Chase, who with two companions traveled from Chicago to Milwaukee in December 1834, states that they crossed twenty-four streams, big and little, "getting mired in most of them." When this happened they would wade ashore with the baggage and pull the wagon out by hand, their single horse having all it could do to extricate itself. Another visitor to Milwaukee in the summer of 1835 tells a similar story of repeated bogging down in the mire, prying the wagon free with handspikes, and the men walking most of the way.

They arrived to find the Milwaukee of July 1835 a town of several stores and dwellings where there had been none at the opening of the season. Instead of a single town, hopeful promoters had started several, and the rivalries and quarreling between them disturbed the peace and prosperity of the future metropolis for decades. Near the mouth of the river, where now is one of the busiest industrial centers in the world, the newcomers found a marsh of several hundred acres, so wet that it was impossible to traverse, while to get around it called for a detour of seven miles.

Real-estate speculation was the all-absorbing interest of the populace. "No one thinks of raising anything on the land, but make claims as fast as they can by going on [it] and cutting a few trees, spade up a little ground, and perhaps plant [some] corn." Even the missionary preacher, sent out by the good people of New England to preach the gospel to the heathen of Wisconsin had become "a little tinctured" with the spirit of speculation. Shocking indeed to the fevered speculators must have been the appearance in their midst a year later of a young scientist from Ohio named Increase Lapham, who with scholarly detachment from all financial schemes devoted his time to cataloguing the shells he found along the lake shore and to printing his research in the first scientific publication ever issued west of Lake Michigan.

The visitor of July 1835 from whose story we have already quoted made the hopeful prophecy that Milwaukee would eventually become "a place of considerable business." The boom which set in the following spring seemed to lend assurance to this forecast, yet the panic of 1837 soon intervened to blast the hopes of the city dwellers. By 1839 this had about run its course, leaving the townsmen in a chastened state of mind. From Bishop Jackson Kemper, however, who drove up from Chicago this summer, not all the horrors of a forty-hour stagecoach journey could conceal its future promise. The natural advantages of Milwaukee, he noted, combined with the enterprising character of its inhabitants, left no room to doubt the "future commanding station" of the place.

Meanwhile Congress, in 1838, had appropriated $15,000 for the construction of a road from the Illinois state line northward to Green Bay, and the preliminary report of Lieutenant Cram, whose survey of the Michigan-Wisconsin boundary has been noted in an earlier chapter, sheds interesting light both upon the condition of the road and the country through which it passed. For somewhat less than $100 per mile a road 158 miles long was to be constructed. From the Illinois line to Saukville, a distance of 68 miles, the belt of woodland along the route was chiefly settled; between Milwaukee and Sheboygan rivers there were several settlers; between Sheboygan and Green Bay, a distance of 63 miles, the only settlement was the one begun at Manitowoc Rapids. To drive a wheeled vehicle north of Milwaukee was impossible; and nowhere between Milwaukee and the Illinois line could a span of horses draw an empty wagon at a faster speed than 25 miles a day. From Green Bay to Milwaukee the mail must be carried on men's backs, and five days' travel were required to negotiate the 158 miles from Green Bay to the Illinois boundary.

The traffic of the Green Bay Road differed materially from that of all the other thoroughfares radiating from Chicago. The Detroit road, as we have seen, was a great highway of travel for settlers pouring into the West. All the others were avenues by which the products of the interior found outlets to the markets of the eastern seaboard and over which flowed the return stream of merchandise of all kinds which the western people required. This double stream of traffic passed through the Chicago gateway, and the toll her merchants took from it grew steadily greater as the population of the interior increased. The Green Bay Road, on the contrary, was paralleled throughout almost its entire extent by the shore of Lake Michigan. Along the shore were scattered at easy intervals such communities as Manitowoc, Kenosha, Racine, Milwaukee, Waukegan and Sheboygan, into whose harbors came the same ships that found their way to Chicago. On the Green Bay Road, therefore, were seen no long processions of farm wagons plodding their weary way to the distant Chicago market. Nor could one see on it the steady stream of emigrant wagons which crowded the Detroit road. The reason for this is obvious. If the settler followed the overland route to the West, he was likely to turn into the interior upon reaching Chicago. If his intended destination was some point in Wisconsin he usually came by water around the lakes and debarked at the point, usually Milwaukee, from which he could most easily proceed to it.

So it came about that the Wisconsin coast of Lake Michigan was dotted with aspiring metropolises while along the Michigan coast there was no comparable development; and since trade and population go hand in hand, the routes of the vessels which came to Lake Michigan ran down the Wisconsin coast. This convenience of access to the Wisconsin shore thus provided a further reason for intending western settlers to locate in Wisconsin rather than in western Michigan.

The rapid settlement of eastern Wisconsin that followed the quieting of the Indian title to the country was breath-taking. As might be expected, the southern counties were occupied first, chiefly by the westward-flowing stream of migrants from the older East. Alien homeseekers, accustomed to the harder conditions of life in the Old World, did not hesitate to plunge into the forest belt which reached southward as far as Milwaukee; and both Yankees and aliens spread inland from the lake shore as time passed. Thus Racine and Kenosha Counties together with their inland neighbors became centers of transplanted Yankeedom, while the Germans, Belgians and others occupied the lake shore from Milwaukee northward.

The head start in settlement which the Wisconsin coast gained over the Michigan side of the lake has never since been overcome, for even if Chicago be omitted from consideration as being in a sense *sui generis,* the cities of the Michigan coast cut a rather sorry figure when compared with their west-coast rivals. For this inferiority Lake Michigan itself bears the chief responsibility. Extending more than 300 miles from north to south, the lake cuts squarely across all east-west lines of traffic, compelling the railroads and truck lines either to end at its shore or to turn southward around it. The reverse is true, of course, of the cities along the Wisconsin coast, but they enjoy the tremendous advantage over those of western Michigan of having a vast hinterland of almost incredible economic richness for which they serve as the gateway to the markets of the East. Compared with it the tributary hinterland served by the east coast cities is extremely limited.

Since railroads are confined to dry land, their builders were baffled for a time by the 300-mile wall which Lake Michigan interposes to their progress from east to west. But the spirit of America is indomitable and eventually a partial victory over the great inland sea was achieved which now demands our attention. Too vast to be bridged, the lake could readily be navigated, and although no one had ever heard of putting to sea with a train of cars on a boat, eventually someone asked, "Why not?" In short, why could not loaded railroad cars be transported across the lake, to resume their journey by rail on the opposite side, more cheaply and inexpensively than their contents could be loaded aboard ship for the voyage and then reloaded on cars when it reached the opposite shore.

Solution of the problem was first demonstrated at Detroit in 1866, when the steel car ferry *Great Western* was placed in service between Detroit and Windsor. Eventually the ferrying of cars across the Detroit and St. Clair rivers developed to enormous proportions and beginning in the early eighties an entire fleet of ferries, operating day and night, conveyed hundreds of cars daily between the Canadian and American shores.[3] The use of car ferries soon spread to the Niagara and other rivers, but a quarter of a century passed before the attempt was made to employ such craft on the wider waters of the open lakes.

In this development Lake Michigan pioneered the way. The Ann Arbor Railroad in 1892 procured the building at Toledo of two wooden car ferries for transporting its trains between Frankfort, Michigan, and Menominee on Green Bay and Kewaunee on the Wisconsin side of the lake. Although these pioneer ferries were crude affairs, they possessed the supreme virtue of demonstrating the feasibility of ferrying cars across large bodies of water such as Lake Michigan. The natural result followed that other railway lines imitated the action of the Ann Arbor road, and new and better car ferries were placed in service from time to time. Today such service is maintained between Milwaukee and Muskegon and Ludington, Michigan; between Manitowoc, Wisconsin, and Ludington and Frankfort, Michigan; between Frankfort and Menominee on Green Bay; and between Frankfort and Manistique in the Upper Peninsula. Older than any of these is the ferry service maintained between Mackinac and St. Ignace.

In the operation of railroad ferries Lake Michigan so far outranks all other bodies of water in the world that there can hardly be said to be a second. The ferries are powerful deep-hulled steel ships built to navigate the year round in all kinds of weather. For them alone there is no closed season on the lakes. Although Lake Michigan never freezes over, ice forms along the shores, at times extending out twenty miles or more into the lake; while fields of floating ice may extend to mid-lake. The winter gales drive the ice floes back and forth, or pile them in great masses along the shore and the car ferries must either crush a way through the solid ice or shove the floes aside in order to accomplish their scheduled voyages. Occasionally a vessel is stalled in a field of ice, but others come to the rescue and break open a passageway to the imprisoned ship.

The cars are carried on several parallel tracks laid lengthwise through the interior of the ship. A great apron at the stern, similar to the ones in use on wartime landing barges, lets down to run the cars on or off the boat, and is raised to fasten them in securely during the voyage. According to Plumb, the first car ferries in service on Lake Michigan had no aprons and the vessel was thus exposed to inundation from the open rear. The story is told that in a violent storm the water invaded the engine room, "every piece of machinery seemed to threaten to break away from its fastenings and finally the cars got loose and two or three went off the stern."[4]

The advent of the automobile age produced a marked effect upon the construction and use of the car ferries. In earlier decades these had been built strictly for use as railroad ferries, and any passengers bold enough to take passage on them were tolerated as a nuisance and little or no provision was made for their accommodation and comfort. Gradually, however, as Americans flocked en masse to the ribbons of cement which lured them to strange scenes and distant places the idea dawned upon the railroad operators that a new source of revenue might be developed by ferrying both passengers and their automobiles across the lake.

To attract such traffic the newer ferries were equipped with comfortable cabins, and convenient arrangements for embarking and debarking passengers and autos were established. Peak of this development to date is the *City of Midland,* launched at Manitowoc in 1941 and proudly proclaimed as the new "Queen of the Lakes." Another interesting consequence of the automobile era has been the development in recent years by the state of Michigan of an extensive auto-ferrying service across the Straits of Mackinac, to accommodate the throngs of summer vacationers and autumn hunters who clamor for passage, with their cars, from the one peninsula to the other. Instead of building its own auto ferries the state has purchased several Lake Michigan car ferries from the Pere Marquette and other railroads and placed them in service as auto ferries on the run across the Straits.

Modern Racine and Kenosha, Wisconsin's south shore cities, are thriving industrial centers with great factories whose products are household words throughout America. Although the Chicago Treaty of 1833 by which the Potawatomi sold this region to the white man guaranteed the natives three years' further possession of it, settlers began flocking into the country in advance of 1836, eager to "preempt" promising mill and town sites. One of the most promising locations between Milwaukee and Chicago was the mouth of Root River. Here Gilbert Knapp, who, as captain for several years of the first U. S. revenue cutter on the Upper Lakes, had become familiar with the spot, in the summer of 1834 built perhaps the first cabin of a bona fide settler in southeastern Wisconsin. The following year, when he had admitted two other promoters into partnership, the town of "Port Gilbert" was platted—later to be known as Racine.

The adjacent countryside was settled with astonishing rapidity and before many years all southeastern Wisconsin was dotted over with settlers' holdings and villages.

The story of Kenosha's beginnings is even more interesting. About the time Knapp was completing his log cabin at Racine, the western fever infected a group of enthusiasts in Oswego County, New York, and in February 1835 they organized the Western Emigration Company, with 800 shares of stock of $10 par value. The mania of speculation so gripped the community that old and young, and "even unmarried females who were employed as house servants" rushed to purchase shares in the enterprise.[5]

A month later a committee of three departed to explore the western shore of Lake Michigan in search of a suitable site for the projected colony. At Racine they found the Knapp partnership already in possession of the river mouth, and an effort to buy their holding led to much subsequent bickering. Two of the committee now returned to New York, leaving the third member, Charles W. Turner, at Racine to look after the company's interests. Discord soon ensued and Turner, washing his hands of the company, set out upon an exploration of his own, descending the Rock River valley to Dixon, Illinois, and thence turning eastward to Chicago. Here he decided to examine once more the western shore line of the lake. In attempting to ford Pike River both horse and rider were engulfed in the quicksand, escaping to solid land wet and bedraggled. The explorer spent the night under the stars, expecting to resume his journey next morning. When morning dawned, however, some further observation convinced him that here was the ideal town site he had been seeking. With an ax he proceeded to blaze his claim and on June 10, 1835, the town of Pike River was born.

Much claim jumping and other bickering followed, for details of which we need not pause. The Western Emigration Company, having failed in an effort to oust Turner from his property, proceeded to mark out a town site a mile or so to the southward at the mouth of Pike Creek, to which they gave the name of Southport, as being the southernmost port of Wisconsin. A decade and a half later this was replaced by the beautiful Indian name of Kenosha, which some of the settlers had advocated in the beginning.

Once started, Southport throve amazingly as a center of transplanted Yankeedom. In 1839 a newspaper, the Southport *Telegraph,* was started by a man whose permanent claim to fame is the invention of the typewriter. In 1842 publication of a general literary magazine was begun[6] while the town was yet a mere village, and a few years later still the first free public school in Wisconsin was established. In infant Kenosha, too, was conceived the notable Fourierite colony whose story is told in another chapter.

An early newcomer to Southport who was destined to influence world history was Christopher Latham Sholes. Although he was a native of Pennsylvania, he was of purest New England lineage, being a direct descendant of John Alden, the hero of Longfellow's tale of *The Courtship of Miles Standish.* At the age of fourteen he was apprenticed to a printer, and in 1837, having completed his term of service, he followed his older brother Charles to Green Bay, where the latter had acquired a newspaper.

Before long he went to Madison, where he worked on another paper and served for a short time as a clerk to the infant Wisconsin legislature. Thus equipped by training and experience, at the ripe age of twenty he became editor of the Southport *Telegraph* in 1839. In early Wisconsin politics and journalism went hand in hand, and although Sholes was poorly fitted by temperament for the rough contacts of public life, for over a quarter of a century he mingled the work of journalism with the avocation of politics, serving several terms in the legislature, holding the office of postmaster at Kenosha and Milwaukee, and being appointed Collector of the Port of Milwaukee by President Lincoln.

Fortunately for mankind, this appointment marked the end of Sholes's connection with journalism. An inventive genius, he found in the relative leisure of the collector's office comparatively late in life the time and detachment from routine business which the cultivation of his brain children required. Long since, as a practical printer, he had invented the mailing machine used in printing the names of subscribers on the margins of newspapers. Now, with a group of kindred-minded associates, he began resorting to a small machine shop in Milwaukee kept by a German machinist named Kleinsteuber.

If the achievements of peace are worthy of remembrance the humble shop of C. F. Kleinsteuber should remain forever famous; here in the closing years of the Civil War several inventors were at work upon their respective dream children, and one of them was Sholes. He and Samuel Soule were working on a paging machine, which was patented in September 1864. Henry W. Roby, a shorthand reporter and teacher, was trying to invent a magician's clock, while Carlos Glidden was making a spading machine with which he hopefully expected to supplant the plow in farming.

Roby tells the story.

"One day when we were all four in the shop together working on our favorite hobbies, there came an hour of mutual weariness in our work when we all, together with Mr. Kleinsteuber, the owner of the shop, and Matthias Schwalbach, the pattern maker, stood by Mr. Sholes' bench listening to one of his brilliant outbursts on the history and hardships of invention. During that conversation he told us that he hoped for a better fate for his paging machine than had befallen Eli Whitney and his cotton gin, then he said that about the greatest need of the world was a writing machine. Mr. Glidden broke in with the inquiry, 'Mr. Sholes, why can't you make a machine that will print words as well as figures? If you can make a paging machine, you ought to make a writing machine.' "[7]

The answer was, "I can. I have thought about it a great deal and I am going to try it as soon as I get through with this paging machine." A week or so later he came into Roby's office and said: "Last night I had a cough that kept me awake nearly all night and tired me out but I spent the time in working out the writing machine that I have been so long dreaming about. It has puzzled me a long time, but I think I have the right idea at last."

Soon the entire group—Soule, Roby, Sholes and Glidden—were at work on the invention, Sholes generously inviting all to have a hand in it, as the job was big enough for all.

"The work . . . progressed slowly with many halts and hitches and many parts tried and discarded and many changes of form in the parts retained. The engraving of the letters on the points of the typebars, each at a different angle from all its fellows, gave us great trouble. Everything was slowly and imperfectly done. . . . Many of the first ones were spoiled and many others set awry on the bars. Some overran and some fell short on the alignment, but at last, when all was ready, our gray-haired wizard sat down and wrote, 'C. Latham Sholes, Sept. 1867,' and we had a great time of rejoicing."

Increase A. Lapham, another great and modest Milwaukeean, to whose foresight we are indebted for the early development of the weather bureau, was invited to witness the performance and he exclaimed, "Mr. Sholes, you have a hundred fortunes there." But none of the original group of workers on the new machine ever reaped a fortune from it. There were still many obstacles to surmount, and to procure the necessary capital to perfect the machine and place it on the market called for capacity of a different order than they possessed. Another pioneer Wisconsin editor, James Densmore, whom Sholes had known for many years, was invited to take an interest in the invention. Huge of body, and with a thick-skinned aggressiveness which nothing could daunt or defeat, he carried the enterprise to the point where in 1873 it was taken up by the Remington Arms Company, under whose able and resourceful management it was introduced to a waiting but none too eager world.

One of the earliest purchasers of a typewriter was Mark Twain, and his story of his experiences with it is interesting, although not necessarily accurate. In Boston, he relates:

"Nasby and I saw the machine through a window and went in to look at it. The salesman explained it to us, showed us samples of its work, and said it could do fifty-seven words a minute—a statement which we frankly confessed that we did not believe. So he put his type girl to work and we timed her by the watch. She actually did the fifty-seven in sixty seconds. We were partly convinced, but said it probably couldn't happen again. But it did. We timed the girl over and over again, with the same result always—she won out. She did her work on narrow slips of paper and we pocketed them as fast as she turned them out, to show as curiosities. The price of the machine was $125. I bought one and we went away, very much excited.

"At the hotel we got out our slips and were a little disappointed to find they all contained the same words. The girl had economized her time and labor by using a formula which she knew by heart.

"At home I played with the toy, repeating and repeating and repeating "The Boy stood on the Burning Deck" until I could turn that boy's adventure out at the rate of twelve words a minute; then I resumed the pen, for business, and only worked the machine to astonish inquiring visitors. They carried off reams of the boy and his burning deck."[8]

Meanwhile Sholes, the inventor, whose dream had emancipated mankind from its age-long slavery to the pen and womankind from her age-long humiliation of economic dependence, had lost all title to his great invention. With little money and less health he lived on until February 17, 1890, when his gentle eyes closed for the last time and he took his departure from life "whispering the lines he had so many thousands of times clicked off on his several machines:

" "There is a tide in the affairs of men
Which taken at the flood, leads on to fortune.' "

Although his work as an inventor had brought him little profit, he had realized his ambition of becoming a benefactor to the human race. For a third of a century his body rested in an unmarked grave in Forest Home Cemetery, Milwaukee. A few years since, however, funds were collected for the erection of a suitable monument to the memory of the great inventor.

The beginning of Norwegian settlement in America is largely a Lake Michigan story, which should not be omitted here. During the Napoleonic Wars a number of Norwegian soldiers were carried as prisoners to England. There Lars Larson learned the English language and coming into contact with some kindhearted Quakers became a convert to their faith. Returning to Norway upon his release from captivity, he converted some of his neighbors to Quakerism, thereby bringing down upon them the wrath of the Lutheran State Church.

The usual consequence followed, and in 1825 a party of fifty-two of the persecuted sect sailed in a tiny sloop for America. Here they found a home near Rochester, New York, but the soil was poor and although the colonists managed to exist, prosperity was slow to dawn upon them. In 1834 a second party of Norwegians arrived and settled in La Salle County, Illinois. Here, after some preliminary hardships, they prospered, and their enthusiastic letters to friends and relatives at home provoked a new stream of emigration. From Fox River, says Blegen, the newcomers "advanced from one frontier to another, swarming to the farm lands and towns of Wisconsin, Iowa, and Minnesota and trekking to the Great Plains in the mood of Per Hansa as portrayed in *Giants in the Earth,* Rolvaag's novel about Norwegian land-takers." By 1930, a century later, more than 750,000 persons of Norwegian birth or ancestry were living in America. Although they are widely scattered over the country their principal strength is still found in the group of states west of Lake Michigan. Beginning in the late thirties, Wisconsin was long the chief center of Norwegian settlement. Despite early poverty and prejudices[9] no other European nationality has adapted itself more readily to America.

How the first immigrants were diverted from Illinois, their intended destination, to Wisconsin is related in an amusing story which has been preserved. They had reached Milwaukee, where an enterprising local booster appeared before them with a novel exhibit. It consisted of two men, one exceedingly seedy and emaciated, the other of generous girth and evident prosperity. The half-starved man, the booster explained, was a resident of Illinois where crops were scanty, the climate hot, and fevers and ague abundant; the fat man was from Wisconsin, where cooling breezes fanned the brow and abundant crops repaid the toil of the husbandman. Convinced by this demonstration of the folly of settling in fever-ridden Illinois, the Norsemen remained at Milwaukee to locate in the enchanting Wisconsin countryside.

They settled at Muskego Lake in near-by Waukesha County, and by 1850 over half the Norwegians in America were living in southern Wisconsin. At Muskego the first Norwegian newspaper in the New World was founded in 1847 and here was built the first church. Here, too, were gathered many notable early Norwegian-American leaders, whose names are held high in the estimation of their fellow countrymen to the present day.

A seafaring people, the Norwegians who came to America early turned their attention to the Great Lakes, and from the later thirties on, Chicago, Milwaukee, Racine and other ports on Lake Michigan became centers of Norwegian settlement. Wages on the lakes were much higher than sailors in the homeland were paid, while the conditions of lake navigation made it possible for a family man to make frequent visits to his home. Both as ship operators and as sailors working for wages the Norwegians have figured prominently in the nautical activities of the lakes for practically a century.[10]

---

1 For an account of the crimes of the two Indian murderers see M. M. Quaife, "Capital Punishment in Detroit," *Burton Historical Collection Leaflet*, IV, 46-47; W. W. Blume (ed.), *Transactions of the Supreme Court of the Territory of Michigan* (Ann Arbor, 1938), Vols. III and IV, index references.

2 Their retreat is described in Chapter 4 of the present work.

3 In recent decades, the Michigan Central Railway, largest single operator at Detroit, has transported its cars by a tunnel under the river.

4 Ralph G. Plumb, *Lake Michigan* (Manitowoc, 1941), Chap. VIII.

5 "Early History of Kenosha," in *Wisconsin Historical Collections*, III, 370-394.

6 See M. M. Quaife, "Wisconsin's First Literary Magazine," in *Wisconsin Magazine of History*, V, 43-56.

7 M. M. Quaife (ed.) *Henry W. Roby's Story of the Invention of the Typewriter* (Menasha, Wis., 1925).

8 *Harper's Weekly*, March 18, 1905.

9 In the Wisconsin Territorial Council of 1846 it was gravely debated whether they were superior or inferior to Negroes, one brilliant lawmaker affirming the latter to be "more intelligent, more civilized, better acquainted with our institutions than the Norwegians."

10 Knut Gjerset, *Norwegian Sailors on the Great Lakes* (Northfield, Minnesota, 1928).

Chapter 29

Eighth Wonder of the World

THE ancient world had seven wonders and modern America has one. However, the seven are now with Caesar's ghost while Chicago, the city Lake Michigan incubated, is still in the early flush of her adolescence, facing a future to which no discernible limits can be set.

So masterful is Chicago and so overwhelming her achievements that the mind finds difficulty in appreciating them. A tiny outpost in the heart of the wilderness only 111 years ago, she has long since become the New World's second city; while today her admirers confidently anticipate that before the close of another quarter century she will become the foremost metropolis of the globe.

A simple story may help to convey the remarkable character of this development. A quarter of a century ago, the present writer knew a charming old lady, Mrs. Emily Lebeau, who had come to Chicago in babyhood in 1826. She was a resident of seven years' standing when the modern city was born, and in her old age she still remembered the Potawatomi tongue she had learned in her early childhood. She remembered, too, the era when wilderness was king at Chicago, when wolves and bears roamed over the heart of the present city and throngs of blanketed red men assembled periodically to receive the payments doled out by the Great Father at Washington. Her dying gaze rested upon a city of two and a half million souls, and if the writer shall chance to survive to witness the anticipated development of 1968 her life and his own will have spanned the entire progress from virgin wilderness to world metropolis.

Mark Beaubien, Mrs. Lebeau's father, established Chicago's first hotel, which he named for his friend, Billy Caldwell, the local Potawatomi chief. "You are a great man," said Mark to Billy. "I name him for you, by gar." Since Billy was a half-breed his copper-hued subjects called him "the Sauganash," meaning the Englishman. So the Sauganash House it became. In 1833, Charles J. Latrobe, an

344

aristocratic English traveler, reckoned it a "vile two-storied barrack" in which "most appalling confusion, filth and racket" reigned. Patrick Sherriff, an Irish farmer, who visited Chicago at the same time as Latrobe, found much to extenuate conditions. But even to this more philosophical observer they seemed bad enough. The food, although ample, was "indifferently" cooked and "served still more so." Upon retiring the guest was assigned a dirty pallet in the corner of a tiny room in which were two beds already occupied, and before morning he was roused from his slumber by an angry voice "mouthing horrid imprecations" and demanding to share his bed. Less than a hundred years later the largest hotel in the world replaced the Sauganash; in it were guest rooms enough to enable a lodger to occupy one alone each working day in the week for ten successive years without sleeping twice in the same room; during the war years of 1942-1943 it provided housing for 12,000 soldiers.

Yet another story may help to reflect the change which a century has wrought beside the sleepy Garlic. The first strolling troupe of actors which made Chicago found lodging in the tavern and utilized its dining room as a theater. One of the actors was a young Irishman who for some breach of discipline was discharged by the manager and told to go his way. "And where can I go," he retorted bitterly, "with Lake Michigan howling on one side and the bloody wolves on the other?"

A Canal Commission was created to construct the canal across the portage which had been visioned by Jolliet in 1673, and the first step in the development of the modern city was the platting of a townsite under its authority on a portion of Section 9 of the U. S. land survey in the summer of 1830. The surveyor employed by the commission chose to plat less than one-half of the entire section, reaching northward from Madison to Kinzie Street and westward from State to Des Plaines. Within this area forty-eight blocks and fractional blocks were laid out on the familiar checkerboard plan, with all but a few of them lying south of the main river or west of its North and South Branches.

The plat was filed for record on August 4, 1830, and a public sale of the land was held the following month. One hundred and twenty-six lots brought an average price of $35, while two eighty-acre tracts adjoining the townsite were sold for $1.25 an acre. Some of the purchasers were local residents who were buying in their homesites upon which they had "squatted" without legal title.

A comparison of some of the prices paid at the sale of 1830 with the valuation of the same properties in 1853 suggests the futility of ordinary human foresight. Thomas Hartzell's eighty-acre tract, acquired for $120 on the earlier date, might have been sold for $800,000 on the later one. James Knight's eighty was valued at $600,000 in 1853, while John H. Kinzie's investment of $119 had multiplied itself to $163,000.

Such figures imply, of course, a great increase in population and commercial importance over the twenty-three-year period. Yet there was no real growth until the summer of 1833, when a considerable boom developed, to be followed in the later thirties by a sickening collapse. In October 1833 the "School Section," lying between State and Halstead from Madison south to Roosevelt Road, was auctioned. It embraces today most of the Chicago Loop, probably the most congested business district on earth. It had been divided into 144 blocks of about four acres each, which were purchased, chiefly on credit, at an average price of $6.72 per acre.

As yet, it will be noted, there was but slight indication of the speculative enthusiasm which, beginning in 1835, mounted to fantastic heights. To feed the mania the blocks of the School Section were divided into lots and thrown on the market, after which ever fresh "additions" were hastily platted and offered for sale. Nor was the mania confined to Chicago, for all around Lake Michigan in every inlet and creek, as well as for scores of miles inland, townsites were platted and the lots laid out were eagerly bartered at ever-mounting prices. The pioneer historian of La Salle County relates that he one day called at a log cabin where half a dozen persons were assembled. They had evidently been engaged in high speculation throughout the day for one of them, addressing the newcomer, with a complacent slap of the thigh, said: "I have made $10,000 today, and I will make twice as much tomorrow." Further conversation disclosed that he had been the least successful financier of the entire company.

The fantastic boom was soon succeeded by a collapse which to the desperate "investors" seemed permanent. But some wiser men knew better. Although Chicago would have her ups and downs like any other city, Nature herself had fixed upon the place her guarantee of future greatness. This was never better stated than by Charles Butler, a shrewd New York capitalist who came to Chicago in 1833 in search of a promising field for investment.

To the east lay Michigan Territory with a population of about 40,000, almost all of it gathered in the vicinity of Detroit. The northern half of Indiana contained only a few scattered settlers, while westward from Lake Michigan stretched a vast unoccupied expanse of virgin wilderness awaiting the plow of the farmer.

Butler later wrote:

"One could not fail to be greatly impressed with this scene ... and to see there the germ of that future when these vast plains would be occupied and cultivated ... and sustaining their millions of population. Lake Michigan lay there 320 miles in length from north to south, and it was clear to my mind that the productions of that vast country lying west and northwest of it on their way to the eastern market ... would necessarily be tributary to Chicago, in the site of which the experienced observer ... saw the germ of a city destined ... to become the largest commercial emporium of the United States."

On August 5, 1833, an election was held to determine whether the townsmen favored incorporation as a village, at which thirteen votes were cast, all but one in the affirmative. Five days later, when town trustees were chosen, the entire body of voters, twenty-eight in number, came to the polls and thirteen of them modestly consented to appear in the role of candidates for office. In November a code of ordinances for the new town was adopted and about the same time the first prison, a log structure, was erected on the square where the twin City and County Building still stands. The first debt was incurred in 1834, when the sum of sixty dollars was borrowed for the drainage and improvement of State Street.

In the autumn of 1836 under the influence of the expansive ideas of the period a movement was begun to secure from the legislature a charter for a city. It was successful and on March 4, 1837, the change to the new form of government was made. Although the population was but little over 4,000 the corporate limits were drawn to include all the territory from Twenty-second Street to North Avenue and from the lake westward to Wood Street, an area of ten square miles.

For three years the new city stagnated, but in 1840 it began the upward march which still continues, and by 1857, twenty years after its incorporation, the population had mounted to 93,000. The significance of this twenty-three-fold increase in two decades can scarcely be overestimated. Through it Chicago had become the giant of the Northwest and had stamped the country west of Lake Michigan with the seal of her commercial supremacy.

Explanation of this achievement is not obscure or difficult. Commerce is the lifeblood of an industrial city, and highways are the arterial system through which it circulates. Eastward from Chicago stretched the Great Lakes, affording throughout most of the year a waterway of unlimited capacity. To reach it the Illinois and Michigan Canal had been constructed, tapping the produce of the Mississippi Valley, and in the twenty-year period that opened with 1833 a series of highways by land radiating fanlike from Chicago had been developed. They were soon replaced by the vastly greater development of iron roads which in another quarter century fixed upon Chicago for all time the distinction of being "the commercial emporium of the United States."

A great commercial and constitutional issue first fixed the eyes of the nation upon Chicago just a century ago, launching her at the same time upon her career as the mother of conventions. Although the Constitution gives to Congress the control of commerce with foreign countries and between the states, only belatedly did the concept gain recognition that it was the duty of the Federal Government to improve the navigation of its inland lakes and rivers no less than to safeguard its sea-borne trade. But the newer West insistently demanded such recognition of its needs, and when President Polk in 1846 vetoed the current River and Harbor Bill an agitation was promptly begun for holding a popular convention of protest.

Although Chicago in 1846 had but 15,000 residents, most of whom had arrived since 1840, its location at the head of navigation of the Upper Lakes, at the point where lakes and rivers systems met, pointed

CHICAGO IN FLAMES

This view is from a contemporary sketch published in *Harper's Weekly*, showing the rush of fugitives across Randolph Street Bridge.

Photograph by Kaufmann-Fabry

CHICAGO LAKE FRONT

This view of the Chicago sky line shows Grant Park and the band shell where summer concerts are given.

Courtesy of Underwood and Underwood

OLD TIME VIEW OF THE CHICAGO RIVER

The picture shows the junction of the North and South Branches. On the left is a vessel coming from the North Branch in tow of a tug.

to it as the ideal place for such a gathering. The date was fixed for July 5, 1847, the City Council appropriated $10,000 for the entertainment of visitors and elaborate preparations were made for their reception. At the appointed time 20,000 strangers descended upon Chicago, coming from all over the northern and western states and including in their number many of the most influential figures in public life. Among the throng was a tall and comparatively unknown Illinoisan named Abraham Lincoln, who gained his first opportunity to observe at close range many of the leading figures of America.

Although both Whigs and Democrats sought to turn the convention to their own political advantage, its outstanding purpose was achieved by the unanimous adoption of a resolution that the internal commerce of the country should be fostered and protected no less than its trade with foreign nations. The real beginning of harbors and other navigational aids on the Great Lakes dates from this time, and the commercial advantages of Chicago were advertised by her visitors throughout the nation.

But the opening and improvement of overland highways was no less urgent, and the age of the Iron Horse was already dawning. For Chicago the year 1848 was marked by two important achievements: the canal connecting the waters of Lake Michigan with those of the Illinois was completed; more important augury for the future, Chicago's first railroad, the Galena and Chicago Union, was opened as far as the Des Plaines River, a distance of ten miles. Somewhere on the ceremonial journey of the first train over the route, the dignitaries aboard the baggage car spied a farmer plodding townward behind his slow-moving ox team. They purchased his wagonload of wheat and hides and loaded it on the car, and so the first freight ever brought into Chicago by rail was delivered.

Once begun, the development of the railroads was pushed with breath-taking speed. In February 1854 the Rock Island was completed to the city of that name. Fifteen years later it reached Council Bluffs on the Missouri, from the opposite bank of which the Union Pacific led westward from Omaha to San Francisco. The Illinois Central was opened southward to Cairo on the Ohio in 1856, and in 1873 through rail connection with New Orleans was established. The Burlington Road was opened to Quincy in 1856, and ultimately was pushed across Iowa to Council Bluffs where connection was effected with lines running to the Pacific Coast.

The Galena and Chicago Union, Chicago's pioneer railroad, reached Freeport in 1853. There its direct progress ended, and it presently evolved into the Chicago and Northwestern. Wisconsin's pioneer road, the Milwaukee and Mississippi, was being pushed westward from Milwaukee during these years, reaching the Mississippi in 1857 and being later extended across Iowa and Minnesota. Between the Milwaukee line, pride of the city whose name it bore, and the Northwestern a sharp struggle was waged for the control of the rich traffic of Wisconsin and Minnesota. Eventually the two lines were brought under a single management and the Milwaukee, extended southward to Chicago, added its stream of commerce to the wealth of that city.

Meanwhile eastern railroads were pushing westward toward Lake Michigan and Chicago and within the space of two days in the spring of 1852 passenger trains of the Michigan Central and the Michigan Southern arrived in the city. The story of this development and of the establishment of through rail connection between Chicago and New York City has been told in an earlier chapter.

A quarter century had sufficed to make Chicago the foremost railroad center of the world. In ancient times all roads led to Rome, but in modern America they lead to Chicago, the crossroads of the nation. From all points of the compass literally hundreds of trains dash toward it daily, pouring the goods and the travelers of the nation into the maelstrom of humanity which converges at the head of Lake Michigan. But no train runs through the city, whose continued prosperity and importance is as certain as the future of America herself.

Then came the fire. Since 1840 the city had multiplied itself seventy-five times, to a metropolis of 300,000 in 1870, while the original Yankee element had become submerged by a congeries of Old World breeds which as early as 1850 comprised fifty-four percent of the population. Whether Yankee-born or alien, all Chicagoans were intensely proud of their city and unconscious of any enterprise to which it was unequal or any obstacle which it could not overcome.

Illustrative of this attitude is a story told of P. D. Armour, the great packer and merchant. In the early seventies when Italy was in a state of political turmoil and talk of the Pope seeking an asylum outside the peninsula was heard, Armour one day encountered an Irish friend, William J. Onahan, on the street and calmly proposed that the latter undertake the task of bringing the Holy See to Chicago. Onahan endeavored to explain something of the Pope's responsibilities and the impossibility of removing him from the Eternal City to the Windy City, to which the merchant replied: "How much would it cost to provide all these buildings? Look here," he continued. "You know how to manage these things. You get the Pope to come to Chicago. We will get a big tract of land, 10,000 or 20,000 acres, outside the city; we will build all the necessary offices, a palace, a great cathedral, whatever is needed. With half that land set apart for the Pope, we will make enough out of the other half to pay for the whole business."

Needless to say, the Papacy did not come to the shore of Lake Michigan, although two decades later the dreamers evoked from the sands of Jackson Park a magic city as amazing and beautiful as the Eternal one. But despite her pride of brawn and bigness Chicago was preparing for the world, in her years of mushroom growth, a fearful lesson in the art of city building. Across the broad plain which skirts the river, buildings by the thousands were extended, constructed with no thought of the greatest menace which confronts a modern city. Even the sidewalks, made of resinous pine and elevated upon stringers, were as combustible, almost, as a powder fuse. The single pumping station which supplied the mains with water was covered with a shingled roof. If ever a city invited disaster it was the Chicago of 1871.

The summer was one of excessive dryness. Up from the plains of the far Southwest blew week after week a scorching wind which withered the growing crops and turned the smiling green of the prairies to a dull brick red. In the forests of Wisconsin and Michigan conflagrations of unexampled magnitude raged, devastating entire districts and slaying hundreds of human beings. The fires which consumed the living pine in the forests would not long be balked by the seasoned pine of wooden-housed Chicago.

About the Great Fire of October 8-9 volumes have been written which here must be condensed to a page. Where it started is clear; how it started no man knows. Living in a shack at the corner of Jefferson and De Koven Streets was a poor Irish family by the name of O'Leary. The story commonly told is that Mrs. O'Leary went out to the barn, carrying a lamp, to see her cow; the lamp was upset and cow, stable and Chicago were engulfed in one common ruin. A careful reporter even assured the world that the cow "accidentally" kicked over the lamp; apparently the barnyard pet was questioned as to her motives in the brief interval between the fatal kick and her own prompt demise. Modest Mrs. O'Leary, far from coveting the honor of starting the fire, testified under oath that she was safe abed and knew nothing about it until called by a friend of the family.

Once started, it moved onward with resistless tread to the north and east until there was nothing more to burn. Between nine o'clock on Sunday evening and ten-thirty the following night an area of three and a half square miles, including the business section and much of the western and northern portions of the city, was burned, over 17,000 buildings were destroyed, and 100,000 people were rendered homeless. From Taylor Street to Lincoln Park, from the river to the lake, the city lay in ruins. The direct property loss was about $200,-000,000. The estimate of lives lost is commonly about 300.

While the embers of his vanished office still barred access to the site, W. D. Kerfoot put up a small shack in the middle of Washington Street on which he tacked this sign, scratched on a shingle: "All gone but Wife Children and ENERGY." It was the first structure erected after the fire and the inscription notified the world that Chicago would rise from her ashes to become a new and grander city. The material results of a generation of effort had vanished, yet the setting provided by nature and the energy of the townsmen remained unimpaired, and with these assets the future was secure.

Expressions of sympathy and generous offerings of material assistance poured in from all over the nation and even from across the sea.[1] Without waiting to learn what remained in their glowing safes the banks reopened for business and within a week after the fire had struck them down they resumed payments dollar for dollar. The members of the Board of Trade, who might legally have repudiated their contracts, voted unanimously to execute them. The refuse from the business district was dumped into the lagoon which lay between the lake shore and the Illinois Central Railroad tracks and so was begun the development of imposing Grant Park.

Never reticent about advertising its wares, as soon after the fire as the city caught its breath it erected a great Exposition Building on the lake front to house an Interstate Industrial Exposition, which was continued for many years. Meanwhile the city continued to grow, and the approaching four-hundredth anniversary of the discovery of America suggested to the local boosters the idea of staging an exposition which should outclass all others ever held, as completely as the fire had dwarfed all other holocausts. In 1885 the Directors of the Interstate Exposition formally voted that a great world's fair should be held at Chicago in 1892. In 1889 a World's Columbian Exposition Company was organized and the next year a bill was introduced in Congress providing for staging such an enterprise. New York and several other cities now became exposition-conscious and sought to obtain the prize for themselves, but Chicago's head start and obvious advantages of location could not be overcome.

So was held, although postponed to the summer of 1893, the World's Columbian Exposition, memories of whose breath-taking magic old men and women still cherish after the lapse of half a century. Under the able leadership of Daniel H. Burnham the artistic and architectural resources of the nation were marshaled to transform the sand dunes of Jackson Park into a city of orderly beauty whose like had not been seen since the days of ancient Rome. To its portals flocked millions from all over the world to marvel and admire. The ugly duckling of the American frontier whose loud boasting and smug self-satisfaction had for a generation offended the susceptibilities even of go-getting America had evoked a miracle of magic beauty.

Although the "City White" vanished from earth a few months later, its influence still marches on. From it dates the renaissance of architecture and the birth of orderly city planning in America. From the Columbian Exposition Burnham moved on to other triumphs, among the more notable being his work for the beautification of Washington and his promotion of the City Plan of Chicago. The objective of the latter was to make Chicago the finest commercial city in the world, where people should labor and live under the most perfect conditions possible to achieve. In 1909, after three years of preparation and discussion, the new plan was presented to the public. For its realization a generation of citizens must first be trained in the public schools, but almost from the beginning the citizenry approved the stupendous design, voting taxes and bond issues for the purchase of thousands of acres of park land, creating playgrounds, cutting broad thoroughfares through blighted districts, filling miles of lake-front parkways and rearranging hampering railroad terminals and yards. Despite foreign wars and domestic crises the great work forges ahead toward the noteworthy goal of creating a city worthy to bear the distinction of metropolis of the world.

In 1933 Chicago staged another characteristic show. Economic depression gripped the world, financial institutions were crashing on every hand and careers built up through decades of arduous endeavor were ending in ostracism and suicide. In short, the end of an era seemed at hand when Chicago chose the moment to stage her Century of Progress Exposition.

So great was its success that it was continued through a second year, and for perhaps the only time in the history of such enterprises the exposition wound up its affairs without a financial deficit. Unlike the Columbian Exposition forty years earlier, the Century of Progress created no great stir in foreign lands, but Americans attended it in throngs to view the progress in science and industry which a century had wrought.

In outward setting no two expositions could have been more unlike than those Chicago incubated. In place of the harmony and order which characterized the White City of the nineties, the Century of Progress assailed the senses with possibly the most diverse display of raucous modernity ever assembled. From the "breathing" dome of the Transportation Building to the petty sandwich and hot-dog stands a riot of contrasting colors and architectural forms assailed the eye. The shouts of the hawkers mingled with the blare of bands and the penetrating voices of loudspeakers to weary and confuse the ear. The directors of the exposition had encouraged architects and exhibitors to give vent to their secret dreams, and the resultant display was a bedlam which seemed to belie all we have said about the influence of the earlier exposition upon the public taste. It had the redeeming merits, however, that for once artists and creative workers enjoyed an opportunity for free and frank experimentation on a wholesale scale, and the material creations they evoked, like the buildings of the Columbian Exposition, were consigned to early oblivion.

Apt illustration of the enterprise which is synonymous with Chicago is afforded by the story of the prodigious efforts the city has made to solve her sewerage problem. Until 1855 there was no sewerage system whatever and the annual death rate assumed appalling proportions. Driven by necessity, the first Board of Sewerage Commissioners was appointed and under its authority Chief Engineer Chesborough planned and carried out a system which emptied the sewage into the river and thence into the lake, from which the city water was drawn.[2] Although the sanitary situation seemed solved for the moment, the relief was only temporary, for the city continued to grow rapidly and the river became an increasingly noisome open sewer which the current was too feeble to purify. Within a decade conditions were so bad that a law was procured from the State Legislature permitting the city to deepen the summit development of the Illinois and Michigan Canal by which water from Lake Michigan could be utilized to create a current sufficient to cleanse the river.

After four years of construction at a cost of over $3,000,000 the new cut was completed and on July 15, 1871, the water was turned into the South Branch. The improvement produced was so marked that shortsighted optimists believed the city's sanitary problem was now permanently solved. Yet within another dozen years the river was again an odorous open sewer, and partial relief from the pollution of the drinking water was obtained only by extending the intakes of the water system far out into the lake.

With every passing year conditions became worse and in 1889 the Chicago Sanitary District was organized, embracing an area far larger than the city itself. If the sewage was not to continue to go into the lake it eventually must be diverted across the Continental Divide and down the Illinois River, where dilution with water and exposure to air and sun would gradually purify it. Construction of the Drainage Canal was begun in 1892, and on January 2, 1900, the last bulkhead was cut through and the Chicago River, turned backward in its course, was made to flow toward the Mexican Gulf instead of the Gulf of St. Lawrence. As in 1871, the sanitary improvement was marked, and the typhoid death rate which had stood at 174 per 100,000 population before the canal was opened fell so low that in recent decades physicians may practice for years without encountering a single case. Again, as in 1871, it was hopefully believed that the city's sanitary problem was permanently solved.

But the works of man are painfully fleeting and each new achievement becomes but a steppingstone on the pathway of further progress. Although Chicago had cleaned her own doorstep she had done it at the expense of the down-river cities, which soon began to protest the flow of Chicago sewerage past their doors. When it was proposed to alleviate the nuisance by diverting a larger flow of water from the lake the states adjoining the Great Lakes made even more violent protest. In this they were joined by Canada and thus the problem of Chicago's sewage-disposal system assumed international proportions.

Meanwhile, in addition to the main Drainage Canal, a channel had been constructed from the lake at Wilmette to the North Branch of the Chicago to relieve that stream of its sewage, and on the far south side the Calumet-Sag Channel reversed the current of the sewer-laden Calumet River to empty into the main canal. But Chicago could not indefinitely dump her raw sewage on the down-river communities and many years ago new measures were formulated at vast expense to care for the city of 5,000,000 people anticipated by 1950. These involved the construction of several great sewage-disposal plants, each adequate to the needs of a population of 1,000,000 or more. Even such facilities will in their turn prove inadequate, for the physical problems of a growing city are never-ending.

In a limited way all Lake Michigan cities have been seaports since the opening of the Erie and Welland Canals, over a century ago. The immense advantage of freer access to the ocean is so obvious that practically all dwellers around the Great Lakes are advocates of improving the routes that lead to the sea. More than any other city, Chicago looks two ways—to the Atlantic by way of an improved Welland

Canal-St. Lawrence River route and to the Gulf of Mexico by way of the Illinois-Mississippi River waterway. Although the Drainage Canal was constructed primarily for sanitary reasons, its navigational value was not forgotten. The Chicago River was widened to 200 feet and deepened to 26, admitting the largest vessels on the lakes, and for a distance of 33 miles from Lake Michigan the canal was given a minimum width of 160 feet and a depth of 24. The state now proceeded to canalize the Des Plaines and Illinois rivers as far as Utica, an additional 61 miles, to permit 1,000-ton barges to come from the Mississippi to Chicago. By these measures an important start was made upon the huge task of providing a deepwater channel from Lake Michigan to the Gulf of Mexico.

Life is more than meat, and this is true of a city no less than of an individual. Like all other new cities, early Chicago was raw and crude, for the men who lay the foundations of civilization in a wilderness must of necessity devote their major energy to material tasks, and only later, when an adequate physical environment has been created, can leisure and room be found for the cultivation of things of the spirit. So the mythical citizen who observed that when Chicago got around to it she would "make culture hum" expressed a great truth. First things must come first, and for pioneer Chicago this meant raising the city bodily out of the morass in which it was founded, providing a harbor for ships and highway connections with the outside world, solving the well-nigh insoluble sanitary problem, and, in short, creating all the material properties of a modern city.

Half a century of effort sufficed to lay the foundations of the metropolis of today and to plant the seeds of certain institutions which are the glory of the twentieth-century city. The Historical Society, established in 1857 by leaders of the pioneer generation, has triumphed over no less than three fires to develop one of America's finest historical museums. Northwestern University was established in 1855 at Evanston where eight of its twelve schools are still housed on a campus of great beauty. The professional schools and a university college occupy an imposing group of buildings on a newer campus in the heart of downtown Chicago. Assets of scores of millions of dollars, chiefly accumulated through the gifts of generous individuals, testify the pride of Chicagoans in this great institution of learning.

Original founder of the University of Chicago was Stephen A. Douglas, one of the nation's most notable men. In 1855 when a number of citizens asked his aid in establishing such an institution he responded with a gift of ten acres of ground at Thirty-fourth Street, not far from his present grave and monument. Thereafter much of his thought and attention were given to the institution during his few remaining years of life. Although the university flourished for a time, financial difficulties brought its operations to an end in the eighties, to be revived on another site through the enlightened philanthropy of John D. Rockefeller in 1890. The period of renaissance then effected continues to this day, and long since the rejuvenated University of Chicago gained recognition as one of the world's foremost institutions of learning. Under the dynamic leadership of President Harper from 1890 to 1905 the university assumed a position of leadership, breaking many an educational sacred tradition. Under the like dynamic leadership of President Hutchins during the last decade and a half it has continued to mark out new intellectual pathways.

Other institutions deserving a chapter each can here be barely mentioned. Loyola is one of the great chain of Jesuit universities located with rare statesmanship in the leading metropolises of America. Illinois Institute of Technology, with a campus still in process of development, has evolved within half a decade from the consolidation of Lewis and Armour Institutes, founded by generous businessmen of nineteenth-century Chicago. The Art Institute, besides having one of the country's chief collections of art, maintains the largest art school in America. The Chicago Museum of Natural History, formerly the Field Museum, and the Rosenwald Industrial Museum are gigantic and world-famous institutions, also founded by successful businessmen of Chicago. Two of the world's great reference libraries are the John Crerar and the Walter L. Newberry, founded by the citizens whose names they bear.

In striking contrast to these activities is Chicago's malodorous reputation in the realm of government. As in medieval Florence or Venice, the energies of the townsmen find outlet in gargantuan exhibitions of vice and crime no less than in the development of splendid libraries and universities. The stately Newberry Library looks down upon Bedbug Square, a favorite resort of the hoboes of half a continent; while a mile or so to the north stands the drab garage which served as the execution chamber for the victims of the St. Valentine's Day massacre of 1929, for which no perpetrator was ever punished. The physical environment of the library suggests the extremes—from the heights of culture and learning to the depths of poverty and outlawry—which characterize the life of the great city.

In the realms of disorder and lawlessness the reputation of Chicago is world-wide. "Chicago Pianos" made the tommy gun renowned in almost every underworld resort from New York to Hong Kong and Timbuctoo. It was Chicago that provided the stage for the country's most notable upheaval of anarchy; it was a Chicago sausage maker who conceived the ingenious plan of disposing of the corpse of his murdered wife by rendering it in the sausage vats he used to manufacture food for his customers; and it was two pampered gold-coast youths of a subsequent generation who acquainted the country with the practice of murder for a thrill. It was Chicago, also, that two decades since provided the theater for the unspeakable Al Capone, whose sense of lawless power rose to such a height he could coolly propose to the authorities that he would rid the city of all other gangsters if his own nefarious activities might continue unmolested.

Yet the city is less violent than popular reputation pictures it, and only naïve strangers really believe that scenes of slaughter and sudden death are common on its streets. The present writer lived in Chicago for almost a decade without once observing a crime of violence, and only after removing to Detroit did he gaze popeyed into the muzzle of a revolver held by a nervous thug whose forefinger threatened momentarily to press convulsively the trigger upon which it rested. Focal point of the most progressive nation on earth, seething with vitality and energy, and rich beyond the power of imagination to conceive, Chicago combines magnificent virtues with vices of comparable magnitude. Life here may be hectic but it is never dull. Here La Salle, stormy eighteenth-century empire dreamer and builder, if permitted to return to earth, would feel completely at home.

---

[1] Queen Victoria and some of her subjects presented several thousand books to the city. Temporarily stored in the tank which had been the reservoir for the South Side waterworks, they became the nucleus of the Chicago Public Library. Ironically enough, it was the shelves of this library which a subsequent mayor of the city undertook to purge by making a public bonfire of the books of those historians who had endeavored to tell the truth about the American Revolution. He threatened to "bust King George on the snoot" if the grandson of Victoria should be so rash as to venture to visit the city. The tide of culture at Chicago, which sometimes stands at flood, can on occasion sink very low.

[2] Surveys disclosed that the ground adjoining the river was only three or four feet above lake level. To keep the sewers underground, therefore, a minimum street elevation of ten feet was adopted, and during the next few years the buildings were elevated to this grade. While the work was in progress the city streets presented an exceedingly odd appearance, with some buildings raised to the new level while others remained at the old. "Chicago datum" was established by the Canal Commissioners in 1847 at the low level of the lake in that year. Since over a period of years the lake level varies several feet, the calculations upon which the existing street grade was established were not ideally adequate. To have fixed it higher at the time would have been simple: to do so now is practically unthinkable.

Conclusion

O ENDS our 300-year story. At its beginning a French explorer from Quebec was seeking in the Lake Michigan wilderness the domain of the Emperor of China. Its close finds the civilized dwellers around the Great Lakes engaged as allies of the Chinese Republic in the war to preserve freedom throughout the world.

As we write these lines the return of another Easter season heralds the awakening of Nature from her annual sleep. Again "the flowers appear on the earth, the time of the singing of birds is come." But around the Great Lakes an earlier and surer harbinger of spring is the renewed hum of activity in the shipyards. On Erie and Michigan the great drab ships lie restlessly at their docks in readiness for instant departure, while from captain to cabin boy their crews wait eagerly for the word that the channels of the St. Clair and the St. Marys, along with Whitefish Bay, Green Bay and the Straits, are open to begin their northward dash for distant Escanaba, Marquette and Duluth. Assisting the action of Mother Nature the greatest fleet of icebreakers in the world leads the van of the procession, hurling its ponderous bulk in repeated onslaughts upon ice fields twenty or more inches thick in the stern determination to clear the channels at the earliest possible moment.

This season the struggle has a deeper meaning than ever before, for unless the ore comes down in ample quantity from the Minnesota and Wisconsin mines to feed the ravenous mills around Lake Michigan and Lake Erie, America's armed forces will be sadly crippled and the cause of freedom throughout the world will be correspondingly imperiled. In 1942 the all-time record of more than 92,000,000 tons of ore carried down the lakes was established. Last year a shorter season of navigation was chiefly responsible for reducing the tonnage to 84,404,852. This year the government has set a goal of 90,000,000 or more, and to forward its realization provision has been made for the launching during the year of twenty-five great new ships, sixteen of them ore carriers. To reinforce the fleet of icebreakers the *Mackinaw,* displacing 5,090 tons and costing $10,000,000, was launched at Toledo at the beginning of March. Driven by Diesel engines and manned by a crew of 176, she is the world's most powerful icebreaker.

As if in approval of such efforts Mother Nature advanced the unlocking of the channels of navigation two weeks or more ahead of the usual season. Early in March the clearing of the St. Clair River was begun and on March 23 the icebreakers plowed past Port Huron into the open lake beyond. On the twenty-eighth a carrier laden with limestone sailed from Indiana City for Port Inland at the northern end of Lake Michigan. A week later, on April 4, two great freighters from South Chicago entered the Escanaba harbor, while a fleet of four icebreakers battled to reopen a passage through the straits where no less than twenty-eight vessels had been marooned by the closing of the temporarily opened channel.

But the sternest struggle was waged in the St. Marys River and Whitefish Bay, where ice twenty inches thick still sealed the channel. Led by the package freighter *Hamonic,* the *William G. Mather,* the *William H. Downer* and other ships, moving through the twenty-inch ice at the rate of seven miles in twenty-four hours, grimly battered their way upriver and into Whitefish Bay. Here they were baffled for a time, while dozens of vessels crowded in their rear impatiently awaiting the clearing of a pathway to open water in the lake beyond. As these lines are being penned (April 10) a letter, written on April 8 by an observer at the Sault, arrives: "There are about 30 vessels above the Sault and some 40 below, all battling ice, some of which is yet 20 inches thick near Whitefish Point, trying to reach Duluth and other upper Lake Superior ports. A steady stream of vessels passed upbound within a few hundred feet of this hotel yesterday. . . ." Announcement of the final victory was dispatched by telegraph from the Sault the same day. Before noon of April 11, 122 ships had passed through the locks into Lake Superior, while the *Youngstown* had already raced back from Marquette with the first ore cargo of the season for the lower lakes, 17 days earlier than the first ship locked down in 1943.

All of this makes doleful news for Dictator Shickelgruber and his minions. Although no blood was shed in the battle with the ice of the St. Marys and Whitefish Bay, the victory achieved by the *Hamonic*

and her sister ships marked a major defeat for the sinking Axis cause.
To paraphrase an ancient jingle:

> We've got the ships,
> We've got the men,
> We've got the iron, too ...

... and the miners and sailors and other workers around and on the
Great Lakes are helping to fashion the coffins that are being prepared
for Messrs. Hitler and Hirohito.

ACKNOWLEDGMENTS

Mr. D. L. Chambers, the publisher, and his competent staff of workers have labored patiently and intelligently to transform my frequently imperfect manuscript into an attractive book. Their watchful oversight has saved me from numerous errors. Dr. F. Clever Bald of Ann Arbor has answered many questions and has generously placed at my disposal his valuable manuscript study of the early years of American rule at Detroit. Mr. Willard C. Wichers, Director of the Netherlands Museum at Holland, and his staff have provided information, criticism and photographs. The Honorable Wilbur M. Brucker placed at my disposal his set of the official records of the trial of King Benjamin Purnell. The Detroit Public Library, the Michigan State Historical Commission, the Chicago Historical Society and the William L. Clements Library have provided me with information and pictures. John E. Poole of Van Dyke, diligent collector of Great Lakes lore, has patiently answered my many questions. Alfred T. Goslin has typed my hundreds of pages of deplorably illegible penmanship. To each of these helpers my acknowledgment of appreciation and gratitude is cheerfully tendered.

BIBLIOGRAPHICAL NOTE

Many of the sources of information for the present volume are indicated in the footnotes appended to its several chapters. For original documents concerning the period of exploration and later consult R. G. Thwaites (ed.), *The Jesuit Relations* (Cleveland, 1896-1901), 73 vols.; Pierre Margry, *Découvertes et établissements des Français* (Paris, 1876-1786), 6 vols.; *The Michigan Pioneer and Historical Collections;* and *The Wisconsin Historical Collections.* The story of Lake Michigan belongs to the regional history of the Old Northwest. Valuable secondary histories for this area are C. W. Alvord, *The Illinois Country,* 1683-1818, Vol. I of *Illinois Centennial History* (Springfield, 1920); M. M. Quaife, *Wisconsin. Its History and Its People,* 2 vols. (Chicago, 1924); Louise P. Kellogg, *The French Régime in Wisconsin and the Northwest* (Madison, 1925); and *The British Régime in Wisconsin and the Northwest* (Madison, 1935).

For the entire French-English background in North America the classic account is contained in Francis Parkman's thirteen volumes. A condensed narrative covering the same ground as Parkman is George M. Wrong, *The Rise and Fall of New France,* 2 vols. (Toronto, 1928). Briefer and more popular in character are several of the excellent little volumes of *The Chronicles of Canada Series:* see especially Stephen Leacock, *The Mariner of St. Malo;* Charles W. Colby, *The Founder of New France;* Thomas G. Guthrie, *The Jesuit Missions;* Thomas Chapais, *The Great Intendant;* Charles W. Colby, *The Fighting Governor;* William Wood, *The War with the United States;* and Thomas Marquis, *The War Chief of the Ottawa.*

The many town and county histories for the region adjacent to Lake Michigan contain, as might be expected, a vast amount of lore pertaining to the story of the lake. Worthy of particular mention are Deborah B. Martin's *History of Brown County, Wisconsin* (including Green Bay); Bessie L. Pierce, *A History of Chicago,* Vols. I and II (Chicago, 1937-1940); M. M. Quaife, *Chicago and the Old Northwest,* 1673-1835 (Chicago, 1913); and E. O. Wood, *Historic Mackinac,* 2 vols. (New York, 1918). In this connection too should be noted *The Wisconsin Magazine of History, The Michigan History Magazine,* and certain volumes of The Buffalo Historical Society *Publications,* of The Chicago Historical Society *Collections* and of *The Illinois Historical Collections.* Two books of special character are Calvin Goodrich, *The First Michigan Frontier* (Ann Arbor, 1940), which undertakes to picture the life and society of Michigan at the close of the French period, and M. M. Quaife, *Chicago's Highways Old and New. From Indian Trail to Motor Road* (Chicago, 1923), which depicts the life of Chicago's great radial highways in the pre-railroad era.

Bearing directly upon ships and shipping activities are the useful annual reports and monthly bulletins of the Lake Carriers' Association. Among secondary descriptive volumes easily the most important is J. B. Mansfield, *History of the Great Lakes,* Vol. I (Chicago, 1899). Although it contains numerous errors it is encyclopediac in scope, and one can only admire the industry of the author in assembling its contents. James C. Mills, *Our Inland Seas* (Chicago, 1910); George A. Cuthbertson, *Freshwater* (Toronto, 1931); and Ralph G. Plumb, *Lake Michigan* (Manitowoc, 1941) are also worth reading. The latter little book, incidentally, appears to be the only one ever written heretofore with the sole object of telling the story of Lake Michigan. The author is a lifelong lover of the lake, but only an amateur historian, and the book reflects both the merits and the defects of these respective qualifications.

Much of the data essential to any thoroughgoing study of the Great Lakes still exists only in manuscript; a much greater quantity can be found only in the newspaper files, which now run back for a century and a quarter at Detroit, and for periods of a century or more at Cleveland, Chicago, Buffalo and other lake cities. The two outstanding collections of manuscripts are those of the Buffalo Historical Society and the Burton Historical Collection of the Detroit Public Library. The State Historical Society of Wisconsin, the Chicago Historical Society and certain other institutions possess more or less manuscript material dealing with Lake Michigan.

In what follows some comments will be offered upon the subject matter of some of the individual chapters. Father Vimont's brief tribute to Jean Nicolet in *Jesuit Relations,* Vol. XXIII, contains about all we know concerning this explorer. There are numerous editions of Champlain's works, most recent and most notable being the Champlain Society Edition edited by H. P. Biggar, in 7 vols. (Toronto, 1922-1936). The journals of Marquette's Mississippi River and Illinois expeditions are in *Jesuit Relations,* Vol. LIX, where also is Jolliet's map of New France, on which Lake Michigan in its entirety is first shown.

The literature concerning La Salle, Tonty and Father Hennepin is extensive and frequently controversial. Francis Parkman's biography of La Salle, first issued three-quarters of a century ago, still remains the classic treatment of the subject, although in recent decades it has been sharply criticized, especially by writers of the Roman Catholic faith. Although scholars have been aware for many years of some of the misrepresentations of Father Hennepin all existing accounts of his narrative and career must be revised in the light of Jean Delanglez's recent study, "Hennepin's Description of Louisiana, a Critical Essay," printed in *Mid-America,* Vol. XII.

For original documents concerning the first cities around Lake Michigan see *The Jesuit Relations* and Margry, *Découvertes,* especially Cadillac's *Memoir* on the Upper Country. On early-day St. Joseph see "The St. Joseph Baptismal Register," edited by Reverend George Paré and M. M. Quaife, in *Mississippi Valley Historical Review,* XIII, 20-39, and "The St. Joseph Mission" by George Paré in the same periodical, XVII, 24-54. For the broader picture of the entire French period in the Northwest, with particular emphasis on Wisconsin, see L. P. Kellogg, *French Régime in Wisconsin and the Northwest.* On seventeenth-century Chicago see Reverend G. J. Garraghan, *Chapters in Frontier History* (Milwaukee, 1934), Chap. II, and M. M. Quaife, *Checagou. From Indian Wigwam to Modern City* (Chicago, 1933), Chap. II. Original documents pertaining to the activities of Marquette, Jolliet and La Salle are in *The Jesuit Rela-*

tions and in Margry, *Découvertes*. The excellent *Memoir* on the Illinois Country by the Sieur Deliette is published in *Illinois Historical Collections,* XXIII.

Practically the only detailed critical studies of the period of the Fox Wars are M. M. Quaife, *Wisconsin* . . . Vol. I, Chaps. VIII and IX, and L. P. Kellogg, *French Régime* . . . Chaps. XIII-XV. Numerous original documents are printed in *Wisconsin Historical Collections;* Stanley Faye, "The Foxes Fort," in *Illinois State Historical Society Journal,* XXVIII, 123-163, supplies the best account of the Fox defeat of 1730. The story of Kiala's self-sacrifice remains unknown to poets, dramatists and hero worshipers. It is a great pity.

The classic account of the Pontiac War, now a century old and in various respects outmoded, is Francis Parkman's *Conspiracy of Pontiac.* A biography of that chieftain, still in manuscript, by Dr. Howard Peckham of the University of Michigan, when published will correct, and for the scholarly reader supersede, Parkman's earlier study. Reprint editions of Alexander Henry's *Travels and Adventures* . . . *Between the Years 1760 and 1776* (New York, 1809) have been edited by James Bain (Toronto, 1901) and by M. M. Quaife (Chicago, 1921). Two important contemporary journals of the siege of Detroit, both partial in scope and both anonymous, are F. B. Hough (ed.), *Diary of the Siege of Detroit in the War with Pontiac* (Albany, 1860), and M. Agnes Burton (ed.), *Journal of Pontiac's Conspiracy* (Detroit, 1912). Numerous original documents are printed in the *Michigan Pioneer and Historical Collections* and in the *Wisconsin Historical Collections.* For Robert Rogers and conditions at Mackinac in the later 1760's see Allan Nevins, *Ponteach,* (Chicago, 1914); M. M. Quaife, "Robert Rogers," *Burton Historical Collection Leaflet,* VII, 1-16, and *Wisconsin* . . . Vol. I, Chap. XII; L. P. Kellogg, *British Régime in Wisconsin,* Chaps. III-VII. The Journal of Dr. Daniel Morison exists only in typed manuscript form in the Detroit Public Library.

But little attention has been given by historians to the role of the British navy on the Great Lakes in the decades following the conquest of Canada. For a preliminary study of the subject see M. M. Quaife, "The Royal Navy of the Upper Lakes," in *Burton Historical Collection Leaflet,* II, 49-64.

The best account of the American occupation of Detroit and the Upper Lakes in 1796 is F. Clever Bald's study of the subject, unfortunately still unpublished. On the career of the *Adams* and the early years at Fort Dearborn see articles by M. M. Quaife in *Burton Historical Collection Leaflet,* especially Vols. V, VII and VIII. On the War of 1812 around

Lake Michigan see the same writer's *Chicago and the Old Northwest,* and *Wisconsin* . . . Vol. I. For the remarkable exploits of Sergeant James Keating see M. M. Quaife, "A Forgotten Hero of Rock Island," in *Illinois State Historical Society Journal,* XXIII, 652-663.

About the only information in print concerning Oliver Newberry, "Admiral of the Lakes" a century ago, is George B. Catlin's article in *Michigan Historical Magazine,* Vol. XVII. There is an abundance of material on the development of lake shipping and commerce in the nineteenth century. *Merchant Steam Vessels of the United States, 1807-1856* is a tabular list arranged by years showing names, tonnage, etc. of vessels under U. S. registry. The *Report of Israel D. Andrews . . . upon the Trade of the Great Lakes and Rivers* (Washington, 1854) supplies information for the shipping of the mid-nineteenth century. James L. Barton, *Letter in Relation to the Value and Importance of the Commerce of the Great Western Lakes* (Buffalo, 1845) summarizes statistics on Great Lakes shipping to the date of publication. Ralph G. Plumb, *History of Navigation on the Great Lakes* (Washington, 1911) is a useful concise account of the subject treated.

Information upon the fur trade of the Northwest is abundant. Numerous original documents are printed in the *Wisconsin Historical Collections,* the *Michigan Pioneer and Historical Collections, The John Askin Papers,* etc. Several valuable autobiographic narratives dealing with the fur trade are included in The Lakeside Classics Series of annual volumes (Chicago, 1904 ——), edited since 1916 by the present writer.

The evolution of state boundaries in the Old Northwest is treated in the standard histories of the several states. For monographic material, consult *Michigan Pioneer and Historical Collections,* Vols. XXVII, XXX, and XXXVIII; *Wisconsin Historical Collections,* Vols. XI and XXVI; Indiana Historical Society *Publications,* Vol. VII. The only comprehensive firsthand story of the Mormon kingdom founded by James J. Strang is M. M. Quaife, *The Kingdom of Saint James* (New Haven, 1930).

Data concerning shipping disasters and lake tempests is abundant in the contemporary newspaper files. The best account of the *Phoenix* disaster is by William O. Van Eyck in *Wisconsin Magazine of History,* Vol. VII. The same volume contains Frances Stover's story of "The Steamer that Sunk the Lady Elgin."

Our present chapter supplies the first essay at a comprehensive account of the career of King Benjamin Purnell and his colony. Information concerning the prior colony of Prince Michael Mills at Detroit is contained in the contemporary file of the Detroit *Free Press* and in the Supreme

Court decision upholding his conviction, printed in 94 Michigan Reports, 630-644. Numerous journalistic exposures of King Ben's colony have been published in the Chicago and Detroit papers, particularly the Detroit *Free Press.* The most important single source of information on the subject is the 5,000-page printed record of the prosecution of King Ben by the State of Michigan in 1927, and the 191-page opinion of Judge Fead, analyzing this mass of testimony. Beginning with Joanna Southcott, the successive "Angelic Messengers" of the cult have published numerous books and pamphlets, usually difficult of access and few of which the present writer has seen. Among the more important seem to be *The Flying Roll* by James Jazreel, from which the cult acquired the nickname of "Flying Rollers," and the *Star of Bethlehem,* King Ben's initial publication. For the Supreme Court decision vacating Judge Fead's order for the appointment of a receiver for the colony see 246 Michigan Reports, 606-619.

On the Dutch settlements of Michigan and Wisconsin see articles by Gerrit Van Schelven and Gerrit Dykema in *Michigan History Magazine,* Vol. I, and by Reverend Chrysostom Ver Wyst in Wisconsin Historical Society *Proceedings* for 1916. A comprehensive history of the Holland, Michigan, colony is Aleida J. Pieters, *A Dutch Settlement in Michigan* (Grand Rapids, 1923). George A. Brennan, *The Wonders of the Dunes* (Indianapolis, 1923), although the work of an amateur enthusiast, contains much useful information on the Indiana dunes; charming characterizations of their frequently odd inhabitants are supplied by the books of Earl H. Reed (*The Dune Country, Sketches in Duneland,* and *Tales of a Vanishing River*).

All serious historical investigation is infinitely laborious and ideal perfection in its pursuit is never attained. Our footnotes and bibliographical note will serve to introduce the reader to some of the sources of information about Lake Michigan. Many more, of which no mention is made, have been utilized, and neither footnotes nor the present sketch make any pretense to inclusiveness.

EXPLANATORY NOTE

SEVERAL READERS of the first edition of *Lake Michigan* have questioned the identification of the ballad "The Wreck of the Julie Plante" with Lake St. Clair. I regret that the footnote in my longhand manuscript copy of Chapter XXII giving credit to Mr. William H. Drummond's delightful version of the ballad was inadvertently omitted from the printed book. This detail aside, it is quite certain that the French-Canadian folk tales were no less familiar to the dwellers beside the Detroit than to those along the lower St. Lawrence. *Legends of Le Détroit,* published in 1884 by Marie Caroline Watson Hamlin, assembles a considerable number of them. Still others may be found in histories of Detroit and in other local publications.

There is nothing surprising about this, for Detroit was originally wholly French and the blood of France still flows in the veins of thousands of its citizens. The issue that has been raised concerns the question whether the ballad of the *Julie Plante* is wholly Dr. Drummond's original creation or whether he merely put into literary form a French-Canadian folk tale current on the St. Lawrence and the Great Lakes. Mr. W. W. Boyd of Montreal stoutly affirms the former. Professor Ivan H. Walton of the University of Michigan, who has given much attention to the lore of the lakes, observes that although the song is usually attributed to Drummond, "there is evidence that the French scowmen on the Detroit River sang it before Dr. Drummond's day." (*Michigan History Magazine,* XIX, Autumn, 1935 number, 368). Mr. Earl C. Beck supplies further evidence that the ballad was current in Michigan, at least in recent decades, while it is known to have been a favorite subject of recital by Peter White, nestor of Marquette, who died in 1908. Since Dr. Drummond's poem was first published in 1897, if the tale was actually original with him the circumstances we have recited afford an interesting illustration of the quick appropriation of an entirely new story by the ballad singers of a region remote from its place of origin.

For our purpose in *Lake Michigan* it is unnecessary to determine the historical issue that has been raised. Although some of the language employed is local to the lower St. Lawrence, the setting of the poem is no less appropriate to Lake St. Clair; while as a moving illustration of the terrors of shipwreck it serves the purpose of our opening paragraphs.

INDEX

Aberdeen, 265
Accau, Michael, 39-40
Adams, the, 112-114, 118-121
Adams, George J., 243-244
Adams, John Quincy, 243, 322
Adams, Samuel, 243
Admiral, the, 250
Alden, John, 338
Allegan, 297-298
Allouez, Father Claude, 24, 51-54, 63, 69
Amelia, the, 133
America, the, 251
American Fur Company, 137, 177-183, 204
American Guide Series, 289-290
American Notes, 252
Amherstburg, 42, 169, 252
Anderson, Thomas G., 206
Andreas, A. T., 331
Angelica, the, 106, 110
Angelic Messengers, 262-278
Angélique, ——, 203
Angels, 241. *See also* Angelic Messengers
Angelus, 202
Ann Arbor, 226, 264
Ann Arbor Conventions, 215-216
Ann Arbor Railroad, 334-335
Apostle of the Dunes, 303
Apples, 281-282
Archange, the, 100, 110, 200
Archangel, the, 106
Ark, the, House of David building, 268
Armour Institute, 358
Armour, P. D., 350-351
Army rule, 92-99, 321-324
Army trail, 145
Arndt, Judge John P., 321
Ashland, O., 267, 278
Ashland, Wis., 24, 51
Askin, Catherine, 107
Askin, John, 100, 107, 113, 200, 282
Askin, John, Jr., 282-283
Astor, John Jacob, 177
Atlantic, the, 163
Audubon, John James, 195-196
Augel, Antoine, 39-40
Augusta, the, 259-261
Austerlitz, the, 149
Australia, 268
Austrian Succession War, 75
Automobiles, 335-336
Aveneau, Father Claude, 54-55

Bacon, Rev. David, 283-284

Bacon, Leonard, 284
Bailly, Joseph, 115
Baillytown, 306
Baird, Mrs. Elizabeth, 202, 207
Bald, Prof. F. C., 111
Baltimore, 223
Bangs, Anson, 316
Bank of Michigan, 153
Baptisms for the dead, 243
Barges, 167
Baseball, 270-271, 276
Bateaux, 175, 185
Battle of Lake Erie, 120, 129
Battle of the Thames, 129
Baushke, Albert, 267, 278
Baushke, Louis, 267, 278
Bay of the Puants, *see* Green Bay
Bay of the Stinking Water, *see* Green Bay
Bay View Assembly, 284
Beach House, 225
Bears, 188-190, 287-288, 328, 344
Beaubien, Mark, 344-345
Beaumont, Dr. William, 137
Beaver Islands (*Isles du Castor*), 253,
    288-290; in Pontiac War, 83-84, 86,
    282; Mormon kingdom, 243-247
Bedbug Square, 359
Bedford, Thomas, 246-247
Belgians, 326-327, 333
Belle Isle, 142, 251, 256
Bellestre, Capt. Francis Marie Picote, Sieur
    de, 88
Beloit, 145
Bennett, Lieut. Thomas, 102-103, 109
Benton Harbor, House of David colony,
    262-278
Benzie County, 196
Berrien County, 211, 281-282
Bessemer process, 165
Bethlehem, House of David building, 268
Beulah, 286, 290
Bickle, Bernice, 263-264
Big Bay de Noc, 314
Big Rapids, 294
Binneteau, Father Julien, 66
Biplanes, 308-309
Bird life, 186
Black, Cicely, 127
Black Hawk War, 140-146
Black Lake, 297
Black Peter, 294
Black River, 297-298
Black Rock, 120, 135-140

371